WOMEN ARTISTS, WOMEN EXILES

THE AMERICAN WOMEN WRITERS SERIES

Joanne Dobson, Judith Fetterley, and Elaine Showalter, series editors

The American Women Writers Series makes available for the first time in decades the work of the most significant, influential, and popular American women writers from the 1820s to the 1920s. Coming during a period of explosive growth in women's studies, this ongoing series challenges many assumptions about our twentieth-century objectivity, the sacred nature of the American literary canon, and nineteenth-century history and culture. Each volume in the series is edited by a major scholar in the field and has been entirely retypeset and redesigned.

ALTERNATIVE ALCOTT
Louisa May Alcott
Elaine Showalter, editor

STORIES FROM THE COUNTRY
OF LOST BORDERS
Mary Austin
Marjorie Pryse, editor

CLOVERNOOK SKETCHES
AND OTHER STORIES
Alice Cary
Judith Fetterley, editor

HOBOMOK AND OTHER
WRITINGS ON INDIANS
Lydia Maria Child
Carolyn L. Karcher, editor

"HOW CELIA CHANGED HER
MIND" AND SELECTED STORIES
Rose Terry Cooke
Elizabeth Ammons, editor

RUTH HALL AND OTHER
WRITINGS
Fanny Fern
Joyce Warren, editor

QUICKSAND AND *PASSING*
Nella Larsen
Deborah E. McDowell, editor

HOPE LESLIE
Catharine Maria Sedgwick
Mary Kelley, editor

THE HIDDEN HAND
E.D.E.N. Southworth
Joanne Dobson, editor

OLDTOWN FOLKS
Harriet Beecher Stowe
Dorothy Berkson, editor

WOMEN ARTISTS, WOMEN
EXILES: "MISS GRIEF" AND
OTHER STORIES
Constance Fenimore Woolson
Joan Myers Weimer, editor

WOMEN ARTISTS, WOMEN EXILES
"Miss Grief" and Other Stories

CONSTANCE FENIMORE WOOLSON

Edited and with an Introduction by

JOAN MYERS WEIMER

RUTGERS UNIVERSITY PRESS

New Brunswick and London

Library of Congress Cataloging-in-Publication Data

Woolson, Constance Fenimore, 1840–1894.
Women artists, women exiles : "Miss Grief" and other stories / Constance Fenimore
Woolson : edited with an introduction by Joan Myers Weimer.

p.   cm — (The American women writers series)
Bibliography: p.
ISBN 0-8135-1347-2. ISBN 0-8135-1348-0 (pbk.)
1. Women artists—Fiction.   2. Women—Fiction.   3. Artists—
Fiction.   4. Exiles—Fiction.   I. Weimer, Joan Myers.   II. Title.
III. Series.
PS3361.W45 1988
813'.4—dc19   88-6421
                                                                                CIP

British Cataloging-in-Publication Data Available

CONTENTS

ACKNOWLEDGMENTS

FOR PERMISSION TO PRINT portions of Woolson's unpublished corre-spondence and journals, I am grateful to the Rare Book and Manuscript Library at Columbia University, Duke University Library, Houghton Li-brary at Harvard University, the Pierpont Morgan Library in New York, Princeton University Library, Rollins College, and the Western Reserve Historical Society. The staffs at these libraries were most helpful, as was Signor Murbidelli, director of the Protestant Cemetery in Rome, who made available to me documents in the Benedict Library there. I am also grateful to Doris Faber for sharing her unpublished biography of Con-stance Fenimore Woolson with me; to Barry Qualls for suggestions on interpreting "Castle Nowhere"; to Jean Scully for assisting my research and threatening that if I didn't write a book about Woolson she would; to my students at Drew University for their enthusiasm about Woolson, especially to Martina Nowak and Jennifer Taylor for helping me interpret "Felipa"; to the reference and interlibrary loan staff at the Drew Univer-sity Library for their endless patience; to Kathleen Reich, archivist at Rollins College Library, for enthusiastic sleuthing in the Woolson collec-tion; to Michael Hodges, director of the Drew University London Pro-gram, for sharing his office and computer with me when I urgently needed both; to Mary Felstiner for astutely commenting on the introduction; and to David Weimer for suggesting I prepare this anthology and for providing the essential human and scholarly support while I did so.

INTRODUCTION

IN JANUARY OF 1894, ill with typhoid fever, possibly delirious, Constance Fenimore Woolson leapt or fell from her balcony in Venice and died without regaining consciousness. She was fifty-three years old. The violence of her death horrified her intimate friend Henry James, who believed that she had committed suicide. Thirteen years later, he was still making pilgrimages to her grave in the Protestant Cemetery in Rome, which he found "the most beautiful thing in Italy . . . that very particular spot below the great grey wall, the cypresses and time-silvered pyramid. It is tremendously, inexhaustibly touching—its effect never fails to overwhelm" (Edel 3: 377).

Woolson was, however, a number of contradictory women besides the one whose life had so touched and whose death had so overwhelmed Henry James. One was a novelist so successful in her day that *Harper's* gave her a thousand-dollar bonus on her first novel and begged her for more fiction than she could produce,[1] yet so obscure today that even feminist scholars ignore her. Another was a major innovator in American literary realism, yet singled out for her essential conservatism (James 178). She was adventurous and independent, spending the last fourteen years of her life in Florence and Venice, Oxford and London, Switzerland and Egypt; but she also longed for a little cottage in Florida with all her own things about her. Most paradoxically, Woolson was a highly articulate spokeswoman for the first generation of American women writers who saw themselves as artists, even while she remained strongly male-identified, leaning on her connection with her famous great-uncle James Fenimore Cooper[2] and attaching herself to the most important male writers of her own time.

Trying to understand Woolson through her male connections, however, is to see her through a distorting androcentric lens. Her response to Cooper, James, and other male literary giants was as critical and analytical as it was admiring; by appropriating and transforming some of their key images and themes, she critiqued and revised their work. Furthermore, she was at least as much affected by her personal and literary relations with women as she was by her links with men—so much so that her life and work comprise a complex response to the male and female cultures and literary traditions available to a woman writer after the Civil War.[3]

Woolson saw clearly that all these contexts were charged with conflict for women writers. Her fiction and letters show such women caught between their desire to compete with male artists and their ingrained sense of their own inadequacy; between their vision of a society that suppressed and silenced women and their need to write what male editors would publish and pay for; between their sense of the isolation and alienation of "woman's sphere" and their desire for homes and children. She saw too that women writers were torn between their admiration for male writers and texts and their need to reject or revise them in order to clear a space for their own art. Her life and work answer her own question: "Why do literary women break down so?" (letter to Stedman, 23 July 1876).

WOOLSON'S OWN struggle to prevent physical and emotional breakdown can be traced to the beginning of her life. Within three weeks of her birth in Claremont, New Hampshire, in 1840, scarlet fever killed three of her five older sisters. Her mother could never talk about the tragedy, and her father told the children that "a 'something' went out of her that week that was lost forever" (Benedict 3: 42). Woolson's birthdays must always have been celebrated in the shadow of her sisters' deaths and her mother's sad alteration. By the time she reached puberty, sixth-born Constance had become the eldest. She had watched three other sisters die, one in infancy, one after three months of marriage, one after giving birth to her second child. As she approached womanhood, she came to associate marriage and childbearing with death. These experiences may help explain why she later avoided intimacy with men, whose love seemed to kill, or with women, who died and left her.

Woolson's solitary habits also have roots in her intense relations with her parents. She adored her handsome, dashing father. Shortly after his death when she was twenty-nine, she prepared "A Brief Sketch of the Life of Charles Jarvis Woolson. Written by his daughter" (Benedict 3: 94–101). In the "Brief Sketch," Woolson emphasized traits of his that the two of them shared: a talent for "close observation of nature," a love of adventurous travel, a "ready wit, and keen sense of humour," and "the fortitude with which he bore the trials of life," trials she also shared (loss of loved ones, deafness, depression, financial insecurity). She describes her father as a paragon of physical and intellectual superiority; it seems she could never find a man who was his equal. She wrote to her friend Edmund Clarence Stedman, "My idea of love is, unfortunately, so high, that, like my idea of the office of minister, nothing or nobody ever comes up to it" (23 July 1876).

Much of Woolson's early fiction features father-daughter relations. While the bonds between fathers and daughters are very strong, almost incestuous, the fathers themselves are remarkably weak, as in *Anne* (1880) and *For the Major* (1882). Their deficiencies leave a vacuum in which their daughters must exercise power, just as Jarvis Woolson's death enabled his daughter to discover that she could earn her living by her pen. The incompetence of these adored fictive fathers may also come from Woolson's sense of her father's inability to protect his children from early deaths, while the criminality of the father in "Castle Nowhere" (1875, reprinted here) suggests that she saw her father's love as an attempt to expiate this weakness.

Mothers are much less prominent in Woolson's fiction, although their surrogates are everywhere: guardians, aunts both benevolent and vicious, and independent spinsters who nurture young women. This displacement may reflect Woolson's strong ambivalence toward her own mother. On the positive side was Hannah's role as a literary precursor, both as a niece of Fenimore Cooper and in her own right. Hannah's talent for close observation, her good memory, lively imagination, and deft turn of phrase appear in a large manuscript volume of "Recollections" of her childhood and early years of marriage, writings which Constance greatly admired. At the height of her own career, she wrote her niece about "the desire I have to arrange and publish—probably added to one of my own books—a few of the pages included in the MS volume of her 'recollections' that Mother bequeathed to you. . . . They have a simplicity and reality of style that is very remarkable, and that my best efforts cannot approach" (Benedict 3: 120). Woolson appears to have seen herself as fulfilling her mother's literary ambitions.

The negative side of Hannah's legacy lay in her conspicuous preference for her one son over her many but short-lived daughters. Hannah's longing for a son probably determined the unusually large size of her family; she recalled that she "could not persuade Mr. Woolson to feel as disappointed" as she about the sex of their first eight children (Benedict 3: 161). When she finally produced a male heir, Hannah wrote, "Congratulations poured in—after eight little girls comes the one boy: predictions of wonderful things by him to be accomplished, verses written upon his birth, etc." (Benedict 3: 166). Named for his father, Charly was always the center of his mother's life. In her late thirties, after nearly a decade of devoting herself to her mother's care, Constance wrote bitterly that her mother's "whole happiness, even her life I might almost say, depends, and always has depended upon how Charly is and how he feels" (letter to Samuel Mather, 24 Feb. 1877). Woolson appears to have driven herself all her life to outstrip her living sister and brother while trying to fulfill the promise of her six dead sisters.

However, her childhood was far from grim. The happier side of it can be glimpsed in her mother's account of a home where the family gathers "after tea with games and stories for the little ones until their bedtime, then music or reading or conversation with pleasant 'callers' for the older ones" (Benedict 3: 149). As a schoolgirl at the Cleveland Seminary, Woolson was "the center of a select admiring group, a girl at once fun-loving and dignified . . . whose school essays read in her low, cultivated voice held [her schoolmates] in rapt attention" (Guilford, "Notes").

Woolson took these early writings very seriously. A classmate remembered "the flush of pleasure on Connie's face as her audience breaks into open applause after one of her characteristic essays" was read aloud (Guilford, *Story of a Cleveland School* 76–77). Many years later, she thanked her remarkable teacher Linda Guilford for "the pains you took with my crude compositions; the clearness with which you made my careless eyes notice the essential differences between a good style and a bad one" (Benedict 3: 42). When she graduated at the head of her class at Madame Chegaray's fashionable New York school, and her father took the family on a long celebratory trip to "the fashionable resorts around Boston," she seemed to care more about writing when and where she pleased than about her success as "great belle."

Woolson was twenty-one when the Civil War broke out. She wrote that "the war was the heart and spirit of my life, and everything has seemed tame to me since" (letter to Stedman, 1 Oct. 1876). That excitement extended to a young soldier who had been a childhood friend, but it was only the "glamor that the war threw over the young officers who left their homes to fight" that "made me fancy I cared for him" (letter to Samuel Mather, Jan. 1891). She never again admitted to a romantic attachment to any man.

Very little is known about Woolson in her twenties. She lived with her family in Cleveland, helped run a fair to raise money for medical supplies for Union troops, visited New York, went driving with her father and walking and rowing by herself, and described herself half-ironically to a girlhood friend as a "desolate spinster" (Benedict 2: 19). Certainly she continued her avid reading; probably she began to experiment with writing in different literary genres. But like many other women of her time, only when her father's death left her and her mother with "precarious means" (Benedict 3: 19) did she find the occasion and opportunity, and perhaps the excuse, to publish essays and stories. Their quality suggests she had been working on them for some time.

Within a year of her father's death, when she was thirty, she broke into *Harper's New Monthly Magazine* with "The Happy Valley," a sketch of the Zoarites in Ohio, whom she had visited with her father, and into *Putnam's Magazine* with a sketch of Mackinac Island, where the family had vacationed. She also wrote lively accounts, "From Our Special Woman Correspondent," for the *Daily Cleveland Herald,* based on impressions gathered while she and her mother lived in New York after the family home in Cleveland was broken up.

Within five years, she could write of the "success that has come to me, limited of course, but very great when you think that it lifts all pecuniary cares off my mind. With the money I earn by my pen, Mother and I are entirely comfortable in our quiet way; without it, we should be very much cramped, and every day an anxiety" (Benedict 3: 119). She is obviously proud of her ability to take over her father's role as provider for her mother and herself.

Uncertain where her talents lay, she experimented for a long time with the available literary genres. A successful early venture was in children's literature; her first book, *The Old Stone House* (1873), won a prize of $1000. This genre was very congenial to her: "All of my life . . . I have been a teller of stories to children. Endless stories; stories that went on for months and years,—oral serials" (letter to Mary Mapes Dodge). But she had greater ambitions. In the same year, she published her first two stories for adults. Both "Solomon" and "St. Clair Flats" (reprinted here) feature women stranded in the wilderness with visionary husbands. By 1877 Woolson was also publishing anonymous reviews and criticism in the "Contributor's Club" of the *Atlantic Monthly*. She was deeply interested in the theater, and in the 1880s considered collaborating on a play with Henry James. She published a great deal of poetry, mostly undistinguished except in its effort to present American locales, legends, and dialects in elaborate meters like Poe's.[4]

The best of Woolson's work grows out of her interest in a distinctly female genre: the regional sketch, which aimed to describe as faithfully as possible a narrow piece of life.[5] Because she led a nomadic life in the South and in Europe from the time she began to write for a living, she never focused, as most of the women regionalists did, on a single geographic area. But she entered deeply and seriously into every place she lived or visited. She set most of her early stories in the American equivalents of desert islands: Mackinac Island in Lake Michigan, a mining camp on an island in Lake Superior, a solitary house in a salt marsh on Lake Huron, a cotton plantation abandoned after Sherman's march, a Southern cemetery for Union soldiers. Many of these stories focus on the relations of people who are geographically, socially, and emotionally stranded with visitors from less isolated situations, dramatizing the effect that dominant and muted cultures have on each other.[6] The isolated settings also function as metaphors for women's various forms of exile—from themselves, from their society, from their art—and for Woolson's sense of herself as a home-less outcast.

That feeling seemed to take root during the decade she spent wandering with her mother in the South after her father died. New York had proved too cold for Hannah's health, and too expensive, so they visited Virginia, the Carolinas, Tennessee, and Georgia, eventually settling in St. Augustine, Florida. Living in boarding houses, they met interesting literary figures such as Edmund Clarence Stedman and Elizabeth Stuart Phelps, and fabulously wealthy visitors who interested Woolson only as objects of satire.[7] To a friend's hint that she might be engaged, she replied, "Nobody is at my feet at all, do'nt be satirical. . . . I am as truly out of that kind of talk as a nun. I go about a great deal, but always as an 'observer,' 'a very superior person,' and that sort of thing" (Benedict 2: 242).

Increasingly, she disliked going into society. By age thirty-six she had decided that "To enjoy society a woman must be either personally attractive, gifted with conversational powers, or else must *think* herself one or both, whether she is in reality or not. I do not come under any of those heads. Result: do'nt care for society at all. . . . I keep away from all chance callers and flee all invitations. . . . I am very strongly 'New Hampshire' in all my ways. I have a row of tall solemn Aunts up there, silent, reserved, solitary, thin, and a little grim; I am as much like them as the kind of life I lead will allow" (Hubbell 732).

Her niece Clare Benedict, however, who lived with Woolson for months at a time and was an intimate friend, describes her in totally different terms: "Holding a curiously low opinion of her own personal appearance, she was nevertheless considered by others to be unusually attractive, physically . . . her charm was potent and well-nigh irresistible. . . . [She was] endowed by nature with a passionate, even stormy temperament, together with a keenly analytical mind. . . . Like all creative artists, she suffered from periodical fits of acute depression, but her powers of enjoyment were correspondingly high, and her interests were many and catholic" (Benedict 2: xiii–xv). Even allowing for the niece's inclination to canonize her aunt, Benedict's description of Woolson's personal attractiveness, complex temperament, and capacity for charm matches the woman who emerges from Woolson's letters and photographs much better than the satiric self-portraits. Woolson's self-rejection may have grown in part from the guilty survivor's sense of worthlessness, while her solitary inclinations were reinforced by her decade of displacement in the South.

An important aspect of that displacement was cultural. She found Southern literary taste impossibly provincial, and Southern politics painful, writing to her friend, the Southern poet Paul Hamilton Hayne, "Do'nt you think that for a red hot abolitionist, republican and hard-money advocate, I have behaved well down here in Dixie during these last three long years?" (Easter 1876). She behaved well too in accommodating to the dull routines of her mother's life, but repeatedly described herself as "starving" for culture (letter to Hayne, 14 May 1876). She also found a rich source of untouched material for fiction in the South's struggles to recover from the Civil War five years after the surrender at Appomattox. Although one of the Harper brothers warned her "'of all things' to avoid the subject of the war in connection with the South" (letter to Stedman, 23 July 1876), she ignored his advice and found material there for some of her strongest fiction, such as "Rodman the Keeper" (1877) and "In the Cotton Country" (1876, reprinted here).[8]

Her ability to treat both Northerners and Southerners with balanced sympathy and irony probably grew from her feeling that they were linked by the emotional intensity of the Civil War years. She wrote Hayne, "What days they were. After all, we *lived* then. It is in vain for our generation to hope to be any other than 'people who remember'" (23 July 1875).

Still, she longed to break away from the South and to travel abroad. Resigned and somewhat resentful, she was stuck with her mother in the South while her brother Charly was making trips to Europe and to California, writing to ask her for money, and destroying his health—with morphine, Woolson believed. His letters so "appalled" and "terrified" his sister that she lived "in a state of constant trouble and dread" (letter to Samuel Mather, 30 Jan. 1877).

Such sibling and oedipal tensions animate much of Woolson's fiction. In "The South Devil" (1880, *Rodman the Keeper*), for instance, a hard-working man sacrifices himself for his thoroughly selfish and immature younger brother because the lad reminds him of his own lost beloved—as Charly reminded Constance of her father. Woolson identifies with both brothers, giving the younger her own artistic temperament and her long-ings for flight and irresponsibility. While such feelings—stunningly trans-formed into images of a deadly but beautiful swamp—give this story its force, they pushed all her novels but one into melodrama.[9]

Woolson's compulsive focus on the interrelated themes of irrational guilt, self-sacrifice, and the refusal of love can be traced to her clearly understood but unresolved family drama: passion for her father ambiva-lently transferred to her brother, guilt and inordinate expectations of her-self growing out of her sisters' deaths, longing for her mother's love mixed with resentment of her mother's preference for the men of the family. At the same time, she knew that these themes could empower literature, and she used them deliberately: "The most dramatic effects are those that indicate suppressed passion—hounds are ready to slip the leash. They are utilized by Browning; they channelize the Puritan repression in Haw-thorne" (Benedict 2: 108).

She also understood and shared Hawthorne's guilt over using as material for art the experience of other human beings who could not be intimately observed without damaging their lives and the observer's own integrity. In her own fiction Woolson revises Hawthorne's major tales about this "unpardonable sin"—*The Scarlet Letter* in "Peter the Parson" (1874) and "Rappaccini's Daughter" in "Castle Nowhere" (1875). She also creates women narrators who prey on their subject matter like vampires in such stories as "Jeannette" (1874), "Wilhelmena" (1874), and "In the Cotton Country."[10]

In her guilt as an artist, as well as her guilt as a daughter and sister, can be found the roots of Woolson's self-rejection and reclusiveness. It would certainly have been hard for a woman so entangled in these conflicts to accept herself or to form adult attachments. Here too are sources, along with her biological inheritance from her father and grandfather, of the devastating depressions that darkened her life for months at a time and that contributed to her early death, probably by suicide.

THE DEPRESSIONS BEGAN during her thirties. She "lost a whole year and more, owing to the depressed state of my mind" after finishing her first novel *Anne* (letter to Stedman, 16 Sept. 1877). She wrote to her girlhood friend Arabella Washburn, "Don't fancy I am sad all the time. Oh no. I am much too busy and too full of plans of all kinds. But at times, in spite of all I can do, this deadly enemy of mine creeps in, and once in, he is master. I think it is constitutional, and I know it is inherited" (Benedict 3: 244). She also inherited another cause of depression from her father—deafness, which came to her in her forties. It added to her isolation—"It is only old friends who will take the trouble to speak in a trumpet"—and soon she was not well enough to see anyone because of prolonged infections brought on by attempts to use artificial eardrums whose pain made her think she "should be mad, or dead, before morning" (letter to Baldwin, 5 Feb. 1892).

She struggled fiercely against depression, and developed three remedies for it. The first was simply to hang on and outlive despair with "simple courage. . . . (I am determined never to outlive my own)" (letter to Baldwin, 15 June 1892). The second was travel, which she used extensively, and successfully, most of her life. After the death of her mother, when she was forty, she left for Europe and never returned to America. Until her own death in 1894, she spent cool months in Italy, warm months in England and Switzerland, and traveled to other exotic locales. She sometimes disliked this rootless life—"it is a curious fate that has made the most domestic woman in the world . . . a wanderer for nearly twenty years" (letter to Katherine Mather, 2 July 1893)—and was often tempted to return to America. But she also loved "the romance & color" of Europe: "What do you say to my trying Algiers next winter? Would'nt that be a bold move!" (Petry 47).

Her third remedy for depression, the "evil spirit that haunts all creative minds," was to pump up one's self-esteem. She advised the poet Paul Hamilton Hayne, ill, impoverished, and despairing, to "Think of yourself highly. . . . The greatest artists are nerved to their greatest works by a sublime consciousness of a belief in their own powers" (10 Jan. 1876).

Unsurprisingly, she saw depression as an occupational hazard for women writers, for whom such self-esteem was all but impossible. Although she must have known that male writers broke down too, she thought women who wrote were predisposed to depression. When she heard that the writer Elizabeth Stoddard was ill, she asked Edmund Stedman, "Why do literary women break down so? . . . It almost seems as though only the unhappy women took to writing" (23 July 1876). Some illnesses came from the physical work of writing long manuscripts by hand. "Too constant pen-work" (letter to Stedman, 24 Feb. 1887) brought considerable pain and a right arm whose muscles "tangle themselves with the nerves of the same locality and the two hold a witches' dance together that sends me to bed and keeps me there" (Benedict 2: 41). Some women even lost the ability to use words. Woolson notes that her "(comparatively) small trouble of lameness sinks into nothingness beside the terrible nervous prostration" her friend Frances Hodgson Burnett suffered every time she finished writing a book; bedridden for six months, she could not produce the right names for things (letter to Samuel Mather, n.d.). Such a loss of control over language, or over one's writing arm, vividly expresses the "anxiety of authorship" that Gilbert and Gubar (49) believe afflicted nineteenth-century women writers.[11]

Women writers also suffered, Woolson thought, from losing their femininity. After spending an evening with Elizabeth Stoddard and Mary Mapes Dodge at the home of Edmund Stedman, she wrote to him:

> How much prettier and lovelier a thousand times over was Mrs. Stedman in every motion, look and tone than the best we other three could do! What *is* the reason that if we take up a pen we seem to lose so much in other ways? . . . But perhaps it is 'compensation'; as we gain money, or fame, just so surely must we lose that which in our hearts we prize a great deal more. (28 Sept. 1874)

One might dismiss this uncharacteristically formulaic language as a mixture of flattery and fishing if Woolson hadn't also presented herself to another spinster as an old maid whose necessary literary labors unfitted her to attract a man and reap the usual womanly rewards. She wrote Guilford from Oxford on the birth of a niece, "Oxford and rooms and writing a novel are poor things compared to a baby" (Guilford, "Notes").

While she regretted not having children and a home, she showed no signs of willingness to exchange her independent, adventurous life for them. Although often lonely, she never formed a "Boston marriage" as so many of her contemporaries did, finding the love and support indispensable to the artist in a long-term relationship with another woman. She saw such a partnership close up in the relationship of Alice James and Katherine Loring, and must have known of many others, but she never lived for extended periods with any woman but her mother, nor is there much correspondence to be found with women other than her relatives, although there may well be letters that have been lost. She seems to have rejected the domestic world of womanly bonds which had sustained her mother out of a complex mixture of feelings: resentment at the ways that world had disappointed her as daughter and sister and as artist; longing for a wider, more adventurous life of independence and travel; and fear from childhood of losing women she loved.

She never participated directly in the women's movement, but she showed a cautious sympathy with it. She satirized herself, in a very funny letter, for giving in to her sister and spending a lot of money on a silk suit, which failed to conceal her identity as a literary (and therefore dowdy) woman; but she also laughed at Elizabeth Stuart Phelps for adopting dress reform.[12] She sent her sonnet "To George Eliot" to the *New Century for Women,* a journal supporting woman suffrage. And while she let Henry James think she "would never lend her voice to the plea . . . for a revolution which should place her sex in the thick of the struggle for power" ("Miss Woolson," reprinted here), she wrote his sister Alice that she was in favor of medical education for women but that men and women should receive such education together. "It is the only way, in my opinion, to widen the feminine mind. . . . Do not suppose from that that I think the feminine mind inferior to the masculine. For I do not. But it has been kept back, & enfeebled, & limited, by ages of ignorance, & almost servitude" (Strouse 260).

Most of Woolson's deep attachments were to men, mostly distinguished in or connected with the arts, all safely married except for the entrenched bachelor, Henry James. Correspondence attests to the complex relations she had with Dr. William Wilberforce Baldwin, an American physician living in Florence who treated such noted Americans as Henry James, Samuel Clemens, Edith Wharton, and William Dean Howells (Petry 57n3); with Edmund Clarence Stedman, the eminent critic and poet; with John Hay, who held high posts in the Lincoln, McKinley, and Roosevelt administrations, and who wrote sketches, fiction, and verse as well as a ten-volume study of Lincoln; and with Paul Hamilton Hayne. Her sustained friendships with these remarkable men indicate how readily she was accepted as writer, thinker, and woman, as well as her ambition to achieve eminence like theirs, possibly with their help.[13]

Her hope of meeting Henry James was one factor that impelled her to travel to Europe in 1879. Despite her devastation from her mother's recent death and despite her habitual aversion to society, she managed before leaving America to obtain a letter of introduction to James from his cousin, Henrietta Pell-Clark. James was then the distinguished author of stories, articles, reviews, and several novels, though he had not yet written his major work. Woolson was then the established author of two volumes of short stories and a novel appearing serially in *Harper's*. They met in Florence in the spring of 1880, where despite James's numerous social and professional obligations, "he found time to come in the mornings and take me out; sometimes to the galleries or churches, and sometimes just for a walk in the beautiful green Cascine. . . . He has been perfectly charming to me" (Benedict 2: 184–185).

Woolson had long been fascinated by James's work. Only a few months before they met, she had written a perceptive and appreciative review of his novel *The Europeans* for the *Atlantic*. Three years later she could tell him that "The deepest charm of your writings to me" is that "they voice for me—as nothing else ever has—my own feelings. . . . Your writings . . . are my true country, my real home. And nothing else ever fully is—try as I may to think so" (7 May 1883). For four months in 1886 and 1887 she and James actually shared a home, a villa she was renting outside Florence. Although James told Woolson's sister that these had been "the most charmed and appeased, the most gratified and rewarded and beguiled days that [Woolson] . . . ever passed" (Benedict 3: 338n), they must also have been replete with powerful and mixed feelings on both sides.

For Woolson saw James's personal limitations with her usual clarity, and let him know about them. She told him gently in letters, indirectly in a group of stories about women artists (reprinted here), and with devastating accuracy in journals that James read after her death:

Imagine a man endowed with an absolutely unswerving will; extremely intelligent, he *comprehends* passion, affection, unselfishness and self-sacrifice, etc., perfectly, though he is himself cold and a pure egoist. He has a charming face, a charming voice, and he can, when he pleases, counterfeit all these feelings so exactly that he gets all the benefits that are to be obtained by them.   (Benedict 2: 135)

She was as openly ambivalent toward the writer as she was toward the man. In the four letters she wrote him that James failed to destroy, she grovels before his genius, and then tells him how she hates him for it. She insists that "the utmost best of my work cannot touch the hem of your first or poorest" (30 Aug. 1882). But she also writes with astounding frankness,

I do'nt think you appreciated . . . the laudation your books received in America, as they came out one by one. We little fish did! We little fish became worn to skeletons owing to the constant admonitions we received to regard the beauty, the grace, the incomparable perfec- tions of all sorts and kinds of the proud salmon of the pond; we ended by hating that salmon.   (12 Feb. 1882)

In many ways, Woolson's relationship with James exemplifies ten- sions between male and female writers of their time. For example, James expresses his own mixed feelings about Woolson as woman and as writer, and about successful women writers generally, in his revealing essay "Miss Woolson" (1888, reprinted here). He contrasts women's struggle for ad- mission to "various offices, colleges, functions, and privileges" with their success in gaining "admission into the world of literature: they are there in force; they have been admitted, with all the honours, on a perfectly equal footing. In America, at least, one feels tempted to exclaim that they are in themselves the world of literature." He is sure that Woolson shares his opinion, that except for the "strength of the current which today carries both sexes" to write books, she would not be "competing for the literary laurel" because she believes that women are "by their very nature only too much exposed"—he doesn't say to what—even in their confinement in the home. James claims that she would not "lend her voice to the plea for further exposure—for a revolution which should place her sex in the thick of the struggle for power."

James's essay warns Woolson against struggling for power, against competing with him, against exposing her feelings, while praising her fe- male characters who "try and provide for the happiness of others (when they adore them) even to their own injury." After Woolson's death, James came to believe that she had made such sacrifices for him and that in his egotism he had refused to see her love or seize the salvation it offered him. He dramatized this very situation in "The Beast in the Jungle," whose central theme he took from an entry he found in Woolson's journal—"To imagine a man spending his life looking for and waiting for his 'splendid moment.' . . . But the moment never comes" (Benedict 2: 144−45)—and whose climactic scene of revelation he set at Woolson's grave.

James seemed to think that Woolson had sacrificed opportunities to meet and marry other men because of her absorption in him, but it is doubtful that she could ever have married anyone. Still, she did compromise herself in a way for James. She told him, "I do not come in as a literary woman at all, but as a sort of—admiring aunt. I think that expresses it" (letter to James, 12 Feb. 1882). What this comment expressed was her need to avoid rejection as both a literary competitor and a demanding woman, a need so great that she was willing to sacrifice her literary and sexual identities to it. This denial injured her personally and professionally and surely contributed—along with her ill health, financial worry, history of depression, and philosophical approval of suicide as "the open door"[14]—to her violent death at age fifty-three.

Just after her death, her stricken and guilty friends described her life as wretched. John Hay saw her as a "thoroughly good, and most unhappy woman, with a great talent, bedeviled by disordered nerves. She . . . had not as much happiness as a convict" (Petry 17). And James saw her as never perfectly sane, always so depressed that his feeling for her was largely concern and anxiety (Edel 3: 361). Her own accounts confirm that she was often desperately unhappy.[15] But she was also a witty, irreverent, impertinent woman who enjoyed life passionately. Her psychological doubleness—anguished and amused, home-rooted and restless—was underlined by her complicated dual national identities—a Northerner in the South, an American in Europe. She transforms these facts of her life into the insights of her fiction.

FROM THE 1870s to the early 1890s, a wide and varied readership eagerly awaited stories and novels by Constance Fenimore Woolson as they appeared in the leading American literary magazines. Her contemporaries placed her among the best writers of their time. Alice James asked to have Woolson's story "Dorothy" read to her in the last days of her life, and Henry James wrote to William Dean Howells that the only English language writers he read were Howells himself and Woolson. By putting his essay on her with studies of George Eliot, Turgenev, Emerson, Stevenson, and Maupassant in his *Partial Portraits,* James indicated that he thought her equally worthy of consideration. By today's standards, she deserves to be ranked with such contemporaries as Sarah Orne Jewett, Mary E. Wilkins Freeman, Rebecca Harding Davis, Elizabeth Stuart Phelps, and Kate Chopin. The five novels, four volumes of short stories, and numerous sketches, poems, and reviews she published in her lifetime show her to be an extraordinary observer, a superb stylist, and a shrewd and witty critic of prevailing mores and ideologies.

Why was Woolson so prominent in her own time and so invisible in ours? Possibly she has been misread, in both periods, as a conservative advocate of womanly repression in the name of self-control, and of masochistic self-sacrifice in the name of goodness. Woolson's contemporaries had been taught to admire women like her "heroic" characters who endured "great sacrifice" and "intense suffering with so much fortitude" (Benedict, *Appreciations* 87). Although some women writers saw that such sacrifices were "actually demoralizing and debilitating" (Kelley 251), such widely read novelists as Augusta Evans Wilson and Caroline Lee Hentz glorified such self-abnegating women. By adding their voices to the chorus of approval for selfless women, they helped to console women for their loss of a wider world than the home, while discouraging them from forsaking their assigned domestic sphere.

Modern readers have failed to perceive that Woolson's fiction is not an endorsement but a radical critique of this ideology, and a brilliant analysis of the dynamics of self-sacrifice in women's lives. Her most complex analysis of female selflessness is in her best novel, *East Angels* (1886), whose heroine conceals her struggle for freedom and her rebellion against male authority behind the unassailable veneer of self-sacrifice. Woolson's pervasive irony is subtle enough in this novel that so astute a critic as James could choose to overlook it and praise the book for making "real and natural a transcendent, exceptional act . . . in which the sense of duty is raised to exaltation" ("Miss Woolson"). Woolson's journals, however, make explicit what James missed: "Self-denial is giving up what one really likes. Search for the secret taste of each person, and see if *that* is indulged! If it is, there is no self-denial, no matter how ascetic the man (or woman) may appear to be" (Benedict 2: 110).[16]

Woolson scrutinizes not only the main pillar of domestic ideology, self-sacrifice, but also its base: love. In her fiction, heterosexual love infantilizes women, although the love of daughters and sisters for their fathers and siblings empowers them. In *Jupiter Lights* (1889), for example, a woman capable of shooting a crazed alcoholic and rescuing a baby from a drifting boat in a tempest is reduced, when she falls in love, to the helpless child her lover wants her to be. But in *Horace Chase* (1893), a crippled woman finds the strength to haul her sister off a mountain ledge. In her fiction love sometimes excuses women for venturing beyond prescribed roles, as in *Anne,* where the heroine has to become a detective to clear her lover's name. Or it requires a woman to exaggerate prescribed roles, as when Madame Carroll imitates the ideal of the child-woman to preserve her husband's vital illusions in *For the Major.* But in no case does Woolson accept the patriarchal love plot in which the heroine finds earthly salvation through the love of a good man.

THE STORIES REPRINTED HERE represent the range of Woolson's best work, and feature her most characteristic theme: women's struggles against the isolation and alienation that she saw as inevitable consequences of confinement to the places and ideas of "woman's sphere." Her expanding vision of this struggle unites the three regions she made her own—the Great Lakes, the South, and Europe. The first three stories, from her first volume of collected fiction, *Castle Nowhere: Lake-Country Sketches* (1875), center on isolated women living on tiny islands in the Great Lakes. While the later stories feature women artists who struggle with the patriarchal norms that silence women's voices, these early stories examine the male literary texts that encode women's marginality. By alluding to the work of Francis Bacon, Hawthorne, Bret Harte, and the literary domestics,[17] she makes them her own, revises their assumptions about women, and creates her own art in the space she has cleared. Of all her precursors, her great-uncle Cooper pressed hardest on her imagination.

Annette Kolodny points out that before women writers could construct their own fantasies of the meaning of the wilderness, they had to deal with the mythic figure who already dominated that terrain: the solitary hunter based on Daniel Boone and given imaginative form by Cooper (224). Literary domestics writing frontier fiction, such as E.D.E.N. Southworth and Maria Cummins, tamed and refined the mighty hunter by bringing him "out of the woods and into town" and by redefining the meaning of the hunt (Kolodny 224).

Woolson, however, went much further; she undermined the hero's claim to heroism. She turns Cooper's solitary woodsman into a recreational hunter and parodies as Romantic affectation his desire to live "close to the great heart of nature." She turns Leatherstocking's sententious morality into the religious fanaticism of Waiting Samuel in "St. Clair Flats" or the tortured theology of Old Fog in "Castle Nowhere." She transforms his obtusely clear conscience into the haunted consciousness of Reuben Mitchell in "The Lady of Little Fishing." Most important, she brings Cooper's marginalized, silenced women to the center of her narratives, sometimes as realistic characters who tell their own stories of loss and endurance, sometimes as mythic figures enacting symbolic dramas. As she creates new tales out of old texts, she reveals the effects on a woman writer of the literary traditions available to her.

"The Lady of Little Fishing" (1874) contains a brilliant image of a writer simultaneously demolishing the work of her predecessors and nourishing herself on it. Woolson's narrator uses buildings of an abandoned town on an island in Lake Superior as fuel to cook his meals while shaping a story from the events that took place there. By giving this action to a man, Woolson evades its aggressiveness, but at the same time she confronts directly the most indigestible part of Cooper's legacy: his portrait of the ideal female as a pious half-wit. Woolson transforms his Hetty Hunter, who thinks she can persuade the Indians to stop taking scalps by reading the Bible to them, into an eloquent woman missionary who imposes civilized behavior on Indians as well as on hunters and trappers, and who, like Hetty, is not harmed by them.

Woolson rewrites *The Deerslayer* to explore the possibility that men might listen to a full-witted woman—say, to a writer like herself. She concludes that even lawless, depraved men will hang on a woman's words just as long as they see the woman as an angel, a sexless, wholly spiritual being. Then they will even cook for this madonna, nurse her when she's ill, build a meetinghouse for her to conduct services, and become docile, sexless children for her. But once she falls in love with one of them, she loses her power over both the man and herself. When she throws herself at the feet of a man who does not love her, her rhetorical degradation is as great as her personal fall: "Oh, take me with you! Let me be your servant—your slave—anything—anything, so that I am not parted from you, my lord and master, my only, only love!" Although love is shown to be a terrible affliction, the Lady dies not of love but of shame.

Love leads the Lady not only to the loss of her dignity and verbal power but also to the devastating revelation that she was not God's instrument in the wildernesses of America and of men's hearts. The story thus comments not only on Cooper but on the strategy of some of Woolson's female precursors, the so-called literary domestics, who excused their unladylike entry into man's public sphere by claiming that they wrote because God had called on them to save souls (Kelley 295). Woolson suggests not only that God's instruments may be deluded, but that they can retain their power only by sacrificing their capacity for love. The story also undercuts the ideology of the woman as "the angel of the house." Woolson's angelic Lady is not confined to any home but takes the whole wilderness for her sphere. Her role is not to sacrifice herself for men but to save them by her preaching. And the story subverts the stand of the literary domestics that a woman's selfless love of one man gives her power over him, and through him, in the world. In Woolson's tale, neither love nor moral influence gives a woman power or security. The Lady fades into a troubling memory about whom men construct stories of their own.[18]

The second of the *Lake-Country Sketches* reprinted here, "Castle Nowhere" (1875), also focuses on love and religion, but in this story the woman knows nothing of good and evil. The theologian, called Old Fog, is a murderer who thinks he expiates his crime by tenderly raising an abandoned child, although he commits further murders because the girl's "delicate life must be delicately nurtured." In a review in the *Atlantic,* William Dean Howells objected to the "subtle confusion of all the conceptions of right and wrong" created by Old Fog's morality (737), and the character's disbelief in eternal punishment brought Woolson "at least twenty awful letters. . . . Is it possible that I am to be held personally responsible for the theology and morality of all my characters?" (Benedict 2: 20).

She was herself ambivalent about "Castle Nowhere," writing to Stedman that trying "to make the new story more 'ideal' . . . makes me feel as though I was telling a thousand lies" (20 Jan. 1875), while telling Hayne that she thought "it is my best" (letter of May 1875). The story—a novella, in fact—is a remarkable record of Woolson's confrontation as a committed realist with the possibilities of the mythic and romantic. She here rejects the romantic idea that one can escape a historical identity as "somebody" and become "nobody" or "anybody." She tests the assertion of her young hunter Jarvis Waring, that "we can be anybody we please," by confronting him with the ultimate "nobody"—Old Fog, who has deliberately destroyed his civilized identity—and the ultimate "anybody"—Fog's daughter Silver, whose identity is only potential because she has grown up on a floating castle surrounded by deep water, knowing only four people and five books.

Woolson also entertained and rejected the possibility of being "nowhere" rather than one particular "somewhere"—a possibility that challenges the basis of regionalist writing. "Nowhere" is outside geography, history, religion, society, and culture. There, sinful father and innocent daughter can live happily together until "somebody"—a potential suitor for the daughter—invades, bringing with him a variety of cultural "somewheres" that eventually destroy "nowhere." Jarvis brings the world of Scripture to the wilderness when he identifies Silver as Rachel and himself as Esau, and explains to Silver the meaning of death and resurrection. The world of mythology enters through allusions to Sisyphus, Psyche, and Sleeping Beauty. The world of patriarchy is exemplified by the polygamous Mormons on nearby Beaver Island, while Silver's name indicates that she, like Mormon women, is merely a medium of exchange between men. The world of art is only another form of struggle between men and of male dominance over women: Fog steals Jarvis's copy of Shakespeare's sonnets and a Titian miniature for Silver, who learns "womanly feelings" from the way male art structures love and loss. The sole female influence to balance this male perspective is a doubly disqualified woman—a mute ex-slave.

Whether she is "nowhere" or "somewhere," then, a woman's effort to become "somebody" is severely constrained. But in this novella Woolson does clear a space where women's identities can develop by revising two prominent male fictions in which women are severely repressed: Hawthorne's "Rappaccini's Daughter" and, once more, Cooper's *Deerslayer*. Her critique of Cooper here goes beyond changing a female born with weak brains into a normal woman kept ignorant by a man. While featuring in her title the floating castle prominent in *The Deerslayer*, Woolson centers her tale on what is peripheral in Cooper: the relations of a criminal father and the daughter he raises in the wilderness. She turns the antagonism Cooper imagined between the Hutter girls and Tom into a possessive love between father and daughter whose incestuous tendencies must be halted by a young suitor. And unlike Tom Hutter's horrible slow death from scalping—exactly what he deserves for scalping Indian women and children for bounties—Old Fog dies peacefully in Silver's loving arms. The suggestion is that Woolson, and possibly God, can forgive crimes committed in the name of devotion.

Her use of Hawthorne is more searching. As in "Rappaccini's Daughter," the heroine of "Castle Nowhere" lives in a bower of flowering plants which she kisses and talks to because her father's crimes have deprived her of all human companionship. Like Dr. Rappaccini, Fog is a father willing to sacrifice other men as he has sacrificed his daughter to his own objectives. But unlike the poisonous Beatrice, whose soul may or may not be pure, Silver is utterly innocent. And unlike Hawthorne, Woolson questions whether men of the world could really be satisfied with the pure, cloistered women who were their ideal.

To this end, she loads Silver with archetypes of female innocence until the girl staggers under the weight. Silver is even more innocent than the unfallen Eve, because her father has withheld from her all knowledge of death and of God's word. She is like Sleeping Beauty, with her purity guarded by a hedge of water instead of thorns, like Psyche kept in solitude for the delight of one man and mysteriously provided with delicate food and gorgeous gowns. Woolson's tale makes it clear that the cultural ideal of female innocence limits both male and female development by preventing women's self-realization and by mating men with grown-up children. Silver may have no more opportunity to develop or express herself than Rappaccini's daughter or the Hutter girls, but Woolson, in her strenuous revision of patriarchal texts, has prepared a space where women's identities may develop, where their voices may eventually be heard.

A woman tells her own experience of the wilderness in the last of the *Lake-Country Sketches* reprinted here. The heroine of "St. Clair Flats" (1873) has given up her parents, her baby's grave, and even mementoes of life in civilization because her husband considers them "vanity." He has changed her first as well as last name, and even taken away her title of "Mrs." presumably because the spirits that led him into the wilderness tell him that marital relations are also "vanity." Although Samuel belittles Roxana's domain—he tells visiting hunters that the "woman will attend to your earthly concerns"—Roxana has come to like the spirits who tell Samuel of a thousand years of joy about to begin in America, when it becomes a new Eden. But she also does her best to realize Eden in the present, miraculously providing fresh butter and down pillows on a tiny island at the center of a labyrinth of marshy channels.

Woolson makes this remote spot speak not only of the conflict between flesh and spirit, but also of the related struggles between female and male, the practical and the visionary, the comic and the romantic, the mobile and the stationary, the historic and the mythic. These concerns are superbly illustrated by the imagery of the St. Clair Flats, and by an astonishing range of allusion to myth and legend, Old and New Testament, history and literature. Like the effect of these male texts on a woman writer, the Flats are beautiful but bewildering, fascinating but disorienting: "It is an ocean full of land,—a prairie full of water,—a desert full of verdure."

The story is an elegy for two American myths, one essentially male, the other female. When Woolson's hunter returns to the Flats several years later, he finds no sign of the new American Eden Samuel had waited for, but rather a victory of commerce over the spirit. An ugly and efficient canal cuts through the beautiful channels of the marsh; a lighthouse of "new and prosaic brick" replaces the picturesque fortress on stilts. Nor has Roxana's fantasy of making the wilderness into a domestic garden prevailed; she and Samuel have vanished, and her cheerful home is a ruin. Woolson's lyrical prose is her tribute to the beauty and futility of these dreams.

Introduction

THE NEXT THREE STORIES reprinted here, collected in 1880 in *Rodman the Keeper: Southern Sketches,* are set in the post–Civil War South. They all feature women artists who are exiles not only from their homes but from themselves, cut off from self-knowledge and relationships so devastating that solitude is preferable. Ultimately, these repressions exile them from their own art. But while the plots depict female failure, the style and point of view assert Woolson's growing self-consciousness and self-confidence. She replaces the male narrators of the *Lake-Country Sketches* with female narrators or with a female character's point of view. And she analyzes the debilitation of her women artists in an authorial voice that is assured, ironic, and in control. This striking discrepancy between form and content raises questions about the degree to which Woolson identified herself with these failed women artists.

The comedy that dances around "Miss Elisabetha" (1875) indicates Woolson's distance from a woman who exercises her art exclusively in the domestic sphere. In her characteristic comic style, prominent in all her novels but rare in her short stories, Woolson reveals the absurdities of the elderly spinster while simultaneously evoking sympathy for her. Perfectly confident in her superiority as a descendant of an old New York Dutch family, Miss Elisabetha marches along dusty Florida roads in her ancient brocade dress, accompanied by a bodyguard of black children, prepared to "grind to powder" the opera singer who threatens to take away the spinster's talented ward, Doro. But this beautiful prima donna also gets comic treatment. A parody of male fantasies of female perfection, she materializes on a beach sitting on a tiger skin, dressed in purple velvet, singing like an angel. In reality she is very much like Miss Elisabetha in her self-importance.

Woolson's technique is to point out such similarities in apparently opposite characters. These women confront each other as representatives of two different social orders, one based on old family distinction, the other on new individual accomplishment. They also represent the differing worlds of high art and domestic art. But in fact their common ground as women is more important than the difference in the music they admire and perform; both women are brilliant performers of roles invented by others, and both obey the rules of male art. Miss Elisabetha is merely out-of-date. She reproduces the stylized trills and quavers her music master taught her forty years before, because she has lived in a cultural vacuum and has not heard newer music. In the same way, she practices female domestic arts, along with their supporting values of self-sacrifice and self-satisfaction, because she does not know that the young man for whom she labors will find other women's arts more appealing than hers.

While Woolson respects the domestic art that enables Miss Elisabetha to offer a comfortable life and a wider future to Doro, she sees that it is doomed to fail along with the rigid system of values it expresses because they make no allowance for nature or spontaneity. When Doro chooses marriage to a Minorcan girl over a life as an opera singer or as a cultivated gentleman, high art, bourgeois art, and domestic art all fall before the simple melody she sings in a voice "as full of rich tones as a peach is full of lusciousness." But his choice of luscious nature is no more fulfilling than Elisabetha's choice of puritanical discipline. If Doro is caged by the limits of the sensuous life he chooses, his guardian is enslaved by her rigid habits that keep her laboring even after Doro's death, and in silence—a sure sign that her arts, and the domestic and familial values that supported them, have failed in a world that doesn't value them.

WOOLSON STANDS in no such distant relationship to the would-be woman artist who narrates "In the Cotton Country" (1876). This narrator is a slightly fictionalized version of Woolson herself at that time: a displaced Northerner in the post–Civil War South, a "solitary pedestrian" whose own sense of homelessness is so great that she follows a flock of crows, thinking, "The crows at home—that would be something worth seeing." They lead her not to their home but to a house whose wretched situation "all alone on a desolate waste . . . inspired me with—let us call it interest and I went forward." One might also call it a fascination with solitude even greater than her own, and a need to discover if such deprivation could be endured. The narrator seems to be looking for an image of what she herself would become if she succumbed to her own inclinations toward solitude.

What she finds is a terrifying image of immobilized despair. A once-wealthy Southern woman is living in the dilapidated cabin of her former overseer, unable even to find relief in work like Miss Elisabetha because of her training in pride and indolence on a prosperous plantation. Two-thirds of the story is the bitter monologue forced from her by the narrator. The other third deals with the narrator's compulsive need to hear the other woman's story, and to find a way out of her own isolation by retelling it to an audience she urgently invokes. "I have written stories of imagination, but this is a story of fact, and I want you to believe it. It is true, every word of it, save the names given, and, when you read it, you whose eyes are now upon these lines, stop and reflect that it is only one of many life-stories like unto it." Abandoning her fictional frame, asserting the truth of her narrative, seizing the reader by the shoulders, Woolson indicates that she is seeking a way out of her own isolation by reaching an audience through the pain of a woman even more exiled than herself.

The situation vividly recalls Hawthorne's admission that he hoped through his writing to "open an intercourse with the world" (preface to *Twice Told Tales,* 587), and his conviction that "somewhere among your fellow creatures, there is a heart that will receive yours into itself" (Blodgett 182). Woolson's story also documents the guilt that accompanies this strategy. To conceal from herself the fact that she is actually exploiting the Southern woman's loneliness and despair, the narrator tells herself that she is a "Sister of Charity . . . bearing balm and wine and oil for those who suffer." [19]

The third Southern story reprinted here is one of Woolson's finest, and her most courageous confrontation of the connection between art and sexuality. In "The Lady of Little Fishing," Woolson had suggested that a woman who allows herself to love a man becomes an ordinary woman whose words have no weight with men. In "Felipa" (1876), she indicates that lovelessness limits a woman artist as much as love, and that love for other women is likely to be as disabling as love for men. What appears to us as lesbian or bisexual feeling in "Felipa" would not have startled Woolson's contemporaries, since women's romantic friendships were not regarded with suspicion until a later era. Two years after writing "Felipa," Woolson drew attention to the power of the love women can feel for each other in a review she wrote for the *Atlantic* of Alice Perry's novel *Esther Pennefather* (1878). She called the novel a ridiculous book with an original subject: "the singular power one woman sometimes has over another" until they marry and look back at "that old adoration which was so intense and so pure, so self-sacrificing and so far away" (503). "Felipa" dramatizes what the review suggests: women who love women lose them to men. This story, like "In the Cotton Country," confirms Woolson's conviction that intimacy with either men or women cannot last but can only betray. It also reveals her conviction that the best protection against such loss is accepting homelessness and habitual solitude, while trying to forge an art that links the writer with the human community.

Catherine, the heroine of "Felipa," describes herself as an "artist, poor and painstaking," living a "poor gray life" in the shadow of her friend Christine, who uses her to show off her own beauty and power over others. If Christine is Catherine's foil, her alter ego is Felipa, the Minorcan child they meet in Florida, who rejects patriarchal forms of religion and art by making a goddess out of palmetto leaves and worshipping her. In her passionate attachment to both Christine and her suitor Edward, Felipa also rejects approved heterosexual behavior. Felipa's sexual ambiguity, implied by her name and made explicit by her equal passion for the man and the woman, is secretly shared by Catherine, but the woman artist is properly socialized to repress such desires, to be "gentle," "quiet and good," to accept a "respectable, orderly doll" as an adequate representation of female possibilities, and to do her modest sketching at the seashore, where women who are no man's mate can occupy a sliver of no-man's-land.

Catherine thinks she can escape her smoldering sexual longings by turning to art, which she uses to evade her feelings rather than to understand or transform them. But Felipa understands that art can poison when it is used to repress rather than to express feeling. When Christine finally accepts Edward's marriage proposal, Catherine pretends to be glad, but Felipa eats the "poison things" in Catherine's paint box, and then stabs Edward's arm with Catherine's little dagger. Catherine insists that since Felipa loved the man and the woman "both alike," her love "is nothing; she does not know." But the child's grandfather realizes that "it was two loves, and the stronger thrust the knife." Catherine also has "two loves," and "does not know" what she feels because she cannot admit to any of her feelings. A failed woman and a failed artist, her attempts to capture on canvas the subtleties of the salt-marsh or Felipa's complex character can only be "hopeless efforts."

Woolson's identification with her women artist characters is more

Introduction

complex in this story than in either "Miss Elisabetha" or "In the Cotton Country" because here both the repressed woman painter and her wild alter ego Felipa represent parts of Woolson herself. The story is their joint production, with its energy and passion coming from the child, and its form from the woman. Transforming these Dionysian and Apollonian tendencies into female terms, Woolson decides that neither one by itself can produce art. For the rest of her career, she would continue to search for ways in which they could collaborate.

THE LAST THREE STORIES come from Woolson's years abroad, when her own personal and artistic horizons were expanding. As she continued to explore ways women might wield power through words, she kept raising chilling questions about women and art. If a woman wants passionately to be an artist, but is told she lacks talent, what kind of life can she make for herself in the shadow of great art and criticism by men? The heroine of "The Street of the Hyacinth" (1882) is an independent New Woman with the courage to confront male-sanctified artistic taste from the time of the Romans to her own, but when men convince her that her work is hopelessly mediocre, she abandons it. What use can a woman artist make of the genius of women of another age? "At the Château of Corinne" (1886) invokes the most influential female texts affirming women's art—Elizabeth Barrett Browning's *Aurora Leigh* and Madame de Staël's *Corinne*—but neither their words nor their examples can save the woman artist of the story from having to marry and give up her writing. If a woman writer has enormous power, would her work be perceived as being so flawed by the anomaly of genius in woman that it would fail to find an audience? In "'Miss Grief'" (1880) the only satisfaction possible for a woman genius is to die happily deceived that her work has at last found a publisher.

These stories were written in the early years of Woolson's difficult relationship with Henry James and feature successful male writers and critics who resemble James. Their complex realism shows James's positive effect on Woolson's technique, while their plots insist on the negative effect of his arrogance and the patriarchy that sustained it. In two of the stories, the heroine marries the James-like character, but it is clear in both cases that this solution is a "downfall."

Introduction

Ettie Macks comes from her tiny Western town to live in "The Street of the Hyacinth" in Rome to study masterpieces by men as part of her education as a painter. A series of male mentors persuade her that she has not a shred of talent, and at the end she succumbs to marriage to an art critic she loves but cannot respect. The imagery of hyacinths throughout suggests that rather than finding fulfillment, she has suffered "a great downfall" from her "superhuman" heights of integrity. She is like the street of the Hyacinth, pulled down so it would no longer "disfigure" the Pantheon ("the magnificent old Pagan temple" it adjoined). In "Pagan" mythology, Hyacinthus suffered a downfall worse than Ettie's at the hands of his loving mentor, Apollo, who accidentally killed him while teaching him to throw the discus. In this story, the Apollonian principle is purely destructive. On the street of the Hyacinth, Ettie's mentor has slain his beloved's faith in herself as artist and woman. Her female self-assertion would evidently "disfigure" the monumental principles of male culture which her mentor upholds as both art critic and suitor. Nor is the Dionysian principle more enabling, since Ettie's passion for her destructive mentor contributes to her "downfall."

Ettie's independence and seriousness of purpose are like Woolson's own, while her ambivalent relationship with her mentor reflects Woolson's experience with Henry James. But in Ettie's social and intellectual naïveté, her inability to find an audience that can appreciate her art, or her eventual belief in its hopeless mediocrity, there is no resemblance to Woolson. Woolson may here be speculating about what might happen if she married James, and concluding that marriage would end her career without satisfying her desire to love a man she could also respect, a "downfall" on both counts.

WOOLSON CREATED ANOTHER male mentor who persuades a woman to give up her artistic ambitions, not because her writing is judged to be bad—Woolson never reveals its quality—but because he believes that genius in women is a disfigurement or a delusion. In the character of John Ford in "At the Château of Corinne," Woolson combines Henry James's arrogant charm and dislike of women writers with Edmund Stedman's "entire disbelief in the possibility of true fiery genius in women" (letter to Stedman, 23 July 1876). The story's heroine, Katharine Winthrop, is less like Woolson than any of her other artist heroines, in her artistic dilettantism, leisured life, and abundant suitors.

The plot centers on Katharine's need to choose between independence and literary ambition on the one hand, and marriage to John Ford on the other—a man who detests the idea of female genius and dislikes female independence. Both these attributes are symbolized by Madame de Staël and her heroine Corinne. They were admired by women as different as Elizabeth Cady Stanton and Harriet Beecher Stowe, and also attacked in a popular magazine of the time which warned that while women with minds "equal to any human undertaking" exist, "happily these giants of their kind are rare" (*Young Lady's Companion,* Welter 76). The magazine reflected the popular wisdom that women who go beyond male-defined limitations become monsters. Ford expresses this view in a torrent of misogyny which recalls a similar speech, with a similar ironic function, in Elizabeth Barrett Browning's immensely influential verse novel, *Aurora Leigh.*[20] The overblown rhetoric Woolson assigns Ford is a clear sign of her disapproval of his stereotypical masculinity, while the space she gives his violent opinions indicates her belief that such opinions were a very serious obstacle to women writers.

The structure of the story indicates Woolson's regret that modern women lack the means of a Madame de Staël to develop their genius. The story is built on four visits to Staël's place of exile at Coppet, each marking a decline in Staël's influence and Katharine's independence. Her story, worked out in Staël's shadow, has the same outcome as Ettie's, in the shadow of the Pantheon and the galleries of great male painters. Neither male nor female models of greatness seem of much help to women who would be artists but are persuaded that they have no talent and that their only recourse is marriage to men unable to accept independence or talent in women.

Woolson wrote one tale about a woman writer of undisputed genius. "'Miss Grief'" (1880) is narrated by a self-satisfied male author who models himself on Balzac but writes only "delightful little studies of society." He misreads the name of the woman seeking his help in getting her play published, turning Miss Crief into Miss Grief. And she does bring grief to him. Although he tells himself that he is fortunate because "she, with the greater power, failed—I with the less, succeeded," he knows, like the corrupted artist in Henry James's "The Lesson of the Master" (1888), what it means to have everything but "the great thing . . . the sense of having done the best" (135).

Miss Crief's first name, Aaronna, is also significant: "My father was much disappointed that I was not a boy, and gave me as nearly as possible the name he had prepared—Aaron." That name would have linked the child with the authority of the first high priest of Israel. Because Aaron had the verbal powers Moses lacked, God empowered him to lead and judge his people along with Moses. Woolson implicitly compares Aaronna's works to Aaron's elaborate priestly garb when her narrator likens the woman's writings to "a case of jeweller's wares set before you, with each ring unfinished, each bracelet too large or too small for its purpose, each breastpin without its fastening, each necklace purposely broken." When assumed by a woman, the ornaments which symbolized priestly power appear to male eyes only as ruined treasures. Woolson's simile also recalls the "rings of gold" Aaron collected from the Israelites and "fashioned . . . with a graving tool" into a golden calf. Aaron, however, evades responsibility for this act of artistry, telling Moses that he "threw the gold into the fire and there came out this calf" (Exodus 32:24). But Aaronna cannot escape the consequences of her conscious and deliberate artistry. For the discrepancy between her vision and male-defined norms, she is punished with obscurity and poverty.

This story recasts the relation between the Dionysian and the Apollonian artist which Woolson first considered in "Felipa." This time the wild genius belongs to a mature woman, but it succeeds no more than when it belonged to a wild child. In "'Miss Grief,'" however, the socially conforming male artist wins a measure of love and success, both of which were denied to Catherine, his female equivalent in "Felipa." Mediocre men fare much better in Woolson's fiction than either mediocre or brilliant women.

Woolson here imagines a more direct collaboration between the genius and the conformist than in "Felipa." The male narrator of "'Miss Grief'" tries to correct what he sees as disfiguring faults in the woman's brilliant play, to make it acceptable to a publisher. He finds, however, that at least for a man of his limited talents, the flaws are inseparable from the genius. It is like "taking out one especial figure in a carpet: that is impossible, unless you unravel the whole." As Leon Edel has observed, James took Woolson's metaphor of the "figure in a carpet" for the title of his own tale about the elusive nature of genius. But James gave his male genius, Hugh Vereker, fame and disciples. Miss Crief has neither, because in a woman, genius is perceived as deforming. Her Dionysian imagination, which is "unrestrained, large, vast, like the skies or the wind," cannot be tamed enough to communicate with the public she needs, and brings her only grief.

Characteristically, given her paradoxical and divided nature, Woolson identified with both these characters, and separated herself from both of them. She shared Miss Crief's grief but neither her genius nor her failure. She shared the narrator's success but not his complacent obtuseness. She may have identified with his failure to do the best work of which he was capable, not from lack of dedication but from a fear that her own wildness, like Miss Crief's genius, would have alienated the audience she so urgently needed. Unlike her male mentors, Woolson believed in women's genius, but saw it as so compromised by the patriarchy of her time that it could appear only in distorted forms, and could bring only grief to its possessors.

She believed that women in the past had produced art of distinctive greatness, which could inspire women's genius in the future. Early in her career, she wrote a sonnet, "To George Eliot" (1876), which describes a woman's genius as a combination of the "colossal" power of a Michelangelo with the "finely traced" beauty created by "woman-hands," and concludes, "A myriad women light have seen, / And courage taken, because *thou* has been!" This mixture of power and tenderness is what Woolson hoped her own legacy would be. A month before her death, she thought again of the "giant's work" that a woman could do, and wrote, "I should like to turn into a peak when I die, to be a beautiful purple mountain, which would please the tired, sad eyes of thousands of human beings for ages" (Benedict 2: xvi). Woolson's mountain is not like Shelley's Mont Blanc, embodying the male poet's verbal and sexual power, but like her conception of George Eliot's genius, both maternal and masculine. It suggests that she saw the struggles between gender and genre as not only damaging but also as fruitful.

1. Biographical material on Woolson is very limited. Unless otherwise indicated, my discussion is based on the following sources: *Five Generations (1785–1923)*, the three-volume collection of Woolson family documents edited by Woolson's niece Clare Benedict, and indicated henceforth as Benedict; *Appreciations*, Benedict's collection of readers' responses to those volumes; *The Life of Henry James* by Leon Edel and his edition of James's letters; John D. Kern, *Constance Fenimore Woolson: Literary Pioneer;* Rayburn S. Moore, *Constance Fenimore Woolson;* and Doris Faber's unpublished biography of Woolson. Unpublished letters are designated in the bibliography by the collections in which they appear.

2. Woolson's uncertainty about her ability to equal Cooper as well as her desire to hitch a ride on his fame appear in an early letter to a publisher: "I would rather not have my name appear with the article, but if it is necessary, please give only 'Constance Fenimore' as I have taken that for a nom de plume" (letter to Mary L. Booth, 2 Feb. 1871).

3. Woolson discussed in her reviews and letters and debated in her fiction the work of her immediate male and female predecessors. Her "gods" are Dickens, Cooper, Emerson, Hawthorne, and Turgenev; Madame de Staël, Charlotte Brontë, George Eliot, George Sand, and Elizabeth Barrett Browning. Of her contemporaries, she finds more to admire in the work of men than of women. She praises Bret Harte's Western tales but insists she is not imitating him; reads and reprints as epigraphs to her stories poems by young Southern men; admires the criticism, fiction, and biography written by her eminent friends Edmund Clarence Stedman and John Hay; reviews the writings of Henry James and tells him they form "my true country, my real home" (Edel 3: 93). She is neutral about or critical of many of her women contemporaries. In her journal, she told herself, "Have all the scenes as distinctly American as S. Jewett, and Miss Wilkins . . . but more

realistic," and faulted Rebecca Harding Davis for creating unbelievable characters ("Mottoes"). In letters, she mentions Elizabeth Stuart Phelps, Louisa May Alcott, Mary Mapes Dodge, Frances Hodgson Burnett, Violet Paget ("Vernon Lee"), Elizabeth Stoddard, and Mrs. Oliphant, without giving any opinion of their work. She marvels however that anyone can read the mass of "words, words, words" Augusta Evans Wilson inflicted on her readers, and wonders how readers who liked such writing could ever like her own (letter to Hayne, 10 Jan. 1876).

4. An ambitious book-length poem, *Two Women* (1872), interesting for its reversal of stereotypes, contrasts an experienced woman's generosity with an innocent woman's narcissism. Even more interesting is "The Florida Beach" (1874, Benedict 3: 458), which identifies the woman writer with a lighthouse keeper, suggesting that she is visible, even essential, to an audience she cannot see from her position where land meets sea at the margins of culture.

5. For a suggestive account of regionalism as a women's art form, see Ammons xx–xxii.

6. The distinction between "muted" and "dominant" cultures is made by Shirley and Edwin Ardener, and used by Elaine Showalter to describe the relationship between male and female cultures (261).

7. "Aspinwalls, Stewarts, Rhinelanders, Astors . . . are arriving and we are beginning to breathe that tiresome atmosphere of gold dust and ancestors which has oppressed us for two long winters. I always feel like a fraud when I go sailing with, say, six or eight incomes of six figures and the like" (Benedict 3: 235, 247).

8. Woolson set all her novels in different parts of the South, and prided herself on letters she received from Southerners "about the truthfulness of the 'Southern' part" of *East Angels*. "It is indeed exactly accurate; I have described nothing that is not a literal transcript from life" (letter to Samuel Mather, 18 Mar. 1886).

9. The heroine of her first novel, *Anne*, also written during the years when Charly was writing "appalling" letters, chooses as her lover a man as indolent, careless, irresponsible, and immature as Charly, a character who seems to exist only to give Anne opportunities to show her superior strength and character. An adored scapegrace son provides the complications of the plot of Woolson's second novel, *For the Major* (1883); the heroine of Woolson's fourth novel, *Jupiter Lights* (1889), is tormented by her incestuous passion for her father, her brother, and her brother's son; and her last novel, *Horace Chase* (1893), features the death of a brother from brain fever. Only *East Angels* (1886) is free of these concerns.

10. I discuss these stories and themes in my "Women Artists as Exiles" 6.

11. In *The Madwoman in the Attic*, Gilbert and Gubar argue that women writers had to develop strategies to evade their own anxiety about their right to write at all, in the face of patriarchal assumptions that only men had the necessary authority to be authors.

12. "I did not want the thing at all, but there are so many grand people

here, and Clara does not like it unless I am respectable. I could ill afford the gown, and hated paying for it dreadfully. . . . What remark do you suppose was made about that time by two ladies staying in the same house who did not know me at all? 'Is not that lady opposite us at table a literary person? We have felt sure she was an authoress, and not only that, but there is something about her which makes us think that she was the daughter of a clergyman!' Now then, *they* had on short black alpaca gowns, their noses were sharp and red at the tips, and they wore glasses and had gristly hands. Ages 40 and 50 perhaps. Wasn't it disgusting? After all my trouble and spent money! Elizabeth Stuart Phelps is here again this winter and she is 'Dress Reform.' I am going to be 'Dress Reform' hereafter, in spite of Clara. Dress Reform means two dresses, *et praeterea nihil*" (Benedict 3: 242).

13. More letters have survived to these four men than to Woolson's closest male friend, Henry James, because he destroyed all but four of her letters as well as his letters to her which were in her possession when she died. Despite the paucity of extant correspondence, this relationship has received extensive treatment in Leon Edel's biography of James. But Edel distorts the relationship nearly as much as he misrepresents Woolson's writing, which he describes as "prosy and banal . . . without style, and with an extreme literalness," lacking "ease and the richer verbal imagination . . . minute and cluttered" (2: 203). He presents Woolson as desperately "reaching out to a man younger than herself" (2: 87) who was grateful for her devotion but evasive of the demands of a woman Edel calls an "elderly spinster" though she was only three years older than James. The reality is less stereotypical and more complex.

14. Woolson heavily marked a passage in her copy of *The Teaching of Epictetus* (135) which justifies suicide:

"when, it may be, that the necessary things are no longer supplied, that is the signal for retreat: the door is opened, and God saith to thee, *Depart*.

" 'Whither?'

"To nothing dreadful, but to the place from whence thou camest—to things friendly and akin to thee, to the elements of Being."

Someone—probably Clare Benedict—cut out the pages on death and suicide before donating the volume to the Woolson Collection at Rollins College.

15. When Charly died in his thirties in 1883, for example, the news of the death of this brother whom she had hardly seen as an adult "made me suffer more than I have ever suffered in my life. . . . For a time, it seemed to me that I could not rally from the depression it caused; and that it was hardly worth while to try" (letter to Samuel Mather, 16 Jan. 1884).

16. The wretched ascetic minister in "Peter the Parson" (1874, *Castle Nowhere*), for example, seems to sacrifice physical comforts and love for his religion. But when he dies trying to save a thief who had crippled him from a lynch mob, Woolson shows that he is not a martyr but a suicide. He hates his life because he has failed to conquer either the miners' disbelief or his own "proud, evil body."

Woolson's readers thought he deserved better, but she stuck to her guns: "under the abuse which has been showered upon me for my 'brutal' killing of 'Peter the Parson,' I have steadily maintained to myself that both in an artistic and truthful-to-life point of view my ending of the story was better than the conversion of the miners, the plenty to eat, and the happy marriage proposed by my critics" (Benedict 2: 23).

17. Mary Kelley gives this name to the best-selling women writers of the 1850s, 1860s, and 1870s, who published fiction that affirmed the values of women's domestic sphere.

18. "The Lady of Little Fishing" has long been admired, but for the wrong reasons. Fred L. Pattee thinks that Woolson improved on Bret Harte's story, "The Luck of Roaring Camp"—which tells of a group of rough miners reformed by their responsibility for a baby—because of the superiority of the "real motif of [her] story": that women perversely care only for the men who care nothing for them (*Short Story* 255). The story's "real motif" is not that, and Woolson directly criticized Harte's sentimental Victorian idea that a miner could be brought to salvation by an innocent baby—or a pure woman. More radically, Woolson corrected Harte's depiction of the baby's unwed mother as "a very sinful woman" whose death in childbirth was a divine punishment for her sins (69); the chasteness of Woolson's Lady implies that her own death is a punishment for her sin of thinking herself above such human necessities as love and sex.

19. Woolson's longing to interact with the women whose misery she studies in this and other stories such as "Jeannette" and "Wilhelmena" (*Castle Nowhere*) contrasts with Hawthorne's inclination to be an invisible observer. In an early sketch, "Sights from a Steeple," his narrator thinks that "the most desirable mode of existence might be that of a spiritualized Paul Pry, hovering invisible round men and women, witnessing their deeds, searching into their hearts, borrowing brightness from their felicity and shade from their sorrow, and retaining no emotion peculiar to himself" (404). Hawthorne later resisted this tendency in himself, and in later works he showed such isolated observers as Ethan Brand, Roger Chillingworth, Rappaccini, and Young Goodman Brown as damned souls.

20. This story is a tribute to Elizabeth Barrett Browning as well as to Madame de Staël. Woolson was annoyed by Stedman's condescension to Elizabeth Barrett Browning: "Mr. Stedman does not really believe in woman's genius. His disbelief peeps through every line of the criticism below, whose essence is—'She did wonderfully well for a woman'" (Benedict 2: 93).

SELECTED BIBLIOGRAPHY

MAJOR WORKS BY CONSTANCE FENIMORE WOOLSON

Anne. 1880. New York: Harper, 1882.

Castle Nowhere: Lake-Country Sketches. Boston: Osgood, 1875.

Dorothy and Other Italian Stories. New York: Harper, 1896.

East Angels. New York: Harper, 1886.

For the Major. New York: Harper, 1883.

The Front Yard and Other Italian Stories. New York: Harper, 1895.

Horace Chase. New York: Harper, 1894.

Jupiter Lights. New York: Harper, 1889.

Letters to Dr. William Wilberforce Baldwin. MA 3564. The Pierpont Morgan Library, New York.

Letter to Mary L. Booth. 2 Feb. 1871. General MSS Misc., Princeton University Library.

Letter to Mary Mapes Dodge. n.d. Donald and Robert M. Dodge Collection of Mary Mapes Dodge. Princeton University Library.

Letters to John Hay in Alice Hall Petry, "'Always, Your Attached Friend': The Unpublished Letters of Constance Fenimore Woolson to John and Clara Hay." *Books at Brown* 29–30 (1982–83): 11–108.

Letters to Paul Hamilton Hayne. Duke University Library.

Letters to Henry James. William James Papers. Houghton Library, Harvard University.

Letters to Katherine and Samuel Mather. Mather Family Papers. Western Reserve Historical Society, Cleveland.

Letters to Edmund Clarence Stedman. Edmund Clarence Stedman Papers, Rare Book and Manuscript Library, Butler Library, Columbia University.

"'Miss Grief.'" *Lippincott's Magazine* 25 (May 1880): 574–85.

"Mottoes. Maxims. Reflections." Woolson Papers. Rollins College.

Review of *Esther Pennefather*. Contributors' Club, *Atlantic* 42 (Oct. 1878): 502–03. Benedict 2: 65–67.

Review of Henry James's *The Europeans*. Contributors' Club, *Atlantic* 43 (Feb. 1879): 259. Benedict 2: 55–56.

Rodman the Keeper: Southern Sketches. 1880. Harper, 1886.

"To George Eliot." *The New Century for Women* 2 (20 May 1876): 1.

Two Women. 1862. New York: Appleton, 1877, 1890.

Note: A complete bibliography of Woolson's works is in Kern 180–94.

SOURCES AND FURTHER READINGS

Ammons, Elizabeth, ed. *How Celia Changed Her Mind and Selected Stories*. By Rose Terry Cook. New Brunswick: Rutgers UP, 1986.

Auerbach, Nina. Rev. of *Rediscovered Fiction by American Women: A Personal Selection*. Ed. Elizabeth Hardwick. *Nineteenth Century Fiction* 33 (Mar. 1979): 475–83.

Benedict, Clare, ed. *Appreciations*. London: privately printed, 1941.

———, ed. *Five Generations (1785–1923)*. 3 vols. London: privately printed, 1930, 1932.

Blodgett, Harold. "Hawthorne as Poetry Critic: Six Unpublished Letters to Lewis Mansfield." *American Literature* 30 (Mar. 1958): 37–59.

Browning, Elizabeth Barrett. *Aurora Leigh*. Ed. Cora Kaplan. London: Women's Press, 1982.

Dean, Sharon. "Constance Fenimore Woolson and Henry James: The Literary Relationship." *Massachusetts Studies in English* 7.3 (1980): 1–9.

Edel, Leon. *The Life of Henry James*. 5 vols. Philadelphia: Lippincott, 1953–72.

Selected Bibliography

Epictetus. *The Teaching of Epictetus: Being the "Encheiridion" of Epictetus, with Selections from the "Dissertations" and "Fragments."* Trans. and ed. T. W. Rolleston. London: Walter Scott, 1888.

Gilbert, Sandra, and Susan Gubar. *The Madwoman in the Attic.* New Haven: Yale UP, 1979.

Guilford, Linda T. "Notes in Memory of Miss Woolson." TS. Western Reserve Historical Society, Cleveland.

————. *The Story of a Cleveland School from 1848 to 1881.* Cambridge: John Wilson, 1890.

Harte, Bret. "The Luck of Roaring Camp." *Poems and Prose of Bret Harte.* London: War, Lock and Tyler, 1872.

Hawthorne, Nathaniel. *Selected Tales and Sketches.* Ed. Hyatt Waggoner. New York: Holt, 1970.

Howells, William Dean. Review of "Castle Nowhere." *Atlantic* 35 (June 1875): 736–37.

Hubbell, Jay B. "Some New Letters of Constance Fenimore Woolson." *New England Quarterly* 14 (Dec. 1941): 715–35.

James, Henry. "The Lesson of the Master" (1888) in *Henry James: Stories of Writers and Artists,* ed. F. O. Matthiessen. New York: New Directions, n.d.

————. *Henry James: Letters.* Ed. Leon Edel. 3 vols. Cambridge: Harvard UP, 1974, 1975, 1980.

————. "Miss Woolson." First published as "Miss Constance Fenimore Woolson" in *Harper's Weekly* 31 (12 Feb. 1887): 114–15. Rpt. in *Partial Portraits.* London: Macmillan, 1888.

Kelley, Mary. *Private Woman, Public Stage: Literary Domesticity in Nineteenth-Century America.* New York: Oxford UP, 1984.

Kennedy, Elizabeth Marie. *Constance Fenimore Woolson and Henry James: Friendship and Reflections.* Diss. Yale U, 1983.

Kern, John D. *Constance Fenimore Woolson: Literary Pioneer.* Philadelphia, U of Pennsylvania P, 1934.

Kolodny, Annette. *The Land before Her: Fantasy and Experience of the American Frontier 1630–1860.* Chapel Hill: U of North Carolina P, 1984.

Moore, Rayburn S. *Constance Fenimore Woolson.* New York: Twayne, 1963.

Pattee, Fred Lewis. "Constance Fenimore Woolson and the South." *South Atlantic Quarterly* 38 (1939): 131–41.

————. *The Development of the American Short Story: An Historical Survey.* New York: Harper, 1923.

Petry, Alice Hall. "'Always, Your Attached Friend': The Unpublished Letters of Constance Fenimore Woolson to John Hay." *Books at Brown* 29–30 (1982–83): 11–108.

Showalter, Elaine. "Feminist Criticism in the Wilderness." *Feminist Criticism: Essays on Women, Literature and Theory.* Ed. Elaine Showalter. New York: Pantheon, 1985.

Strouse, Jean. *Alice James: A Biography.* Boston: Houghton, 1980.

Weimer, Joan Myers. "Women Artists as Exiles in the Fiction of Constance Fenimore Woolson." *Legacy* 3.1 (Fall 1986): 3–15.

Weir, Sybil B. "Southern Womanhood in the Novels of Constance Fenimore Woolson." *Mississippi Quarterly* (1976): 559–68.

Welter, Barbara. "Anti-Intellectualism and the American Woman 1800–1860." In *Dimity Convictions: The American Woman in the Nineteenth Century.* Athens: Ohio UP, 1976.

Wood, Ann Douglas. "The Literature of Impoverishment: The Women Local Colorists in America 1865–1914." *Women's Studies* 1 (1972): 3–45.

A NOTE ON THE TEXT

THE STORIES in this anthology are arranged according to the chronology of the volumes in which they were collected either by Woolson or, after her death, by Harper's. Woolson's stories were not always published or collected in the order in which she wrote them; "At the Château of Corinne," for example, was published seven years after Harper's accepted it, and "'Miss Grief'" was not reprinted in any volume of Woolson's collected stories in the nineteenth century.

The publication history of the pieces is as follows: "The Lady of Little Fishing," *Atlantic* 34 (Sept. 1874), rpt. in *Castle Nowhere: Lake-Country Sketches* (1875); "Castle Nowhere," no periodical publication, *Castle Nowhere;* "St. Clair Flats," *Appleton's* 10 (4 Oct. 1873), rpt. in *Castle Nowhere;* "Miss Elisabetha," *Appleton's* 13 (13 Mar. 1875), rpt. in *Rodman the Keeper: Southern Sketches* (1880); "In the Cotton Country," *Appleton's* 15 (29 Apr. 1876), rpt. in *Rodman the Keeper;* "Felipa," *Lippincott's* 17 (June 1876), rpt. in *Rodman the Keeper;* "The Street of the Hyacinth," *Century* 2 (May, June 1882), rpt. in *The Front Yard and Other Italian Stories* (1895); "At the Château of Corinne," *Harper's* 75 (Oct. 1887), rpt. in *Dorothy and Other Italian Stories* (1896); "'Miss Grief,'" *Lippincott's* 25 (May 1880), no rpt.

Stories anthologized by Woolson are reprinted from the anthology in which they appeared. Spelling and punctuation, including her idiosyncratic use of apostrophes, are unchanged.

The text of Henry James's essay, "Miss Woolson," is from his 1888 collection, *Partial Portraits.*

WOMEN ARTISTS, WOMEN EXILES

THE LADY OF LITTLE FISHING

IT WAS AN ISLAND in Lake Superior.

I beached my canoe there about four o'clock in the afternoon, for the wind was against me and a high sea running. The late summer of 1850, and I was coasting along the south shore of the great lake, hunting, fishing, and camping on the beach, under the delusion that in that way I was living "close to the great heart of nature,"—whatever that may mean. Lord Bacon[1] got up the phrase; I suppose he knew. Pulling the boat high and dry on the sand with the comfortable reflection that here were no tides to disturb her with their goings-out and comings-in, I strolled through the woods on a tour of exploration, expecting to find bluebells, Indian pipes, juniper rings, perhaps a few agates along-shore, possibly a bird or two for company. I found a town.

It was deserted; but none the less a town, with three streets, residences, a meeting-house, gardens, a little park, and an attempt at a fountain. Ruins are rare in the New World; I took off my hat. "Hail, homes of the past!" I said. (I cultivated the habit of thinking aloud when I was living close to the great heart of nature.) "A human voice resounds through your arches" (there were no arches,—logs won't arch; but never mind) "once more, a human hand touches your venerable walls, a human foot presses your deserted hearth-stones." I then selected the best half of the meeting-house for my camp, knocked down one of the homes for fuel, and kindled a

3

glorious bonfire in the park. "Now that you are illuminated with joy, O Ruin," I remarked, "I will go down to the beach and bring up my supplies. It is long since I have had a roof over my head; I promise you to stay until your last residence is well burned; then I will make a final cup of coffee with the meeting-house itself, and depart in peace, leaving your poor old bones buried in decent ashes."

The ruin made no objection, and I took up my abode there; the roof of the meeting-house was still water-tight (which is an advantage when the great heart of nature grows wet). I kindled a fire on the sacerdotal hearth, cooked my supper, ate it in leisurely comfort, and then stretched myself on a blanket to enjoy an evening pipe of peace, listening meanwhile to the sounding of the wind through the great pine-trees. There was no door to my sanctuary, but I had the cosey far end; the island was uninhabited, there was not a boat in sight at sunset, nothing could disturb me unless it might be a ghost. Presently a ghost came in.

It did not wear the traditional gray tarlatan armor of Hamlet's father, the only ghost with whom I am well acquainted; this spectre was clad in substantial deer-skin garments, and carried a gun and loaded game-bag. It came forward to my hearth, hung up its gun, opened its game-bag, took out some birds, and inspected them gravely.

"Fat?" I inquired.

"They'll do," replied the spectre, and forthwith set to work preparing them for the coals. I smoked on in silence. The spectre seemed to be a skilled cook, and after deftly broiling its supper, it offered me a share; I accepted. It swallowed a huge mouthful and crunched with its teeth; the spell was broken, and I knew it for a man of flesh and blood.

He gave his name as Reuben,[2] and proved himself an excellent camping companion; in fact, he shot all the game, caught all the fish, made all the fires, and cooked all the food for us both. I proposed to him to stay and help me burn up the ruin, with the condition that when the last timber of the meeting-house was consumed, we should shake hands and depart, one to the east, one to the west, without a backward glance. "In that way we shall not infringe upon each other's personality," I said.

"Agreed," replied Reuben.

He was a man of between fifty and sixty years, while I was on the sunny side of thirty; he was reserved, I was always generously affable; he was an excellent cook, while I—well, I was n't; he was taciturn, and so, in payment for the work he did, I entertained him with conversation, or rather monologue, in my most brilliant style. It took only two weeks to burn up the town, burned we never so slowly; at last it came the turn of the meeting-house, which now stood by itself in the vacant clearing. It was a cool September day; we cooked breakfast with the roof, dinner with the sides, supper with the odds and ends, and then applied a torch to the frame-work. Our last camp-fire was a glorious one. We lay stretched on our blankets, smoking and watching the glow. "I wonder, now, who built the old shanty," I said in a musing tone.

"Well," replied Reuben, slowly, "if you really want to know, I will tell you. I did."

"You!"

"Yes."

"You did n't do it alone?"

"No; there were about forty of us."

"Here?"

"Yes; here at Little Fishing."

"Little Fishing?"

"Yes; Little Fishing Island. That is the name of the place."

"How long ago was this?"

"Thirty years."

"Hunting and trapping, I suppose?"

"Yes; for the Northwest and Hudson Bay Companies." [3]

"Was n't a meeting-house an unusual accompaniment?"

"Most unusual."

"Accounted for in this case by—"

"A woman."

"Ah!" I said in a tone of relish; "then of course there is a story?"

"There is."

"Out with it, comrade. I scarcely expected to find the woman and her story up here; but since the irrepressible creature would come, out with her by all means. She shall grace our last pipe together, the last timber of our meeting-house, our last night on Little Fishing. The dawn will see us far from each other, to meet no more this side heaven. Speak then, O comrade mine! I am in one of my rare listening moods!"

I stretched myself at ease and waited. Reuben was a long time beginning, but I was too indolent to urge him. At length he spoke.

"They were a rough set here at Little Fishing, all the worse for being all white men; most of the other camps were full of half-breeds and Indians. The island had been a station away back in the early days of the Hudson Bay Company; it was a station for the Northwest Company while that lasted; then it went back to the Hudson, and stayed there until the company moved its forces farther to the north. It was not at any time a regular post; only a camp for the hunters. The post was farther down the lake. O, but those were wild days! You think you know the wilderness, boy; but you know nothing, absolutely nothing. It makes me laugh to see the airs of you city gentlemen with your fine guns, improved fishing-tackle, elaborate paraphernalia, as though you were going to wed the whole forest, floating up and down the lake for a month or two in the summer! You should have seen the hunters of Little Fishing going out gayly when the mercury was down twenty degrees below zero, for a week in the woods. You should have seen the trappers wading through the hard snow, breast high, in the gray dawn, visiting the traps and hauling home the prey. There were all kinds of men here, Scotch, French, English, and American; all classes, the high and the low, the educated and the ignorant; all sorts, the lazy and the hard-working. One thing only they all had in common,— badness. Some had fled to the wilderness to escape the law, others to escape order; some had chosen the wild life because of its wildness, others had drifted into it from sheer lethargy. This far northern border did not attract the plodding emigrant, the respectable settler. Little Fishing held none of that trash; only a reckless set of fellows who carried their lives in their hands, and tossed them up, if need be, without a second thought."

"And other people's lives without a third," I suggested.

"Yes; if they deserved it. But nobody whined; there was n't any nonsense here. The men went hunting and trapping, got the furs ready for the bateaux,* ate when they were hungry, drank when they were thirsty, slept when they were sleepy, played cards when they felt like it, and got angry and knocked each other down whenever they chose. As I said before, there was n't any nonsense at Little Fishing,—until *she* came."

6

"Ah! the she!"

"Yes, the Lady,—our Lady, as we called her. Thirty-one years ago; how long it seems!"

"And well it may," I said. "Why, comrade, I was n't born then!"

This stupendous fact seemed to strike me more than my companion; he went on with his story as though I had not spoken.

"One October evening, four of the boys had got into a row over the cards; the rest of us had come out of our wigwams to see the fun, and were sitting around on the stumps, chaffing them, and laughing; the campfire was burning in front, lighting up the woods with a red glow for a short distance, and making the rest doubly black all around. There we all were, as I said before, quite easy and comfortable, when suddenly there appeared among us, as though she had dropped from heaven, a woman!

"She was tall and slender, the firelight shone full on her pale face and dove-colored dress, her golden hair was folded back under a little white cap, and a white kerchief lay over her shoulders; she looked spotless. I stared; I could scarcely believe my eyes; none of us could. There was not a white woman west of the Sault Ste. Marie.[5] The four fellows at the table sat as if transfixed; one had his partner by the throat, the other two were disputing over a point in the game. The lily lady glided up to their table, gathered the cards in her white hands, slowly, steadily, without pause or trepidation before their astonished eyes, and then, coming back, she threw the cards into the centre of the glowing fire. 'Ye shall not play away your souls,' she said in a clear, sweet voice. 'Is not the game sin? And its reward death?'[6] And then, immediately, she gave us a sermon, the like of which was never heard before; no argument, no doctrine, just simple, pure entreaty. 'For the love of God,' she ended, stretching out her hands towards our silent, gazing group,—'for the love of God, my brothers, try to do better.'

"We did try; but it was not for the love of God. Neither did any of us feel like brothers.

"She did not give any name; we called her simply our Lady, and she accepted the title. A bundle carefully packed in birch-bark was found on the beach. 'Is this yours?' asked black Andy.

"'It is,' replied the Lady; and removing his hat, the black-haired giant carried the package reverently inside her lodge. For we had given her our best wigwam, and fenced it off with pine saplings so that it looked like a miniature fortress. The Lady did not suggest this stockade; it was our own idea, and with one accord we worked at it like beavers, and hung up a gate with a ponderous bolt inside.

"'Mais, ze can nevare farsen eet wiz her leetle fingares,' said Frenchy, a sallow little wretch with a turn for handicraft; so he contrived a small spring which shot the bolt into place with a touch. The Lady lived in her fortress; three times a day the men carried food to her door, and, after tapping gently, withdrew again, stumbling over each other in their haste. The Flying Dutchman,[7] a stolid Holland-born sailor, was our best cook, and the pans and kettles were generally left to him; but now all wanted to try their skill, and the results were extraordinary.

"'She's never touched that pudding, now,' said Nightingale Jack, discontentedly, as his concoction of berries and paste[8] came back from the fortress door.

"'She will starve soon, I think,' remarked the Doctor, calmly; 'to my certain knowledge she has not had an eatable meal for four days.' And he lighted a fresh pipe. This was an aside, and the men pretended not to hear it; but the pans were relinquished to the Dutchman from that time forth.

"The Lady wore always her dove-colored robe, and little white cap, through whose muslin we could see the glimmer of her golden hair. She came and went among us like a spirit; she knew no fear; she turned our life inside out, nor shrank from its vileness. It seemed as though she was not of earth, so utterly impersonal was her interest in us, so heavenly her pity. She took up our sins, one by one, as an angel might; she pleaded with us for our own lost souls, she spared us not, she held not back one grain of denunciation, one iota of future punishment. Sometimes, for days, we would not see her; then, at twilight, she would glide out among us, and, standing in the light of the camp-fire, she would preach to us as though inspired. We listened to her; I do not mean that we were one whit better at heart, but still we listened to her, always. It was a wonderful sight, that lily face under the pine-trees, that spotless woman standing alone in the glare of the fire, while around her lay forty evil-minded, lawless men, not one of whom but would have killed his neighbor for so much as a disrespectful thought of her.

"So strange was her coming, so almost supernatural her appearance in this far forest, that we never wondered over its cause, but simply accepted it as a sort of miracle; your thoroughly irreligious men are always superstitious. Not one of us would have asked a question, and we should never have known her story had she not herself told it to us; not immediately, not as though it was of any importance, but quietly, briefly, and candidly as a child. She came, she said, from Scotland, with a band of God's people. She had always been in one house, a religious institution of some kind, sewing for the poor when her strength allowed it, but generally ill, and suffering much from pain in her head; often kept under the influence of soothing medicines for days together. She had no father or mother, she was only one of this band; and when they decided to send out missionaries to America, she begged to go, although but a burden; the sea voyage restored her health; she grew, she said, in strength and in grace, and her heart was as the heart of a lion. Word came to her from on high that she should come up into the northern lake-country and preach the gospel there; the band were going to the verdant prairies. She left them in the night, taking nothing but her clothing; a friendly vessel carried her north; she had preached the gospel everywhere. At the Sault the priests had driven her out, but nothing fearing, she went on into the wilderness, and so, coming part of the way in canoes, part of the way along-shore, she had reached our far island. Marvellous kindness had she met with, she said; the Indians, the half-breeds, the hunters, and the trappers had all received her, and helped her on her way from camp to camp. They had listened to her words also. At Portage they had begged her to stay through the winter, and offered to build her a little church for Sunday services. Our men looked at each other. Portage was the worst camp on the lake, notorious for its fights; it was a mining settlement.

"'But I told them I must journey on towards the west,' continued our Lady. 'I am called to visit every camp on this shore before the winter sets in; I must soon leave you also.'

"The men looked at each other again; the Doctor was spokesman. 'But, my Lady,' he said, 'the next post is Fort William, two hundred and thirty-five miles away on the north shore.'

"'It is almost November; the snow will soon be six and ten feet deep. The Lady could never travel through it,—could she, now?' said Black Andy, who had begun eagerly, but in his embarrassment at the sound of his own voice, now turned to Frenchy and kicked him covertly into answering.

"'Nevare!' replied the Frenchman; he had intended to place his hand upon his heart to give emphasis to his word, but the Lady turned her calm eyes that way, and his grimy paw fell, its gallantry wilted.

"'I thought there was one more camp,—at Burnt-Wood River,' said our Lady in a musing tone. The men looked at each other a third time; there was a camp there, and they all knew it. But the Doctor was equal to the emergency.

"'That camp, my Lady,' he said gravely,—'that camp no longer exists!' Then he whispered hurriedly to the rest of us, 'It will be an easy job to clean it out, boys. We 'll send over a party to-night; it 's only thirty-five miles.'

"We recognized superior genius; the Doctor was our oldest and deepest sinner. But what struck us most was his anxiety to make good his lie. Had it then come to this,—that the Doctor told the truth?

"The next day we all went to work to build our Lady a church; in a week it was completed. There goes its last cross-beam now into the fire; it was a solid piece of work, was n't it? It has stood this climate thirty years. I remember the first Sunday service: we all washed, and dressed ourselves in the best we had; we scarcely knew each other, we were so fine. The Lady was pleased with the church, but yet she had not said she would stay all winter; we were still anxious. How she preached to us that day! We had made a screen of young spruces set in boxes, and her figure stood out against the dark green background like a thing of light. Her silvery voice rang through the log-temple, her face seemed to us like a star. She had no color in her cheeks at any time; her dress, too, was colorless. Although gentle, there was an iron inflexibility about her slight, erect form. We felt, as we saw her standing there, that if need be she would walk up to the lion's jaws, the cannon's mouth, with a smile. She took a little book from her pocket and read to us a hymn,—'O come, all ye faithful,' the old 'Adeste Fideles.' Some of us knew it; she sang, and gradually, shamefacedly, voices joined in. It was a sight to see Nightingale Jack solemnly singing away about 'choirs of angels'; but it was a treat to hear him, too,—what a voice he had! Then our Lady prayed, kneeling down on the little platform in front of the evergreens, clasping her hands, and lifting her eyes to heaven. We did not know what to do at first, but the Doctor gave us a severe look and bent his head, and we all followed his lead.

"When service was over and the door opened, we found that it had been snowing; we could not see out through the windows because white cloth was nailed over them in place of glass.

"'Now, my Lady, you will have to stay with us,' said the Doctor. We all gathered around with eager faces.

"'Do you really believe that it will be for the good of your souls?' asked the sweet voice.

"The Doctor believed—for us all.

"'Do you really hope?'

"The Doctor hoped.

"'Will you try to do your best?'

"The Doctor was sure he would.

"'I will,' answered the Flying Dutchman, earnestly. 'I moost not fry de meat any more; I moost broil!'

"For we had begged him for months to broil, and he had obstinately refused; broil represented the good, and fry the evil, to his mind; he came out for the good according to his light; but none the less did we fall upon him behind the Lady's back, and cuff him into silence.

"She stayed with us all winter. You don't know what the winters are up here; steady, bitter cold for seven months, thermometer always below, the snow dry as dust, the air like a knife. We built a compact chimney for our Lady, and we cut cords of wood into small, light sticks, easy for her to lift, and stacked them in her shed; we lined her lodge with skins, and we made oil from bear's fat and rigged up a kind of lamp for her. We tried to make candles, I remember, but they would not run straight; they came out hump-backed and sidling,[9] and burned themselves to wick in no time. Then we took to improving the town. We had lived in all kinds of huts and lean-to shanties; now nothing would do but regular log-houses. If it had been summer, I don't know what we might not have run to in the way of piazzas and fancy steps; but with the snow five feet deep, all we could accomplish was a plain, square log-house, and even that took our whole force. The only way to keep the peace was to have all the houses exactly alike; we laid out the three streets, and built the houses, all facing the meeting-house, just as you found them."

"And where was the Lady's lodge?" I asked, for I recalled no stockaded fortress, large or small.

My companion hesitated a moment. Then he said abruptly, "It was torn down."

"Torn down!" I repeated. "Why, what—"

Reuben waved his hand with a gesture that silenced me, and went on with his story. It came to me then for the first time, that he was pursuing the current of his own thoughts rather than entertaining me. I turned to look at him with a new interest. I had talked to him for two weeks, in rather a patronizing way; could it be that affairs were now, at this last moment, reversed?

"It took us almost all winter to build those houses," pursued Reuben. "At one time we neglected the hunting and trapping to such a degree, that the Doctor called a meeting and expressed his opinion. Ours was a voluntary camp, in a measure, but still we had formally agreed to get a certain amount of skins ready for the bateaux by early spring; this agreement was about the only real bond of union between us. Those whose houses were not completed scowled at the Doctor.

"'Do you suppose I'm going to live like an Injun when the other fellows has regular houses?' inquired Black Andy, with a menacing air.

"'By no means,' replied the Doctor, blandly. 'My plan is this: build at night.'

"'At night?'

"'Yes; by the light of pine fires.'

"We did. After that, we faithfully went out hunting and trapping as long as daylight lasted, and then, after supper, we built up huge fires of pine logs, and went to work on the next house. It was a strange picture: the forest deep in snow, black with night, the red glow of the great fires, and our moving figures working on as complacently as though daylight, balmy air, and the best of tools were ours.

"The Lady liked our industry. She said our new houses showed that the 'new cleanliness of our inner man required a cleaner tabernacle for the outer.' I don't know about our inner man, but our outer was certainly much cleaner.

"One day the Flying Dutchman made one of his unfortunate remarks. 'De boys t'inks you 'll like dem better in nize houses,' he announced when, happening to pass the fortress, he found the Lady standing at her gate gazing at the work of the preceding night. Several of the men were near enough to hear him, but too far off to kick him into silence as usual; but they glared at him instead. The Lady looked at the speaker with her dreamy, far-off eyes.

"'De boys t'inks you like dem,' began the Dutchman again, thinking she did not comprehend; but at that instant he caught the combined glare of the six eyes, and stopped abruptly, not at all knowing what was wrong, but sure there was something.

"'Like them,' repeated the Lady, dreamily; 'yea, I do like them. Nay, more, I love them. Their souls are as dear to me as the souls of brothers.'

"Say, Frenchy, have you got a sister?' said Nightingale Jack, confidentially, that evening.

"'Mais oui,' said Frenchy.

"'You think all creation of her, I suppose?'

"'We fight like four cats and one dog; *she* is the cats,' said the Frenchman concisely.

"'You don't say so!' replied Jack. 'Now, I never had a sister,—but I thought perhaps—' He paused, and the sentence remained unfinished.

"The Nightingale and I were house-mates. We sat late over our fire not long after that; I gave a gigantic yawn. 'This lifting logs half the night is enough to kill one,' I said, getting out my jug. 'Sing something, Jack. It's a long time since I've heard anything but hymns.'

"Jack always went off as easily as a music-box: you had only to wind him up; the jug was the key. I soon had him in full blast. He was giving out

'The minute gun at sea,—the minute gun at sea,'

with all the pathos of his tenor voice, when the door burst open and the whole population rushed in upon us.

"'What do you mean by shouting this way, in the middle of the night?'

"'Shut up your howling, Jack.'

"'How do you suppose any one can sleep?'

"'It's a disgrace to the camp!'

"'Now then, gentlemen,' I replied, for my blood was up (whiskey, perhaps), 'is this my house, or is n't it? If I want music, I'll have it. Time was when you were not so particular.'

"It was the first word of rebellion. The men looked at each other, then at me.

"'I'll go and ask her if she objects,' I continued, boldly.

"'No, no. You shall not.'

"'Let him go,' said the Doctor, who stood smoking his pipe on the outskirts of the crowd. 'It is just as well to have that point settled now. The Minute Gun at Sea is a good moral song in its way,—a sort of marine missionary affair.'

"So I started, the others followed; we all knew that the Lady watched late; we often saw the glimmer of her lamp far on towards morning. It was burning now. The gate was fastened, I knocked; no answer. I knocked again, and yet a third time; still, silence. The men stood off at a little distance and waited. 'She shall answer,' I said angrily, and going around to the side where the stockade came nearer to the wall of the lodge, I knocked loudly on the close-set saplings. For answer I thought I heard a low moan; I listened, it came again. My anger vanished, and with a mighty bound I swung myself up to the top of the stockade, sprung down inside, ran around, and tried the door. It was fastened; I burst it open and entered. There, by the light of the hanging lamp, I saw the Lady on the floor, apparently dead. I raised her in my arms; her heart was beating faintly, but she was unconscious. I had seen many fainting fits; this was something different; the limbs were rigid. I laid her on the low couch, loosened her dress, bathed her head and face in cold water, and wrenched up one of the warm hearth-stones to apply to her feet. I did not hesitate; I saw that it was a dangerous case, something like a trance or an 'ecstasis.' Somebody must attend to her, and there were only men to choose from. Then why not I?

"I heard the others talking outside; they could not understand the delay; but I never heeded, and kept on my work. To tell the truth, I had studied medicine, and felt a genuine enthusiasm over a rare case. Once my patient opened her eyes and looked at me, then she lapsed away again into unconsciousness in spite of all my efforts. At last the men outside came in, angry and suspicious; they had broken down the gate. There we all stood, the whole forty of us, around the deathlike form of our Lady.

"What a night it was! To give her air, the men camped outside in the snow with a line of pickets in whispering distance from each other from the bed to their anxious group. Two were detailed to help me,—the Doctor (whose title was a sarcastic D.D.) and Jimmy, a gentle little man, excellent at bandaging broken limbs. Every vial in the camp was brought in,—astonishing lotions, drops, and balms; each man produced something; they did their best, poor fellows, and wore out the night with their anxiety. At dawn our Lady revived suddenly, thanked us all, and assured us that she felt quite well again; the trance was over. 'It was my old enemy,' she said, 'the old illness of Scotland, which I hoped had left me forever. But I am thankful that it is no worse; I have come out of it with a clear brain. Sing a hymn of thankfulness for me, dear friends, before you go.'

"Now, we sang on Sunday in the church; but then she led us, and we had a kind of an idea that after all she did not hear us. But now, who was to lead us? We stood awkwardly around the bed, and shuffled our hats in our uneasy fingers. The Doctor fixed his eyes upon the Nightingale; Jack saw it and cowered. 'Begin,' said the Doctor in a soft voice; but gripping him in the back at the same time with an ominous clutch.

" 'I don't know the words,' faltered the unhappy Nightingale.

" 'Now thank we all our God,
With hearts and hands and voices,'

began the Doctor, and repeated Luther's[10] hymn with perfect accuracy from beginning to end. 'What will happen next? The Doctor knows hymns!' we thought in profound astonishment. But the Nightingale had begun, and gradually our singers joined in; I doubt whether the grand old choral was ever sung by such a company before or since. There was never any further question, by the way, about that minute gun at sea; it stayed at sea as far as we were concerned.

"Spring came, the faltering spring of Lake Superior. I won't go into my own story, but such as it was, the spring brought it back to me with new force. I wanted to go,—yet I did n't. 'Where,' do you ask? To see her, of course,—a woman, the most beautiful,—well, never mind all that. To be brief, I loved her; she scorned me; I thought I had learned to hate her—but—I was n't sure about it now. I kept myself aloof from the others and gave up my heart to the old sweet, bitter memories; I did not even go to church on Sundays. But all the rest went; our Lady's influence was as great as ever. I could hear them singing; they sang better now that they could have the door open; the pent-up feeling used to stifle them. The time for the bateaux drew near, and I noticed that several of the men were hard at work packing the furs in bales, a job usually left to the *voyageurs*[11] who came with the boats. 'What's that for?' I asked.

"'You don't suppose we're going to have those bateaux rascals camping on Little Fishing, do you?' said Black Andy, scornfully. 'Where are your wits, Reub?'

"And they packed every skin, rafted them all over to the mainland, and waited there patiently for days, until the train of slow boats came along and took off the bales; then they came back in triumph. 'Now we're secure for another six months,' they said, and began to lay out a park, and gardens for every house. The Lady was fond of flowers; the whole town burst into blossom. The Lady liked green grass; all the clearing was soon turfed over like a lawn. The men tried the ice-cold lake every day, waiting anxiously for the time when they could bathe. There was no end to their cleanliness; Black Andy had grown almost white again, and Frenchy's hair shone like oiled silk.

"The Lady stayed on, and all went well. But, gradually, there came a discovery. The Lady was changing,—had changed! Gradually, slowly, but none the less distinctly to the eyes that knew her every eyelash. A little more hair was visible over the white brow, there was a faint color in the cheeks, a quicker step; the clear eyes were sometimes downcast now, the steady voice softer, the words at times faltering. In the early summer the white cap vanished, and she stood among us crowned only with her golden hair; one day she was seen through her open door sewing on a white robe! The men noted all these things silently; they were even a little troubled as at something they did not understand, something beyond their reach. Was she planning to leave them?

"'It's my belief she's getting ready to ascend right up into heaven,' said Salem.

"Salem was a little 'wanting,'[12] as it is called, and the men knew it; still, his words made an impression. They watched the Lady with an awe which was almost superstitious; they were troubled, and knew not why.

But the Lady bloomed on. I did not pay much attention to all this; but I could not help hearing it. My heart was moody, full of its own sorrows; I secluded myself more and more. Gradually I took to going off into the mainland forests for days on solitary hunting expeditions. The camp went on its way rejoicing; the men succeeded, after a world of trouble, in making a fountain which actually played, and they glorified themselves exceedingly. The life grew quite pastoral. There was talk of importing a cow from the East, and a messenger was sent to the Sault for certain choice supplies against the coming winter. But, in the late summer, the whisper went round again that the Lady had changed, this time for the worse. She looked ill, she drooped from day to day; the new life that had come to her vanished, but her former life was not restored. She grew silent and sad, she strayed away by herself through the woods, she scarcely noticed the men who followed her with anxious eyes. Time passed, and brought with it an undercurrent of trouble, suspicion, and anger. Everything went on as before; not one habit, not one custom was altered; both sides seemed to shrink from the first change, however slight. The daily life of the camp was outwardly the same, but brooding trouble filled every heart. There was no open discussion, men talked apart in twos and threes; a gloom rested over everything, but not one said, 'What is the matter?'

"There was a man among us,—I have not said much of the individual characters of our party, but this man was one of the least esteemed, or rather liked; there was not much esteem of any kind at Little Fishing. Little was known about him; although the youngest man in the camp, he was a mooning, brooding creature, with brown hair and eyes and a melancholy face. He was n't hearty and whole-souled, and yet he was n't an out-and-out rascal; he was n't a leader, and yet he was n't a follower either. He would n't be; he was like a third horse, always. There was no goodness about him; don't go to fancying that that was the reason the men did not like him, he was as bad as they were, every inch! He never shirked his work, and they could n't get a handle on him anywhere; but he was just— unpopular. The why and the wherefore are of no consequence now. Well, do you know what was the suspicion that hovered over the camp? It was this: our Lady loved that man!

"It took three months for all to see it, and yet never a word was spoken. All saw, all heard; but they might have been blind and deaf for any sign they gave. And the Lady drooped more and more.

"September came, the fifteenth; the Lady lay on her couch, pale and thin; the door was open and a bell stood beside her, but there was no line of pickets whispering tidings of her state to an anxious group outside. The turf in the three streets had grown yellow for want of water, the flowers in the little gardens had drooped and died, the fountain was choked with weeds, and the interiors of the houses were all untidy. It was Sunday, and near the hour for service; but the men lounged about, dingy and unwashed.

"'A'n't you going to church?' said Salem, stopping at the door of one of the houses; he was dressed in his best, with a flower in his button-hole.

"'See him now! See the fool,' said Black Andy. 'He's going to church, he is! And where's the minister, Salem? Answer me that!'

"'Why,—in the church, I suppose,' replied Salem, vacantly.

"'No, she a'n't; not she! She's at home, a-weeping, and a-wailing, and a-ger-nashing of her teeth,'[13] replied Andy with bitter scorn.

"'What for?' said Salem.

"'What for? Why, that's the joke! Hear him, boys; he wants to know what for!'

"The loungers laughed,—a loud, reckless laugh.

"'Well, I'm going any way,' said Salem, looking wonderingly from one to the other; he passed on and entered the church.

"'I say, boys, let's have a high old time,' cried Andy, savagely. 'Let's go back to the old way and have a jolly Sunday. Let's have out the jugs and the cards and be free again!'

"The men hesitated; ten months and more of law and order held them back.

"'What are you afraid of?' said Andy. 'Not of a canting hypocrite, I hope. She's fooled us long enough, I say. Come on!' He brought out a table and stools, and produced the long-unused cards and a jug of whiskey. 'Strike up, Jack,' he cried; 'give us old Fiery-Eyes.'

"The Nightingale hesitated. Fiery-Eyes was a rollicking drinking song; but Andy put the glass to his lips and his scruples vanished in the tempting aroma. He began at the top of his voice, partners were chosen, and, trembling with excitement and impatience, like prisoners unexpectedly set free, the men gathered around, and made their bets.

"'What born fools we've been,' said Black Andy, laying down a card.

"'Yes,' replied the Flying Dutchman, 'porn fools!' And he followed suit.

"But a thin white hand came down on the bits of colored pasteboard. It was our Lady. With her hair disordered, and the spots of fever in her cheeks, she stood among us again; but not as of old. Angry eyes confronted her, and Andy wrenched the cards from her grasp. 'No, my Lady,' he said, sternly; 'never again!'

"The Lady gazed from one face to the next, and so all around the circle; all were dark and sullen. Then she bowed her head upon her hands and wept aloud.

"There was a sudden shrinking away on all sides, the players rose, the cards were dropped. But the Lady glided away, weeping as she went; she entered the church door and the men could see her taking her accustomed place on the platform. One by one they followed; Black Andy lingered till the last, but he came. The service began, and went on falteringly, without spirit, with palpable fears of a total breaking down which never quite came; the Nightingale sang almost alone, and made sad work with the words; Salem joined in confidently, but did not improve the sense of the hymn. The Lady was silent. But when the time for the sermon came she rose and her voice burst forth.

"'Men, brothers, what have I done? A change has come over the town, a change has come over your hearts. You shun me! What have I done?'

"There was a grim silence; then the Doctor rose in his place and answered,—

"'Only this, madam. You have shown yourself to be a woman.'

"'And what did you think me?'

"'A saint.'

"'God forbid!' said the Lady, earnestly. 'I never thought myself one.'

"'I know that well. But you were a saint to us; hence your influence. It is gone.'

"'Is it all gone?' asked the Lady, sadly.

"'Yes. Do not deceive yourself; we have never been one whit better save through our love for you. We held you as something high above ourselves; we were content to worship you.'

"'O no, not me!' said the Lady, shuddering.

"'Yes, you, you alone! But—our idol came down among us and showed herself to be but common flesh and blood! What wonder that we stand aghast? What wonder that our hearts are bitter? What wonder (worse than all!) that when the awe has quite vanished, there is strife for the beautiful image fallen from its niche?'

"The Doctor ceased, and turned away. The Lady stretched out her hands towards the others; her face was deadly pale, and there was a bewildered expression in her eyes.

"'O, ye for whom I have prayed, for whom I have struggled to obtain a blessing,—ye whom I have loved so,—do *ye* desert me thus?' she cried.

"'*You* have deserted us,' answered a voice.

"'I have not.'

"'You have,' cried Black Andy, pushing to the front. 'You love that Mitchell! Deny it if you dare!'

"There was an irrepressible murmur, then a sudden hush. The angry suspicion, the numbing certainty had found voice at last; the secret was out. All eyes, which had at first closed with the shock, were now fixed upon the solitary woman before them; they burned like coals.

"'Do I?' murmured the Lady, with a strange questioning look that turned from face to face,—'do I?—Great God! I do.' She sank upon her knees and buried her face in her trembling hands. 'The truth has come to me at last.—I do!'

"Her voice was a mere whisper, but every ear heard it, and every eye saw the crimson rise to the forehead and redden the white throat.

"For a moment there was silence, broken only by the hard breathing of the men. Then the Doctor spoke.

"'Go out and bring him in,' he cried. 'Bring in this Mitchell! It seems he has other things to do,—the blockhead!'

"Two of the men hurried out.

"'He shall not have her,' shouted Black Andy. 'My knife shall see to that!' And he pressed close to the platform. A great tumult arose, men talked angrily and clinched their fists, voices rose and fell together. 'He shall not have her,—Mitchell! Mitchell!'

"'The truth is, each one of you wants her himself,' said the Doctor.

"There was a sudden silence, but every man eyed his neighbor jealously. Black Andy stood in front, knife in hand, and kept guard. The Lady had not moved; she was kneeling, with her face buried in her hands.

"'I wish to speak to her,' said the Doctor, advancing.

"'You shall not,' cried Andy, fiercely interposing.

"'You fool! I love her this moment ten thousand times more than you do. But do you suppose I would so much as touch a woman who loved another man?'

"The knife dropped; the Doctor passed on and took his place on the platform by the Lady's side. The tumult began again, for Mitchell was seen coming in the door between his two keepers.

"'Mitchell! Mitchell!' rang angrily through the church.

"'Look, woman!' said the Doctor, bending over the kneeling figure at his side. She raised her head and saw the wolfish faces below.

"'They have had ten months of your religion,' he said.

"It was his revenge. Bitter, indeed; but he loved her.

"In the mean time the man Mitchell was hauled and pushed and tossed forward to the platform by rough hands that longed to throttle him on the way. At last, angry himself, but full of wonder, he confronted them, this crowd of comrades suddenly turned madmen! 'What does this mean?' he asked.

"'Mean! mean!' shouted the men; 'a likely story! He asks what this means!' And they laughed boisterously.

"The Doctor advanced. 'You see this woman,' he said.

"'I see our Lady.'

"'Our Lady no longer; only a woman like any other,—weak and fickle. Take her,—but begone.'

"'Take her!' repeated Mitchell, bewildered,—'take our Lady! And where?'

"'Fool! Liar! Blockhead!' shouted the crowd below.

"'The truth is simply this, Mitchell,' continued the Doctor quietly. 'We herewith give you up our Lady,—ours no longer; for she has just confessed, openly confessed, that she loves you.'

"Mitchell started back. 'Loves me!'

"'Yes.'

"Black Andy felt the blade of his knife. 'He'll never have her alive,' he muttered.

"'But,' said Mitchell, bluntly confronting the Doctor, 'I don't want her.'

"'You don't want her?'

"'I don't love her.'

"'You don't love her?'

"'Not in the least,' he replied, growing angry, perhaps at himself. 'What is she to me? Nothing. A very good missionary, no doubt; but *I* don't fancy woman-preachers. You may remember that *I* never gave in to her influence; *I* was never under her thumb. *I* was the only man in Little Fishing who cared nothing for her!'

"'And that is the secret of *her* liking,' murmured the Doctor. 'O woman! woman! the same the world over!'

"In the mean time the crowd had stood stupefied.

"'He does not love her!' they said to each other; 'he does not want her!'

"Andy's black eyes gleamed with joy; he swung himself up on to the platform. Mitchell stood there with face dark and disturbed, but he did not flinch. Whatever his faults, he was no hypocrite. 'I must leave this to-night,' he said to himself, and turned to go. But quick as a flash our Lady sprang from her knees and threw herself at his feet. 'You are going,' she cried. 'I heard what you said,—you do not love me! But take me with you,—oh, take me with you! Let me be your servant,—your slave—anything—anything, so that I am not parted from you, my lord and master, my only, only love!'

"She clasped his ankles with her thin, white hands, and laid her face on his dusty shoes.

"The whole audience stood dumb before this manifestation of a great love. Enraged, bitter, jealous as was each heart, there was not a man but would at that moment have sacrificed his own love that she might be blessed. Even Mitchell, in one of those rare spirit-flashes when the soul is shown bare in the lightning, asked himself, 'Can I not love her?' But the soul answered, 'No.' He stooped, unclasped the clinging hands, and turned resolutely away.

"'You are a fool,' said the Doctor. 'No other woman will ever love you as she does.'

"'I know it,' replied Mitchell.

"He stepped down from the platform and crossed the church, the silent crowd making a way for him as he passed along; he went out into the sunshine, through the village, down towards the beach,—they saw him no more.

"The Lady had fainted. The men bore her back to the lodge and tended her with gentle care one week,—two weeks,—three weeks. Then she died.

"They were all around her; she smiled upon them all, and called them all by name, bidding them all farewell. 'Forgive me,' she whispered to the Doctor. The Nightingale sang a hymn, sang as he had never sung before. Black Andy knelt at her feet. For some minutes she lay scarcely breathing; then suddenly she opened her fading eyes. 'Friends,' she murmured, 'I am well punished. I thought myself holy,—I held myself above my kind,—but God has shown me I am the weakest of them all.'

"The next moment she was gone.

"The men buried her with tender hands. Then, in a kind of blind fury against Fate, they tore down her empty lodge and destroyed its every fragment; in their grim determination they even smoothed over the ground and planted shrubs and bushes, so that the very location might be lost. But they did not stay to see the change. In a month the camp broke up of itself, the town was abandoned, and the island deserted for good and all; I doubt whether any of the men ever came back or even stopped when passing by. Probably I am the only one. Thirty years ago,—thirty years ago!"

"That Mitchell was a great fool," I said, after a long pause. "The Doctor was worth twenty of him; for that matter, so was Black Andy. I only hope the fellow was well punished for his stupidity."

"He was."

"O, you kept track of him, did you?"

"Yes. He went back into the world, and the woman he loved repulsed him a second time, and with even more scorn than before."

"Served him right."

"Perhaps so; but after all, what could he do? Love is not made to order. He loved one, not the other; that was his crime. Yet,—so strange a creature is man,—he came back after thirty years, just to see our Lady's grave."

"What! Are you—"

"I am Mitchell,—Reuben Mitchell."

CASTLE NOWHERE

※ ※ ※ ※ ※ ※

NOT MANY YEARS AGO the shore bordering the head of Lake Michigan, the northern curve of that silver sea, was a wilderness unexplored. It is a wilderness still, showing even now on the school-maps nothing save an empty waste of colored paper, generally a pale, cold yellow suitable to the climate, all the way from Point St. Ignace to the iron ports on the Little Bay de Noquet, or Badderknock in lake phraseology, a hundred miles of nothing, according to the map-makers, who, knowing nothing of the region, set it down accordingly, withholding even those long-legged letters, "Chip-pe-was," "Ric-ca-rees," that stretch accommodatingly across so much townless territory farther west. This northern curve is and always has been off the route to anywhere; and mortals, even Indians, prefer as a general rule, when once started, to go somewhere. The earliest Jesuit explorers and the captains of yesterday's schooners had this in common, that they could not, being human, resist a cross-cut; and thus, whether bark canoes of two centuries ago or the high, narrow propellers of to-day, one and all, coming and going, they veer to the southeast or west, and sail gayly out of sight, leaving this northern curve of ours unvisited and alone. A wilderness still, but not unexplored; for that railroad of the future which is to make of British America[1] a garden of roses, and turn the wild trappers of the Hudson's Bay Company into gently smiling congressmen, has it not sent its missionaries thither, to the astonishment and joy of the beasts that dwell therein? According to tradition, these men surveyed the territory, and then crossed over (those of them at least whom the beasts had spared)

25

to the lower peninsula, where, the pleasing variety of swamps being added to the labyrinth of pines and sand-hills, they soon lost themselves, and to this day have never found what they lost. As the gleam of a camp-fire is occasionally seen, and now and then a distant shout heard by the hunter passing along the outskirts, it is supposed that they are in there some-where, surveying still.

Not long ago, however, no white man's foot had penetrated within our curve. Across the great river and over the deadly plains, down to the burning clime of Mexico and up to the arctic darkness, journeyed our countrymen, gold to gather and strange countries to see; but this little pocket of land and water passed they by without a glance, inasmuch as no iron mountains rose among its pines, no copper lay hidden in its sand ridges, no harbors dented its shores. Thus it remained an unknown region, and enjoyed life accordingly. But the white man's foot, well booted, was on the way, and one fine afternoon came tramping through. "I wish I was a tree," said to himself this white man, one Jarvis Waring by name. "See that young pine, how lustily it grows, feeling its life to the very tip of each green needle! How it thrills in the sun's rays, how strongly, how completely it carries out the intention of its existence! *It* never has a headache, it—Bah! what a miserable, half-way thing is man, who should be a demigod, and is—a creature for the very trees to pity!" And then he built his camp-fire, called in his dogs, and slept the sleep of youth and health, none the less deep because of that Spirit of Discontent that had driven him forth into the wilderness; probably the Spirit of Discontent knew what it was about. Thus for days, for weeks, our white man wandered through the forest and wandered at random, for, being an exception, he preferred to go nowhere; he had his compass, but never used it, and, a practised hunter, eat what came in his way and planned not for the morrow. "Now am I living the life of a good, hearty, comfortable bear," he said to himself with satisfaction.

"No, you are not, Waring," replied the Spirit of Discontent, "for you know you have your compass in your pocket and can direct yourself back to the camps on Lake Superior or to the Sault for supplies, which is more than the most accomplished bear can do."

"O come, what do you know about bears?" answered Waring; "very likely they too have their depots of supplies,—in caves perhaps—"

"No caves here."

"In hollow trees, then."

"You are thinking of the stories about bears and wild honey," said the pertinacious Spirit.

"Shut up, I am going to sleep," replied the man, rolling himself in his blanket; and then the Spirit, having accomplished his object, smiled blandly and withdrew.

Wandering thus, all reckoning lost both of time and place, our white man came out one evening unexpectedly upon a shore; before him was water stretching away grayly in the fog-veiled moonlight; and so successful had been his determined entangling of himself in the webs of the wilderness, that he really knew not whether it was Superior, Huron, or Michigan that confronted him, for all three bordered the eastern end of the upper peninsula. Not that he wished to know; precisely the contrary. Glorifying himself in his ignorance, he built a fire on the sands, and leaning back against the miniature cliffs that guard the even beaches of the inland seas, he sat looking out over the water, smoking a comfortable pipe of peace, and listening, meanwhile, to the regular wash of the waves. Some people are born with rhythm in their souls, and some not; to Jarvis Waring everything seemed to keep time, from the songs of the birds to the chance words of a friend; and during all this pilgrimage through the wilderness, when not actively engaged in quarrelling with the Spirit, he was repeating bits of verses and humming fragments of songs that kept time with his footsteps, or rather they were repeating and humming themselves along through his brain, while he sat apart and listened. At this moment the fragment that came and went apropos of nothing was Shakespeare's sonnet,

> "When to the sessions of sweet silent thought,
> I summon up remembrance of things past." [2]

Now the small waves came in but slowly, and the sonnet, in keeping time with their regular wash, dragged its syllables so dolorously that at last the man woke to the realization that something was annoying him.

> "When to—the ses—sions of—sweet si—lent thought,"

chanted the sonnet and the waves together.

"O double it, double it, can't you?" said the man, impatiently; "this way:—

'When to the ses—sions of sweet si—lent thought, te-tum,—te-tum,
te-tum.'"

But no; the waves and the lines persisted in their own idea, and the listener finally became conscious of a third element against him, another sound which kept time with the obstinate two and encouraged them in their obstinacy,—the dip of light oars somewhere out in the gray mist.

"When to—the ses—sions of—sweet si—lent thought,
I sum—mon up—remem—brance of—things past,"

chanted the sonnet and the waves and the oars together, and went duly on, sighing the lack of many things they sought, away down to that "dear friend," who in some unexplained way made all their "sorrows end." Even then, while peering through the fog and wondering where and what was this spirit boat that one could hear but not see, Waring found time to make his usual objections. "This summoning up remembrance of things past, sighing the lack, weeping afresh, and so forth, is all very well," he remarked to himself, "we all do it. But that friend who sweeps in at the death with his opportune dose of comfort is a poetical myth whom I, for one, have never yet met."

"That is because you do not deserve such a friend," answered the Spirit, briskly reappearing on the scene. "A man who flies into the wilderness to escape—"

"Spirit, are you acquainted with a Biblical personage named David?" interrupted Waring, executing a flank movement.

The Spirit acknowledged the acquaintance, but cautiously, as not knowing what was coming next.

"Did he or did he not have anything to say about flying to wildernesses and mountain-tops?[3] Did he or did he not express wishes to sail thither in person?"

"David had a voluminous way of making remarks," replied the Spirit, "and I do not pretend to stand up for them all. But one thing is certain; whatever he may have wished, in a musical way, regarding wildernesses and mountain-tops, when it came to the fact he did not go. And why? Because he—"

"Had no wings," said Waring, closing the discussion with a mighty yawn. "I say, Spirit, take yourself off. Something is coming ashore, and were it old Nick[4] in person I should be glad to see him and shake his clawed hand."

As he spoke, out of the fog and into the glare of the fire shot a phantom skiff, beaching itself straight and swift at his feet, and so suddenly that he had to withdraw them like a flash to avoid the crunch of the sharp bows across the sand. "Always let the other man speak first," he thought; "this boomerang of a boat has a shape in it, I see."

The shape rose, and, leaning on its oar, gazed at the camp and its owner in silence. It seemed to be an old man, thin and bent, with bare arms, and a yellow handkerchief bound around its head, drawn down almost to the eyebrows, which, singularly bushy and prominent, shaded the deep-set eyes and hid their expression.

"But, supposing he won't, don't stifle yourself," continued Waring; then aloud, "Well, old gentleman, where do you come from?"

"Nowhere."

"And where are you going?"

"Back there."

"Could n't you take me with you? I have been trying all my life to go nowhere, but never could learn the way; do what I would, I always found myself going in the opposite direction, namely, somewhere."

To this the shape replied nothing, but gazed on.

"Do the nobodies reside in Nowhere, I wonder," pursued the smoker; "because if they do, I am afraid I shall meet all my friends and relatives. What a pity the somebodies could not reside there! But perhaps they do; cynics would say so."

But at this stage the shape waved its oar impatiently and demanded, "Who are you?"

"Well, I do not exactly know. Once I supposed I was Jarvis Waring, but the wilderness has routed that prejudice. We can be anybody we please; it is only a question of force of will; and my latest character has been William Shakespeare. I have been trying to find out whether I wrote my own plays. Stay to supper and take the other side; it is long since I have had an argument with flesh and blood. And you are that,—are n't you?"

But the shape frowned until it seemed all eyebrow. "Young man," it said, "how came you here? By water?"

"No; by land."

"Alongshore?"

"No; through the woods."

"Nobody ever comes through the woods."

"Agreed; but I am somebody."

"Do you mean that you have come across from Lake Superior on foot?"

"I landed on the shore of Lake Superior a month or two ago, and struck inland the same day; where I am now I neither know nor want to know."

"Very well," said the shape,—"very well." But it scowled more gently. "You have no boat?"

"No."

"Do you start on to-morrow?"

"Probably; by that time the waves and 'the sessions of sweet silent thought' will have driven me distracted between them."

"I will stay to supper, I think," said the shape, unbending still further, and stepping out of the skiff.

"Deeds before words then," replied Waring, starting back towards a tree where his game-bag and knapsack were hanging. When he returned the skiff had disappeared; but the shape was warming its moccasined feet at the fire in a very human sort of way. They cooked and eat with the appetites of the wilderness, and grew sociable after a fashion. The shape's name was Fog, Amos⁵ Fog, or old Fog, a fisherman and a hunter among the islands farther to the south; he had come inshore to see what that fire meant, no person had camped there in fifteen long years.

"You have been here all that time, then?"

"Off and on, off and on; I live a wandering life," replied old Fog; and then, with the large curiosity that solitude begets, he turned the conversation back towards the other and his story. The other, not unwilling to tell his adventures, began readily; and the old man listened, smoking meanwhile a second pipe produced from the compact stores in the knapsack. In the web of encounters and escapes, he placed his little questions now and then; no, Waring had no plan for exploring the region, no intention of settling there, was merely idling away a summer in the wilderness and would then go back to civilization never to return, at least, not that way; might go west across the plains, but that would be farther south. They talked on, one much, the other little; after a time, Waring, whose heart had been warmed by his flask, began to extol his ways and means.

"Live? I live like a prince," he said. "See these tin cases; they contain concentrated stores of various kinds. I carry a little tea, you see, and even a few lumps of white sugar as a special treat now and then on a wet night."

"Did you buy that sugar at the Sault?" said the old man, eagerly.

"O no; I brought it up from below. For literature I have this small edition of Shakespeare's sonnets, the cream of the whole world's poetry; and when I am tired of looking at the trees and the sky, I look at this, Titian's lovely daughter with her upheld salver of fruit. Is she not beautiful as a dream?"

"I don't know much about dreams," replied old Fog, scanning the small picture with curious eyes; "but is n't she a trifle heavy in build? They dress like that nowadays, I suppose,—flowered gowns and gold chains around the waist?"

"Why, man, that picture was painted more than three centuries ago."

"Was it now? Women don't alter much, do they?" said old Fog, simply. "Then they don't dress like that nowadays?"

"I don't know how they dress, and don't care," said the younger man, repacking his treasures.

Old Fog concluded to camp with his new friend that night and be off at dawn. "You see it is late," he said, "and your fire's all made and everything comfortable. I've a long row before me to-morrow: I'm on my way to the Beavers."

"Ah! very intelligent animals, I am told. Friends of yours?"

"Why, they're islands, boy; Big and Little Beaver! What do you know, if you don't know the Beavers?"

"Man," replied Waring. "I flatter myself I know the human animal well; he is a miserable beast."

"Is he?" said old Fog, wonderingly; "who'd have thought it!" Then, giving up the problem as something beyond his reach,—"Don't trouble yourself if you hear me stirring in the night," he said; "I am often mighty restless." And rolling himself in his blanket, he soon became, at least as regards the camp-fire and sociability, a nonentity.

"Simple-minded old fellow," thought Waring, lighting a fresh pipe; "has lived around here all his life, apparently. Think of that,—to have lived around here all one's life! I, to be sure, am here now; but then, have I not been—" And here followed a revery of remembrances, that glittering network of gayety and folly which only young hearts can weave, the network around whose border is written in a thousand hues, "Rejoice, young man, in thy youth, for it cometh not again."[6]

> "Alas, what sighs from our boding hearts
> The infinite skies have borne away!"

sings a poet of our time; and the same thought lies in many hearts unexpressed, and sighed itself away in this heart of our Jarvis Waring that still foggy evening on the beach.

The middle of the night, the long watch before dawn; ten chances to one against his awakening! A shape is moving toward the bags hanging on the distant tree. How the sand crunches,—but he sleeps on. It reaches the bags, this shape, and hastily rifles them; then it steals back and crosses the sand again, its moccasined feet making no sound. But, as it happened, that one chance (which so few of us ever see!) appeared on the scene at this moment and guided those feet directly towards a large, thin, old shell masked with newly blown sand; it broke with a crack; Waring woke, and gave chase. The old man was unarmed, he had noticed that; and then such a simple-minded, harmless old fellow! But simple-minded, harmless old fellows do not run like mad if one happens to wake; so the younger pursued. He was strong, he was fleet; but the shape was fleeter, and the space between them grew wider. Suddenly the shape turned and darted into the water, running out until only its head was visible above the surface, a dark spot in the foggy moon-light. Waring pursued, and saw meanwhile another dark spot beyond, an empty skiff which came rapidly inshoreward until it met the head, which forthwith took to itself a body, clambered in, lifted the oars, and was gone in an instant. "Well," said Waring, still pursuing down the gradual slope of the beach, "will a phantom bark come at my call, I wonder? At any rate I will go out as far as he did, and see." But no; the perfidious beach at this instant shelved off suddenly and left him afloat in deep water. Fortunately he was a skilled swimmer, and soon regained the shore, wet and angry. His dogs were whimpering at a distance, both securely fastened to trees, and the light of the fire had died down; evidently the old Fog was not, after all, so simple as some other people!

"I might as well see what the old rogue has taken," thought Waring; "all the tobacco and whiskey, I'll be bound." But nothing had been touched save the lump-sugar, the little book, and the picture of Titian's daughter! Upon this what do you suppose Waring did? He built a boat.

When it was done, and it took some days and was nothing but a dug-out after all (the Spirit said that), he sailed out into the unknown; which being interpreted means that he paddled southward. From the conformation of the shore, he judged that he was in a deep curve, protected in a measure from the force of wind and wave. "I'll find that ancient mariner,"[7] he said to himself, "if I have to circumnavigate the entire lake. My book of sonnets, indeed, and my Titian picture! Would nothing else content him? This voyage I undertake from a pure inborn sense of justice——"

"Now, Waring, you know it is nothing of the kind," said the Spirit who had sailed also. "You know you are tired of the woods and dread going back that way, and you know you may hit a steamer off the islands; besides, you are curious about this old man who steals Shakespeare and sugar, leaving tobacco and whiskey untouched."

"Spirit," replied the man at the paddle, "you fairly corrupt me with your mendacity. Be off and unlimber yourself in the fog; I see it coming in."

He did see it indeed; in it rolled upon him in columns, a soft silvery cloud enveloping everything, the sunshine, the shore, and the water, so that he paddled at random, and knew not whither he went, or rather saw not, since knowing was long since out of the question. "This is pleasant," he said to himself when the morning had turned to afternoon and the afternoon to night, "and it is certainly new. A stratus of tepid cloud a thousand miles long and a thousand miles deep, and a man in a dug-out paddling through! Sisyphus[8] was nothing to this." But he made himself comfortable in a philosophic way, and went to the only place left to him,—to sleep.

At dawn the sunshine colored the fog golden, but that was all; it was still fog, and lay upon the dark water thicker and softer than ever. Waring eat some dried meat, and considered the possibilities; he had reckoned without the fog, and now his lookout was uncomfortably misty. The provisions would not last more than a week; and though he might catch fish, how could he cook them? He had counted on a shore somewhere; any land, however desolate, would give him a fire; but this fog was muffling, and unless he stumbled ashore by chance he might go on paddling in a circle forever. *"Bien,"* he said, summing up, "my part at any rate is to go on; *I,* at least, can do my duty."

"Especially as there is nothing else to do," observed the Spirit.

Having once decided, the man kept at his work with finical precision. At a given moment he eat a lunch, and very tasteless it was too, and then to work again; the little craft went steadily on before the stroke of the strong arms, its wake unseen, its course unguided. Suddenly at sunset the fog folded its gray draperies, spread its wings, and floated off to the southwest, where that night it rested at Death's Door and sent two schooners to the bottom; but it left behind it a released dug-out, floating before a log fortress which had appeared by magic, rising out of the water with not an inch of ground to spare, if indeed there was any ground; for might it not be a species of fresh-water boat, anchored there for clearer weather?

"Ten more strokes and I should have run into it," thought Waring as he floated noiselessly up to this watery residence; holding on by a jutting beam, he reconnoitred the premises. The building was of logs, square, and standing on spiles, its north side, under which he lay, showed a row of little windows all curtained in white, and from one of them peeped the top of a rose-bush; there was but one story, and the roof was flat. Nothing came to any of these windows, nothing stirred, and the man in the dug-out, being curious as well as hungry, decided to explore, and touching the wall at intervals pushed his craft noiselessly around the eastern corner; but here was a blank wall of logs and nothing more. The south side was the same, with the exception of two loopholes, and the dug-out glided its quietest past these. But the west shone out radiant, a rude little balcony overhanging the water, and in it a girl in a mahogany chair, nibbling something and reading.

"My sugar and my sonnets, as I am alive!" ejaculated Waring to himself.

The girl took a fresh bite with her little white teeth, and went on reading in the sunset light.

"Cool," thought Waring.

And cool she looked truly to a man who had paddled two days in a hot sticky fog, as, clad in white, she sat still and placid on her airy perch. Her hair, of the very light fleecy gold seldom seen after babyhood, hung over her shoulders unconfined by comb or ribbon, falling around her like a veil and glittering in the horizontal sunbeams; her face, throat, and hands were white as the petals of a white camelia, her features infantile, her cast-down eyes invisible under the full-orbed lids. Waring gazed at her cynically, his boat motionless; it accorded with his theories that the only woman he had seen for months should be calmly eating and reading stolen sweets. The girl turned a page, glanced up, saw him, and sprang forward smiling; as she stood at the balcony, her beautiful hair fell below her knees.

"Jacob," she cried, gladly, "is that you at last?"

"No," replied Waring, "it is not Jacob; rather Esau. Jacob was too tricky for me. The damsel Rachel,[9] I presume!"

"My name is Silver," said the girl, "and I see you are not Jacob at all. Who are you, then?"

"A hungry, tired man who would like to come aboard and rest awhile."

"Aboard? This is not a boat."

"What then?"

"A castle,—Castle Nowhere."

"You reside here?"

"Of course; where else should I reside? Is it not a beautiful place?" said the girl, looking around with a little air of pride.

"I could tell better if I was up there."

"Come, then."

"How?"

"Do you not see the ladder?"

"Ah, yes,—Jacob had a ladder,[10] I remember; he comes up this way, I suppose?"

"He does not; but I wish he would."

"Undoubtedly. But you are not Leah all this time?"

35

"I am Silver, as I told you before; I know not what you mean with your Leah."

"But, mademoiselle, your Bible——"

"What is Bible?"

"You have never read the Bible?"

"It is a book, then. I like books," replied Silver, waving her hand comprehensively; "I have read five, and now I have a new one."

"Do you like it,—your new one?" asked Waring, glancing towards his property.

"I do not understand it all; perhaps you can explain to me?"

"I think I can," answered the young man, smiling in spite of himself; "that is, if you wish to learn."

"Is it hard?"

"That depends upon the scholar; now, some minds——" Here a hideous face looked out through one of the little windows, and then vanished. "Ah," said Waring, pausing, "one of the family?"

"That is Lorez, my dear old nurse."

The face now came out on to the balcony and showed itself as part of an old negress, bent and wrinkled with age.

"He came in a boat, Lorez," said Silver, "and yet you see he is not Jacob. But he says he is tired and hungry, so we will have supper now, without waiting for father."

The old woman smiled and nodded, stroking the girl's glittering hair meanwhile with her black hand.

"As soon as the sun has gone it will be very damp," said Silver, turning to her guest; "you will come within. But you have not told me your name."

"Jarvis," replied Waring, promptly.

"Come, then, Jarvis." And she led the way through a low door into a long narrow room with a row of little square windows on each side all covered with little square white curtains. The walls and ceiling were planked, and the workmanship of the whole rude and clumsy; but a gay carpet covered the floor, a chandelier adorned with lustres hung from a hook in the ceiling, large gilded vases and a mirror in a tarnished gilt frame adorned a shelf over the hearth, mahogany chairs stood in ranks against the wall under the little windows, and a long narrow table ran down the centre of the apartment from end to end. It all seemed strangely familiar; of what did it remind him? His eyes fell upon the table-legs; they were riveted to the floor. Then it came to him at once,—the long narrow cabin of a lake steamer.

"I wonder if it is not anchored after all," he thought.

"Just a few shavings and one little stick, Lorez," said Silver; "enough to give us light and drive away the damp."

Up flared the blaze and spread abroad in a moment the dear home feeling. (O hearth-fire, good genius of home, with thee a log-cabin is cheery and bright, without thee the palace a dreary waste!)

"And now, while Lorez is preparing supper, you will come and see my pets," said Silver, in her soft tone of unconscious command.

"By all means," replied Waring. "Anything in the way of mermaidens?"

"Mermaidens dwell in the water, they cannot live in houses as we can; did you not know that? I have seen them on moonlight nights, and so has Lorez; but Aunt Shadow never saw them."

"Another member of the family,—Aunt Shadow?"

"Yes," replied Silver; "but she is not here now. She went away one night when I was asleep. I do not know why it is," she added, sadly, "but if people go away from here in the night they never come back. Will it be so with you, Jarvis?"

"No; for I will take you with me," replied the young man, lightly.

"Very well; and father will go too, and Lorez," said Silver.

To this addition, Waring, like many another man in similar circumstances, made no reply. But Silver did not notice the omission. She had opened a door, and behold, they stood together in a bower of greenery and blossom, flowers growing everywhere,—on the floor, up the walls, across the ceiling, in pots, in boxes, in baskets, on shelves, in cups, in shells, climbing, crowding each other, swinging, hanging, winding around everything,—a riot of beauty with perfumes for a language. Two white gulls stood in the open window and gravely surveyed the stranger.

"They stay with me almost all the time," said the water-maiden; "every morning they fly out to sea for a while, but they always come back."

Then she flitted to and fro, kissed the opening blossoms and talked to them, tying back the more riotous vines, and gravely admonishing them.

"They are so happy here," she said; "it was dull for them on shore. I would not live on the shore! Would you?"

"Certainly not," replied Waring, with an air of having spent his entire life upon a raft. "But you did not find all these blossoms on the shores about here, did you?"

"Father found them,—he finds everything; in his boat almost every night is something for me. I hope he will come soon; he will be so glad to see you."

"Will he? I wish I was sure of that," thought Waring. Then aloud, "Has he any men with him?" he asked, carelessly.

"O no; we live here all alone now,—father, Lorez, and I."

"But you were expecting a Jacob?"

"I have been expecting Jacob for more than two years. Every night I watch for him, but he comes not. Perhaps he and Aunt Shadow will come together,—do you think they will?" said Silver, looking up into his eyes with a wistful expression.

"Certainly," replied Waring.

"Now am I glad, so glad! For father and Lorez will never say so. I think I shall like you, Jarvis." And, leaning on a box of mignonette, she considered him gravely with her little hands folded.

Waring, man of the world,—Waring, who had been under fire,— Waring the impassive,—Waring the unflinching,—turned from this scrutiny.

Supper was eaten at one end of the long table; the dishes, tablecloth, and napkins were marked with an anchor, the food simple but well cooked.

"Fish, of course, and some common supplies I can understand," said the visitor; "but how do you obtain flour like this, or sugar?"

"Father brings them," said Silver, "and keeps them locked in his storeroom. Brown sugar we have always, but white not always, and I like it so much! Don't you?"

"No; I care nothing for it," said Waring, remembering the few lumps and the little white teeth.

The old negress waited, and peered at the visitor out of her small bright eyes; every time Silver spoke to her, she broke into a radiance of smiles and nods, but said nothing.

"She lost her voice some years ago," explained the little mistress when the black had gone out for more coffee; "and now she seems to have forgotten how to form words, although she understands us."

Lorez returned, and, after refilling Waring's cup, placed something shyly beside his plate, and withdrew into the shadow. "What is it?" said the young man, examining the carefully folded parcel.

"Why, Lorez, have you given him that!" exclaimed Silver as he drew out a scarlet ribbon, old and frayed, but brilliant still. "We think it must have belonged to her young master," she continued in a low tone. "It is her most precious treasure, and long ago she used to talk about him, and about her old home in the South."

The old woman came forward after a while, smiling and nodding like an animated mummy, and taking the red ribbon threw it around the young man's neck, knotting it under the chin. Then she nodded with treble radiance and made signs of satisfaction.

"Yes, it *is* becoming," said Silver, considering the effect thoughtfully, her small head with its veil of hair bent to one side, like a flower swayed by the wind.

The flesh-pots of Egypt[11] returned to Jarvis Waring's mind; he remembered certain articles of apparel left behind in civilization, and murmured against the wilderness. Under the pretense of examining the vases, he took an early opportunity of looking into the round mirror. "I am hideous," he said to himself, uneasily.

"Decidedly so," echoed the Spirit in a cheerful voice. But he was not; only a strong dark young man of twenty-eight, browned by exposure, clad in a gray flannel shirt and the rough attire of a hunter.

The fire on the hearth sparkled gayly. Silver had brought one of her little white gowns, half finished, and sat sewing in its light, while the old negress came and went about her household tasks.

"So you can sew?" said the visitor.

"Of course I can. Aunt Shadow taught me," answered the water-maiden, threading her needle deftly. "There is no need to do it, for I have so many dresses; but I like to sew, don't you?"

"I cannot say that I do. Have you so many dresses, then?"

"Yes; would you like to see them? Wait."

Down went the little gown trailing along the floor, and away she flew, coming back with her arms full,—silks, muslins, laces, and even jewelry. "Are they not beautiful?" she asked, ranging her splendor over the chairs.

"They are indeed," said Waring, examining the garments with curious eyes. "Where did you get them?"

"Father brought them. O, there he is now, there he is now! I hear the oars. Come, Lorez."

She ran out; the old woman hastened, carrying a brand from the hearth; and after a moment Waring followed them. "I may as well face the old rogue at once," he thought.

The moon had not risen and the night was dark; under the balcony floated a black object, and Lorez, leaning over, held out her flaming torch. The face of the old rogue came out into the light under its yellow handkerchief, but so brightened and softened by loving gladness that the gazer above hardly knew it. "Are you there, darling, well and safe?" said the old man, looking up fondly as he fastened his skiff.

"Yes, father; here I am and so glad to see you," replied the water-maiden, waiting at the top of the ladder. "We have a visitor, father dear; are you not glad, so glad to see him?"

The two men came face to face, and the elder started back. "What are you doing here?" he said, sternly.

"Looking for my property."

"Take it, and begone!"

"I will, to-morrow."

All this apart, and with the rapidity of lightning.

"His name is Jarvis, father, and we must keep him with us," said Silver.

"Yes, dear, as long as he wishes to stay; but no doubt he has home and friends waiting for him."

They went within, Silver leading the way. Old Fog's eyes gleamed and his hands were clinched. The younger man watched him warily.

"I have been showing Jarvis all my dresses, father, and he thinks them beautiful."

"They certainly are remarkable," observed Waring, coolly.

Old Fog's hands dropped, he glanced nervously towards the visitor.

"What have you brought for me to-night, father dear?"

"Nothing, child; that is, nothing of any consequence. But it is growing late; run off to your nest."

"O no, papa; you have had no supper, nor—"

"I am not hungry. Go, child, go; do not grieve me," said the old man in a low tone.

"Grieve you? Dear papa, never!" said the girl, her voice softening to tenderness in a moment. "I will run straight to my room.—Come, Lorez."

The door closed. "Now for us two," thought Waring.

But the cloud had passed from old Fog's face, and he drew up his chair confidentially. "You see how it is," he began in an apologetic tone; "that child is the darling of my life, and I could not resist taking those things for her; she has so few books, and she likes those little lumps of sugar."

"And the Titian picture?" said Waring, watching him doubtfully.

"A father's foolish pride; I knew she was lovelier, but I wanted to see the two side by side. She is lovelier, is n't she?"

"I do not think so."

"Don't you?" said old Fog in a disappointed tone. "Well, I suppose I am foolish about her; we live here all alone, you see: my sister brought her up."

"The Aunt Shadow who has gone away?"

"Yes; she was my sister, and—and she went away last year," said the old man. "Have a pipe?"

"I should think you would find it hard work to live here."

"I do; but a poor man cannot choose. I hunt, fish, and get out a few furs sometimes; I traffic with the Beaver Island people now and then. I bought all this furniture in that way; you would not think it, but they have a great many nice things down at Beaver."

"It looks like steamboat furniture."

"That is it; it is. A steamer went to pieces down there, and they saved almost all her furniture and stores; they are very good sailors, the Beavers."

"Wreckers, perhaps?"

"Well, I would not like to say that; you know we do have terrible storms on these waters. And then there is the fog; this part of Lake Michigan is foggy half the time, why, I never could guess; but twelve hours out of the twenty-four the gray mist lies on the water here and outside, shifting slowly backwards and forwards from Little Traverse to Death's Door, and up into this curve, like a waving curtain. Those silks, now, came from the steamer; trunks, you know. But I have never told Silver; she might ask where were the people to whom they belonged. You do not like the idea? Neither do I. But how could we help the drowning when we were not there, and these things were going for a song down at Beaver. The child loves pretty things; what could a poor man do? Have a glass of punch; I'll get it ready in no time." He bustled about, and then came back with the full glasses. "You won't tell her? I may have done wrong in the matter, but it would kill me to have the child lose faith in me," he said, humbly.

"Are you going to keep the girl shut up here forever?" said Waring, half touched, half disgusted; the old fellow had looked abject as he pleaded.

"That is it; no," said Fog, eagerly. "She has been but a child all this time, you see, and my sister taught her well. We did the best we could. But as soon as I have a little more, just a little more, I intend to move to one of the towns down the lake, and have a small house and everything comfortable. I have planned it all out, I shall have——"

He rambled on, garrulously detailing all his fancies and projects while the younger man sipped his punch (which was very good), listened until he was tired, fell into a doze, woke and listened awhile longer, and then, wearied out, proposed bed.

"Certainly. But, as I was saying——"

"I can hear the rest to-morrow," said Waring, rising with scant courtesy.

"I am sorry you go so soon; could n't you stay a few days?" said the old man, lighting a brand. "I am going over to-morrow to the shore where I met you. I have some traps there; you might enjoy a little hunting."

"I have had too much of that already. I must get my dogs, and then I should like to hit a steamer or vessel going below."

"Nothing easier; we'll go over after the dogs early in the morning, and then I'll take you right down to the islands if the wind is fair. Would you like to look around the castle,——I am going to draw up the ladders. No? This way, then; here is your room."

It was a little side-chamber with one window high up over the water; there was an iron bolt on the door, and the walls of bare logs were solid. Waring stood his gun in one corner, and laid his pistols by the side of the bed,——for there was a bed, only a rude framework like a low-down shelf, but covered with mattress and sheets none the less,—and his weary body longed for those luxuries with a longing that only the wilderness can give,—the wilderness with its beds of boughs, and no undressing. The bolt and the logs shut him in safely; he was young and strong, and there were his pistols. "Unless they burn down their old castle," he said to himself, "they cannot harm me." And then he fell to thinking of the lovely childlike girl, and his heart grew soft. "Poor old man," he said, "how he must have worked and stolen and starved to keep her safe and warm in this far-away nest of his hidden in the fogs! I won't betray the old fellow, and I'll go to-morrow. Do you hear that, Jarvis Waring? I'll go to-morrow!"

And then the Spirit, who had been listening as usual, folded himself up silently and flew away.

To go to sleep in a bed, and awake in an open boat drifting out to sea, is startling. Waring was not without experiences, startling and so forth, but this exceeded former sensations; when a bear had him, for instance, he at least understood it, but this was not a bear, but a boat. He examined the craft as well as he could in the darkness. "Evidently boats in some shape or other are the genii of this region," he said; "they come shooting ashore from nowhere, they sail in at a signal without oars, canvas, or crew, and now they have taken to kidnapping. It is foggy too, I'll warrant; they are in league with the fogs." He looked up, but could see nothing, not even a star. "What does it all mean anyway? Where am I? Who am I? Am I anybody? Or has the body gone and left me only an any?" But no one answered. Finding himself partly dressed, with the rest of his clothes at his feet, he concluded that he was not yet a spirit; in one of his pockets was a match, he struck it and came back to reality in a flash. The boat was his own dug-out, and he himself and no other was in it: so far, so good. Everything else, however, was fog and night. He found the paddle and began work. "We shall see who will conquer," he thought, doggedly, "Fate or I!" So he paddled on an hour or more.

Then the wind arose and drove the fog helter-skelter across to Green Bay, where the gray ranks curled themselves down and lay hidden until morning. "I'll go with the wind," thought Waring, "it must take me some-where in time." So he changed his course and paddled on. The wind grew strong, then stronger. He could see a few stars now as the ragged dark clouds scudded across the heavens, and he hoped for the late moon. The wind grew wild, then wilder. It took all his skill to manage his clumsy boat. He no longer asked himself where he was or who; he knew,—a man in the grasp of death. The wind was a gale now, and the waves were pressed down flat by its force as it flew along. Suddenly the man at the paddle, almost despairing, espied a light, high up, steady, strong. "A lighthouse on one of the islands," he said, and steered for it with all his might. Good luck was with him; in half an hour he felt the beach under him, and landed on a shore; but the light he saw no longer. "I must be close in under it," he thought. In the train of the gale came thunder and lightning. Waring sat under a bush watching the powers of the air in conflict, he saw the fury of their darts and heard the crash of their artillery, and mused upon the wonders of creation, and the riddle of man's existence. Then a flash came, different from the others in that it brought the human element upon the scene; in its light he saw a vessel driving helplessly before the gale. Down from his spirit-heights he came at once, and all the man within him was stirred for those on board, who, whether or not they had ever perplexed themselves over the riddle of their existence, no doubt now shrank from the violent solution offered to them. But what could he do? He knew nothing of the shore, and yet there must be a harbor somewhere, for was there not the light? Another flash showed the vessel still nearer, drifting broadside on; involuntarily he ran out on the long sandy point where it seemed that soon she must strike. But sooner came a crash, and a grinding sound; there was a reef outside then, and she was on it, the rocks cutting her, and the waves pounding her down on their merciless edges. "Strange!" he thought. "The harbor must be on the other side I suppose, and yet it seems as though I came this way." Looking around, there was the light high up behind him, burning clearly and strongly, while the vessel was breaking to pieces below. "It is a lure," he said, indignantly, "a false light." In his wrath he spoke aloud; suddenly a shape came out of the darkness, cast him down, and tightened a grasp around his throat. "I know you," he muttered, strangling. One hand was free, he drew out his pistol, and fired; the shape fell back. It was old Fog. Wounded? Yes, badly.

Waring found his tinder-box, made a blaze of driftwood, and bound up the bleeding arm and leg roughly. "Wretch," he said, "you set that light."

Old Fog nodded.

"Can anything be done for the men on board? Answer, or I'll end your miserable life at once; I don't know why, indeed, I have tried to save it."

Old Fog shook his head. "Nothing," he murmured; "I know every inch of the reef and shore."

Another flash revealed for an instant the doomed vessel, and Waring raged at his own impotence as he strode to and fro, tears of anger and pity in his eyes. The old man watched him anxiously. "There are not more than six of them," he said; "it was only a small schooner."

"Silence!" shouted Waring; "each man of the six now suffering and drowning is worth a hundred of such as you!"

"That may be," said Fog.

Half an hour afterwards he spoke again. "They're about gone now, the water is deadly cold up here. The wind will go down soon, and by daylight the things will be coming ashore; you'll see to them, won't you?"

"I'll see to nothing, murderer!"

"And if I die, what are you?"

"An avenger."

"Silver must die too then; there is but little in the house, she will soon starve. It was for her that I came out to-night."

"I will take her away; not for your sake, but for hers."

"How can you find her?"

"As soon as it is daylight I will sail over."

"Over? Over where? That is it, you do not know," said the old man, eagerly, raising himself on his unwounded arm. "You might row and sail about here for days, and I'll warrant you'd never find the castle; it's hidden away more carefully than a nest in the reeds, trust me for that. The way lies through a perfect tangle of channels and islands and marshes, and the fog is sure for at least a good half of the time. The sides of the castle towards the channel show no light at all; and even when you're once through the outlying islets, the only approach is masked by a movable bed of sedge which I contrived, and which turns you skilfully back into the marsh by another way. No; you might float around there for days, but you'd never find the castle."

"I found it once."

"That was because you came from the north shore. I did not guard that side, because no one has ever come that way; you remember how quickly I saw your light and rowed over to find out what it was. But you are miles away from there now."

The moon could not pierce the heavy clouds, and the night continued dark. At last the dawn came slowly up the east and showed an angry sea, and an old man grayly pallid on the sands near the dying fire; of the vessel nothing was to be seen.

"The things will be coming ashore, the things will be coming ashore," muttered the old man, his anxious eyes turned towards the water that lay on a level with his face; he could not raise himself now. "Do you see things coming ashore?"

Waring looked searchingly at him. "Tell me the truth," he said, "has the girl no boat?"

"No."

"Will any one go to rescue her; does any one know of the castle?"

"Not a human being on this earth."

"And that aunt,—that Jacob?"

"Did n't you guess it? They are both dead. I rowed them out by night and buried them,—my poor old sister, and the boy who had been our serving-lad. The child knows nothing of death. I told her they had gone away."

"Is there no way for her to cross to the islands or mainland?"

"No; there is a circle of deep water all around the castle, outside."

"I see nothing for it, then, but to try and save your justly forfeited life," said Waring, kneeling down with an expression of repugnance. He was something of a surgeon, and knew what he was about. His task over, he made up the fire, warmed some food, fed the old man, and helped his waning strength with the contents of his flask. "At least you placed all my property in the dug-out before you set me adrift," he said; "may I ask your motive?"

"I did not wish to harm you; only to get rid of you. You had provisions, and your chances were as good as many you had had in the woods."

"But I might have found my way back to your castle?"

"Once outside, you could never do that," replied the old man, securely.

"I could go back along-shore."

"There are miles of piny-wood swamps where the streams come down; no, you could not do it, unless you went away round to Lake Superior again, and struck across the country as you did before. That would take you a month or two, and the summer is almost over. You would not risk a Northern snowstorm, I reckon. But say, do you see things coming ashore?"

"The poor bodies will come, no doubt," said Waring, sternly.

"Not yet; and they don't often come in here, any way; they're more likely to drift out to sea."

"Miserable creature, this is not the first time, then!"

"Only four times,—only four times in fifteen long years, and then only when she was close to starvation," pleaded the old man. "The steamer was honestly wrecked,—the Anchor, of the Buffalo line,—honestly, I do assure you; and what I gathered from her—she did not go to pieces for days—lasted me a long time, besides furnishing the castle. It was a god-send to me, that steamer. You must not judge me, boy; I work, I slave, I go hungry and cold, to keep her happy and warm. But times come when everything fails and starvation is at the door. She never knows it, none of them ever knew it, for I keep the keys and amuse them with little mysteries; but, as God is my judge, the wolf has been at the door, and is there this moment unless I have luck. Fish? There are none in shore where they can catch them. Why do I not fish for them? I do; but my darling is not accustomed to coarse fare, her delicate life must be delicately nourished. O, you do not know, you do not know! I am growing old, and my hands and eyes are not what they were. That very night when I cam home and found you there, I had just lost overboard my last supplies, stored so long, husbanded so carefully! If I could walk, I would show you my cellar and storehouse back in the woods. Many things that they have held were honestly earned, by my fish and my game, and one thing and another. I get out timber and raft it down to the islands sometimes, although the work is too hard for an old man alone; and I trade my furs off regularly at the settlements on the islands and even along the mainland,—a month's work for a little flour or sugar. Ah, how I have labored! I have felt my muscles crack, I have dropped like a log from sheer weariness. Talk of tortures; which of them have I not felt, with the pains and faintness of exposure and hunger racking me from head to foot? Have I stopped for snow and ice? Have I stopped for anguish? Never; I have worked, worked, worked, with the tears of pain rolling down my cheeks, with my body gnawed by hunger. That night, in some way, the boxes slipped and fell overboard as I was shifting them; just slipped out of my grasp as if on purpose, they knowing all the time that they were my last. Home I came, empty-handed, and found you there! I would have taken your supplies, over on the north beach, that night, yes, without pity, had I not felt sure of those last boxes; but I never rob needlessly. You look at me with scorn? You are thinking of those dead men? But what are they to Silver,—the rough common fellows,—and the wolf standing at the castle door! Believe me, though, I try everything before I resort to this, and only twice out of the four times have I caught anything with my tree-hung light; once it was a vessel loaded with provisions, and once it was a schooner with grain from Chicago, which washed overboard and was worthless. O, the bitter day when I stood here in the biting wind and watched it float by out to sea! But say, has anything come ashore? She will be waking soon, and we have miles to go."

But Waring did not answer; he turned away. The old man caught at his feet. "You are not going," he cried in a shrill voice,—"you are not going? Leave me to die,—that is well; the sun will come and burn me, thirst will come and madden me, these wounds will torture me, and all is no more than I deserve. But Silver? If I die, she dies. If you forsake me, you forsake her. Listen; do you believe in your Christ, the dear Christ? Then, in his name I swear to you that you cannot reach her alone, that only I can guide you to her. O save me, for her sake! Must she suffer and linger and die? O God, have pity and soften his heart!" The voice died away in sobs, the weak slow sobs of an old man.

But Waring, stern in avenging justice, drew himself from the feeble grasp, and walked down towards the boats. He did not intend fairly to desert the miserable old creature. He hardly knew what he intended, but his impulse was to put more space between them, between himself and this wretch who gathered his evil living from dead men's bones. So he stood gazing out to sea. A faint cry roused him, and, turning, he saw that the old man had dragged himself half across the distance between them, marking the way with his blood, for the bandages were loosened by his movements. As Waring turned, he held up his hands, cried aloud, and fell as if dead on the sands. "I am a brute," said Waring. Then he went to work and brought back consciousness, rebound the wounds, lifted the body in his strong arms and bore it down the beach. A sail-boat lay in a cove, with a little skiff in tow. Waring arranged a couch in the bottom, and placed the old man in an easy position on an impromptu pillow made of his coat. Fog opened his eyes. "Anything come ashore?" he asked faintly, trying to turn his head towards the reef. Conquering his repugnance, the young man walked out on the long point. There was nothing there; but farther down the coast barrels were washing up and back in the surf, and one box had stranded in shallow water. "Am I, too, a wrecker?" he asked himself, as with much toil and trouble he secured the booty and examined it. Yes, the barrels contained provisions.

Old Fog, revived by the sight, lay propped at the stern, giving directions. Waring found himself a child obeying the orders of a wiser head. The load on board, the little skiff carrying its share behind, the young man set sail and away they flew over the angry water; old Fog watching the sky, the sail, and the rudder, guiding their course with a word now and then, but silent otherwise.

"Shall we see the castle soon?" asked Waring, after several hours had passed.

"We may be there by night, if the wind does n't shift."

"Have we so far to go, then? Why, I came across in the half of a night."

"Add a day to the half and you have it. I let you down at dawn and towed you out until noon; then I spied that sail beating up, and I knew there would be a storm by night, and—and things were desperate with me. So I cast you off and came over to set the light. It was a chance I did not count on, that your dug-out should float this way; I calculated that she would beach you safely on an island farther to the south."

"And all this time, when you were letting me down— By the way, how did you do it?"

"Lifted a plank in the floor."

"When you were letting me down, and towing me out, and calculating chances, what was I, may I ask?"

"O, just a body asleep, that was all; your punch was drugged, and well done too! Of course I could not have you at the castle; that was plain."

They flew on a while longer, and then veered short to the left. "This boat sails well," said Waring, "and that is your skiff behind I see. Did you whistle for it that night?"

"I let it out by a long cord while you went after the game-bag, and the shore-end I fastened to a little stake just under the edge of the water on that long slope of beach. I snatched it up as I ran out, and kept hauling in until I met it. You fell off that ledge, did n't you? I calculated on that. You see I had found out all I wanted to know; the only thing I feared was some plan for settling along that shore, or exploring it for something. It is my weak side; if you had climbed up one of those tall trees you might have caught sight of the castle,—that is, if there was no fog."

"Will the fog come up now?"

"Hardly; the storm has been too heavy. I suppose you know what day it is?" continued the old man, peering up at his companion from under his shaggy eyebrows.

"No; I have lost all reckonings of time and place."

"Purposely?"

"Yes."

"You are worse than I am, then; I keep a reckoning, although I do not show it. To-day is Sunday, but Silver does not know it; all days are alike to her. Silver has never heard of the Bible," he added, slowly.

"Yes, she has, for I told her."

"You told her!" cried old Fog, wringing his hands.

"Be quiet, or you will disturb those bandages again. I only asked her if she had read the book, and she said no; that was all. But supposing it had not been all, what then? Would it harm her to know of the Bible?"

"It would harm her to lose faith in me."

"Then why have you not told her yourself?"

"I left her to grow up as the flowers grow," said old Fog, writhing on his couch. "Is she not pure and good? Ah, a thousand times more than any church or school could make her!"

"And yet you have taught her to read?"

"I knew not what might happen. I could not expose her defenceless in a hard world. Religion is fancy, but education is like an armor. I cannot tell what may happen."

"True. You may die, you know; you are an old man."

The old man turned away his face.

They sailed on, eating once or twice; afternoon came, and then an archipelago closed in around them; the sail was down, and the oars out. Around and through, across and back, in and out they wound, now rowing, now poling, and now and then the sail hoisted to scud across a space of open water. Old Fog's face had grown gray again, and the lines had deepened across his haggard cheek and set mouth; his strength was failing. At last they came to a turn, broad and smooth like a canal. "Now I will hoist the sail again," said Waring.

But old Fog shook his head. "That turn leads directly back into the marsh," he said. "Take your oar and push against the sedge in front."

The young man obeyed, and lo! it moved slowly aside and disclosed a narrow passage westward; through this they poled their way long to open water, then set the sail, rounded a point, and came suddenly upon the castle. "Well, I am glad we are here," said Waring.

Fog had fallen back. "Promise," he whispered with gray lips,— "promise that you will not betray me to the child." And his glazing eyes fixed themselves on Waring's face with the mute appeal of a dying animal in the hands of its captor.

"I promise," said Waring.

But the old man did not die; he wavered, lingered, then slowly rallied,—very slowly. The weeks had grown into a month and two before he could manage his boat again. In the mean time Waring hunted and fished for the household, and even sailed over to the reef with Fog on a bed in the bottom of the boat, coming back loaded with the spoil; not once only, not twice did he go; and at last he knew the way, even through the fog, and came and went alone, bringing home the very planks and beams of the ill-fated schooner. "They will make a bright fire in the evenings," he said. The dogs lived on the north shore, went hunting when their master came over, and the rest of the time possessed their souls in patience. And what possessed Waring, do you ask? His name for it was "necessity." "Of course I cannot leave them to starve," he said to himself.

Silver came and went about the castle, at first wilfully, then sub-missively, then shyly. She had folded away all her finery in wondering silence, for Waring's face had shown disapproval, and now she wore always her simple white gown. "Can you not put up your hair?" he had asked one day; and from that moment the little head appeared crowned with braids. She worked among her flowers and fed her gulls as usual, but she no longer talked to them or told them stories. In the evenings they all sat around the hearth, and sometimes the little maiden sang; Waring had taught her new songs. She knew the sonnets now, and chanted them around the castle to tunes of her own; Shakespeare would not have known his stately measures, dancing along to her rippling melodies.

The black face of Orange[12] shone and simmered with glee; she nod-ded perpetually, and crooned and laughed to herself over her tasks by the hour together,—a low chuckling laugh of exceeding content.

And did Waring ever stop to think? I know not. If he did, he forgot the thoughts when Silver came and sat by him in the evening with the light of the hearth-fire shining over her. He scarcely saw her at other times, except on her balcony, or at her flower-window as he came and went in his boat below; but in the evenings she sat beside him in her low chair, and laid sometimes her rose-leaf palm in his rough brown hand, or her pretty head against his arm. Old Fog sat by always; but he said little, and his face was shaded by his hand.

The early autumn gales swept over the lakes, leaving wreck and disaster behind; but the crew of the castle stayed safely at home and lis-tened to the tempest cosily, while the flowers bloomed on, and the gulls brought all their relations and colonized the balcony and window-sills, fed daily by the fair hand of Silver. And Waring went not.

Then the frosts came, and turned the forests into splendor; they rowed over and brought out branches, and Silver decked the long room with scarlet and gold. And Waring went not.

The dreary November rains began, the leaves fell, and the dark water surged heavily; but a store of wood was piled on the flat roof, and the fire on the hearth blazed high. And still Waring went not.

At last the first ice appeared, thin flakes forming around the log foundations of the castle; then old Fog spoke. "I am quite well now, quite strong again; you must go to-day, or you will find yourself frozen in here. As it is, you may hit a late vessel off the islands that will carry you below. I will sail over with you, and bring back the boat."

"But you are not strong enough yet," said Waring, bending over his work, a shelf he was carving for Silver; "I cannot go and leave you here alone."

"It is either go now, or stay all winter. You do not, I presume, intend to make Silver your wife,—Silver, the daughter of Fog the wrecker."

Waring's hands stopped; never before had the old man's voice taken that tone, never before had he even alluded to the girl as anything more than a child. On the contrary, he had been silent, he had been humble, he had been openly grateful to the strong young man who had taken his place on sea and shore, and kept the castle full and warm. "What new thing is this?" thought Waring, and asked the same.

"Is it new?" said Fog. "I thought it old, very old. I mean no mystery, I speak plainly. You helped me in my great strait, and I thank you; perhaps it will be counted unto you for good in the reckoning up of your life. But I am strong again, and the ice is forming. You can have no intention of making Silver your wife?"

Waring looked up, their eyes met. "No," he replied slowly, as though the words were being dragged out of him by the magnetism of the old man's gaze, "I certainly have no such intention."

Nothing more was said; soon Waring rose and went out. But Silver spied him from her flower-room, and came down to the sail-boat where it lay at the foot of the ladder. "You are not going out this cold day," she said, standing by his side as he busied himself over the rigging. She was wrapped in a fur mantle, with a fur cap on her head, and her rough little shoes were fur-trimmed. Waring made no reply. "But I shall not allow it," continued the maiden, gayly. "Am I not queen of this castle? You yourself have said it many a time. You cannot go, Jarvis; I want you here." And with her soft hands she blinded him playfully.

"Silver, Silver," called old Fog's voice above, "come within; I want you."

After that the two men were very crafty in their preparations.

The boat ready, Waring went the rounds for the last time. He brought down wood for several days and stacked it, he looked again at all the provisions and reckoned them over; then he rowed to the north shore, visited his traps, called out the dogs from the little house he had made for them, and bade them good by. "I shall leave you for old Fog," he said; "be good dogs, and bring in all you can for the castle."

The dogs wagged their tails, and waited politely on the beach until he was out of sight; but they did not seem to believe his story, and went back to their house tranquilly without a howl. The day passed as usual. Once the two men happened to meet in the passageway. "Silver seems restless, we must wait till darkness," said Fog in a low tone.

"Very well," replied Waring.

At midnight they were off, rowing over the black water in the sail-boat, hoping for a fair wind at dawn, as the boat was heavy. They journeyed but slowly through the winding channel, leaving the sedge-gate open; no danger now from intruders; the great giant, Winter, had swallowed all lesser foes. It was cold, very cold, and they stopped awhile at dawn on the edge of the marsh, the last shore, to make a fire and heat some food before setting sail for the islands.

"Good God!" cried Waring.

A boat was coming after them, a little skiff they both knew, and in it, paddling, in her white dress, sat Silver, her fur mantle at her feet where it had fallen unnoticed. They sprang to meet her, knee-deep in the icy water; but Waring was first, and lifted her slight form in his arms.

"I have found you, Jarvis," she murmured, laying her head down upon his shoulder; then the eyes closed, and the hand she had tried to clasp around his neck fell lifeless. Close to the fire, wrapped in furs, Waring held her in his arms, while the old man bent over her, chafing her hands and little icy feet, and calling her name in an agony.

"Let her but come back to life, and I will say not one word, not one word more," he cried with tears. "Who am I that I should torture her? You shall go back with us, and I will trust it all to God,—all to God."

"But what if I will not go back, what if I will not accept your trust?" said Waring, turning his head away from the face pillowed on his breast.

"I do not trust you, I trust God; he will guard her."

"I believe he will," said the young man, half to himself. And then they bore her home, not knowing whether her spirit was still with them, or already gone to that better home awaiting it in the next country.

That night the thick ice came, and the last vessels fled southward. But in the lonely little castle there was joy; for the girl was saved, barely, with fever, with delirium, with long prostration, but saved!

When weeks had passed, and she was in her low chair again, propped with cushions, pallid as a snow-drop, weak and languid, but still *there,* she told her story, simply and without comprehension of its meaning.

"I could not rest that night," she said, "I know not why; so I dressed softly and slipped past Orange asleep on her mattress by my door, and found you both gone,—you, father, and you, Jarvis. You never go out at night, and it was very cold; and Jarvis had taken his bag and his knapsack, and all the little things I know so well. His gun was gone from the wall, his clothes from his empty room, and that picture of the girl holding up the fruit was not on his table. From that I knew that something had happened; for it is dear to Jarvis, that picture of the girl," said Silver with a little quiver in her voice. With a quick gesture Waring drew the picture from his pocket and threw it into the fire; it blazed, and was gone in a moment. "Then I went after you," said Silver with a little look of gratitude. "I know the passage through the south channels, and something told me you had gone that way. It was very cold."

That was all, no reasoning, no excuse, no embarrassment; the flight of the little sea-bird straight to its mate.

Life flowed on again in the old channel, Fog quiet, Silver happy, and Waring in a sort of dream. Winter was full upon them, and the castle beleaguered with his white armies both below and above, on the water and in the air. The two men went ashore on the ice now, and trapped and hunted daily, the dogs following. Fagots were cut and rough roads made through the forest. One would have supposed they were planning for a lifelong residence, the young man and the old, as they came and went together, now on the snow-crust, now plunging through breast-deep into the light dry mass. One day Waring said, "Let me see your reckoning. Do you know that to-morrow will be Christmas?"

"Silver knows nothing of Christmas," said Fog, roughly.

"Then she shall know," replied Waring.

Away he went to the woods and brought back evergreen. In the night he decked the cabin-like room, and with infinite pains constructed a little Christmas-tree and hung it with everything he could collect or contrive.

"It is but a poor thing, after all," he said, gloomily, as he stood alone surveying his work. It was indeed a shabby little tree, only redeemed from ugliness by a white cross poised on the green summit; this cross glittered and shone in the firelight,—it was cut from solid ice.

"Perhaps I can help you," said old Fog's voice behind. "I did not show you this, for fear it would anger you, but—but there must have been a child on board after all." He held a little box of toys, carefully packed as if by a mother's hand,—common toys, for she was only the captain's wife, and the schooner a small one; the little waif had floated ashore by itself, and Fog had seen and hidden it.

Waring said nothing, and the two men began to tie on the toys in silence. But after a while they warmed to their work and grew eager to make it beautiful; the old red ribbon that Orange had given was considered a precious treasure-trove, and, cut in fragments, it gayly held the little wooden toys in place on the green boughs.

Fog, grown emulous, rifled the cupboards and found small cakes freshly baked by the practised hand of the old cook; these he hung ex-ultingly on the higher boughs. And now the little tree was full, and stood bravely in its place at the far end of the long room, while the white cross looked down on the toys of the drowned child and the ribbon of the slave, and seemed to sanctify them for their new use.

Great was the surprise of Silver the next morning, and many the questions she asked. Out in the world, they told her, it was so; trees like that were decked for children.

"Am I a child?" said Silver, thoughtfully; "what do you think, papa?"

"What do *you* think?" said Waring, turning the question.

"I hardly know; sometimes I think I am, and sometimes not; but it is of no consequence what I am as long as I have you,—you and papa. Tell me more about the little tree, Jarvis. What does it mean? What is that white shining toy on the top? Is there a story about it?"

"Yes, there is a story; but—but it is not I who should tell it to you," replied the young man, after a moment's hesitation.

"Why not? Whom have I in all the world to tell me, save you?" said fondly the sweet child-voice.

They did not take away the little Christmas-tree, but left it on its pedestal at the far end of the long room through the winter; and as the cross melted slowly, a new one took its place, and shone aloft in the firelight. But its story was not told.

February came, and with it a February thaw; the ice stirred a little, and the breeze coming over the floes was singularly mild. The arctic winds and the airs from the Gulf Stream had met and mingled, and the gray fog appeared again, waving to and fro. "Spring has come," said Silver; "there is the dear fog." And she opened the window of the flower-room, and let out a little bird.

"It will find no resting-place for the sole of its foot, for the snow is over the face of the whole earth," said Waring. "Our ark has kept us cosily through bitter weather, has it not, little one?" (He had adopted a way of calling her so.)

"Ark," said Silver; "what is that?"

"Well," answered Waring, looking down into her blue eyes as they stood together at the little window, "it was a watery residence like this; and if Japheth,—he was always my favorite of the three—had had you there, my opinion is that he would never have come down at all, but would have resided permanently on Ararat." [13]

Silver looked up into his face with a smile, not understanding what he said, nor asking to understand; it was enough for her that he was there. And as she gazed her violet eyes grew so deep, so soft, that the man for once (give him credit, it was the first time) took her into his arms. "Silver," he whispered, bending over her, "do you love me?"

"Yes," she answered in her simple, unconscious way, "you know I do, Jarvis."

No color deepend in her fair face under his ardent gaze; and, after a moment, he released her, almost roughly. The next day he told old Fog that he was going.

"Where?"

"Somewhere, this time. I've had enough of Nowhere."

"Why do you go?"

"Do you want the plain truth, old man? Here it is, then: I am growing too fond of that girl,—a little more and I shall not be able to leave her."

"Then stay; she loves you."

"A child's love."

"She will develop—"

"Not into my wife if I know myself," said Waring, curtly.

Old Fog sat silent a moment. "Is she not lovely and good?" he said in a low voice.

"She is; but she is your daughter as well."

"She is not."

"She is not! What then?"

"I—I do not know; I found her, a baby, by the wayside."

"A foundling! So much the better, that is even a step lower," said the younger man, laughing roughly. And the other crept away as though he had been struck.

Waring set about his preparations. This time Silver did not suspect his purpose. She had passed out of the quick, intuitive watchfulness of childhood. During these days she had taken up the habit of sitting by herself in the flower-room, ostensibly with her book or sewing; but when they glanced in through the open door, her hands were lying idle on her lap and her eyes fixed dreamily on some opening blossom. Hours she sat thus, without stirring.

Waring's plan was a wild one; no boat could sail through the ice, no foot could cross the wide rifts made by the thaw, and weeks of the bitterest weather still lay between them and the spring. "Along-shore," he said.

"And die of cold and hunger," answered Fog.

"Old man, why are you not afraid of me?" said Waring, pausing in his work with a lowering glance. "Am I not stronger than you, and the master, if I so choose, of your castle of logs?"

"But you will not so choose."

"Do not trust me too far!"

"I do not trust you,—but God."

"For a wrecker and a murderer, you have, I must say, a remarkably serene conscience," sneered Waring.

Again the old man shrank, and crept silently away.

But when in the early dawn a dark figure stood on the ice adjusting its knapsack, a second figure stole down the ladder. "Will you go, then," it said, "go and leave the child?"

"She is no child," answered the younger man, sternly; "and you know it."

"To me she is."

"I care not what she is to you; but she shall *not* be more to me."

"More to you?"

"No more than any other pretty piece of waxwork," replied Waring, striding away into the gray mist.

Silver came to breakfast radiant, her small head covered from forehead to throat with the winding braids of gold, her eyes bright, her cheeks faintly tinged with the icy water of her bath. "Where is Jarvis?" she asked.

"Gone hunting," replied old Fog.

"For all day?"

"Yes; and perhaps for all night. The weather is quite mild, you know."

"Yes, papa. But I hope it will soon be cold again; he cannot stay out long then," said the girl, gazing out over the ice with wistful eyes.

The danger was over for that day; but the next morning there it was again, and with it the bitter cold.

"He must come home soon now," said Silver, confidently, melting the frost on one of the little windows so that she could see out and watch for his coming. But he came not. As night fell the cold grew intense; deadly, clear, and still, with the stars shining brilliantly in the steel-blue of the sky. Silver wandered from window to window, wrapped in her fur mantle; a hundred times, a thousand times she had scanned the ice-fields and the snow, the lake and the shore. When the night closed down, she crept close to the old man who sat by the fire in silence, pretending to mend his nets, but furtively watching her every movement. "Papa," she whispered, "where is he,—where is he?" And her tears fell on his hands.

"Silver," he said, bending over her tenderly, "do I not love you? Am I not enough for you? Think, dear, how long we have lived here, and how happy we have been. He was only a stranger. Come, let us forget him, and go back to the old days."

"What! Has he gone, then? Has Jarvis gone?" Springing to her feet she confronted him with clinched hands and dilated eyes. Of all the words she had heard but one; he had gone! The poor old man tried to draw her down again into the shelter of his arms, but she seemed turned to stone, her slender form was rigid. "Where is he? Where is Jarvis? What have you done with him,—you, you!"

The quick unconscious accusation struck to his heart. "Child," he said in a broken voice, "I tried to keep him. I would have given him my place in your love, in your life, but he would not. He has gone, he cares not for you; he is a hard, evil man."

"He is not! But even if he were, I love him," said the girl, defiantly.

Then she threw up her arms toward heaven (alas! it was no heaven to her, poor child) as if in appeal. "Is there no one to help me?" she cried aloud.

"What can we do, dear?" said the old man, standing beside her and smoothing her hair gently. "He would not stay,—I could not keep him!"

"*I* could have kept him."

"You would not ask him to stay, if he wished to go?"

"Yes, I would; he must stay, for my sake."

"But if he had loved you, dear, he would not have gone."

"Did he say he did not love me?" demanded Silver, with gleaming eyes.

Old Fog hesitated.

"Did he say he did not love me? Did Jarvis say that?" she repeated, seizing his arm with grasp of fire.

"Yes; he said that."

But the lie meant to rouse her pride, killed it; as if struck by a visible hand, she swayed and fell to the floor.

The miserable old man watched her all the night. She was delirious, and raved of Waring through the long hours. At daylight he left her with Orange, who, not understanding these white men's riddles, and sorely perplexed by Waring's desertion, yet cherished her darling with dumb untiring devotion, and watched her every breath.

Following the solitary trail over the snow-covered ice and thence along-shore towards the east journeyed old Fog all day in the teeth of the wind, dragging a sledge loaded with furs, provisions, and dry wood; the sharp blast cut him like a knife, and the dry snow-pellets stung as they touched his face, and clung to his thin beard coated with ice. It was the worst day of the winter, an evil, desolate, piercing day; no human creature should dare such weather. Yet the old man journeyed patiently on until nightfall, and would have gone farther had not darkness concealed the track; his fear was that new snow might fall deeply enough to hide it, and then there was no more hope of following. But nothing could be done at night, so he made his camp, a lodge under a drift with the snow for walls and roof, and a hot fire that barely melted the edges of its icy hearth. As the blaze flared out into the darkness, he heard a cry, and followed; it was faint, but apparently not distant, and after some search he found the spot; there lay Jarvis Waring, helpless and nearly frozen. "I thought you farther on," he said, as he lifted the heavy, inert body.

"I fell and injured my knee yesterday; since then I have been freezing slowly," replied Waring in a muffled voice. "I have been crawling backwards and forwards all day to keep myself alive, but had just given it up when I saw your light."

All night the old hands worked over him, and they hated the body they touched; almost fiercely they fed and nourished it, warmed its blood, and brought back life. In the dawning Waring was himself again; weak, helpless, but in his right mind. He said as much, and added, with a touch of his old humor, "There is a wrong mind you know, old gentleman."

The other made no reply; his task done, he sat by the fire waiting. He had gone after this fellow, driven by fate; he had saved him, driven by fate. Now what had fate next in store? He warmed his wrinkled hands mechanically and waited, while the thought came to him with bitterness that his darling's life lay at the mercy of this man who had nothing better to do, on coming back from the very jaws of death, than make jests. But old Fog was mistaken; the man had something better to do, and did it. Perhaps he noted the expression of the face before him; perhaps he did not, but was thinking, young-man fashion, only of himself; at any rate this is what he said: "I was a fool to go. Help me back, old man; it is too strong for me,—I give it up."

"Back,—back where?" said the other, apathetically.

Waring raised his head from his pillow of furs. "Why do you ask, when you know already? Back to Silver, of course; have you lost your mind?"

His harshness came from within; in reality it was meant for himself; the avowal had cost him something as it passed his lips in the form of words; it had not seemed so when in the suffering, and the cold, and the approach of death, he had seen his own soul face to face and realized the truth.

So the two went back to the castle, the saved lying on the sledge, the savior drawing it; the wind was behind them now, and blew them along. And when the old man, weary and numb with cold, reached the ladder at last, helped Waring, lame and irritable, up to the little snow-covered balcony, and led the way to Silver's room,—when Silver, hearing the step, raised herself in the arms of the old slave and looked eagerly, not at him, no, but at the man behind,—did he shrink? He did not; but led the reluctant, vanquished, defiant, half-angry, half-shamed lover forward, and gave his darling into the arms that seemed again almost unwilling, so strong was the old opposing determination that lay bound by love's bonds.

Silver regained her life as if by magic; not so Waring, who lay suffering and irritable on the lounge in the long room, while the girl tended him with a joy that shone out in every word, every tone, every motion. She saw not his little tyrannies, his exacting demands, his surly tempers; or rather she saw and loved them as women do when men lie ill and helpless in their hands. And old Fog sat apart, or came and went unnoticed; hours of the cold days he wandered through the forests, visiting the traps mechanically, and making tasks for himself to fill up the time; hours of the cold evenings he paced the snow-covered roof alone. He could not bear to see them, but left the post to Orange, whose black face shone with joy and satisfaction over Waring's return.

But after a time fate swung around (as she generally does if impatient humanity would but give her a chance). Waring's health grew, and so did his love. He had been like a strong man armed, keeping his palace; but a stronger than he was come, and, the combat over, he went as far the other way, and adored the very sandals of the conqueror. The gates were open, and all the floods were out.

And Silver? As he advanced, she withdrew. (It is always so in love, up to a certain point; and beyond that point lies, alas! the broad monotonous country of commonplace.)

This impetuous, ardent lover was not the Jarvis she had known, the Jarvis who had been her master, and a despotic one at that. Frightened, shy, bewildered, she fled away from all her dearest joys, and stayed by herself in the flower-room with the bar across the door, only emerging timidly at meal-times and stealing into the long room like a little wraith; a rosy wraith now, for at last she had learned to blush. Waring was angry at this desertion, but only the more in love; for the face had lost its infantile calm, the violet eyes veiled themselves under his gaze, and the unconscious child-mouth began to try to control and conceal its changing expressions, and only succeeded in betraying them more helplessly than ever. Poor little solitary maiden-heart!

Spring was near now; soft airs came over the ice daily, and stirred the water beneath; then the old man spoke. He knew what was coming, he saw it all, and a sword was piercing his heart; but bravely he played his part. "The ice will move out soon, in a month or less you can sail safely," he said, breaking the silence one night when they two sat by the fire, Waring moody and restless, for Silver had openly repulsed him, and fled away early in the evening. "She is trifling with me," he thought, "or else she does not know what love is. By heavens, I will teach her though——" As far as this his mind had journeyed when Fog spoke. "In a month you can sail safely, and I suppose you will go for good this time?"

"Yes."

Fog waited. Waring kicked a fallen log into place, lit his pipe, then let it go out, moved his chair forward, then pushed it back impatiently, and finally spoke. "Of course I shall take Silver; I intend to make Silver my wife."

"At last?"

"At last. No wonder you are glad——"

"Glad!" said old Fog,——"glad!" But the words were whispered, and the young man went on unheeding.

"Of course it is a great thing for you to have the child off your hands and placed in a home so high above your expectations. Love is a strange power. I do not deny that I have fought against it, but—but—why should I conceal? I love Silver with all my soul, she seems to have grown into my very being."

It was frankly and strongly uttered; the good side of Jarvis Waring came uppermost for the moment.

Old Fog leaned forward and grasped his hand. "I know you do," he said. "I know something of men, and I have watched you closely, Waring. It is for this love that I forgive— I mean that I am glad and thankful for it, very thankful."

"And you have reason to be," said the younger man, withdrawing into his pride again. "As my wife, Silver will have a home, a circle of friends, which— But you could not understand; let it pass. And now, tell me all you know of her."

The tone was a command, and the speaker leaned back in his chair with the air of an owner as he relighted his pipe. But Fog did not shrink. "Will you have the whole story?" he asked humbly.

"As well now as ever, I suppose, but be as brief as possible," said the young man in a lordly manner. Had he not just conferred an enormous favor, an alliance which might be called the gift of a prince, on this dull old backwoodsman?

"Forty years ago or thereabouts," began Fog in a low voice, "a crime was committed in New York City. I shall not tell you what it was, there is no need; enough that the whole East was stirred, and a heavy reward was offered for the man who did the deed. I am that man."

Waring pushed back his chair, a horror came over him, his hand sought for his pistol; but the voice went on unmoved. "Shall I excuse the deed to you, boy? No, I will not. It was done and I did it; that is enough, the damning fact that confronts and silences all talk of motive or cause. This much only will I say; to the passion of the act deliberate intention was not added, and there was no gain for the doer; only loss, the black eternal loss of everything in heaven above, on the earth beneath, or in the waters that are under the earth, for hell itself seemed to spew me out. At least so I thought as I fled away, the mark of Cain upon my brow; [14] the horror was so strong upon me, that I could not kill myself, I feared to join the dead. I went to and fro on the earth, and walked up and down in it; [15] I fled to the uttermost parts of the sea, [16] and yet came back again, moved by a strange impulse to be near the scene of my crime. After years had passed, and with them the memory of the deed from the minds of others, though not from mine, I crept to the old house where my one sister was living alone, and made myself known to her. She left her home, a forlorn place, but still a home, and followed me with a sort of dumb affection,—poor old woman. She was my senior by fifteen years, and I had been her pride; and so she went with me from the old instinct, which still remained, although the pride was dead, crushed by slow horror. We kept together after that, two poor hunted creatures instead of one; we were always fleeing, always imagining that eyes knew us, that fingers pointed us out. I called her Shadow, and together we took the name of Fog, a common enough name, but to us meaning that we were nothing, creatures of the mist, wandering to and fro by night, but in the morning gone. At last one day the cloud over my mind seemed to lighten a little, and the thought came to me that no punishment can endure forever, without impugning the justice of our great Creator. A crime is committed, perhaps in a moment; the ensuing suffering, the results, linger on earth, it may be for some years; but the end of it surely comes sooner or later, and it is as though it had never been. Then, for that crime, shall a soul suffer forever,—not a thousand years, a thousand ages if you like, but forever? Out upon the monstrous idea! Let a man do evil every moment of his life, and let his life be the full threescore years and ten; shall there not come a period in the endless cycles of eternity when even his punishment shall end? What kind of a God is he whom your theologians have held up to us,—a God who creates us at his pleasure, without asking whether or not we wish to be created, who endows us with certain wild passions and capacities for evil, turns us loose into a world of suffering, and then, for our misdeeds there, our whole lives being less than one instant's time in his sight, punishes us forever! Never-ending tortures throughout the countless ages of eternity for the little crimes of threescore years and ten! Heathendom shows no god so monstrous as this. O great Creator, O Father of our souls, of all the ills done on the face of thy earth, this lie against thy justice and thy goodness, is it not the greatest? The thought came to me, as I said, that no punishment could endure forever, that somewhere in the future I, even I, should meet pardon and rest. That day I found by the wayside a little child, scarcely more than a baby; it had wandered out of the poorhouse, where its mother had died the week before, a stranger passing through the village. No one knew anything about her nor cared to know, for she was almost in rags, fair and delicate once they told me, but wasted with illness and too far gone to talk. Then a second thought came to me,—expiation. I would take this forlorn little creature and bring her up as my own child, tenderly, carefully,—a life for a life. My poor old sister took to the child wonderfully, it seemed to brighten her desolation into something that was almost happiness; we wandered awhile longer, and then came westward through the lakes, but it was several years before we were fairly settled here. Shadow took care of the baby and made her little dresses; then, when the time came to teach her to sew and read, she said more help was needed, and went alone to the towns below to find a fit servant, coming back in her silent way with old Orange, another stray lost out of its place in the world, and suffering from want in the cold Northern city. You must not think that Silver is totally ignorant; Shadow had the education of her day, poor thing, for ours was a good old family as old families go in this new country of ours, where three generations of well-to-do people constitute aristocracy. But religion, so called, I have not taught her. Is she any the worse for its want?"

"I will teach her," said Waring, passing over the question (which was a puzzling one), for the new idea, the strange interest he felt in the task before him, the fair pure mind where his hand, and his alone, would be the first to write the story of good and evil.

"That I should become attached to the child was natural," continued old Fog; "but God gave it to me to love her with so great a love that my days have flown; for her to sail out over the stormy water, for her to hunt through the icy woods, for her to dare a thousand deaths, to labor, to save, to suffer,—these have been my pleasures through all the years. When I came home, there she was to meet me, her sweet voice calling me father, the only father she could ever know. When my poor old sister died, I took her away in my boat by night and buried her in deep water; and so I did with the boy we had here for a year or two, saved from a wreck. My darling knows nothing of death; I could not tell her."

"And those wrecks," said Waring; "how do you make them balance with your scheme of expiation?"

The old man sat silent a moment; then he brought his hand down violently on the table by his side. "I will not have them brought up in that way, I tell you I will not! Have I not explained that I was desperate?" he said in an excited voice. "What are one or two miserable crews to the delicate life of my beautiful child? And the men had their chances, too, in spite of my lure. Does not every storm threaten them with deathly force? Wait until you are tempted, before you judge me, boy. But shall I tell you the whole? Listen, then. Those wrecks were the greatest sacrifices, the most bitter tasks of my hard life, the nearest approach I have yet made to the expiation. Do you suppose I wished to drown the men? Do you suppose I did not know the greatness of the crime? Ah, I knew it only too well, and yet I sailed out and did the deed! It was for her,—to keep her from suffering; so I sacrificed myself unflinchingly. I would murder a thousand men in cold blood, and bear the thousand additional punishments without a murmur throughout a thousand ages of eternity, to keep my darling safe and warm. Do you not see that the whole was a self-immolation, the greatest, the most complete I could make? I vowed to keep my darling tenderly. I have kept my vow; see that you keep yours."

The voice ceased, the story was told, and the teller gone. The curtain over the past was never lifted again; but often, in after years, Waring thought of this strange life and its stranger philosophy. He could not judge them. Can we?

The next day the talk turned upon Silver. "I know you love her," said the old man, "but how much?"

"Does it need the asking?" answered Waring with a short laugh; "am I not giving up my name, my life, into her hands?"

"You could not give them into hands more pure."

"I know it; I am content. And yet, I sacrifice something," replied the young man, thinking of his home, his family, his friends.

Old Fog looked at him. "Do you hesitate?" he said, breaking the pause.

"Of course I do not; why do you ask?" replied Waring, irritably. "But some things may be pardoned, I think, in a case like mine."

"I pardon them."

"I can teach her, of course, and a year or so among cultivated people will work wonders; I think I shall take her abroad, first. How soon did you say we could go?"

"The ice is moving. There will be vessels through the straits in two or three weeks," replied Fog. His voice shook. Waring looked up; the old man was weeping. "Forgive me," he said, brokenly, "but the little girl is very dear to me."

The younger man was touched. "She shall be as dear to me as she has been to you," he said; "do not fear. My love is proved by the very struggle I have made against it. I venture to say no man ever fought harder against himself than I have in this old castle of yours. I kept that Titian picture as a counter-charm. It resembles a woman who, at a word, will give me herself and her fortune,—a woman high in the cultivated circles of cities both here and abroad, beautiful, accomplished, a queen in her little sphere. But all was useless. That long night in the snow, when I crawled backwards and forwards to keep myself from freezing, it came to me with power that the whole of earth and all its gifts compared not with this love. Old man, she will be happy with me."

"I know it."

"Did you foresee this end?" asked Waring after a while, watching, as he spoke, the expression of the face before him. He could not rid himself of the belief that the old man had laid his plans deftly.

"I could only hope for it: I saw that she loved you."

"Well, well," said the younger man, magnanimously, "it was natural, after all. Your expiation has ended better than you hoped; for the little orphan child you have reared has found a home and friends, and you yourself need work no more. Choose your abode here or anywhere else in the West, and I will see that you are comfortable."

"I will stay on here."

"As you please. Silver will not forget you; she will write often. I think I will go first up the Rhine and then into Switzerland," continued Waring, going back to himself and his plans with the matter-of-course egotism of youth and love. And old Fog listened.

What need to picture the love-scene that followed? The next morning a strong hand knocked at the door of the flower-room, and the shy little maiden within had her first lesson in love, or rather in its expression, while all the blossoms listened and the birds looked on approvingly. To do him justice, Waring was an humble suitor when alone with her; she was so fair, so pure, so utterly ignorant of the world and of life, that he felt himself unworthy, and bowed his head. But the mood passed, and Silver liked him better when the old self-assertion and quick tone of command came uppermost again. She knew not good from evil, she could not comprehend or analyze the feeling in her heart; but she loved this stranger, this master, with the whole of her being. Jarvis Waring knew good from evil (more of the latter knew he than of the former), he comprehended and analyzed fully the feeling that possessed him; but, man of the world as he was, he loved this little water-maiden, this fair pagan, this strange isolated girl, with the whole force of his nature. "Silver," he said to her, seriously enough, "do you know how much I love you? I am afraid to think what life would seem without you."

"Why think of it, then, since I am here?" replied Silver. "Do you know, Jarvis, I think if I had not loved you so much, you would not have loved me, and then—it would have been—that is, I mean—it would have been different—" She paused; unused to reasoning or to anything like argument, her own words seemed to bewilder her.

Waring laughed, but soon grew serious again. "Silver," he said, taking her into his arms, "are you sure that you can love me as I crave?" (For he seemed at times tormented by the doubt as to whether she was anything more than a beautiful child.) He held her closely and would not let her go, compelling her to meet his ardent eyes. A change came over the girl, a sudden red flashed up into her temples and down into her white throat. She drew herself impetuously away from her lover's arms and fled from the room. "I am not sure but that she is a watersprite, after all," grumbled Waring, as he followed her. But it was a pleasure now to grumble and pretend to doubt, since from that moment he was sure.

The next morning Fog seemed unusually cheerful.

"No wonder," thought Waring. But the character of benefactor pleased him, and he appeared in it constantly.

"We must have the old castle more comfortable; I will try to send up furniture from below," he remarked, while pacing to and fro in the evening.

"Is n't it comfortable now?" said Silver. "I am sure I always thought this room beautiful."

"What, this clumsy imitation of a second-class Western steamer? Child, it is hideous!"

"Is it?" said Silver, looking around in innocent surprise, while old Fog listened in silence. Hours of patient labor and risks not a few over the stormy lake were associated with each one of the articles Waring so cavalierly condemned.

Then it was, "How you do look, old gentleman! I must really send you up some new clothes.—Silver, how have you been able to endure such shabby rags so long? All the years before I came, did it never force itself upon you?"

"I do not know,—I never noticed; it was always just papa, you know," replied Silver, her blue eyes resting on the old man's clothes with a new and perplexed attention.

But Fog bore himself cheerily. "He is right, Silver," he said, "I am shabby indeed. But when you go out into the world, you will soon forget it."

"Yes," said Silver, tranquilly.

The days flew by and the ice moved out. This is the phrase that is always used along the lakes. The ice "moves out" of every harbor from Ogdensburg to Duluth. You can see the great white floes drift away into the horizon, and the question comes, Where do they go? Do they not meet out there the counter floes from the Canada side, and then do they all join hands and sink at a given signal to the bottom? Certainly, there is nothing melting in the mood of the raw spring winds and clouded skies.

"What are your plans?" asked old Fog, abruptly, one morning when the gulls had flown out to sea, and the fog came stealing up from the south.

"For what?"

"For the marriage."

"Aha!" thought Waring, with a smile of covert amusement, "he is in a hurry to secure the prize, is he? The sharp old fellow!" Aloud he said, "I thought we would all three sail over to Mackinac; and there we could be married, Silver and I, by the fort chaplain, and take the first Buffalo steamer; you could return here at your leisure."

"Would it not be a better plan to bring a clergyman here, and then you two could sail without me? I am not as strong as I was; I feel that I cannot bear— I mean that you had better go without me."

"As you please; I thought it would be a change for you, that was all."

"It would only prolong— No, I think, if you are willing, we will have the marriage here, and then you can sail immediately."

"Very well; but I did not suppose you would be in such haste to part with Silver," said Waring, unable to resist showing his comprehension of what he considered the manoeuvres of the old man. Then, waiving further discussion,—"And where shall we find a clergyman?" he asked.

"There is one over on Beaver."

"He must be a singular sort of a divine to be living there!"

"He is; a strayed spirit, as it were, but a genuine clergyman of the Presbyterian church, none the less. I never knew exactly what he represented there, but I think he came out originally as a sort of missionary."

"To the Mormons," said Waring, laughing; for he had heard old Fog tell many a story of the Latter-Day Saints, who had on Beaver Island at that time their most eastern settlement.

"No; to the Indians,—sent out by some of those New England societies, you know. When he reached the islands, he found the Indians mostly gone, and those who remained were all Roman Catholics. But he settled down, farmed a little, hunted a little, fished a little, and held a service all by himself occasionally in an old log-house, just often enough to draw his salary and to write up in his semiannual reports. He is n't a bad sort of a man in his way."

"And how does he get on with the Mormons?"

"Excellently. He lets them talk, and sells them fish, and shuts his eyes to everything else."

"What is his name?"

"Well, over there they call him the Preacher, principally because he does not preach, I suppose. It is a way they have over on Beaver to call people names; they call me Believer."

"Believer?"

"Yes, because I believe nothing; at least so *they* think."

A few days later, out they sailed over the freed water, around the point, through the sedge-gate growing green again, across the channelled marsh, and out towards the Beavers,—Fog and Waring, armed as if for a foray.

"Why?" asked Waring.

"It's safer; the Mormons are a queer lot," was the reply.

When they came in sight of the islands, the younger man scanned them curiously. Some years later an expedition composed of exasperated crews of lake schooners, exasperated fishermen, exasperated mainland settlers, sailed westward through the straits bound for these islands, armed to the teeth and determined upon vengeance and slaughter. False lights, stolen nets, and stolen wives were their grievances; and no aid coming from the general government, then as now sorely perplexed over the Mormon problem,[17] they took justice into their own hands and sailed bravely out, with the stars and stripes floating from the mast of their flag-ship,— an old scow impressed for military service. But this was later; and when

Fog and Waring came scudding into the harbor, the wild little village existed in all its pristine outlawry, a city of refuge for the flotsam vagabondage of the lower lakes.

"Perhaps he will not come with us," suggested Waring.

"I have thought of that, but it need not delay us long," replied Fog; "we can kidnap him."

"Kidnap him?"

"Yes, he is but a small chap," said the old man, tranquilly.

They fastened their boat to the long log-dock, and started ashore. The houses of the settlement straggled irregularly along the beach and inland towards the fields where fine crops were raised by the Saints, who had made here, as is their custom everywhere, a garden in the wilderness; the only defence was simple but strong,—an earthwork on one of the white sand-hills back of the village, over whose rampart peeped two small cannon, commanding the harbor. Once on shore, however, a foe found only a living, moving rampart of flesh and blood, as reckless a set of villains as New World history can produce. But this rampart came together only in times of danger; ordinary visitors, coming by twos and threes, they welcomed or murdered as they saw fit, or according to the probable contents of their pockets, each man for himself and his family. Some of these patriarchal gentlemen glared from their windows at Fog and Waring as they passed along; but the worn clothes not promising much, they simply invited them to dinner; they liked to hear the news, when there was nothing else going on. Old Fog excused himself. They had business, he said, with the Preacher; was he at home?

He was; had anything been sent to him from the East,—any clothes, now, for the Indians?

Old Fog had heard something of a box at Mackinac, waiting for a schooner to bring it over. He was glad it was on the way, it would be of so much use to the Indians,—they wore so many clothes.

The patriarchs grinned, and allowed the two to pass on. Waring had gazed within, meanwhile, and discovered the plural wives, more or less good-looking, generally less; they did not seem unhappy, however, not so much so as many a single one he had met in more luxurious homes, and he said to himself, "Women of the lower class are much better and happier when well curbed." It did not occur to him that possibly the evil tempers of men of the lower class are made more endurable by a system of co-operation; one reed bends, breaks, and dies, but ten reeds together can endure.

The Preacher was at home on the outskirts,—a little man, round and rosy, with black eyes and a cheery voice. He was attired entirely in blanket-cloth, baggy trousers and a long blouse, so that he looked not unlike a Turkish Santa Claus, Oriental as to under, and arctic as to upper rigging. "Are you a clergyman?" said Waring, inspecting him with curious eyes.

"If you doubt it, look at this," said the little man; and he brought out a clerical suit of limp black cloth, and a ministerial hat much the worse for wear. These articles he suspended from a nail, so that they looked as if a very poor lean divine had hung himself there. Then he sat down, and took his turn at staring. "I do not bury the dead," he remarked after a moment, as if convinced that the two shabby hunters before him could have no other errand.

Waring was about to explain, but old Fog stopped him with a glance. "You are to come with us, sir," he said courteously; "you will be well treated, well paid, and returned in a few days."

"Come with you! Where?"

"Never mind where; will you come?"

"No," said the little blanket-man, stoutly.

In an instant Fog had tripped him up, seized a sheet and blanket from the bed, bound his hands and feet with one, and wrapped him in the other. "Now, then," he said shouldering the load, "open the door."

"But the Mormons," objected Waring.

"O, they like a joke, they will only laugh! But if, by any chance, they should show fight, fire at once," replied the old man, leading the way. Waring followed, his mind anything but easy; it seemed to him like running the gantlet. He held his pistols ready, and glanced furtively around as they skirted the town and turned down towards the beach. "If any noise is made," Fog had remarked, "I shall know what to do."

Whereupon the captive swallowed down his wrath and a good deal of woollen fuzz, and kept silence. He was no coward, this little Preacher. He held his own manfully on the Beavers; but no one had ever carried him off in a blanket before. So he silently considered the situation.

When near the boat they came upon more patriarchs. "Put a bold face on it," murmured old Fog. "Whom do you suppose we have here?" he began, as they approached. "Nothing less than your little Preacher; we want to borrow him for a few days."

The patriarchs stared.

"Don't you believe it?—Speak up, Preacher; are you being carried off?"

No answer.

"You had better speak," said Fog, jocosely, at the same time giving his captive a warning touch with his elbow.

The Preacher had revolved the situation rapidly, and perceived that in any contest his round body would inevitably suffer from friend and foe alike. He was not even sure but that he would be used as a missile, a sort of ponderous pillow swung by one end. So he replied briskly, "Yes, I am being carried as you see, dear brethren; I don't care about walking to-day."

The patriarchs laughed, and followed on to the boat, laughing still more when Fog gayly tossed in his load of blanket, and they could hear the little man growl as he came down. "I say, though, when are you going to bring him back, Believer?" said one.

"In a few days," replied Fog, setting sail.

Away they flew; and, when out of harbor, the captive was released, and Waring told him what was required.

"Why did n't you say so before?" said the little blanket-man; "nothing I like better than a wedding, and a drop of punch afterwards."

His task over, Fog relapsed into silence; but Waring, curious, asked many a question about the island and its inhabitants. The Preacher responded freely in all things, save when the talk glided too near himself. The Mormons were not so bad, he thought; they had their faults, of course, but you must take them on the right side.

"Have they a right side?" asked Waring.

"At least they have n't a rasping, mean, cold, starving, bony, freezing, busy-bodying side," was the reply, delivered energetically; whereat Waring concluded the little man had had his own page of history back somewhere among the decorous New England hills.

Before they came to the marsh they blindfolded their guest, and did not remove the bandage until he was safely within the long room of the castle. Silver met them, radiant in the firelight.

"Heaven grant you its blessing, maiden," said the Preacher, becoming Biblical at once. He meant it, however, for he sat gazing at her long with moistened eyes, forgetful even of the good cheer on the table; a gleam from his far-back youth came to him, a snow-drop that bloomed and died in bleak New Hampshire long, long before.

The wedding was in the early morning. Old Fog had hurried it, hurried everything; he seemed driven by a spirit of unrest, and wandered from place to place, from room to room, his eyes fixed in a vacant way upon the familiar objects. At the last moment he appeared with a prayer-book, its lettering old, its cover tarnished. "Have you any objection to using the Episcopal service?" he asked in a low tone. "I—I have heard the Episcopal service."

"None in the world," replied the affable little Preacher.

But he too grew sober and even earnest as Silver appeared, clad in white, her dress and hair wreathed with the trailing arbutus, the first flower of spring, plucked from under the vanishing snows. So beautiful her face, so heavenly its expression, that Waring, as he took her hand, felt his eyes grow dim, and he vowed to himself to cherish her with tenderest love forever.

"We are gathered together here in the sight of God," began the Preacher solemnly; and old Fog, standing behind, shrank into the shadow, and bowed his head upon his hands. But when the demand came, "Who giveth this woman to be married to this man?" he stepped forward, and gave away his child without a tear, nay, with even a smile on his brave old face.

"To love, cherish, and to obey," repeated Silver in her clear sweet voice.

And then Waring placed upon her finger the little ring he himself had carved out of wood. "It shall never be changed," he said, "but coated over with heavy gold, just as it is."

Old Orange, radiant with happiness, stood near, and served as a foil for the bridal white.

It was over; but they were not to start until noon.

Fog put the Preacher almost forcibly into the boat and sailed away with him, blindfolded and lamenting.

"The wedding feast," he cried, "and the punch! You are a fine host, old gentleman."

"Everything is here, packed in those baskets. I have even given you two fine dogs. And there is your fee. I shall take you in sight of the Beavers, and then put you into the skiff and leave you to row over alone. The weather is fine, you can reach there to-morrow."

Remonstrance died away before the bag of money; old Fog had given his all for his darling's marriage-fee. "I shall have no further use for it," he thought, mechanically.

So the little blanket-man paddled away in his skiff with his share of the wedding-feast beside him; the two dogs went with him, and became good Mormons.

Old Fog returned in the sail-boat through the channels, and fastened the sedge-gate open for the out-going craft. Silver, timid and happy, stood on the balcony as he approached the castle.

"It is time to start," said the impatient bridegroom. "How long you have been, Fog!"

The old man made no answer, but busied himself arranging the boat; the voyage to Mackinac would last two or three days, and he had provided every possible comfort for their little camps on shore.

"Come," said Waring, from below.

Then the father went up to say good by. Silver flung her arms around his neck and burst into tears. "Father, father," she sobbed, "must I leave you? O father, father!"

He soothed her gently; but something in the expression of his calm, pallid face touched the deeper feelings of the wakening woman, and she clung to him desperately, realizing, perhaps, at this last moment, how great was his love for her, how great his desolation. Waring had joined them on the balcony. He bore with her awhile and tried to calm her grief, but the girl turned from him and clung to the old man; it was as though she saw at last how she had robbed him. "I cannot leave him thus," she sobbed; "O father, father!"

Then Waring struck at the root of the difficulty. (Forgive him; he was hurt to the core.) "But he is not your father," he said, "he has no claim upon you. I am your husband now, Silver, and you must come with me; do you not wish to come with me, darling?" he added, his voice sinking into fondness.

"Not my father!" said the girl. Her arms fell, and she stood as if petrified.

"No, dear; he is right. I am not your father," said old Fog, gently. A spasm passed over his features, he kissed her hastily, and gave her into her husband's arms. In another moment they were afloat, in two the sail filled and the boat glided away. The old man stood on the castle roof, smiling and waving his hand; below, Orange fluttered her red handkerchief from the balcony, and blessed her darling with African mummeries. The point was soon rounded, the boat gone.

THAT NIGHT, when the soft spring moonlight lay over the water, a sail came gliding back to the castle, and a shape flew up the ladder; it was the bride of the morning.

"O father, father, I could not leave you so, I made him bring me back, if only for a few days! O father, father! for you are my father, the only father I can ever know,—and so kind and good!"

In the gloom she knelt by his bedside, and her arms were around his neck. Waring came in afterwards, silent and annoyed, yet not unkind. He stirred the dying brands into a flame.

"What is this?" he said, starting, as the light fell across the pillow.

"It is nothing," replied Fog, and his voice sounded far away; "I am an old man, children, and all is well."

They watched him through the dawning, through the lovely day, through the sunset, Waring repentant, Silver absorbed in his every breath; she lavished upon him now all the wealth of love her unconscious years had gathered. Orange seemed to agree with her master that all was well. She came and went, but not sadly, and crooned to herself some strange African tune that rose and fell more like a chant of triumph than a dirge. She was doing her part, according to her light, to ease the going of the soul out of this world.

Grayer grew the worn face, fainter the voice, colder the shrivelled old hands in the girl's fond clasp.

"O Jarvis, Jarvis, what is this?" she murmured, fearfully.

Waring came to her side and put his strong arm around her. "My little wife," he said, "this is Death. But do not fear."

And then he told her the story of the Cross; and, as it came to her a revelation, so, in the telling, it became to him, for the first time, a belief.

Old Fog told them to bury him out in deep water, as he had buried the others; and then he lay placid, a great happiness shining in his eyes.

"It is well," he said, "and God is very good to me. Life would have been hard without you, darling. Something seemed to give way when you said good by; but now that I am called, it is sweet to know that you are happy, and sweeter still to think that you came back to me at the last. Be kind to her, Waring. I know you love her; but guard her tenderly,—she is but frail. I die content, my child, quite content; do not grieve for me."

Then, as the light faded from his eyes, he folded his hands. "Is it expiated, O God? Is it expiated?" he murmured.

There was no answer for him on earth.

THEY BURIED HIM as he had directed, and then they sailed away, taking the old black with them. The castle was left alone; the flowers bloomed on through the summer, and the rooms held the old furniture bravely through the long winter. But gradually the walls fell in, and the water entered. The fogs still steal across the lake, and wave their gray draperies up into the northern curve; but the sedge-gate is gone, and the castle is indeed Nowhere.

ST. CLAIR FLATS

IN SEPTEMBER, 1855, I first saw the St. Clair Flats.[1] Owing to Raymond's determination, we stopped there.

"Why go on?" he asked. "Why cross another long, rough lake, when here is all we want?"

"But no one ever stops here," I said.

"So much the better; we shall have it all to ourselves."

"But we must at least have a roof over our heads."

"I presume we can find one."

The captain of the steamer, however, knew of no roof save that covering the little lighthouse set on spiles, which the boat would pass within the half-hour; we decided to get off there, and throw ourselves upon the charity of the lighthouse-man. In the mean time, we sat on the bow with Captain Kidd, our four-legged companion, who had often accompanied us on hunting expeditions, but never before so far westward. It had been rough on Lake Erie,—very rough. We, who had sailed the ocean with composure, found ourselves most inhumanly tossed on the short, chopping waves of this fresh-water sea; we, who alone of all the cabin-list had eaten our four courses and dessert every day on the ocean-steamer, found ourselves here reduced to the depressing diet of a herring and pilot-bread. Captain Kidd, too, had suffered dumbly; even now he could not find comfort, but tried every plank in the deck, one after the other, circling round and round after his tail, dog-fashion, before lying down, and no

79

sooner down than up again for another melancholy wandering about the deck, another choice of planks, another circling, and another failure. We were sailing across a small lake whose smooth waters were like clear green oil; as we drew near the outlet, the low, green shores curved inward and came together, and the steamer entered a narrow, green river.

"Here we are," said Raymond. "Now we can soon land."

"But there is n't any land," I answered.

"What is that, then?" asked my near-sighted companion, pointing toward what seemed a shore.

"Reeds."

"And what do they run back to?"

"Nothing."

"But there must be solid ground beyond?"

"Nothing but reeds, flags, lily-pads, grass, and water, as far as I can see."

"A marsh?"

"Yes, a marsh."

The word "marsh" does not bring up a beautiful picture to the mind, and yet the reality was as beautiful as anything I have ever seen,—an enchanted land, whose memory haunts me as an idea unwritten, a melody unsung, a picture unpainted, haunts the artist, and will not away. On each side and in front, as far as the eye could reach, stretched the low green land which was yet no land, intersected by hundreds of channels, narrow and broad, whose waters were green as their shores. In and out, now running into each other for a moment, now setting off each for himself again, these many channels flowed along with a rippling current; zigzag as they were, they never seemed to loiter, but, as if knowing just where they were going and what they had to do, they found time to take their own pleasant roundabout way, visiting the secluded households of their friends the flags, who, poor souls, must always stay at home. These currents were as clear as crystal, and green as the water-grasses that fringed their miniature shores. The bristling reeds, like companies of free-lances, rode boldly out here and there into the deeps, trying to conquer more territory for the grasses, but the currents were hard to conquer; they dismounted the free-lances, and flowed over their submerged heads; they beat them down with assaulting ripples; they broke their backs so effectually that the bravest had no spirit left, but trailed along, limp and bedraggled. And, if by chance the lances succeeded in stretching their forces across from one little shore to another, then the unconquered currents forced their way between the closely serried ranks of the enemy, and flowed on as gayly as ever, leaving the grasses sitting hopeless on the bank; for they needed solid ground for their delicate feet, these graceful ladies in green.

You might call it a marsh; but there was no mud, no dark slimy water, no stagnant scum; there were no rank yellow lilies, no gormandizing frogs, no swinish mud-turtles. The clear waters of the channels ran over golden sands, and hurtled among the stiff reeds so swiftly that only in a bay, or where protected by a crescent point, could the fair white lilies float in the quiet their serene beauty requires. The flags, who brandished their swords proudly, were martinets down to their very heels, keeping themselves as clean under the water as above, and harboring not a speck of mud on their bright green uniforms. For inhabitants, there were small fish roving about here and there in the clear tide, keeping an eye out for the herons, who, watery as to legs, but venerable and wise of aspect, stood on promontories musing, apparently, on the secrets of the ages.

The steamer's route was a constant curve; through the larger channels of the archipelago she wound, as if following the clew of a labyrinth.[2] By turns she headed toward all the points of the compass, finding a channel where, to our uninitiated eyes, there was no channel, doubling upon her own track, going broadside foremost, floundering and backing, like a whale caught in a shallow. Here, landlocked, she would choose what seemed the narrowest channel of all, and dash recklessly through, with the reeds almost brushing her sides; there she crept gingerly along a broad expanse of water, her paddle-wheels scarcely revolving, in the excess of her caution. Saplings, with their heads of foliage on, and branches adorned with fluttering rags, served as finger-posts to show the way through the watery defiles, and there were many other hieroglyphics legible only to the pilot. "This time, surely, we shall run ashore," we thought again and again, as the steamer glided, head-on, toward an islet; but at the last there was always a quick turn into some unseen strait opening like a secret passage in a castle-wall, and we found ourselves in a new lakelet, heading in the opposite direction. Once we met another steamer, and the two great hulls floated slowly past each other, with engines motionless, so near that the passengers could have shaken hands with each other had they been so disposed. Not that they were so disposed, however; far from it. They gathered on their respective decks and gazed at each other gravely; not a smile was seen, not a word spoken, not the shadow of a salutation given. It was not pride, it was not suspicion; it was the universal listlessness of the traveling American bereft of his business, Othello with his occupation gone. What can such a man do on a steamer? Generally, nothing. Certainly he would never think of any such light-hearted nonsense as a smile or passing bow.

But the ships were, *par excellence,* the bewitched craft, the Flying Dutchmen of the Flats. A brig, with lofty, sky-scraping sails, bound south, came into view of our steamer, bound north, and passed, we hugging the shore to give her room; five minutes afterward the sky-scraping sails we had left behind veered around in front of us again; another five minutes, and there they were far distant on the right; another, and there they were again close by us on the left. For half an hour those sails circled around us, and yet all the time we were pushing steadily forward; this seemed witching work indeed. Again, the numerous schooners thought nothing of sailing overland; we saw them on all sides gliding before the wind, or beating up against it over the meadows as easily as over the water; sailing on grass was a mere trifle to these spirit-barks. All this we saw, as I said before, apparently. But in that adverb is hidden the magic of the St. Clair Flats.

"It is beautiful,—beautiful," I said, looking off over the vivid green expanse.

"Beautiful?" echoed the captain, who had himself taken charge of the steering when the steamer entered the labyrinth,—"I don't see anything beautiful in it!—Port your helm up there; port!"

"Port it is, sir," came back from the pilot-house above.

"These Flats give us more trouble than any other spot on the lakes; vessels are all the time getting aground and blocking up the way, which is narrow enough at best. There's some talk of Uncle Sam's cutting a canal right through,—a straight canal; but he's so slow, Uncle Sam is, and I'm afraid I'll be off the waters before the job is done."

"A straight canal!" I repeated, thinking with dismay of an ugly utilitarian ditch invading this beautiful winding waste of green.

"Yes, you can see for yourself what a saving it would be," replied the captain. "We could run right through in no time, day or night; whereas, now, we have to turn and twist and watch every inch of the whole everlasting marsh." Such was the captain's opinion. But we, albeit neither romantic nor artistic, were captivated with his "everlasting marsh," and eager to penetrate far within its green fastnesses.

"I suppose there are other families living about here, besides the family at the lighthouse?" I said.

"Never heard of any. They'd have to live on a raft if they did."

"But there must be some solid ground."

"Don't believe it; it's nothing but one great sponge for miles.— Steady up there; steady!"

"Very well," said Raymond, "so be it. If there is only the lighthouse, at the lighthouse we'll get off, and take our chances."

"You're surveyors, I suppose?" said the captain.

Surveyors are the pioneers of the lake-country, understood by the people to be a set of harmless monomaniacs, given to building little observatories along-shore, where there is nothing to observe; mild madmen, whose vagaries and instruments are equally singular. As surveyors, therefore, the captain saw nothing surprising in our determination to get off at the lighthouse; if we had proposed going ashore on a plank in the middle of Lake Huron, he would have made no objection.

At length the lighthouse came into view, a little fortress perched on spiles, with a ladder for entrance; as usual in small houses, much time seemed devoted to washing, for a large crane, swung to and fro by a rope, extended out over the water, covered with fluttering garments hung out to dry. The steamer lay to, our row-boat was launched, our traps handed out, Captain Kidd took his place in the bow, and we pushed off into the shallows; then the great paddlewheels revolved again, and the steamer sailed away, leaving us astern, rocking on her waves, and watched listlessly by the passengers until a turn hid us from their view. In the mean time numerous flaxen-haired children had appeared at the little windows of the lighthouse,—too many of them, indeed, for our hopes of comfort.

"Ten," said Raymond, counting heads.

The ten, moved by curiosity as we approached, hung out of the windows so far that they held on merely by their ankles.

"We cannot possibly save them all," I remarked, looking up at the dangling gazers.

"O, they're amphibious," said Raymond; "web-footed, I presume."

We rowed up under the fortress, and demanded parley with the keeper in the following language:—

"If your father here?"

"No; but ma is," answered the chorus.—"Ma! ma!"

Ma appeared, a portly female, who held converse with us from the top of the ladder. The sum and substance of the dialogue was that she had not a corner to give us, and recommended us to find Liakim, and have him show us the way to Waiting Samuel's.

"Waiting Samuel's?" we repeated.

"Yes; he's a kind of crazy man living away over there in the Flats. But there's no harm in him, and his wife is a tidy housekeeper. You be surveyors, I suppose?"

We accepted the imputation in order to avoid a broadside of questions, and asked the whereabouts of Liakim.

"O, he's round the point, somewhere there, fishing!"

We rowed on and found him, a little, round-shouldered man, in an old flat-bottomed boat, who had not taken a fish, and looked as though he never would. We explained our errand.

"Did Rosabel Lee tell ye to come to me?" he asked.

"The woman in the lighthouse told us," I said.

"That's Rosabel Lee, that's my wife; I'm Liakim Lee," said the little man, gathering together his forlorn old rods and tackle, and pulling up his anchor.

> "In the kingdom down by the sea
> Lived the beautiful Annabel Lee,"[3]

I quoted, *sotto voce.*

"And what very remarkable feet had she!" added Raymond, improvising under the inspiration of certain shoes, scow-like in shape, gigantic in length and breadth, which had made themselves visible at the top round of the ladder.

At length the shabby old boat got under way, and we followed in its path, turning off to the right through a network of channels, now pulling ourselves along by the reeds, now paddling over a raft of lily-pads, now poling through a winding labyrinth, and now rowing with broad sweeps across the little lake. The sun was sinking, and the western sky grew bright at his coming; there was not a cloud to make mountain-peaks on the horizon, nothing but the level earth below meeting the curved sky above, so evenly and clearly that it seemed as though we could go out there and touch it with our hands. Soon we lost sight of the little lighthouse; then one by one the distant sails sank down and disappeared, and we were left alone on the grassy sea, rowing toward the sunset.

"We must have come a mile or two, and there is no sign of a house," I called out to our guide.

"Well, I don't pretend to know how far it is, exactly," replied Liakim; "we don't know how far anything is here in the Flats, we don't."

"But are you sure you know the way?"

"O my, yes! We've got most to the boy. There it is!"

The "boy" was a buoy, a fragment of plank painted white, part of the cabin-work of some wrecked steamer.

"Now, then," said Liakim, pausing, "you jest go straight on in this here channel till you come to the ninth run from this boy, on the right; take that, and it will lead you right up to Waiting Samuel's door."

"Are n't you coming with us?"

"Well, no. In the first place, Rosabel Lee will be waiting supper for me, and she don't like to wait; and, besides, Samuel can't abide to see none of us round his part of the Flats."

"But—" I began.

"Let him go," interposed Raymond; "we can find the house without trouble." And he tossed a silver dollar to the little man, who was already turning his boat.

"Thank you," said Liakim. "Be sure you take the ninth run and no other,—the ninth run from this boy. If you make any mistake, you'll find yourselves miles away."

With this cheerful statement, he began to row back. I did not altogether fancy being left on the watery waste without a guide; the name, too, of our mythic host did not bring up a certainty of supper and beds. "Waiting Samuel," I repeated, doubtfully. "What is he waiting for?" I called back over my shoulder; for Raymond was rowing.

"The judgment-day!" answered Liakim, in a shrill key. The boats were now far apart; another turn, and we were alone.

We glided on, counting the runs on the right: some were wide, promising rivers; others wee little rivulets; the eighth was far away; and, when we had passed it, we could hardly decide whether we had reached the ninth or not, so small was the opening, so choked with weeds, showing scarcely a gleam of water beyond when we stood up to inspect it.

"It is certainly the ninth, and I vote that we try it. It will do as well as another, and I, for one, am in no hurry to arrive anywhere," said Raymond, pushing the boat in among the reeds.

"Do you want to lose yourself in this wilderness?" I asked, making a flag of my handkerchief to mark the spot where we had left the main stream.

"I think we are lost already," was the calm reply. I began to fear we were.

For some distance the "run," as Liakim called it, continued choked with aquatic vegetation, which acted like so many devil-fish catching our oars; at length it widened and gradually gave us a clear channel, albeit so winding and erratic that the glow of the sunset, our only beacon, seemed to be executing a waltz all round the horizon. At length we saw a dark spot on the left, and distinguished the outline of a low house. "There it is," I said, plying my oars with renewed strength. But the run turned short off in the opposite direction, and the house disappeared. After some time it rose again, this time on our right, but once more the run turned its back and shot off on a tangent. The sun had gone, and the rapid twilight of September was falling around us; the air, however, was singularly clear, and, as there was absolutely nothing to make a shadow, the darkness came on evenly over the level green. I was growing anxious, when a third time the house appeared, but the willful run passed by it, although so near that we could distinguish its open windows and door. "Why not get out and wade across?" I suggested.

"According to Liakim, it is the duty of this run to take us to the very door of Waiting Samuel's mansion, and it shall take us," said Raymond, rowing on. It did.

Doubling upon itself in the most unexpected manner, it brought us back to a little island, where the tall grass had given way to a vegetable-garden. We landed, secured our boat, and walked up the pathway toward the house. In the dusk it seemed to be a low, square structure, built of planks covered with plaster; the roof was flat, the windows unusually broad, the door stood open,—but no one appeared. We knocked. A voice from within called out, "Who are you, and what do you want with Waiting Samuel?"

"Pilgrims, asking for food and shelter," replied Raymond.

"Do you know the ways of righteousness?"

"We can learn them."

"Will you conform to the rules of this household without murmuring?"

"We will."

"Enter then, and peace be with you!" said the voice, drawing nearer. We stepped cautiously through the dark passage into a room, whose open windows let in sufficient twilight to show us a shadowy figure. "Seat yourselves," it said. We found a bench, and sat down.

"What seek ye here?" continued the shadow.

"Rest!" replied Raymond.

"Hunting and fishing!" I added.

"Ye will find more than rest," said the voice, ignoring me altogether (I am often ignored in this way),—"more than rest, if ye stay long enough, and learn of the hidden treasures. Are you willing to seek for them?"

"Certainly!" said Raymond. "Where shall we dig?"

"I speak not of earthly digging, young man. Will you give me the charge of your souls?"

"Certainly, if you will also take charge of our bodies."

"Supper, for instance," I said, again coming to the front; "and beds."

The shadow groaned; then it called out wearily, "Roxana!"

"Yes, Samuel," replied an answering voice, and a second shadow became dimly visible on the threshold. "The woman will attend to your earthly concerns," said Waiting Samuel.—"Roxana, take them hence." The second shadow came forward, and, without a word, took our hands and led us along the dark passage like two children, warning us now of a step, now of a turn, then of two steps, and finally opening a door and ushering us into a fire-lighted room. Peat was burning upon the wide hearth, and a singing kettle hung above it on a crane; the red glow shone on a rough table, chairs cushioned in bright calico, a loud-ticking clock, a few gayly flowered plates and cups on a shelf, shining tins against the plastered wall, and a cat dozing on a bit of carpet in one corner. The cheery domestic scene, coming after the wide, dusky Flats, the silence, the darkness, and the mystical words of the shadowy Samuel, seemed so real and pleasant that my heart grew light within me.

"What a bright fire!" I said. "This is your domain, I suppose, Mrs.——Mrs.——"

"I am not Mrs.; I am called Roxana," replied the woman, busying herself at the hearth.

"Ah, you are then the sister of Waiting Samuel, I presume?"

"No, I am his wife, fast enough; we were married by the minister twenty years ago. But that was before Samuel had seen any visions."

"Does he see visions?"

"Yes, almost every day."

"Do you see them, also?"

"O no; I'm not like Samuel. He has great gifts, Samuel has! The visions told us to come here; we used to live away down in Maine."

"Indeed! That was a long journey!"

"Yes! And we didn't come straight either. We'd get to one place and stop, and I'd think we were going to stay, and just get things comfortable, when Samuel would see another vision, and we'd have to start on. We wandered in that way two or three years, but at last we got here, and something in the Flats seemed to suit the spirits, and they let us stay."

At this moment, through the half-open door, came a voice.

"An evil beast is in this house. Let him depart."

"Do you mean me?" said Raymond, who had made himself comfortable in a rocking-chair.

"Nay; I refer to the four-legged beast," continued the voice. "Come forth, Apollyon!" [4]

Poor Captain Kidd seemed to feel that he was the person in question, for he hastened under the table with drooping tail and mortified aspect.

"Roxana, send forth the beast," said the voice.

The woman put down her dishes and went toward the table; but I interposed.

"If he must go, I will take him," I said, rising.

"Yes; he must go," replied Roxana, holding open the door. So I ordered out the unwilling Captain, and led him into the passageway.

"Out of the house, out of the house," said Waiting Samuel. "His feet may not rest upon this sacred ground. I must take him hence in the boat."

"But where?"

"Across the channel there is an islet large enough for him; he shall have food and shelter, but here he cannot abide," said the man, leading the way down to the boat.

The Captain was therefore ferried across, a tent was made for him out of some old mats, food was provided, and, lest he should swim back, he was tethered by a long rope, which allowed him to prowl around his domain and take his choice of three runs for drinking-water. With all these advantages, the ungrateful animal persisted in howling dismally as we rowed away. It was company he wanted, and not a "dear little isle of his own"; but then, he was not by nature poetical.

"You do not like dogs?" I said, as we reached our strand again.

"St. Paul wrote, 'Beware of dogs,'"[5] replied Samuel.

"But did he mean——"

"I argue not with unbelievers; his meaning is clear to me, let that suffice," said my strange host, turning away and leaving me to find my way back alone. A delicious repast was awaiting me. Years have gone by, the world and all its delicacies have been unrolled before me, but the memory of the meals I ate in that little kitchen in the Flats haunts me still. That night it was only fish, potatoes, biscuits, butter, stewed fruit, and coffee; but the fish was fresh, and done to the turn of a perfect broil, not burn; the potatoes were fried to a rare crisp, yet tender perfection, not chippy brittleness; the biscuits were light, flaked creamily, and brown on the bottom; the butter freshly churned, without salt; the fruit, great pears, with their cores extracted, standing whole on their dish, ready to melt, but not melted; and the coffee clear and strong, with yellow cream and the old-fashioned, unadulterated loaf-sugar. We ate. That does not express it; we devoured. Roxana waited on us, and warmed up into something like excitement under our praises.

"I *do* like good cooking," she confessed. "It's about all I have left of my old life. I go over to the mainland for supplies, and in the winter I try all kinds of new things to pass away the time. But Samuel is a poor eater, he is;

and so there isn't much comfort in it. I'm mighty glad you've come, and I hope you'll stay as long as you find it pleasant." This we promised to do, as we finished the potatoes and attacked the great jellied pears. "There's one thing, though," continued Roxana; "you'll have to come to our service on the roof at sunrise."

"What service?" I asked.

"The invocation. Dawn is a holy time, Samuel says, and we always wait for it; 'before the morning watch,'⁶ you know,—it says so in the Bible. Why, my name means 'the dawn,' Samuel says; that's the reason he gave it to me. My real name, down in Maine, was Maria,—Maria Ann."

"But I may not wake in time," I said.

"Samuel will call you."

"And if, in spite of that, I should sleep over?"

"You would not do that; it would vex him," replied Roxana, calmly.

"Do you believe in these visions, madam?" asked Raymond, as we left the table, and seated ourselves in front of the dying fire.

"Yes," said Roxana; emphasis was unnecessary,—of course she believed.

"How often do they come?"

"Almost every day there is a spiritual presence, but it does not always speak. They come and hold long conversations in the winter, when there is nothing else to do; that, I think, is very kind of them, for in the summer Samuel can fish, and his time is more occupied. There were fishermen in the Bible, you know; it is a holy calling."

"Does Samuel ever go over to the mainland?"

"No, he never leaves the Flats. I do all the business; take over the fish, and buy the supplies. I bought all our cattle," said Roxana, with pride. "I poled them away over here on the raft, one by one, when they were little things."

"Where do you pasture them?"

"Here, on the island; there are only a few acres, to be sure; but I can cut boat-loads of the best feed within a stone's throw. If we only had a little more solid ground! But this island is almost the only solid piece in the Flats."

"Your butter is certainly delicious."

"Yes, I do my best. It is sold to the steamers and vessels as fast as I make it."

"You keep yourself busy, I see."

"O, I like to work; I could n't get on without it."

"And Samuel?"

"He is not like me," replied Roxana. "He has great gifts, Samuel has. I often think how strange it is that I should be the wife of such a holy man! He is very kind to me, too; he tells me about the visions, and all the other things."

"What things?" said Raymond.

"The spirits, and the sacred influence of the sun; the fiery triangle, and the thousand years of joy. The great day is coming, you know; Samuel is waiting for it."

"Nine of the night. Take thou thy rest. I will lay me down in peace, and sleep, for it is thou, Lord, only, that makest me dwell in safety," chanted a voice in the hall; the tone was deep and not without melody, and the words singularly impressive in that still, remote place.

"Go," said Roxana, instantly pushing aside her half-washed dishes. "Samuel will take you to your room."

"Do you leave your work unfinished?" I said, with some curiosity, noticing that she had folded her hands without even hanging up her towels.

"We do nothing after the evening chant," she said. "Pray go; he is waiting."

"Can we have candles?"

"Waiting Samuel allows no false lights in his house; as imitations of the glorious sun, they are abominable to him. Go, I beg."

She opened the door, and we went into the passage; it was entirely dark, but the man led us across to our room, showed us the position of our beds by sense of feeling, and left us without a word. After he had gone, we struck matches, one by one, and, with the aid of their uncertain light, managed to get into our respective mounds in safety; they were shake-downs on the floor, made of fragrant hay instead of straw, covered with clean sheets and patchwork coverlids, and provided with large, luxurious pillows. O pillow! Has any one sung thy praises? When tired or sick, when discouraged or sad, what gives so much comfort as a pillow? Not your curled-hair brickbats; not your stiff, fluted, rasping covers, or limp cotton cases; but a good, generous, soft pillow, deftly cased in smooth, cool, untrimmed linen! There's a friend for you, a friend who changes not, a friend who soothes all your troubles with a soft caress, a mesmeric touch of balmy forgetfulness.

I slept a dreamless sleep. Then I heard a voice borne toward me as if coming from far over a sea, the waves bringing it nearer and nearer.

"Awake!" it cried; "awake! The night is far spent; the day is at hand. Awake!"

I wondered vaguely over this voice as to what manner of voice it might be, but it came again, and again, and finally I awoke to find it at my side. The gray light of dawn came through the open windows, and Raymond was already up, engaged with a tub of water and crash towels. Again the chant sounded in my ears.

"Very well, very well," I said, testily. "But if you sing before breakfast you'll cry before night, Waiting Samuel."

Our host had disappeared, however, without hearing my flippant speech, and slowly I rose from my fragrant couch; the room was empty save for our two mounds, two tubs of water, and a number of towels hanging on nails. "Not overcrowded with furniture," I remarked.

"From Maine to Florida, from Massachusetts to Missouri, have I travelled, and never before found water enough," said Raymond. "If waiting for the judgment-day raises such liberal ideas of tubs and towels, I would that all the hotel-keepers in the land could be convened here to take a lesson."

Our green hunting-clothes were soon donned, and we went out into the hall; a flight of broad steps led up to the roof; Roxana appeared at the top and beckoned us thither. We ascended, and found ourselves on the flat roof. Samuel stood with his face toward the east and his arms outstretched, watching the horizon; behind was Roxana, with her hands clasped on her breast and her head bowed: thus they waited. The eastern sky was bright with golden light; rays shot upward toward the zenith, where the rose-lights of dawn were retreating down to the west, which still lay in the shadow of night; there was not a sound; the Flats stretched out dusky and still. Two or three minutes passed, and then a dazzling rim appeared above the horizon, and the first gleam of sunshine was shed over the level earth; simultaneously the two began a chant, simple as a Gregorian, but rendered in correct full tones. The words, apparently, had been collected from the Bible:—

> "The heavens declare the glory of God—
>   Joy cometh in the morning!
> In them is laid out the path of the sun—
>   Joy cometh in the morning!
> As a bridegroom goeth he forth;
> As a strong man runneth his race.
> The outgoings of the morning
>   Praise thee, O Lord!
> Like a pelican in the wilderness,
> Like a sparrow upon the house-top,
>   I wait for the Lord.
> It is good that we hope and wait,
>   Wait—wait."

The chant over, the two stood a moment silently, as if in contemplation, and then descended, passing us without a word or sign, with their hands clasped before them as though forming part of an unseen procession. Raymond and I were left alone upon the house-top.

"After all, it is not such a bad opening for a day; and there is the pelican of the wilderness to emphasize it," I said, as a heron flew up from the water, and, slowly flapping his great wings, sailed across to another channel. As the sun rose higher, the birds began to sing; first a single note here and there, then a little trilling solo, and finally an outpouring of melody on all sides,—land-birds and water-birds, birds that lived in the Flats, and birds that had flown thither for breakfast,—the whole waste was awake and rejoicing in the sunshine.

"What a wild place it is!" said Raymond. "How boundless it looks! One hill in the distance, one dark line of forest, even one tree, would break its charm. I have seen the ocean, I have seen the prairies, I have seen the great desert, but this is like a mixture of the three. It is an ocean full of land,—a prairie full of water,—a desert full of verdure."

"Whatever it is, we shall find in it fishing and aquatic hunting to our hearts' content," I answered.

And we did. After a breakfast delicious as the supper, we took our boat and a lunch-basket, and set out. "But how shall we ever find our way back?" I said, pausing as I recalled the network of runs, and the will-o'-the-wisp aspect of the house, the previous evening.

"There is no other way but to take a large ball of cord with you, fasten one end on shore, and let it run out over the stern of the boat," said Roxana. "Let it run out loosely, and it will float on the water. When you want to come back you can turn around and wind it in as you come. *I* can read the Flats like a book, but they're very blinding to most people; and you might keep going round in a circle. You will do better not to go far, anyway. I'll wind the bugle on the roof an hour before sunset; you can start back when you hear it; for it's awkward getting supper after dark." With this musical promise we took the clew of twine which Roxana rigged for us in the stern of our boat, and started away, first releasing Captain Kidd, who was pacing his islet in sullen majesty, like another Napoleon on St. Helena.[7] We took a new channel and passed behind the house, where the imported cattle were feeding in their little pasture; but the winding stream soon bore us away, the house sank out of sight, and we were left alone.

We had fine sport that morning among the ducks,—wood, teal, and canvas-back,—shooting from behind our screens woven of rushes; later in the day we took to fishing. The sun shone down, but there was a cool September breeze, and the freshness of the verdure was like early spring. At noon we took our lunch and a *siesta* among the water-lilies. When we awoke we found that a bittern had taken up his position near by, and was surveying us gravely:—

> "'The moping bittern, motionless and stiff,
> That on a stone so silently and stilly
> Stands, an apparent sentinel, as if
> To guard the water-lily,"

quoted Raymond. The solemn bird, in his dark uniform, seemed quite undisturbed by our presence; yellow-throats and swamp-sparrows also came in numbers to have a look at us; and the fish swam up to the surface and eyed us curiously. Lying at ease in the boat, we in our turn looked down into the water. There is a singular fascination in looking down into a clear stream as the boat floats above; the mosses and twining water-plants seem to have arbors and grottos in their recesses, where delicate marine creatures might live, naiads and mermaids of miniature size; at least we are always looking for them. There is a fancy, too, that one may find some-thing,—a ring dropped from fair fingers idly trailing in the water; a book which the fishes have read thoroughly; a scarf caught among the lilies; a spoon with unknown initials; a drenched ribbon, or an embroidered hand-kerchief. None of these things did we find, but we did discover an old brass breastpin, whose probable glass stone was gone. It was a paltry trinket at best, but I fished it out with superstitious care,—a treasure-trove of the Flats. "'Drowned,'" I said, pathetically, "'drowned in her white robes—'"

"And brass breastpin," added Raymond, who objected to sentiment, true or false.

"You Philistine! Is nothing sacred to you?"

"Not brass jewelry, certainly."

"Take some lilies and consider them,"[8] I said, plucking several of the queenly blossoms floating alongside.

"Cleopatra art thou, regal blossom,
　　Floating in thy galley down the Nile,—
All my soul does homage to thy splendor,
　　All my heart grows warmer in thy smile;
Yet thou smilest for thine own grand pleasure,
　　Caring not for all the world beside,
As in insolence of perfect beauty,
　　Sailest thou in silence down the tide.

"Loving, humble rivers all pursue thee,
　　Wasted are their kisses at thy feet;
Fiery sun himself cannot subdue thee,
　　Calm thou smilest through his raging heat;
Naught to thee the earth's great crowd of blossoms,
　　Naught to thee the rose-queen on her throne;

> Haughty empress of the summer waters,
>   Livest thou, and diest, all alone."

This from Raymond.

"Where did you find that?" I asked.

"It is my own."

"Of course! I might have known it. There is a certain rawness of style and versification which——"

"That's right," interrupted Raymond; "I know just what you are going to say. The whole matter of opinion is a game of 'follow-my-leader'; not one of you dares admire anything unless the critics say so. If I had told you the verses were by somebody instead of a nobody, you would have found wonderful beauties in them."

"Exactly. My motto is, 'Never read anything unless it is by a some-body.' For, don't you see, that a nobody, if he is worth anything, will soon grow into a somebody, and, if he is n't worth anything, you will have saved your time!"

"But it is not merely a question of growing," said Raymond; "it is a question of critics."

"No; there you are mistaken. All the critics in the world can neither make nor crush a true poet."

"What is poetry?" said Raymond, gloomily.

At this comprehensive question, the bittern gave a hollow croak, and flew away with his long legs trailing behind him. Probably he was not of an aesthetic turn of mind, and dreaded lest I should give a ramified answer.

Through the afternoon we fished when the fancy struck us, but most of the time we floated idly, enjoying the wild freedom of the watery waste. We watched the infinite varieties of the grasses, feathery, lance-leaved, tufted, drooping, banner-like, the deer's tongue, the wild-celery, and the so-called wild-rice, besides many unknown beauties delicately fringed, as difficult to catch and hold as thistle-down. There were plants journeying to and fro on the water like nomadic tribes of the desert; there were fleets of green leaves floating down the current; and now and then we saw a wonderful flower with scarlet bells, but could never approach near enough to touch it.

At length, the distant sound of the bugle came to us on the breeze, and I slowly wound in the clew, directing Raymond as he pushed the boat along, backing water with the oars. The sound seemed to come from every direction. There was nothing for it to echo against, but, in place of the echo, we heard a long, dying cadence, which sounded on over the Flats fainter and fainter in a sweet, slender note, until a new tone broke forth. The music floated around us, now on one side, now on the other; if it had been our only guide, we should have been completely bewildered. But I wound the cord steadily; and at last suddenly, there before us, appeared the house with Roxana on the roof, her figure outlined against the sky. Seeing us, she played a final salute, and then descended, carrying the imprisoned music with her.

That night we had our supper at sunset. Waiting Samuel had his meals by himself in the front room. "So that in case the spirits come, I shall not be there to hinder them," explained Roxana. "I am not holy, like Samuel; they will not speak before me."

"Do you have your meals apart in the winter, also?" asked Raymond.

"Yes."

"That is not very sociable," I said.

"Samuel never was sociable," replied Roxana. "Only common folks are sociable; but he is different. He has great gifts, Samuel has."

The meal over, we went up on the roof to smoke our cigars in the open air; when the sun had disappeared and his glory had darkened into twilight, our host joined us. He was a tall man, wasted and gaunt, with piercing dark eyes and dark hair, tinged with gray, hanging down upon his shoulders. (Why is it that long hair on the outside is almost always the sign of something wrong in the inside of a man's head?) He wore a black skull-cap like the *Faust*[9] of the operatic stage.

"Why were the Flats called St. Clair?" I said; for there is something fascinating to me in the unknown history of the West. "There is n't any," do you say? you, I mean, who are strong in the Punic wars! you, too, who are so well up in Grecian mythology. But there is history, only we don't know it. The story of Lake Huron in the times of the Pharaohs, the story of the Mississippi during the reign of Belshazzar, would be worth hearing. But it is lost! All we can do is to gather together the details of our era,—the era when Columbus came to this New World, which was, nevertheless, as old as the world he left behind.

"It was in 1679," began Waiting Samuel, "that La Salle sailed up the Detroit River in his little vessel of sixty tons burden, called the Griffin. He was accompanied by thirty-four men, mostly fur-traders; but there were among them two holy monks, and Father Louis Hennepin, a friar of the Franciscan order. They passed up the river and entered the little lake just south of us, crossing it and these Flats on the 12th of August, which is Saint Clair's day. Struck with the gentle beauty of the scene, they named the waters after their saint, and at sunset sang a *Te Deum* [10] in her honor."

"And who was Saint Clair?"

"Saint Clair, virgin and abbess, born in Italy, in 1193, made superior of a convent by the great Francis, and canonized for her distinguished virtues," said Samuel, as though reading from an encyclopaedia.

"Are you a Roman Catholic?" asked Raymond.

"I am everything; all sincere faith is sacred to me," replied the man. "It is but a question of names."

"Tell us of your religion," said Raymond, thoughtfully; for in religions Raymond was something of a polyglot.

"You would hear of my faith? Well, so be it. Your question is the work of spirit influence. Listen, then. The great Creator has sowed immensity with innumerable systems of suns. In one of these systems a spirit forgot that he was a limited, subordinate being, and misused his freedom; how, we know not. He fell, and with him all his kind. A new race was then created for the vacant world, and, according to the fixed purpose of the Creator, each was left free to act for himself; he loves not mere machines. The fallen spirit, envying the new creature called man, tempted him to sin. What was his sin? Simply the giving up of his birthright, the divine soul-sparkle, for a promise of earthly pleasure. The triune divine deep, the mysterious fiery triangle, which, to our finite minds, best represents the Deity, now withdrew his personal presence; the elements, their balance broken, stormed upon man; his body, which was once ethereal, moving by mere volition, now grew heavy; and it was also appointed unto him to die. The race thus darkened, crippled, and degenerate, sank almost to the level of the brutes, the mind-fire alone remaining of all their spiritual gifts. They lived on blindly, and as blindly died. The sun, however, was left to them, a type of what they had lost.

"At length, in the fullness of time, the world-day of four thousand years, which was appointed by the council in heaven for the regiving of the divine and forfeited soul-sparkle, as on the fourth day of creation the great sun was given, there came to earth the earth's compassionate Saviour, who took upon himself our degenerate body, and revivified it with the divine soul-sparkle, who overcame all our temptations, and finally allowed the tinder of our sins to perish in his own painful death upon the cross. Through him our paradise body was restored, it waits for us on the other side of the grave. He showed us what it was like on Mount Tabor,[11] with it he passed through closed doors, walked upon the water, and ruled the elements; so will it be with us. Paradise will come again; this world will, for a thousand years, see its first estate; it will be again the Garden of Eden. America is the great escaping-place; here will the change begin. As it is written, 'Those who escape to my utmost borders.' As the time draws near, the spirits who watch above are permitted to speak to those souls who listen. Of these listening, waiting souls am I; therefore have I withdrawn my-self. The sun himself speaks to me, the greatest spirit of all; each morning I watch for his coming; each morning I ask, 'Is it to-day?' Thus do I wait."

"And how long have you been waiting?" I asked.

"I know not; time is nothing to me."

"Is the great day near at hand?" said Raymond.

"Almost at its dawning; the last days are passing."

"How do you know this?"

"The spirits tell me. Abide here, and perhaps they will speak to you also," replied Waiting Samuel.

We made no answer. Twilight had darkened into night, and the Flats had sunk into silence below us. After some moments I turned to speak to our host; but, noiselessly as one of his own spirits, he had departed.

"A strange mixture of Jacob Boehmen, chiliastic dreams,[12] Christian-ity, sun-worship, and modern spiritualism," I said. "Much learning hath made the Maine farmer mad."

"Is he mad?" said Raymond. "Sometimes I think we are all mad."

"We should certainly become so if we spent our time in speculations upon subjects clearly beyond our reach. The whole race of philosophers from Plato down are all the time going round in a circle. As long as we are in the world, I for one propose to keep my feet on solid ground; especially as we have no wings. 'Abide here, and perhaps the spirits will speak to you,' did he say? I think very likely they will, and to such good purpose that you won't have any mind left."

"After all, why should not spirits speak to us?" said Raymond, in a musing tone.

As he uttered those words the mocking laugh of a loon came across the dark waste.

"The very loons are laughing at you," I said, rising. "Come down; there is a chill in the air, composed in equal parts of the Flats, the night, and Waiting Samuel. Come down, man; come down to the warm kitchen and common-sense."

We found Roxana alone by the fire, whose glow was refreshingly real and warm; it was like the touch of a flesh-and-blood hand, after vague dreamings of spirit-companions, cold and intangible at best, with the added suspicion that, after all, they are but creations of our own fancy, and even their spirit-nature fictitious. Prime,[13] the graceful *raconteur* who goes a-fishing, says, "firelight is as much of a polisher in-doors as moonlight outside." It is; but with a different result. The moonlight polishes every-thing into romance, the firelight into comfort. We brought up two re-markably easy old chairs in front of the hearth and sat down, Raymond still adrift with his wandering thoughts, I, as usual, making talk out of the present. Roxana sat opposite, knitting in hand, the cat purring at her feet. She was a slender woman, with faded light hair, insignificant features, small dull blue eyes, and a general aspect which, with every desire to state at its best, I can only call commonplace. Her gown was limp, her hands roughened with work, and there was no collar around her yellow throat. O magic rim of white, great is thy power! With thee, man is civilized; without thee, he becomes at once a savage.

"I am out of pork," remarked Roxana, casually; "I must go over to the mainland to-morrow and get some."

If it had been anything but pork! In truth, the word did not chime with the mystic conversation of Waiting Samuel. Yes; there was no doubt about it. Roxana's mind was sadly commonplace.

"See what I have found," I said, after a while, taking out the old breastpin. "The stone is gone; but who knows? It might have been a diamond dropped by some French duchess, exiled, and fleeing for life across these far Western waters; or perhaps that German Princess of Brunswick-Wolfen-something-or-other,[14] who, about one hundred years ago, was dead and buried in Russia, and travelling in America at the same time, a sort of a female wandering Jew,[15] who has been done up in stories ever since."

(The other day, in Bret Harte's "Melons,"[16] I saw the following: "The singular conflicting conditions of John Brown's body and soul were, at that time, beginning to attract the attention of American youth." That is good, is n't it? Well, at the time I visited the Flats, the singular conflicting conditions of the Princess of Brunswick-Wolfen-something-or-other had, for a long time, haunted me.)

Roxana's small eyes were near-sighted; she peered at the empty setting, but said nothing.

"It is water-logged," I continued, holding it up in the firelight, "and it hath a brassy odor; nevertheless, I feel convinced that it belonged to the princess."

Roxana leaned forward and took the trinket; I lifted up my arms and gave a mighty stretch, one of those enjoyable lengthenings-out which belong only to the healthy fatigue of country life. When I drew myself in again, I was surprised to see Roxana's features working, and her rough hands trembling, as she held the battered setting.

"It was mine," she said; "my dear old cameo breastpin that Abby gave me when I was married. I saved it and saved it, and would n't sell it, no matter how low we got, for someway it seemed to tie me to home and baby's grave. I used to wear it when I had baby—I had neck-ribbons then; we had things like other folks, and on Sundays we went to the old meeting-house on the green. Baby is buried there—O baby, baby!" and the voice broke into sobs.

"You lost a child?" I said, pitying the sorrow which was, which must be, so lonely, so unshared.

"Yes. O baby! baby!" cried the woman, in a wailing tone. "It was a little boy, gentlemen, and it had curly hair, and could just talk a word or two; its name was Ethan, after father, but we all called it Robin. Father was mighty proud of Robin, and mother, too. It died, gentlemen, my baby died, and I buried it in the old churchyard near the thorn-tree. But still I thought to stay there always along with mother and the girls; I never supposed anything else, until Samuel began to see visions. Then, everything was different, and everybody against us; for, you see, I would marry Samuel, and when he left off working, and began to talk to the spirits, the folks all said, 'I told yer so, Maria Ann!' Samuel was n't of Maine stock exactly: his father was a sailor, and 't was suspected that his mother was some kind of an East-Injia woman, but no one knew. His father died and left the boy on the town, so he lived round from house to house until he got old enough to hire out. Then he came to our farm, and there he stayed. He had wonderful eyes, Samuel had, and he had a way with him—well, the long and short of it was, that I got to thinking about him, and could n't think of anything else. The folks did n't like it at all, for, you see, there was Adam Rand, who had a farm of his own over the hill; but I never could bear Adam Rand. The worst of it was, though, that Samuel never so much as looked at me, hardly. Well, it got to be the second year, and Susan, my younger sister, married Adam Rand. Adam, he thought he'd break up my nonsense, that's what they called it, and so he got a good place for Samuel away down in Connecticut, and Samuel said he'd go, for he was always restless, Samuel was. When I heard it, I was ready to lie down and die. I ran out into the pasture and threw myself down by the fence like a crazy woman. Samuel happened to come by along the lane, and saw me; he was always kind to all the dumb creatures, and stopped to see what was the matter, just as he would have stopped to help a calf. It all came out then, and he was awful sorry for me. He sat down on the top bar of the fence and looked at me, and I sat on the ground a-crying with my hair down, and my face all red and swollen.

"'I never thought to marry, Maria Ann,' says he.

"'O, please do, Samuel,' says I, 'I'm a real good housekeeper, I am, and we can have a little land of our own, and everything nice—'

"'But I wanted to go away. My father was a sailor,' he began, a-looking away off toward the ocean.

"'O, I can't stand it,—I can't stand it,' says I, beginning to cry again. Well, after that he 'greed to stay at home and marry me, and the folks they had to give in to it when they saw how I felt. We were married on Thanksgiving day, and I wore a pink delaine, purple neck-ribbon, and this very breastpin that sister Abby gave me,—it cost four dollars, and came 'way from Boston. Mother kissed me, and said she hoped I'd be happy.

"'Oh course I shall, mother,' says I. 'Samuel has great gifts; he is n't like common folks.'

"'But common folks is a deal comfortabler,' says mother. The folks never understood Samuel.

"Well, we had a chirk[17] little house and bit of land, and baby came, and was so cunning and pretty. The visions had begun to appear then, and Samuel said he must go.

"'Where?' says I.

"'Anywhere the spirits lead me,' says he.

"But baby could n't travel, and so it hung along; Samuel left off work, and everything ran down to loose ends; I did the best I could, but it was n't much. Then baby died, and I buried him under the thorn-tree, and the visions came thicker and thicker, and Samuel told me as how this time he must go. The folks wanted me to stay behind without him; but they never understood me nor him. I could no more leave him than I could fly; I was just wrapped up in him. So we went away; I cried dreadfully when it came to leaving the folks and Robin's little grave, but I had so much to do after we got started, that there was n't time for anything but work. We thought to settle in ever so many places, but after a while there would always come a vision, and I'd have to sell out and start on. The little money we had was soon gone, and then I went out for days' work, and picked up any work I could get. But many's the time we were cold, and many's the time we were hungry, gentlemen. The visions kept coming, and by and by I got to like 'em too. Samuel he told me all they said when I came home nights, and it was nice to hear all about the thousand years of joy, when there'd be no more trouble, and when Robin would come back to us again. Only I told Samuel that I hoped the world would n't alter much, because I wanted to go back to Maine for a few days and see all the old places. Father and mother are dead, I suppose," said Roxana, looking up at us with a pathetic expression in her small dull eyes. Beautiful eyes are doubly beautiful in sorrow; but there is something peculiarly pathetic in small dull eyes looking up at you, struggling to express the grief that lies within, like a prisoner behind the bars of his small dull window.

"And how did you lose your breastpin?" I said, coming back to the original subject.

"Samuel found I had it, and threw it away soon after we came to the Flats; he said it was vanity."

"Have you been here long?"

"O yes, years. I hope we shall stay here always now,—at least, I mean until the thousand years of joy begin,—for it's quiet, and Samuel's more easy here than in any other place. I've got used to the lonely feeling, and don't mind it much now. There's no one near us for miles, except Rosabel Lee and Liakim; they don't come here, for Samuel can't abide 'em, but sometimes I stop there on my way over from the mainland, and have a little chat about the children. Rosabel Lee has got lovely children, she has! They don't stay there in the winter, though; the winters *are* long, I don't deny it."

"What do you do then?"

"Well, I knit and cook, and Samuel reads to me, and has a great many visions."

"He has books, then?"

"Yes, all kinds; he's a great reader, and he has boxes of books about the spirits, and such things."

"Nine of the night. Take thou thy rest. I will lay me down in peace and sleep; for it is thou, Lord, only, that makest me dwell in safety," chanted the voice in the hall; and our evening was over.[18]

At dawn we attended the service on the roof; then, after breakfast, we released Captain Kidd, and started out for another day's sport. We had not rowed far when Roxana passed us, poling her flat-boat rapidly along; she had a load of fish and butter, and was bound for the mainland village. "Bring us back a Detroit paper," I said. She nodded and passed on, stolid and homely in the morning light. Yes, I was obliged to confess to myself that she *was* common-place.

A glorious day we had on the moors in the rushing September wind. Everything rustled and waved and danced, and the grass undulated in long billows as far as the eye could see. The wind enjoyed himself like a mad creature; he had no forests to oppose him, no heavy water to roll up,—nothing but merry, swaying grasses. It was the west wind,—"of all the winds, the best wind." The east wind was given us for our sins; I have long suspected that the east wind was the angel that drove Adam out of Paradise. We did nothing that day,—nothing but enjoy the rushing breeze. We felt like Bedouins of the desert, with our boat for a steed. "He came flying upon the wings of the wind," is the grandest image of the Hebrew poet.

Late in the afternoon we heard the bugle and returned, following our clew as before. Roxana had brought a late paper, and, opening it, I saw the account of an accident,—a yacht run down on the Sound and five drowned; five, all near and dear to us. Hastily and sadly we gathered our possessions together; the hunting, the fishing, were nothing now; all we thought of was to get away, to go home to the sorrowing ones around the new-made graves. Roxana went with us in her boat to guide us back to the little lighthouse. Waiting Samuel bade us no farewell, but as we rowed away we saw him standing on the house-top gazing after us. We bowed, he waved his hand; and then turned away to look at the sunset. What were our little affairs to a man who held converse with the spirits!

We rowed in silence. How long, how weary seemed the way! The grasses, the lilies, the silver channels—we no longer even saw them. At length the forward boat stopped. "There's the lighthouse yonder," said Roxana. "I won't go over there to-night. Maybe you'd rather not talk, and Rosabel Lee will be sure to talk to me. Good by." We shook hands, and I laid in the boat a sum of money to help the little household through the winter; then we rowed on toward the lighthouse. At the turn I looked back; Roxana was sitting motionless in her boat; the dark clouds were rolling up behind her; and the Flats looked wild and desolate. "God help her!" I said.

A steamer passed the lighthouse and took us off within the hour.

Years rolled away, and I often thought of the grassy sea, and intended to go there; but the intention never grew into reality. In 1870, however, I was travelling westward, and, finding myself at Detroit, a sudden impulse took me up to the Flats. The steamer sailed up the beautiful river and crossed the little lake, both unchanged. But, alas! the canal predicted by the captain fifteen years before had been cut, and, in all its unmitigated ugliness, stretched straight through the enchanted land. I got off at the new and prosaic brick lighthouse, half expecting to see Liakim and his Rosabel Lee; but they were not there, and no one knew anything about them. And Waiting Samuel? No one knew anything about him, either. I took a skiff, and, at the risk of losing myself, I rowed away into the wilderness, spending the day among the silvery channels, which were as beautiful as ever. There were fewer birds; I saw no grave herons, no sombre bitterns, and the fish had grown shy. But the water-lilies were beautiful as of old, and the grasses as delicate and luxuriant. I had scarcely a hope of finding the old house on the island, but late in the afternoon, by a mere chance, I rowed up unexpectedly to its little landing-place. The walls stood firm and the roof was unbroken; I landed and walked up the overgrown path. Opening the door, I found the few old chairs and tables in their places, weather-beaten and decayed, the storms had forced a way within, and the floor was insecure; but the gay crockery was on its shelf, the old tins against the wall, and all looked so natural that I almost feared to find the mortal remains of the husband and wife as I went from room to room. They were not there, however, and the place looked as if it had been uninhabited for years. I lingered in the doorway. What had become of them? Were they dead? Or had a new vision sent them farther toward the setting sun? I never knew, although I made many inquiries. If dead, they were probably lying somewhere under the shining waters; if alive, they must have "folded their tents, like the Arabs, and silently stolen away." [19]

I rowed back in the glow of the evening across the grassy sea. "It is beautiful, beautiful," I thought, "but it is passing away. Already commerce has invaded its borders; a few more years and its loveliness will be but a legend of the past. The bittern has vanished; the loon has fled away. Waiting Samuel was the prophet of the waste; he has gone, and the barriers are broken down. Farewell, beautiful grass-water! No artist has painted, no poet has sung your wild, vanishing charm; but in one heart, at least, you have a place, O lovely land of St. Clair!"

MISS ELISABETHA

In yonder homestead, wreathed with bounteous vines,
A lonely woman dwells, whose wandering feet
Pause oft amid one chamber's calm retreat,
Where an old mirror from its quaint frame shines.
And here, soft wrought in memory's vague designs,
Dim semblances her wistful gaze will greet
Of lost ones that inthrall phantasmally sweet
The mirror's luminous quietude enshrines.

But unto her these dubious forms that pass
With shadowy majesty or dreamy grace,
Wear nothing of ghostliness in mien or guise.
The only ghost that haunts this glimmering glass
Carries the sad reality in its face
Of her own haggard cheeks and desolate eyes!
　　　Edgar Fawcett[1]

OVERLOOKING the tide-water river stands an old house, gleaming white in the soft moonlight; the fragrance of tropic flowers floats out to sea on the land-breeze, coming at sunset over the pine-barrens to take the place of the ocean winds that have blown all day long, bringing in the salt freshness to do battle with the hot shafts of the sun and conquer them. The side of the house toward the river shows stone arches, doorless, opening into a hall; beyond is a large room, lighted by two candles placed on an old-fashioned piano; and full in their yellow radiance sits Miss Elisabetha, playing, with clear, measured touch, an old-time minuet. The light falls upon her face, with its sharp, high-curved features, pale-blue eyes, and the three thin curls of blonde hair on each side. She is not young, our Elisa-betha: the tall, spare form, stiffly erect, the little wisp of hair behind cere-moniously braided and adorned with a high comb, the long, thin hands, with the tell-tale wrist-bones prominent as she plays, and the fine network of wrinkles over her pellucid, colorless cheeks, tell this. But the boy who listens sees it not; to him she is a St. Cecilia,[2] and the gates of heaven open as she plays. He leans his head against the piano, and his thoughts are lost in melody; they do not take the form of words, but sway to and fro with the swell and the ebb of the music. If you should ask him, he could not express what he feels, for his is no analytical mind; attempt to explain it to him, and very likely he would fall asleep before your eyes. Miss Elisabetha plays well—in a prim, old-fashioned way, but yet well; the ancient piano has lost its strength, but its tones are still sweet, and the mistress humors its failings. She tunes it herself, protects its strings from the sea-damps, dusts it carefully, and has embroidered for it a cover in cross-stitch, yellow tulips growing in straight rows out of a blue ground—an heirloom pattern brought from Holland. Yet entire happiness can not be ours in this world, and Miss Elisabetha sometimes catches herself thinking how delightful it would be to use E flat once more; but the piano's E flat is hopelessly gone.

"Is not that enough for this evening, Theodore?" said Miss Elisabetha, closing the manuscript music-book, whose delicate little pen-and-ink notes were fading away with age.

"Oh, no, dear aunt; sing for me, please, 'The Proud Ladye.'"

And so the piano sounded forth again in a prim melody, and the thin voice began the ballad of the knight, who, scorned by his lady-love, went to the wars with her veil bound on his heart; he dies on the field, but a dove bears back the veil to the Proud Ladye, who straightway falls "a-weeping and a-weeping till she weeps her life away." The boy who listens is a slender stripling, with brown eyes, and a mass of brown curls tossed back from a broad, low forehead; he has the outlines of a Greek, and a dark, silken fringe just borders his boyish mouth. He is dressed in a simple suit of dark-blue cotton jacket and trousers, the broad white collar turned down, revealing his round young throat; on his slender feet he wears snowy stockings, knitted by Miss Elisabetha's own hands, and over them a low slipper of untanned leather. His brown hands are clasped over one knee, the taper fingers and almond-shaped nails betraying the artistic temperament—a sign which is confirmed by the unusually long, slender line of the eye-brows, curving down almost to the cheeks.

"A-weeping and a-weeping till she weeps her life away," sang Miss Elisabetha, her voice in soft *diminuendo* to express the mournful end of the Proud Ladye. Then, closing the piano carefully, and adjusting the tulip-bordered cover, she extinguished the candles, and the two went out under the open arches, where chairs stood ready for them nightly. The tide-water river—the Warra—flowed by, the moon-path shining goldenly across it; up in the north palmettos stood in little groups alongshore, with the single feathery pine-trees of the barrens coming down to meet them; in the south shone the long lagoon, with its low islands, while opposite lay the slender point of the mainland, fifteen miles in length, the Warra on one side, and on the other the ocean; its white sand-ridges gleamed in the moonlight, and the two could hear the sound of the waves on its outer beach.

"It is so beautiful," said the boy, his dreamy eyes following the silver line of the lagoon.

"Yes," replied Miss Elisabetha, "but we have no time to waste, Theodore. Bring your guitar and let me hear you sing that *romanza* again; remember the pauses—three beats to the measure."

Then sweetly sounded forth the soft tenor voice, singing an old French *romanza,* full of little quavers, and falls, and turns, which the boy involuntarily slurred into something like naturalness, or gave *staccato* as the mocking-bird throws out his shower of short, round notes. But Miss Elisabetha allowed no such license: had she not learned that very *romanza* from Monsieur Vocard himself forty years before? and had he not carefully taught her every one of those little turns and quavers? Taking the guitar from Theodore's hand, she executed all the flourishes slowly and precisely, making him follow her, note for note. Then he must sing it all over again while she beat the time with her long, slender foot, incased in a black-silk slipper of her own making. The ladies of the Daarg family always wore slippers—the heavy-sounding modern boot they considered a structure suitable only for persons of plebeian origin. A lady should not even step perceptibly; she should glide.

"Miss 'Lisabeet, de toas' is ready. Bress de chile, how sweet he sings to-night! Mos' like de mock-bird's self, Mass' Doro."

So spoke old Viny, the one servant of the house, a broad-shouldered, jet-black, comfortable creature, with her gray wool peeping from beneath a gay turban. She had belonged to Doro's Spanish mother, but, when Miss Elisabetha came South to take the house and care for the orphan-boy, she had purchased the old woman, and set her free immediately.

"It don't make naw difference as I can see, Miss 'Lisabeet," said Viny, when the new mistress carefully explained to her that she was a free agent from that time forth. " 'Pears harnsome in you to do it, but it arn't likely I'll leabe my chile, my Doro-boy, long as I lib—is it, now? When I die, he'll have ole Viny burred nice, wid de priests, an' de candles, an' de singing, an' all."

"Replace your guitar, Theodore," said Miss Elisabetha, rising, "and then walk to and fro between here and the gate ten times. Walk briskly, and keep your mouth shut; after singing you should always guard against the damps."

The boy obeyed in his dreamy way, pacing down the white path, made hard with pounded oyster-shells, to the high stone wall. The old iron-clamped gate, which once hung between the two pomegranate-topped pillars, was gone; for years it had leaned tottering half across the entrance-way, threatening to brain every comer, but Miss Elisabetha had ordered its removal in the twinkling of her Northern eye, and in its place now hung a neat, incongruous little wicket, whose latch was a standing bone of contention between the mistress and the entire colored population of the small village.

"Go back and latch the gate," was her constantly repeated order; "the cows might enter and injure the garden."

"But th' arn't no cows, Miss 'Lisabeet."

"There should be, then," the ancient maiden would reply, severely. "Grass would grow with a little care and labor; look at our pasture. You are much too indolent, good people!"

Theodore stood leaning over the little gate, his eyes fixed on the white sand-hills across the Warra; he was listening to the waves on the outer beach.

"Theodore, Theodore!" called Miss Elisabetha's voice, "do not stand, but pace to and fro; and be sure and keep your mouth closed."

Mechanically the boy obeyed, but his thoughts were following the sound of the water. Following a sound? Yes. Sounds were to him a language, and he held converse with the surf, the winds, the rustling marsh-grass, and the sighing pines of the barrens. The tale of the steps completed, he reentered the house, and, following the light, went into a long, narrow room, one of three which, built out behind the main body of the house, formed with its back-wall a square, surrounding a little courtyard, in whose center stood the well, a ruined fountain, rose- and myrtle-bushes, and two ancient figtrees, dwarfed and gnarled. Miss Elisabetha was standing at the head of the table; before her was a plate containing three small slices of dry toast, crisp and brown, and a decanter of orange-wine, made by her own hands. One slice of the toast was for herself, two were for the boy, who was still supposed to be growing; a Northerner would have said that he was over twenty, but Spanish blood hastens life, and Teodoro in years was actually not yet eighteen. In mind he was still younger, thanks to Miss Elisabetha's care and strict control. It had never even occurred to him that he need not so absolutely obey her; and, to tell the truth, neither had it occurred to her. Doro ate his simple supper standing—the Daarg family never sat down gluttonously to supper, but browsed lightly on some delicate fragments, moving about and chatting meanwhile as though half forgetting they were eating at all. Then Miss Elisabetha refilled his little glass, watched him drink the clear amber liquid to the last drop, and bade him good night in her even voice. He turned at the door and made her a formal bow, not without grace; she had carefully taught him this salutation, and required it of him every night.

"I wish you a blessed rest, Theodore," she said, courtesying in reply; "do not keep the light burning."

Half an hour later, when the ancient maiden glided out of her chamber, clad in a long frilled wrapper, the three curls in papers on each side of her head, she saw no gleam from under the low door of the little room across the hall; she listened, but there was no sound, and, satisfied, she retired to her high couch and closed the gayly flowered curtains around her. But, out on the small balcony which hung like a cage from his eastern window, Doro stood, leaning over the iron railing and listening, listening to the far sound of the sea.

Such had been the life down in the old house for sixteen long, winterless years, the only changes being more difficult music and more toast, longer lessons in French, longer legs to the little blue trousers, increased attention to sea-baths and deportment, and always and ever a careful saving of every copper penny and battered shilling. What became of these coins old Viny did not know; she only knew how patiently they were collected, and how scrupulously saved. Miss Elisabetha attended to the orange-grove in person; not one orange was lost, and the annual waste of the other proprietors, an ancient and matter-of-course waste, handed down from father to son, represented in her purse not a few silver pieces. Pedro, the Minorcan,[3] who brought her fish and sea-food, she had drilled from boyhood in his own art by sheer force of will, paying him by the day, and sending him into the town to sell from door to door all she did not need herself, to the very last clam. The lazy housewives soon grew into the habit of expecting Pedro and his basket, and stood in their doorways chatting in the sun and waiting for him, while the husbands let their black dugouts lie idle, and lounged on the sea-wall, smoking and discussing the last alligator they had shot, or the last ship, a coasting-schooner out of water, which had sailed up their crooked harbor six months before. Miss Elisabetha had learned also to braid palmetto, and her long fingers, once accustomed to the work, accomplished as much in a week as Zanita Perez and both her apprentices accomplished in two; she brought to the task also original ideas, original at least in Beata, where the rude hats and baskets were fac-similes of those braided there two hundred years before by the Spanish women, who had learned the art from the Indians. Thus Miss Elisabetha's wares found ready sale at increased prices, little enough to Northern ideas—sixpence for a hat—one shilling for a basket; but all down the coast, and inland toward the great river, there was a demand for her work, and the lines hung in the garden were almost constantly covered with the drying palmetto. Then she taught music. To whom, do you ask? To the black-eyed daughters of the richer townspeople, and to one or two demoiselles belonging to Spanish families down the coast, sent up to Beata to be educated by the nuns. The good Sisters did their best, but they knew little, poor things, and were glad to call in Miss Elisabetha with her trills and quavers; so the wiry organ in the little cathedral sounded out the ballads and *romanzas* of Monsieur Vocard, and the demoiselles learned to sing them in their broken French, no doubt greatly to the satisfaction of the golden-skinned old fathers and mothers on the plantations down the coast. The *padre* in charge of the parish had often importuned Miss Elisabetha to play this organ on Sundays, as the decorous celebration of high-mass suffered sadly, not to say ludicrously, from the blunders of poor Sister Paula. But Miss Elisabetha briefly refused; she must draw a line somewhere, and a pagan ceremonial she could not countenance. The Daarg family, while abhorring greatly the Puritanism of the New England colonies, had yet held themselves equally aloof from the image-worship of Rome; and they had always considered it one of the inscrutable mysteries of Providence that the French nation, so skilled in polite attitude, so versed in the singing of *romanzas,* should yet have been allowed to remain so long in ignorance of the correct religious mean.

The old house was managed with the nicest care. Its thick coquina-walls[4] remained solid still, and the weak spots in the roof were mended with a thatch of palmetto and tar, applied monthly under the mistress's superintendence by Viny, who never ceased to regard the performance as a wonder of art, accustomed as she was to the Beata fashion of letting roofs leak when they wanted to, the family never interfering, but encamping on the far side of the flow with calm undisturbed. The few pieces of furniture were dusted and rubbed daily, and the kitchen department was under martial law; the three had enough to eat—indeed, an abundance— oysters, fish, and clams, sweet potatoes from the garden, and various Northern vegetables forced to grow under the vigilant nursing they received, but hating it, and coming up as spindling as they could. The one precious cow gave them milk and butter, the well-conducted hens gave them eggs; flour and meal, coffee and tea, hauled across the barrens from the great river, were paid for in palmetto-work. Yes, Miss Elisabetha's household, in fact, lived well, better perhaps than any in Beata; but so measured were her quantities, so exact her reckonings, so long her look ahead, that sometimes, when she was away, old Viny felt a sudden wild desire to toss up fritters in the middle of the afternoon, to throw away yesterday's tea-leaves, to hurl the soured milk into the road, or even to eat oranges without counting them, according to the fashions of the easy old days when Doro's Spanish grandmother held the reins, and everything went to ruin comfortably. Every morning after breakfast Miss Elisabetha went the rounds through the house and garden; then English and French with Doro for two hours; next a sea-bath for him and sailing or walking as he pleased, when the sun was not too hot. Luncheon at noon, followed by a *siesta;* then came a music-lesson, long and charming to both; and, after that, he had his choice from among her few books. Dinner at five, a stroll along the beach, music in the evenings—at first the piano in the parlor, then the guitar under the arches; last of all, the light supper, and good-night. Such was Doro's day. But Miss Elisabetha, meanwhile, had a hundred other duties which she never neglected, in spite of her attention to his welfare—first the boy, then his money, for it was earned and destined for him. Thus the years had passed, without change, without event, without misfortune; the orange-trees had not failed, the palmetto-work had not waned, and the little store of money grew apace. Doro, fully employed, indulged by Viny, amused with his dogs, his parrot, his mocking-birds, and young owls, all the variety of pets the tropical land afforded, even to young alligators clandestinely kept in a sunken barrel up the marsh, knew no *ennui*. But, most of all, the music filled his life, rounding out every empty moment, and making an undercurrent, as it were, to all other occupations; so that the French waltzed through his brain, the English went to marches, the sailing made for itself *gondelieds,*[5] and even his plunges in the Warra were like crashes of fairy octaves, with *arpeggios* of pearly notes in showers coming after.

These were the *ante-bellum* days, before the war had opened the Southern country to winter visitors from the North; invalids a few, tourists a few, came and went, but the great tide, which now sweeps annually down the Atlantic coast to Florida, was then unknown. Beata, lying by itself far down the peninsula, no more looked for winter visitors than it looked for angels; but one day an angel arrived unawares, and Doro saw her.

Too simple-hearted to conceal, excited, longing for sympathy, he poured out his story to Miss Elisabetha, who sat copying from her music-book a certain ballad for the Demoiselle Xantez.

"It was over on the north beach, aunt, and I heard the music and hastened thither. She was sitting on a tiger-skin thrown down on the white sand; purple velvet flowed around her, and above, from embroideries like cream, rose her flower-face set on a throat so white, where gleamed a star of brilliancy; her hair was like gold—yellow gold—and it hung in curls over her shoulders, a mass of radiance; her eyes were blue as the deepest sky-color; and oh! so white her skin, I could scarcely believe her mortal. She was playing on a guitar, with her little hands so white, so soft, and singing—aunt, it was like what I have dreamed."

The boy stopped and covered his face with his hands. Miss Elisabetha had paused, pen in hand. What was this new talk of tiger-skins and golden hair? No one could sing in Beata save herself alone; the boy was dreaming!

"Theodore," she said, "fancy is permitted to us under certain restrictions, but no well-regulated mind will make to itself realities of fancies. I am sorry to be obliged to say it, but the romances must be immediately removed from the shelf."

These romances, three in number, selected and sanctioned by the governess of the Misses Daarg forty years before, still stood in Miss Elisabetha's mind as exemplars of the wildest flights of fancy.

"But this is not fancy, dear aunt," said Doro eagerly, his brown eyes velvet with moisture, and his brown cheeks flushed. "I saw it all this afternoon over on the beach; I could show you the very spot where the tiger-skin lay, and the print of her foot, which had a little shoe so odd— like this," and rapidly he drew the outline of a walking-boot in the extreme of the Paris fashion.

Miss Elisabetha put on her glasses.

"Heels," she said slowly; "I have heard of them."

"There is nothing in all the world like her," pursued the excited boy, "for her hair is of pure gold, not like the people here; and her eyes are so sweet, and her forehead so white! I never knew such people lived—why have you not told me all these years?"

"She is a blonde," replied Miss Elisabetha primly. "I, too, am a blonde, Theodore."

"But not like this, aunt. My lovely lady is like a rose."

"A subdued monotone of coloring has ever been a characteristic of our family, Theodore. But I do not quite understand your story. Who is this person, and was she alone on the beach?"

"There were others, but I did not notice them; I only looked at her."

"And she sang?"

"O aunt, so heavenly sweet—so strange, so new her song, that I was carried away up into the blue sky as if on strong wings—I seemed to float in melody. But I can not talk of it; it takes my breath away, even in thought!"

Miss Elisabetha sat perplexed.

"Was it one of our *romanzas,* Theodore, or a ballad?" she said, running over the list in her mind.

"It was something I never heard before," replied Doro, in a low voice; "it was not like anything else—not even the mocking-bird, for, though it went on and on, the same strain floated back into it again and again; and the mocking-bird, you know, has a light and fickle soul. Aunt, I can not tell you what it was like, but it seemed to tell me a new story of a new world."

"How many beats had it to the measure?" asked Miss Elisabetha, after a pause.

"I do not know," replied the boy dreamily.

"You do not know! All music is written in some set time, Theodore. At least, you can tell me about the words. Were they French?"

"No."

"Nor English?"

"No."

"What then?"

"I know not; angel-words, perhaps.

"Did she speak to you?"

"Yes," replied Doro, clasping his hands fervently. "She asked me if I liked the song, and I said, 'Lady, it is of the angels.' Then she smiled, and asked my name, and I told her, 'Doro'—"

"You should have said, 'Theodore,'" interrupted Miss Elisabetha; "do I not always call you so?"

"And she said it was a lovely name; and could I sing? I took her guitar, and sang to her—"

"And she praised your method, I doubt not?"

"She said, 'Oh, what a lovely voice!' and she touched my hair with her little hands, and I—I thought I should die, aunt, but I only fell at her feet."

"And where—where is this person now?" said the perplexed maiden, catching at something definite.

"She has gone—gone! I stood and watched the little flag on the mast until I could see it no more. She has gone! Pity me, aunt, dear aunt. What shall I do? How shall I live?"

The boy broke into sobs, and would say no more. Miss Elisabetha was strangely stirred; here was a case beyond her rules; what should she do? Having no precedent to guide her, she fell back into her old beliefs gained from studies of the Daarg family, as developed in boys. Doro was excused from lessons, and the hours were made pleasant to him. She spent many a morning reading aloud to him; and old Viny stood amazed at the variety and extravagance of the dishes ordered for him.

"What! chickens ebery day, Miss 'Lisabeet? 'Pears like Mass' Doro hab eberyting now!"

"Theodore is ill, Lavinia," replied the mistress; and she really thought so.

Music, however, there was none; the old charmed afternoons and evenings were silent.

"I can not bear it," the boy had said, with trembling lips.

But one evening he did not return: the dinner waited for him in vain; the orange after-glow faded away over the pine-barrens; and in the pale green of the evening sky arose the star of the twilight; still he came not. Miss Elisabetha could eat nothing.

"Keep up the fire, Lavinia," she said, rising from the table at last.

"Keep up de fire, Miss 'Lisabeet! Till when?"

"Till Theodore comes!" replied the mistress shortly.

"De worl' mus' be coming to de end," soliloquized the old black woman, carrying out the dishes; "sticks of wood no account!"

Late in the evening a light footstep sounded over the white path, and the strained, watching eyes under the stone arches saw at last the face of the missing one.

"O aunt, I have seen her—I have seen her! I thought her gone for ever. O aunt—dear, dear aunt, she has sung for me again!" said the boy, flinging himself down on the stones, and laying his flushed face on her knee. "This time it was over by the old lighthouse, aunt. I was sailing up and down in the very worst breakers I could find, half hoping they would swamp the boat, for I thought perhaps I could forget her down there under the water—when I saw figures moving over on the island-beach. Something in the outlines of one made me tremble; and I sailed over like the wind, the little boat tilted on its side within a hair's-breadth of the water, cutting it like a knife as it flew. It was she, aunt, and she smiled! 'What, my young Southern nightingale,' she said, 'is it you?' And she gave me her hand—her soft little hand."

The thin fingers, hardened by much braiding of palmetto, withdrew themselves instinctively from the boy's dark curls. He did not notice it, but rushed on with his story unheeding:

"She let me walk with her, aunt, and hold her parasol, decked with lace, and she took off her hat and hung it on my arm, and it had a long, curling plume. She gave me sweet things—oh, so delicious! See, I kept some," said Doro, bringing out a little package of bonbons. "Some are of sugar, you see, and some have nuts in them; those are chocolate. Are they not beautiful?"

"Candies, I think," said Miss Elisabetha, touching them doubtfully with the end of her quill.

"And she sang for me, aunt, the same angel's music; and then, when I was afar in heaven, she brought me back with a song about three fishermen who sailed out into the west; and I wept to hear her, for her voice then was like the sea when it feels cruel. She saw the tears, and, bidding me sit by her side, she struck a few chords on her guitar and sang to me of a miller's daughter who grew so dear, so dear. Do you know it, aunt?"

"A miller's daughter? No; I have no acquaintance with any such person," said Miss Elisabetha, considering.

"Wait, I will sing it to you," said Doro, running to bring his guitar; "she taught it to me herself!"

And the the tenor voice rose in the night air, bearing on the lovely melody the impassioned words of the poet. Doro sang them with all his soul, and the ancient maiden felt her heart disquieted within her—why, she knew not. It seemed as though her boy was drifting away whither she could not follow.

"Is it not beautiful, aunt? I sang it after her line by line until I knew it all, and then I sang her all my songs; and she said I must come and see her the day after to-morrow, and she would give me her picture and something else. What do you suppose it is, aunt? She would not tell me, but she smiled and gave me her hand for good-by. And now I can live, for I am to see her at Martera's house, beyond the convent, the day after to-morrow, the day after to-morrow—oh, happy day, the day after to-morrow!"

"Come and eat your dinner, Theodore," said Miss Elisabetha, rising. Face to face with a new world, whose possibilities she but dimly understood, and whose language was to her an unknown tongue, she grasped blindly at the old anchors riveted in years of habit; the boy had always been something of an epicure in his fastidious way, and one of his favorite dishes was on the table.

"You may go, Lavinia," she said, as the old slave lingered to see if her darling enjoyed the dainties; she could not bear that even Viny's faithful eyes should notice the change, if change there was.

The boy ate nothing.

"I am not hungry, aunt," he said, "I had so many delicious things over on the beach. I do not know what they were, but they were not like our things at all." And, with a slight gesture of repugnance, he pushed aside his plate.

"You had better go to bed," said Miss Elisabetha, rising. In her perplexity this was the first thing which suggested itself to her; a good night's rest had been known to work wonders; she would say no more till morning. The boy went readily; but he must have taken his guitar with him, for long after Miss Elisabetha had retired to her couch she heard him softly singing again and again the romance of the miller's daughter. Several times she half rose as if to go and stop him; then a confused thought came to her that perhaps his unrest might work itself off in that way, and she sank back, listening meanwhile to the fanciful melody with feelings akin to horror. It seemed to have no regular time, and the harmony was new and strange to her old-fashioned ears. "Truly, it must be the work of a composer gone mad," said the poor old maid, after trying in vain for the fifth time to follow the wild air. There was not one trill or turn in all its length, and the accompaniment, instead of being the decorous one octave in the bass, followed by two or three chords according to the time, seemed to be but a general sweeping over the strings, with long pauses, and unexpected minor harmony introduced, turning the air suddenly upside down, and then back again before one had time to comprehend what was going on. "Heaven help me!" said Miss Elisabetha, as the melody began again for the sixth time, "but I fear I am sinful enough to hate that miller's daughter." And it was very remarkable, to say the least, that a person in her position "was possessed of a jewel to tremble in her ear," she added censoriously, "not even to speak of a necklace." But the comfort was cold, and, before she knew it, slow, troubled tears had dampened her pillow.

Early the next morning she was astir by candle-light, and, going into the detached kitchen, began preparing breakfast with her own hands, adding to the delicacies already ordered certain honey-cakes, an heirloom in the Daarg family. Viny could scarcely believe her eyes when, on coming down to her domain at the usual hour, she found the great fireplace glowing, and the air filled with the fragrance of spices; Christmas alone had heretofore seen these honey-cakes, and to-day was only a common day!

"I do not care for anything, aunt," said Doro, coming listlessly to the table when all was ready. He drank some coffee, broke a piece of bread, and then went back to his guitar; the honey-cakes he did not even notice.

One more effort remained. Going softly into the parlor during the morning, Miss Elisabetha opened the piano, and, playing over the prelude to "The Proud Ladye," began to sing in her very best style, giving the flourishes with elaborate art, scarcely a note without a little step down from the one next higher; these airy descents, like flights of fairy stairs, were considered very high art in the days of Monsieur Vocard. She was in the middle of "a-weeping and a-weeping," when Doro rushed into the room. "O, aunt," he cried, "please, please do not sing! Indeed, I can not bear it. We have been all wrong about our music; I can not explain it, but I feel it—I know it. If you could only hear her! Come with me to-morrow and hear her, dear aunt, and then you will understand what I mean."

Left to herself again, Miss Elisabetha felt a great resolve come to her. She herself would go and see this stranger, and grind her to powder! She murmured these words over several times, and derived much comfort from them.

With firm hands she unlocked the cedar chest which had come with her from the city seventeen years before; but the ladies of the Daarg family had not been wont to change their attire every passing fashion, and the robe she now drew forth was made in the style of full twenty-five years previous—a stiff drab brocade flowered in white, two narrow flounces around the bottom of the scant skirt, cut half low in the neck with a little bertha, the material wanting in the lower part standing out resplendent in the broad leg-of-mutton sleeves, stiffened with buckram. Never had the full daylight of Beata seen this precious robe, and Miss Elisabetha herself considered it for a moment with some misgivings as to its being too fine for such an occasion. But had not Doro spoken of "velvet" and "embroideries"? So, with solemnity, she arrayed herself, adding a certain Canton-crape scarf of a delicate salmon color, and a Leghorn bonnet with crown and cape, which loomed out beyond her face so that the three curls slanted forward over the full ruche to get outside, somewhat like blinders. Thus clad, with her slippers, her bag on her arm, and lace mits on her hands, Miss Elisabetha surveyed herself in the glass. In the bag were her handkerchief, an ancient smelling-bottle, and a card, yellow indeed, but still a veritable engraved card, with these words upon it:

"Miss ELISABETHA DAARG,
DAARG'S BAY."

The survey was satisfactory. "Certainly I look the gentlewoman," she thought, with calm pride, "and this person, whoever she is, can not fail to at once recognize me as such. It has never been our custom to visit indiscriminately; but in this case I do it for the boy's sake." So she sallied forth, going out by a side-door to escape observation, and walked toward the town, revolving in her mind the words she should use when face to face with the person. "I shall request her—with courtesy, of course—still I shall feel obliged to request her to leave the neighborhood," she thought. "I shall express to her—with kindness, but also with dignity—my opinion of the meretricious music she has taught my boy, and I shall say to her frankly that I really can not permit her to see him again. Coming from me, these words will, of course, have weight, and —"

"Oh, see Miss 'Lisabeet!" sang out a child's voice. "Nita, do but come and see how fine she is!"

Nita came, saw, and followed, as did other children—girls carrying plump babies, olive-skinned boys keeping close together, little blacks of all ages, with go-carts made of turtleshells. It was not so much the splendor—though that was great, too—as it was the fact that Miss Elisabetha wore it. Had they not all known her two cotton gowns as far back as they could remember? Reaching the Martera house at last, her accustomed glide somewhat quickened by the presence of her escort (for, although she had often scolded them over her own gate, it was different now when they assumed the proportions of a body-guard), she gave her card to little Inez, a daughter of the household, and one of her pupils.

"Bear this card to the person you have staying with you, my child, and ask her if she will receive me."

"But there is more than one person, señora," replied Inez, lost in wonder over the brocade.

"The one who sings, then."

"They all sing, Miss 'Lisabeet."

"Well, then, I mean the person—who wears purple velvet and—and embroideries," said the visitor, bringing out these items reluctantly.

"Ah! you mean the beautiful lady," cried Inez. "I run, I run, señora"; and in a few minutes Miss Elisabetha was ushered up the stairs, and found herself face to face with "the person."

"To whom have I the honor of speaking?" said a languid voice from the sofa.

"Madame, my card—"

"Oh, was that a card? Pray excuse me.—Lucille, my glasses." Then, as a French maid brought the little, gold-rimmed toy, the person scanned the name. "Ma'm'selle Dag?" she said inquiringly.

"Daarg, madame," replied Miss Elisabetha. "If you have resided in New York at all, you are probably familiar with the name"; and majestically she smoothed down the folds of the salmon-colored scarf.

"I have resided in New York, and I am not familiar with the name," said the person, throwing her head back indolently among the cushions.

She wore a long, full robe of sea-green silk, opening over a mist of lace-trimmed skirts, beneath whose filmy borders peeped little feet incased in green-silk slippers, with heels of grotesque height; a cord and tassels confined the robe to her round waist; the hanging sleeves, open to the shoulders, revealed superb white arms; and the mass of golden hair was gathered loosely up behind, with a mere *soupçon* of a cap perched on top, a knot of green ribbon contrasting with the low-down golden ripples over the forehead. Miss Elisabetha surveyed the attitude and the attire with disfavor; in her young days no lady in health wore a wrapper, or lolled on sofas. But the person, who was the pet prima donna of the day, English, with a world-wide experience and glory, knew nothing of such traditions.

"I have called, madame," began the visitor, ignoring the slight with calm dignity (after all, how should "a person" know anything of the name of Daarg?), "on account of my—my ward, Theodore Oesterand."

"Never heard of him," replied the diva. It was her hour for *siesta,* and any infringement of her rules told upon the carefully tended, luxuriant beauty.

"I beg your pardon," said Miss Elisabetha, with increased accentuation of her vowels. "Theodore has had the honor of seeing you twice, and he has also sung for you."

"What! you mean my little bird of the tropics, my Southern nightingale!" exclaimed the singer, raising herself from the cushions.—"Lucille, why have you not placed a chair for this lady?—I assure you, I take the greatest interest in the boy, Miss Dag."

"Daarg," replied Miss Elisabetha; and then, with dignity, she took the chair, and seating herself, crossed one slipper over the other, in the attitude number one of her youth. Number one had signified "repose," but little repose felt she now; there was something in the attire of this person, something in her yellow hair and white arms, something in the very air of the room, heavy with perfumes, that seemed to hurt and confuse her.

"I have never heard a tenor of more promise, never in my life; and consider how much that implies, Ma'm'selle! You probably know who I am?"

"I have not that pleasure."

"*Bien,* I will tell you. I am Kernadi."

Miss Elisabetha bowed, and inhaled salts from her smelling-bottle, her little finger elegantly separated from the others.

"You do not mean to say that you have never heard of Kernadi—Cécile Kernadi?" said the diva, sitting fairly erect now in her astonishment.

"Never," replied the maiden, not without a proud satisfaction in the plain truth of her statement.

"Where have you lived, ma'm'selle?"

"Here, Mistress Kernadi."

The singer gazed at the figure before her in its ancient dress, and gradually a smile broke over her beautiful face.

"Ma'm'selle," she said, dismissing herself and her fame with a wave of her white hand, "you have a treasure in Doro, a voice rare in a century; and, in the name of the world, I ask you for him."

Miss Elisabetha sat speechless; she was never quick with words, and now she was struck dumb.

"I will take him with me when I go in a few days," pursued Kernadi; "and I promise you he shall have the very best instructors. His method now is bad—insufferably bad. The poor boy has had, of course, no opportunities; but he is still young, and can unlearn as well as learn. Give him to me. I will relieve you of all expenses, so sure do I feel that he will do me credit in the end. I will even pass my word that he shall appear with me upon either the London or the Vienna stage before two years are out."

Miss Elisabetha had found her words at last.

"Madame," she said, "do you wish to make an opera-singer of the son of Petrus Oesterand?"

"I wish to make an opera-singer of this pretty Doro; and, if this good Petrus is his father, he will, no doubt, give his consent."

"Woman, he is dead."

"So much the better; he will not interfere with our plans, then," replied the diva, gayly.

Miss Elisabetha rose; her tall form shook perceptibly.

"I have the honor to bid you good day," she said, courtesying formally.

The woman on the sofa sprang to her feet.

"You are offended?" she asked; "and why?"

"That you, a person of no name, of no antecedents, a public singer, should presume to ask for my boy, an Oesterand—should dare to speak of degrading him to your level!"

Kernadi listened to these words in profound astonishment. Princes had bowed at her feet, blood-royal had watched for her smile. Who was this ancient creature, with her scarf and bag? Perhaps, poor thing! she did not comprehend! The diva was not bad-hearted, and so, gently enough, she went over her offer a second time, dwelling upon and explaining its advantages. "That he will succeed, I do not doubt," she said; "but in any case he shall not want."

Miss Elisabetha was still standing.

"Want? she repeated; "Theodore want? I should think not."

"He shall have the best instructors," pursued Kernadi, all unheeding. To do her justice, she meant all she said. It is ever a fancy of singers to discover singers—provided they sing other *rôles*.

"Madame, I have the honor of instructing him myself."

"Ah, indeed. Very kind of you, I am sure; but—but no doubt you will be glad to give up the task. And he shall see all the great cities of

Europe, and hear their music. I am down here merely for a short change—
having taken cold in your miserable New York climate; but I have my usual
engagements in London, St. Petersburg, Vienna, and Paris, you know."

"No, madame, I do not know," was the stiff reply.

Kernadi opened her fine eyes still wider. It was true, then, and not a
pretense. People really lived—white people, too—who knew nothing of
her and her movements! She thought, in her vague way, that she really
must give something to the missionaries; and then she went back to Doro.

"It will be a great advantage to him to see artist-life abroad—" she
began.

"I intend him to see it," replied Miss Elisabetha.

"But he should have the right companions—advisers—"

"*I* shall be with him madame."

The diva surveyed the figure before her, and amusement shone in
her eyes.

"But you will find it fatiguing," she said—"so much journeying, so
much change! Nay, ma'm'selle, remain at home in your peaceful quiet, and
trust the boy to me." She had sunk back upon her cushions, and, catching a
glimpse of her face in the mirror, she added, smiling: "One thing more.
You need not fear lest I should trifle with his young heart. I assure you I
will not; I shall be to him like a sister."

"You could scarcely be anything else, unless it was an aunt," replied
the ancient maiden; "I should judge you fifteen years his senior, madame."

Which was so nearly accurate that the beauty started, and for the
first time turned really angry.

"Will you give me the boy?" she said, shortly. "If he were here I
might show you how easily— But, *ciel!* you could never understand such
things; let it pass. Will you give me the boy—yes or no?"

"No."

There was a silence. The diva lolled back on her cushions, and
yawned.

"You must be a very selfish woman—I think the most selfish I have
ever known," she said coolly, tapping the floor with her little slippered
feet, as if keeping time to a waltz.

"I—selfish?"

"Yes, you—selfish. And, by the by, what right have you to keep the boy at all? Certainly, he resembles you in nothing. What relation does he hold to you?"

"He is—he is my ward," answered Miss Elisabetha, nervously re-arranging her scarf. "I bid you, madame, good day."

"Ward!" pursued Kernadi; "that means nothing. Was his mother your sister?"

"Nay; his mother was a Spanish lady," replied the troubled one, who knew not how to evade or lie.

"And the father—you spoke of him—was he a relative?"

A sudden and painful blush dyed the thin old face, creeping up to the very temples.

"Ah," said the singer, with scornful amusement in her voice, "if that is all, I shall take the boy without more ado": and, lifting her glasses, she fixed her eyes full on the poor face before her, as though it was some rare variety of animal.

"You shall not have him; I say you shall not!" cried the elder woman, rousing to the contest like a tigress defending her young.

"Will you let him choose?" said Kernadi, with her mocking laugh. "See! I dare you to let him choose"; and, springing to her feet, she wheeled her visitor around suddenly, so that they stood side by side before the mirror. It was a cruel deed. Never before had the old eyes realized that their mild blue had faded; that the curls, once so soft, had grown gray and thin; that the figure, once sylph-like, was now but angles; and the throat, once so fair, yellow and sinewed. It came upon her suddenly—the face, the coloring, and the dress; a veil was torn away, and she saw it all. At the same instant gleamed the golden beauty of the other, the folds of her flowing robe, the mists of her laces. It was too much. With ashen face the stricken woman turned away, and sought the door-knob; she could not speak; a sob choked all utterance. Doro would choose.

But Cécile Kernadi rushed forward; her better nature was touched.

"No, no," she said impulsively, "you shall not go so. See! I will promise; you shall keep the boy, and I will let him go. He is all you have, perhaps, and I—I have so much! Do you not believe me? I will go away this very day and leave no trace behind. He will pine, but it will pass—a boy's first fancy. I promised him my picture, but you shall take it. There! Now go, go, before I regret what I do. He has such a voice!—but never mind, you shall not be robbed by me. Farewell, poor lady; I, too, may grow old some day. But hear one little word of advice from my lips: The boy has waked up to life; he will never be again the child you have known. Though I go, another will come; take heed!"

That night, in the silence of her own room, Miss Elisabetha prayed a little prayer, and then, with firm hand, burned the bright picture to ashes.

Wild was the grief of the boy; but the fair enchantress was gone. He wept, he pined; but she was gone. He fell ill, and lay feverish upon his narrow bed; but she was none the less gone, and nothing brought her back. Miss Elisabetha tended him with a great patience, and spoke no word. When he raved of golden hair, she never said, "I have seen it"; when he cried, "Her voice, her angel-voice!" she never said, "I have heard it." But one day she dropped these words: "Was she not a false woman, Theodore, who went away not caring, although under promise to see you, and to give you her picture?" And then she walked quietly to her own room, and barred the door, and wept; for the first time in her pure life she had burdened her soul with falsehood—yet would she have done it ten times over to save the boy.

Time and youth work wonders; it is not that youth forgets so soon; but this—time is then so long. Doro recovered, almost in spite of himself, and the days grew calm again. Harder than ever worked Miss Elisabetha, giving herself hardly time to eat or sleep. Doro studied a little listlessly, but he no longer cared for his old amusements. He had freed his pets: the mocking-birds had flown back to the barrens, and the young alligators, who had lived in the sunken barrel, found themselves unexpectedly obliged to earn their own living along the marshes and lagoons. But of music he would have none; the piano stood silent, and his guitar had disappeared.

"It is wearing itself away," thought the old maid; "then he will come back to me." But nightly she counted her secret store, and, angered at its smallness, worked harder and harder, worked until her shoulders ached and her hands grew knotted. "One more year, only one more year," she thought; "then he shall go!" And through all the weary toil these words echoed like a chant—"One more year—only one more!"

Two months passed, and then the spring came to the winterless land—came with the yellow jasmine. "But four months now, and he shall go," said Miss Elisabetha, in her silent musings over the bag of coin. "I have shortened the time by double tasks." Lightly she stepped about the house, counted her orange-buds, and reckoned up the fish. She played the cathedral organ now on Sundays, making inward protest after every note, and sitting rigidly with her back toward the altar in the little high-up gallery during the sermon, as much as to say: "It is only my body which is here. Behold! I do not even bow down in the house of Rimmon."[6] Thus laboring early and late, with heart, and hand, and strength, she saw but little of Doro, save at meals and through his one hour of listless study; but the hidden hope was a comforter, and she worked and trusted on. There was one little gleam of light: he had begun to play again on his guitar, softly, furtively, and as it were in secret. But she heard him, and was cheered.

One evening, toiling home through the white sand after a late music-lesson, laden with a bag of flour which she would not trust Viny to buy, she heard a girl's voice singing. It was a plaintive, monotonous air that she sang, simple as a Gregorian chant; but her voice was a velvet contralto, as full of rich tones as a peach is full of lusciousness. The contralto voice is like the violoncello.

"The voice is not bad," thought Miss Elisabetha, listening critically, "but there is a certain element of the *sauvage* in it. No lady, no person of culture, would permit herself to sing in that way; it must be one of the Minorcans."

Still, in spite of prejudices, the music in her turned her steps toward the voice; her slippers made no sound, and she found it. A young girl, a Minorcan, sat under a bower of jasmine, leaning back against her lover's breast; her dark eyes were fixed on the evening star, and she sang as the bird sings, naturally, unconsciously, for the pure pleasure of singing. She was a pretty child. Miss Elisabetha knew her well—Catalina, one of a thriftless, olive-skinned family down in the town. "Not fourteen, and a lover already," thought the old maid with horror. "Would it be of any use, I wonder, if I spoke to her mother?" Here the lover—the Paul of this Virginia[7]—moved, and the shadows slid off his face; it was Doro!

Alone in her chamber sat Miss Elisabetha. Days had passed, but of no avail. Even now the boy was gone to the tumble-down house in the village where Catalina's little brothers and sisters swarmed out of doors and windows, and the brown, broad mother bade him welcome with a hearty slap on the shoulder. She had tried everything—argument, entreaty, anger, grief—and failed; there remained now only the secret, the secret of years, of much toil and many pains. The money was not yet sufficient for two; so be it. She would stay herself, and work on; but he should go. Before long she would hear his step, perhaps not until late, for those people had no settled hours (here a remembrance of all their ways made her shudder), but come he would in time; this was still his home. At midnight she heard the footfall, and opening the door called gently, "Theodore, Theodore." The youth came, but slowly. Many times had she called him lately, and he was weary of the strife. Had he not told her all—the girl singing as she passed, her voice haunting him, his search for her, and her smile; their meetings in the *chaparral,* where she sang to him by the hour, and then, naturally as the bud opens, their love? It seemed to him an all-sufficient story, and he could not understand the long debates.

"And the golden-haired woman," Miss Elisabetha had said; "she sang to you too, Theodore."

"I had forgotten her aunt," replied the youth simply.

So he came but slowly. This time, however, the voice was gentle, and there was no anger in the waiting eyes. She told him all as he sat there: the story of his father, who was once her friend, she said with a little quiver in her voice, the death of the young widowed mother, her own coming to this far Southern land, and her long labors for him. Then she drew a picture of the bright future opening before him, and bringing forth the bag showed him its contents, the savings and earnings of seventeen years, tied in packages with the contents noted on their labels. "All is for you, dear child," she said, "for you are still but a child. Take it and go. I had planned to accompany you, but I give that up for the present. I will remain and see to the sale of everything here, and then I will join you—that is, if you wish it, dear. Perhaps you will enjoy traveling alone, and—and I have plenty of friends to whom I can go, and shall be quite content, dear—quite content."

"Where it is that you wish me to go, aunt?" asked Doro coldly. They were going over the same ground, then, after all.

"Abroad, dear—abroad, to all the great cities of the world," said the aunt, faltering a little as she met his eyes. "You are well educated, Theodore; I have taught you myself. You are a gentleman's son, and I have planned for you a life suited to your descent. I have written to my cousins in Amsterdam; they have never seen me, but for the sake of the name they will—O my boy, my darling, tell me that you will go!" she burst forth, breaking into entreaty as she read his face.

But Doro shook off her hands. "Aunt," he said, rising, "why will you distress yourself thus? I shall marry Catalina, and you know it; have I not told you so? Let us speak no more on the subject. As to the money, I care not for it; keep it." And he turned toward the door as if to end the discussion. But Miss Elisabetha followed and threw herself on her knees before him.

"Child!" she cried, "give me, give yourself a little delay; only that, a little delay. Take the money—go; and if at the end of the year your mind is still the same, I will say not one word, no, not one, against it. She is but young, too young to marry. O my boy, for whom I have labored, for whom I have planned, for whom I have prayed, will you too forsake me?"

"Of course not, aunt," replied Doro; "I mean you to live with us always"; and with his strong young arms he half led, half carried her back to her arm-chair. She sat speechless. To live with them always—with *them*! Words surged to her lips in a flood—then, as she met his gaze, surged back to her heart again. There was that in the expression of his face which told her all words were vain; the placid, far-away look, unmoved in spite of her trouble, silenced argument and killed hope. As well attack a creamy summer cloud with axes; as well attempt to dip up the ocean with a cup. She saw it all in a flash, as one sees years of past life in the moment before drowning; and she was drowning, poor soul! Yet Doro saw nothing, felt nothing, save that his aunt was growing into an old woman with foolish fancies, and that he himself was sleepy. And then he fell to thinking of his love, and all her enchanting ways—her little angers and quick repentances, the shoulder turned away in pretended scorn, and the sudden waves of tenderness that swept him into paradise. So he stood dreaming, while tearless, silent Miss Elisabetha sat before her broken hopes. At last Doro, coming back to reality, murmured, "Aunt, you will like her when you know her better, and she will take good care of you."

But the aunt only shuddered.

"Theodore, Theodore!" she cried, "will you break my heart? Shall the son of Petrus Oesterand marry so?"

"I do not know what you mean by 'so,' aunt. All men marry, and why not I? I never knew my father; but, if he were here, I feel sure he would see Catalina with my eyes. Certainly, in all my life, I have never seen a face so fair, or eyes so lustrous."

"Child, you have seen nothing—nothing. But I intended, Heaven knows I intended—"

"It makes no difference now, aunt; do not distress yourself about it."

"Theodore, I have loved you long—your youth has not been an unhappy one; will you, for my sake, go for this one year?" she pleaded, with quivering lips.

The young man shook his head with a half smile.

"Dear aunt," he said gently, "pray say no more. I do not care to see the world; I am satisfied here. As to Catalina, I love her. Is not that enough?" He bent and kissed her cold forehead, and then went away to his happy dreams; and, if he thought of her at all as he lingered in the soft twilight that comes before sleep, it was only to wonder over her distress— a wonder soon indolently comforted by the belief that she would be calm and reasonable in the morning. But, across the hall, a gray old woman sat, her money beside her, and the hands that had earned it idle in her lap. God keep us from such a vigil!

And did she leave him? No; not even when the "him" became "them."

The careless young wife, knowing nothing save how to love, queened it right royally over the old house, and the little brown brothers and sisters ran riot through every room. The piano was soon broken by the ignorant hands that sounded its chords at random; but only Doro played on it now, and nothing pleased him so well as to improvise melodies from the plaintive Minorcan songs the little wife sang in her velvet voice. Years passed; the money was all spent, and the house full—a careless, idle, ignorant, happy brood, asking for nothing, planning not at all, working not at all, but loving each other in their own way, contented to sit in the sunshine, and laugh, and eat, and sing, all the day long. The tall, gaunt figure that came and went among them, laboring ceaselessly, striving always against the current, they regarded with tolerating eyes as a species differing from theirs, but good in its way, especially for work. The children loved the still silent old woman, and generously allowed her to take care of them until she tried to teach them; then away they flew like wild birds of the forest, and not one learned more than the alphabet.

Doro died first, a middle-aged man; gently he passed away without pain, without a care. "You have been very good to me, aunt; my life has been a happy one; I have had nothing to wish for," he murmured, as she bent to catch the last look from his dying eyes.

He was gone; and she bore on the burden he had left to her. I saw her last year—an old, old woman, but working still.

IN THE COTTON COUNTRY

The loveliest land that smiles beneath the sky,
The coast-land of our western Italy.
I view the waters quivering; quaff the breeze,
Whose briny raciness keeps an under taste
Of flavorous tropic sweets, perchance swept home
From Cuba's perfumed groves and garden spiceries.

    Paul Hamilton Hayne [1]

Call on thy children of the hill,
Wake swamp and river, coast and rill,
Rouse all thy strength, and all thy skill,
            Carolina!
Tell how the patriot's soul was tried,
And what his dauntless breast defied;
How Rutledge ruled and Laurens died,
            Carolina!

    Henry Timrod [2]

DO YOU KNOW the cotton country—the country of broad levels open to the sun, where the ungainly, ragged bushes stand in long rows, bearing the clothing of a nation on their backs? Not on their backs either, for the white wool is scattered over the branches and twigs, looking, not as if it grew there, but as if it had been blown that way, and had caught and clung at random. When I first came to the cotton country, I used to stand with my chin on the top-rail of the fences, trying to rid my eyes of that first impression. I saw the fields only when the cotton was white, when there were no green leaves left, and the fleecy down did not seem to me a vegetable at all. Starved cows passed through the half-plucked rows untempted, and I said to myself: "Of course. Cows do not eat cotton any more than they eat wool; but what bush is there at the North that they would not nibble if starving?" Accustomed to the trim, soldierly ranks of the Western corn-fields, or the billowy grace of the wheat, I could think of nothing save a parade of sturdy beggarmen unwillingly drawn up in line, when I gazed upon the stubborn, uneven branches, and generally lop-sided appearance of these plants—plants, nevertheless, of wealth, usefulness, and historic importance in the annals of our land. But after a while I grew accustomed to their contrary ways, and I even began to like their defiant wildness, as a contrast, perhaps, to the languorous sky above, the true sky of the cotton country, with its soft heat, its hazy air, and its divine twilight that lingers so long. I always walked abroad at sunset, and it is in the sunset-light that I always see the fields now when far away. No doubt there was plenty of busy, prosaic reality down there in the mornings, but I never saw it; I only saw the beauty and the fancies that come with the soft after-glow and the shadows of the night.

Down in the cotton country the sun shines steadily all day long, and the earth is hot under your feet. There are few birds, but at nightfall the crows begin to fly home in a long line, going down into the red west as though they had important messages to deliver to some imprisoned princess on the edge of the horizon. One day I followed the crows. I said to myself: "The princess is a *ruse;* they probably light not far from here, and I am going to find their place. The crows at home—that would be something worth seeing." Turning from the path, I went westward. "What!" said a country-woman, meeting Wordsworth on the road, "are ye stepping westward, sir?" [3] I, too, stepped westward.

Field after field I crossed; at last the fences ceased, and only old half-filled ditches marked the boundary-lines. The land sloped downward slightly, and after a while the ridge behind me seemed like a line of heights, the old cotton-plants on its top standing out as distinctly as single pine-trees on a mountain-summit outlined against the sky; so comparative is height. The crows still flew westward as I came out upon a second level lower down than the first, and caught a golden gleam through the fringe of bushes in the middle of the plain. I had unwittingly found the river at last, that broad, brown river that I knew was down there somewhere, although I had not seen it with my bodily eyes. I had full knowledge of what it was, though, farther south toward the ocean; I knew the long trestles over the swamps and dark canebrakes that stretched out for miles on each side of the actual stream—trestles over which the trains passed cautiously every day, the Northern passengers looking nervously down at the quaking, spongy surface below, and prophesying accidents as certain some time—

when they were not on board. Up here in the cotton country, however, the river was more docile; there were no tides to come up and destroy the banks, and with the exception of freshets the habits of the stream were orderly. The levels on each side might have been, should have been, rich with plenty. Instead, they were uncultivated and desolate. Here and there a wild, outlawed cotton-bush reared its head, and I could trace the old line of the cart-road and cross-tracks; but the soil was spongy and disintegrated, and for a long time evidently no care had been bestowed upon it. I crossed over to the river, and found that the earth-bank which had protected the field was broken down and washed away in many places; the low trees and bushes on shore still held the straws and driftwood that showed the last freshet's high-water mark.

The river made an irregular bend a short distance below, and I strolled that way, walking now on the thick masses of lespedeza that carpeted the old road-track, and now on the singularly porous soil of the level, a soil which even my inexperienced eyes recognized as worthless, all its good particles having been drained out of it and borne away on the triumphant tide of the freshets. The crows still evaded me, crossing the river in a straight line and flying on toward the west, and, in that arbitrary way in which solitary pedestrians make compacts with themselves, I said, "I will go to that tree at the exact turn of the bend, and not one step farther." I went to that tree at the exact turn of the bend, and then I went—farther; for I found there one solemn, lonely old house. Now, if there had been two, I should not have gone on; I should not have broken my compact. Two houses are sociable and commonplace; but one all alone on a desolate waste like that inspired me with—let us call it interest, and I went forward.

It was a lodge rather than a house; in its best day it could never have been more than a very plain abode, and now, in its worst, it seemed to have fallen into the hands of Giant Despair.[4] "Forlorn" was written over its lintels, and "without hope" along its low roof-edge. Raised high above the ground, in the Southern fashion, on wooden supports, it seemed even more unstable than usual to Northern eyes, because the lattice-work, the valance, as it were, which generally conceals the bare, stilt-like underpinning, was gone, and a thin calf and some melancholy chickens were walking about underneath, as though the place was an arbor. There was a little patch of garden, but no grass, no flowers; everything was gray, the un-painted house, the sand of the garden-beds, and the barren waste stretch-ing away on all sides. At first I thought the place was uninhabited, but as I drew nearer a thin smoke from one of the chimneys told of life within, and I said to myself that the life would be black-skinned life, of course. For I was quite accustomed now to finding the families of the freedmen crowded into just such old houses as this, hidden away in unexpected places; for the freedmen hardly ever live up on the even ground in the broad sunshine as though they had a right there, but down in the hollows or out into the fringes of wood, where their low-roofed cabins, numerous though they may be, are scarcely visible to the passer-by. There was no fence around this house; it stood at large on the waste as though it be-longed there. Take away the fence from a house, and you take away its respectability; it becomes at once an outlaw. I ascended the crazy, sunken steps that led to the front door, and lifted the knocker that hung there as if in mockery; who ever knocked there now save perhaps a river-god with his wet fingers as he hurried by, mounted on the foaming freshet, to ravage and lay waste again the poor, desolate fields? But no spirit came to the door, neither came the swarm of funny little black faces I had expected; instead, I saw before me a white woman, tall, thin, and gray-haired. Si-lently she stood there, her great, dark eyes, still and sad, looking at me as much as to say, "By what right are you here?"

"Excuse me, madam," was my involuntary beginning; then I some-what stupidly asked for a glass of water.

"I would not advise you to drink the water we have here; it is not good," replied the woman. I knew it was not; the water is never good down on the levels. But I was very stupid that day.

"I should like to rest a while," was my next attempt. It brought out a wooden chair, but no cordiality. I tried everything I could think of in the way of subjects for conversation, but elicited no replies beyond monosyl-lables. I could not very well say, "Who are you, and how came you here?" and yet that was exactly what I wanted to know. The woman's face baffled me, and I do not like to be baffled. It was a face that was old and at the same time young; it had deep lines, it was colorless, and the heavy hair was gray; and still I felt that it was not old in years, but that it was like the peaches we find sometimes on the ground, old, wrinkled, and withered, yet showing here and there traces of that evanescent bloom which comes before the ripeness. The eyes haunted me; they haunt me now, the dry, still eyes of immovable, hopeless grief. I thought, "Oh, if I could only help her!" but all I said was, "I fear I am keeping you standing"; for that is the senseless way we human creatures talk to each other.

Her answer was not encouraging.

"Yes," she replied, in her brief way, and said no more.

I felt myself obliged to go.

But the next afternoon I wandered that way again, and the next, and the next. I used to wait impatiently for the hour when I could enter into the presence of her great silence. How still she was! If she had wept, if she had raved, if she had worked with nervous energy, or been resolutely, doggedly idle, if she had seemed reckless, or callous, or even pious; but no, she was none of these. Her old-young face was ever the same, and she went about her few household tasks in a steady, nerveless manner, as though she could go on doing them for countless ages, and yet never with the least increase of energy. She swept the room, for instance, every day, never thoroughly, but in a gentle, incompetent sort of way peculiarly her own; yet she always swept it and never neglected it, and she took as much time to do it as though the task was to be performed with microscopic exactness.

She lived in her old house alone save for the presence of one child, a boy of six or seven years— -a quiet, grave-eyed little fellow, who played all by himself hour after hour with two little wooden soldiers and an empty spool. He seldom went out of the house; he did not seem to care for the sunshine or the open air as other children care, but gravely amused himself in-doors in his own quiet way. He did not make his wooden soldiers talk or demolish each other triumphantly, according to the manner of boys; but he marshaled them to and fro with slow consideration, and the only sound was the click of their little muskets as he moved them about. He seemed never to speak of his own accord; he was strangely silent always. I used to wonder if the two ever talked together playfully as mother and child should talk; and one day, emboldened by a welcome, not warmer, for it was never warm, but not quite so cold perhaps, I said:

"Your little son is very quiet, madam."

"He is not my son."

"Ah!" I replied, somewhat disconcerted. "He is a pretty child; what is his name?"

"His name is John."

The child heard us in his barren corner, but did not look up or speak; he made his two soldiers advance solemnly upon the spool in silence, with a flank movement. I have called the corner barren, because it seemed doubly so when the boy sat there. The poorest place generally puts on something of a homelike air when a little child is in it; but the two bare walls and angle of bare floor remained hopelessly empty and desolate. The room was large, but there was nothing in it save the two wooden chairs and a table; there was no womanly attempt at a rag-carpet, curtains for the windows, or newspaper pictures for the walls—none of those little contrivances for comfort with which women generally adorn even the most miserable abiding-places, showing a kind of courage which is often pathetic in its hopefulness. Here, however, there was nothing. A back-room held a few dishes, some boxes and barrels, and showed on its cavernous hearth the ashes of a recent fire. "I suppose they sleep in a third bare room somewhere, with their two beds, no doubt, standing all alone in the center of the chamber; for it would be too human, of course, to put them up snugly against the wall, as anybody else would do," I said to myself.

In time I succeeded in building up a sort of friendship with this solitary woman of the waste, and in time she told me her story. Let me tell it to you. I have written stories of imagination, but this is a story of fact, and I want you to believe it. It is true, every word of it, save the names given, and, when you read it, you whose eyes are now upon these lines, stop and reflect that it is only one of many life-stories like unto it. "War is cruelty," said our great general.[5] It is. It must be so. But shall we not, we women, like Sisters of Charity, go over the field when the battle is done, bearing balm and wine and oil for those who suffer?

"Down here in the cotton country we were rich once, madam; we were richer than Northerners ever are, for we toiled not for our money, neither took thought for it; it came and we spent it; that was all. My father was Clayton Cotesworth, and our home was twenty miles from here, at the Sand Hills. Our cotton-lands were down on these river levels; this was one of our fields, and this house was built for the overseer; the negro-quarters that stood around it have been carried off piecemeal by the freedmen."

(Impossible to put on paper her accentuation of this title.) "My father was an old man; he could not go to battle himself, but he gave first his eldest son, my brother James. James went away from earth at Fredericksburg. It was in the winter, and very cold. How often have I thought of that passage, 'And pray ye that your flight be not in the winter,'[6] when picturing his sufferings before his spirit took flight! Yes, it was very cold for our Southern boys; the river was full of floating ice, and the raw wind swept over them as they tried to throw up intrenchments on the heights. They had no spades, only pointed sticks, and the ground was frozen hard. Their old uniforms, worn thin by hard usage, hung in tatters, and many of them had no shoes; the skin of their poor feet shone blue, or glistening white, like a dead man's skin, through the covering of rags they made for themselves as best they could. They say it was a pitiful sight to see the poor fellows sitting down in the mornings, trying to adjust these rag-wrappings so that they would stay in place, and fastening them elaborately with their carefully saved bits of string. He was an honored man who invented a new way. My brother was one of the shoeless; at the last, too, it seems that he had no blanket, only a thin counterpane. When night came, hungry and tired as he was, he could only wrap himself in that and lie down on the cold ground to wait for morning. When we heard all this afterward, we said, 'Blessed be the bullet that put him out of his misery!' for poor James was a delicate boy, and had been accustomed to loving, watchful care all his life. Yet, oh, if I could only know that he was warm once, just once, before he died! They told us he said nothing after he was shot save 'How cold! How cold!' They put his poor, stiff body hastily down under the sod, and then the brigade moved on; 'no man knoweth his sepulchre unto this day.'[7]

"Next John went, my second brother. He said good-by, and marched away northward—northward, northward, always northward—to cold, corpse-strewed Virginia, who cried aloud to us continually, 'More! more!' Her roads are marked with death from her Peaks of Otter to the sea, and her great valley ran red. We went to her from all over the South, from Alabama, Florida, and Georgia, and from our own Carolina. We died there by thousands, and by tens of thousands. O Virginia, our dead lie thick in thy tidewater plains, in thy tangled Wilderness, and along thy river-shores, with faces upturned, and hearts still for ever.

"John came back to us once, and wedded the fair girl to whom he was betrothed. It was a sad bridal, although we made it as gay as we could; for we had come to the times of determined gayety then. The tone of society was like the determinedly gay quicksteps which the regimental bands play when returning from a funeral, as much as to say, 'Le roi est mort, vive le roi!'[8] So we turned our old silk dresses, and made a brave appearance; if our shoes were shabby, we hid them under our skirts as well as we could, and held our heads the higher. Maum Sally made a big wedding-cake, as of old, and we went without meat to pay for the spices in it; such luxuries we obtained from the blockade-runners now and then, but they were worth almost their weight in gold. Then John, too, left us. In four months he also was taken—killed by guerrillas, it is supposed, as he rode through a lonely mountain-defile. He was not found for weeks; the snow fell and covered him, mercifully giving the burial the frozen earth denied. After a while the tidings came to us, and poor Mabel slowly wept herself into the grave. She was a loving-hearted little creature, and her life was crushed. She looked at her baby once, called his name John, and then died. The child, that boy yonder, seems to have inherited her grief. He sheds no tears, however; his girl-mother shed them all, both for him and for herself, before ever he saw the light. My turn came next.

"You have been married, madam? Did you love, too? I do not mean regard, or even calm affection; I do not mean sense of duty, self-sacrifice, or religious goodness. I mean love—love that absorbs the entire being. Some women love so; I do not say they are the happiest women. I do not say they are the best. I am one of them. But God made us all; he gave us our hearts—we did not choose them. Let no woman take credit to herself for her even life, simply because it has been even. Doubtless, if he had put her out in the breakers, she would have swayed too. Perhaps she would have drifted from her moorings also, as I have drifted. I go to no church; I can not pray. But do not think I am defiant; no, I am only dead. I seek not the old friends, few and ruined, who remain still above-ground; I have no hope, I might almost say no wish. Torpidly I draw my breath through day and night, nor care if the rain falls or the sun shines. You Northern women would work; I can not. Neither have I the courage to take the child and die. I live on as the palsied animal lives, and if some day the spring fails, and the few herbs within his reach, he dies. Nor do I think he grieves much about it; he only eats from habit. So I.

"It was in the third year of the war that I met Ralph Kinsolving. I was just eighteen. Our courtship was short; indeed, I hardly knew that I loved him until he spoke and asked me to give him myself. 'Marry me, Judith,' he pleaded ardently; 'marry me before I go; let it be my wife I leave behind me, and not my sweetheart. For sweethearts, dear, can not come to us in camp when we send, as we shall surely send soon, that you may all see our last grand review.' So spoke Rafe, and with all his heart he believed it. We all believed it. Never for a moment did we doubt the final triumph of our arms. We were so sure we were right!

" 'Our last grand review,' said Rafe; but he did not dream of that last review at Appomattox, when eight thousand hungry, exhausted men stacked their muskets in the presence of the enemy, whose glittering ranks, eighty thousand strong, were drawn up in line before them, while in the rear their well-filled wagons stood—wagons whose generous plenty brought tears to the eyes of many a poor fellow that day, thinking, even while he eagerly ate, of his desolated land, and his own empty fields at home.

"I did marry my soldier, and, although it was in haste, I had my wedding-dress, my snowy veil; lace and gauze were not needed at the hospitals! But we went without the wedding-cake this time, and my satin slippers were made at home, looking very like a pair of white moccasins when finished.

"In the middle of the ceremony there was an alarm; the slaves had risen at Latto's down the river, and were coming to the village armed with clubs, and, worse still, infuriated with liquor they had found. Even our good old rector paused. There were but few white men at home. It seemed indeed a time for pausing. But Rafe said, quietly, 'Go on!' and, unsheathing his sword, he laid it ready on the chancel-rail. 'To have and to hold, from this day forward, for better for worse, for richer for poorer, in sickness and in health, to love and to cherish, till death us do part,' repeated Rafe, holding my hand in his firm clasp, and looking down into my frightened face so tenderly that I forgot my alarm—everything, indeed, save his love. But when the last word was spoken, and the blessing pronounced over our bowed heads, the shining sword seeming a silent witness, Rafe left me like a flash. The little church was empty when I rose from my knees; the women had hurried home with blanched faces to bar their doors and barricade their windows, and the men had gone for their horses and guns; only my old father waited to give me his blessing, and then we, too, hastened homeward. Our little band of defenders assembled in the main street, and rode gallantly out to meet the negroes, who were as fifty to their one. Rafe was the leader, by virtue of his uniform, and he waved his hand to me as he rode by. 'Cheer up, Judith,' he cried; 'I will soon return.'

"I never saw him again.

"They dispersed the negroes without much difficulty; Latto's slaves had been badly treated for months, they had not the strength to fight long. But Rafe rode to the next town with the prisoners under his charge, and there he met an imploring summons to the coast; the Federal ships had appeared unexpectedly off the harbor, and the little coast-city lay exposed and helpless at the mouth of the river. All good men and true within reach were summoned to the defense. So my soldier went, sending back word to me a second time, 'I will soon return.' But the siege was long, long—one of those bitterly contested little sieges of minor importance, with but small forces engaged on each side, which were so numerous during the middle times of the war—those middle times after the first high hopes had been disappointed, and before the policy of concentration had been adopted by the North—that slow, dogged North of yours that kept going back and beginning over again, until at last it found out how to do it. This little siege was long and weary, and when at last the Federal vessels went suddenly out beyond the bar again, and the town, unconquered, but crippled and suffering, lay exhausted on the shore, there was not much cause for rejoicing. Still I rejoiced; for I thought that Rafe would come. I did not know that his precious furlough had expired while he was shut up in the beleaguered city, and that his colonel had sent an imperative summons, twice repeated. Honor, loyalty, commanded him to go, and go immediately. He went.

"The next tidings that came to me brought word that he loved me and was well; the next, that he loved me and was well; the next, that he loved me and was—dead. Madam, my husband, Ralph Kinsolving, was shot—as a spy!

"You start—you question—you doubt. But spies were shot in those days, were they not? That is a matter of history. Very well; you are face to face now with the wife of one of them.

"You did not expect such an ending, did you? You have always thought of spies as outcasts, degraded wretches, and, if you remembered their wives at all, it was with the idea that they had not much feeling, probably, being so low down in the scale of humanity. But, madam, in those bitter, hurrying days men were shot as spies who were no spies. Nay, let me finish; I know quite well that the shooting was not confined to one side; I acknowledge that; but it was done, and mistakes were made. Now and then chance brings a case to light, so unmistakable in its proof that those who hear it shudder—as now and then also chance brings a coffin to light whose occupant was buried alive, and came to himself when it was too late. But what of the cases that chance does *not* bring to light?

"My husband was no spy; but it had been a trying time for the Northern commanders: suspicion lurked everywhere; the whole North clamored to them to advance, and yet their plans, as fast as they made them, were betrayed in some way to the enemy. An example was needed—my husband fell in the way.

"He explained the suspicious circumstances of his case, but a cloud of witnesses rose up against him, and he proudly closed his lips. They gave him short shrift; that same day he was led out and met his death in the presence of thousands. They told me that he was quite calm, and held himself proudly; at the last he turned his face to the south, as if he were gazing down, down, into the very heart of that land for whose sake he was about to die. I think he saw the cotton-fields then, and our home; I think he saw me, also, for the last time.

"By the end of that year, madam, my black hair was gray, as you see it now; I was an old woman at nineteen.

"My father and I and that grave-eyed baby lived on in the old house. Our servants had left us, all save one, old Cassy, who had been my nurse or 'maumee,' as we called her. We suffered, of course. We lived as very poor people live. The poorest slaves in the old time had more than we had then. But we did not murmur; the greater griefs had swallowed up the less. I said, 'Is there any sorrow like unto my sorrow?'[9] But the end was not yet.

"You have heard the story of the great march, the march to the sea?[10] But there was another march after that, a march of which your own writers have said that its route was marked by a pillar of smoke by day and of flame by night[11]—the march through South Carolina. The Northern soldiers shouted when they came to the yellow tide of the Savannah, and looked across and knew that the other shore was South Carolina soil. They crossed, and Carolina was bowed to the dust. Those were the days we cried in the morning, 'O God, that it were night!' and in the night, 'O God, that it were morning!' Retribution, do you say? It may be so. But love for our State seemed loyalty to us; and slavery was the sin of our fathers, not ours. Surely we have expiated it now.

"'Chile, chile, dey is come!' cried old Cassy, bursting into my room one afternoon, her withered black face grayly pale with fear. I went out. Cavalrymen were sweeping the village of all it contained, the meager little that was left to us in our penury. My father was asleep; how I prayed that he might not waken! Although an old man, he was fiery as a boy, and proudly, passionately rebellious against the fate which had come upon us. Our house was some distance back from the road, and broad grounds separated us from the neighboring residences. Cassy and I softly piled our pillows and cushions against the doors and windows that opened from his room to the piazza, hoping to deaden the sounds outside, for some of our people were resisting, and now and then I heard shouts and oaths. But it was of no use. My dear old father woke, heard the sounds, and rushed out into the street sword in hand; for he had been a soldier too, serving with honor through the Mexican War. Made desperate by my fears for him, I followed. There was a *mêlée* in the road before our house; a high wind blew the thick dust in my eyes and half blinded me, so that I only saw struggling forms on foot and on horseback, and could not distinguish friend or foe. Into this group my father rushed. I never knew the cause of the contest; probably it was an ill-advised attack by some of our people, fiery and reasonless always. But, whatever it was, at length there came one, two, three shots, and then the group broke apart. I rushed forward and received my old father in my arms, dying—dead. His head lay on my shoulder as I knelt in the white road, and his silver hair was dabbled with blood; he had been shot through the head and breast, and lived but a moment.

"We carried him back to the house, old Cassy and I, slowly, and with little regard for the bullets which now whistled through the air; for the first shots had brought together the scattered cavalrymen, who now rode through the streets firing right and left, more at random, I think, than with direct aim, yet still determined to 'frighten the rebels,' and avenge the soldier, one of their number, who had been killed at the beginning of the fray. We laid my father down in the center of the hall, and prepared him for his long sleep. No one came to help us; no one came to sorrow with us; each household gathered its own together and waited with bated breath for what was still to come. I watched alone beside my dead that night, the house-doors stood wide open, and lights burned at the head and foot of the couch. I said to myself, 'Let them come now and take their fill.' But no one disturbed me, and I kept my vigil from midnight until dawn; then there came a sound of many feet, and when the sun rose our streets were full of blue-coated soldiers, thousands upon thousands; one wing of the great army was marching through. There was still hot anger against us for our resistance, and when the commanding officers arrived they ordered guards to be stationed at every house, with orders to shoot any man or boy who showed himself outside of his doorway. All day and night the Federal soldiers would be passing through, and the guards gave notice that if another man was injured twenty rebel lives should answer for it.

"'We must bury my father, you and I together, Cassy,' I said; 'there is no one to help us. Come!'

"The old woman followed me without a word. Had I bidden her go alone, even as far as the door-step, she would have cowered at my feet in abject terror; but, following me, she would have gone unquestioning to the world's end. The family burial-place was on our own grounds, according to the common custom of the South; thither we turned our steps, and in silence hollowed out a grave as best we could. The guard near by watched us with curiosity for some time; at last he approached:

"'What are you two women doing there?'

"'Digging a grave.'

"'For whom?'

"'For my father, who lies dead in the house.'

"He withdrew a short distance, but still watched us closely, and when all was ready, and we returned to the house for our burden, I saw him signal the next guard. 'They will not interrupt us,' I said; 'we are only two women and a dead man.'

"I wrapped my dear father in his cloak, and covered his face; then we bore the lounge on which he lay out into the sunshine down toward the open grave. The weight of this poor frame of ours when dead is marvelous, and we moved slowly; but at length we reached the spot. I had lined the grave with coverlids and a fine linen sheet, and now, with the aid of blankets, we lowered the clay to its last resting-place. Then, opening my prayer-book, I read aloud the service for the burial of the dead, slowly, and without tears, for I was thinking of the meeting above of the old father and his two boys: 'Lord, thou hast been our refuge from one generation to another. Before the mountains were brought forth, or ever the earth and the world were made, thou art God from everlasting.' I took a clod and cast it upon the shrouded breast below. 'Earth to earth, ashes to ashes, dust to dust,' I said, and old Cassy, kneeling opposite, broke forth into low wailing, and rocked her body to and fro. Then we filled the grave. I remember that I worked with feverish strength; if it was not done quickly, I knew I could never do it at all. Can you realize what it would be to stand and shovel the earth with your own hands upon your dead?—to hear the gravel fall and strike?—to see the last shrouded outline disappear under the stifling, heavy clods? All this it was mine to do. When it was over I turned to go, and for the first time lifted my eyes. There at the fence-corner stood a row of Federal soldiers, silent, attentive, and with bared heads; my father was buried with military honors after all.

"During all that day and night the blue-coated ranks marched by; there seemed to be no end to the line of glittering muskets. I watched them passively, holding the orphan-boy on my knee; I felt as though I should never move or speak again. But after the army came the army-followers and stragglers, carrion-birds who flew behind the conquerors and devoured what they had left. They swept the town clean of food and raiment; many houses they wantonly burned; what they could not carry with them they destroyed. My own home did not escape: rude men ransacked every closet and drawer, and cut in ribbons the old portraits on the wall. A German, coming in from the smoke-house, dripping with bacon-juice, wiped his hands upon my wedding-veil, which had been discovered and taken from its box by a former intruder. It was a little thing; but, oh, how it hurt me! At length the last straggler left us, and we remained in the ashes. We could not sit down and weep for ourselves and for our dead; the care of finding wherewithal to eat thrust its coarse necessity upon us, and forced us to our feet. I had thought that all the rest of my life would be but a bowed figure at the door of a sepulchre; but the camp-followers came by, took the bowed figure by the arm, and forced it back to every-day life. We could no longer taste the luxury of tears. For days our people lived on the refuse left by the army, the bits of meat and bread they had thrown aside from their plenty; we picked up the corn with which they had fed their horses, kernel by kernel, and boiled it for our dinner; we groped in the ashes of their camp-fires; little children learned the sagacity of dogs seeking for bones, and quarreled over their findings. The fortune of war, do you say? Yes, the fortune of war! But it is one thing to say, and another thing to feel!

"We came away, madam, for our home was in ashes—old Cassy, the child, and I; we came on foot to this place, and here we have staid. No, the fields are never cultivated now. The dike has been broken down in too many places, and freshets have drained all the good out of the soil; the land is worthless. It was once my father's richest field. Yes, Cassy is dead. She was buried by her own people, who forgave her at the last for having been so spiritless as to stay with 'young missis,' when she might have tasted the glories of freedom over in the crowded hollow where the blacks were enjoying themselves and dying by the score. In six months half of them were gone. They had their freedom—oh, yes, plenty of it; they were quite free—to die! For, you see, madam, their masters, those villainous old masters of theirs, were no longer there to feed and clothe them. Oh! it was a great deliverance for the enfranchised people! Bitter, am I? Put yourself in my place.

"What am I going to do? Nothing. The boy? He must take his chances. Let him grow up under the new *régime,* I have told him nothing of the old. It may be that he will prosper; people do prosper, they tell me. It seems we were wrong, all wrong; then we must be very right now, for the blacks are our judges, councilors, postmasters, representatives, and lawmakers. That is as it should be, isn't it? What! not so? But how can it be otherwise? Ah, you think that a new king will arise who knows not Joseph [12]—that is, that a new generation will come to whom these questions will be things of the past. It may be so; I do not know. I do not know anything certainly any more, for my world has been torn asunder, and I am uprooted and lost. No, you can not help me, no one can help me. I can not adjust myself to the new order of things; I can not fit myself in new soil; the fibers are broken. Leave me alone, and give your help to the young; they can profit by it. The child? Well, if—if you really wish it, I will not oppose you. Take him, and bring him up in your rich, prosperous North; the South has no place for him. Go, and God speed you! But, as for me, I will abide in mine own country. It will not be until such as I have gone from earth that the new blood can come to her. Let us alone; we will watch the old life out with her, and when her new dawning comes we shall have joined our dead, and all of us, our errors, our sins, and our sufferings will be forgotten."

FELIPA

Glooms of the live-oaks, beautiful-braided and woven
With intricate shades of the vines that, myriad cloven,
Clamber the forks of the multiform boughs.

> . . . . Green colonnades

Of the dim sweet woods, of the dear dark woods,
Of the heavenly woods and glades,
That run to the radiant marginal sand-beach within
> The wide sea-marches of Glynn.

> . . . . Free

By a world of marsh that borders a world of sea.
Sinuous southward and sinuous northward the shimmering band
Of the sand-beach fastens the fringe of the marsh to the folds of the land.

Inward and outward to northward and southward the beach-lines linger
> and curl
As a silver-wrought garment that clings to and follows the firm, sweet
> limbs of a girl.
A league and a league of marsh-grass, waist-high, broad in the blade,
Green, and all of a height, and unflecked with a light or a shade.
> *Sidney Lanier.*[1]

CHRISTINE and I found her there. She was a small, dark-skinned, yellow-eyed child, the offspring of the ocean and the heats, tawny, lithe and wild, shy yet fearless—not unlike one of the little brown deer that bounded through the open reaches of the pine-barren behind the house. She did not come to us—we came to her; we loomed into her life like genii from another world, and she was partly afraid and partly proud of us. For were we not her guests? proud thought! and, better still, were we not women? "I have only seen three women in all my life," said Felipa, inspecting us gravely, "and I like women. I am a woman too, although these clothes of the son of Pedro make me appear as a boy; I wear them on account of the boat and the hauling in of the fish. The son of Pedro being dead at a

149

convenient age, and his clothes fitting me, what would you have? It was a chance not to be despised. But when I am grown I shall wear robes long and beautiful like the señora's." The little creature was dressed in a boy's suit of dark-blue linen, much the worse for wear, and torn.

"If you are a girl, why do you not mend your clothes?" I said.

"Do you mend, señora?"

"Certainly: all women sew and mend."

"The other lady?"

Christine laughed as she lay at ease upon the brown carpet of pine-needles, warm and aromatic after the tropic day's sunshine. "The child has divined me already, Catherine," she said.

Christine was a tall, lissome maid, with an unusually long stretch of arm, long sloping shoulders, and a long fair throat; her straight hair fell to her knees when unbound, and its clear flaxen hue had not one shade of gold, as her clear gray eyes had not one shade of blue. Her small, straight, rose-leaf lips parted over small, dazzlingly white teeth, and the outline of her face in profile reminded you of an etching in its distinctness, although it was by no means perfect according to the rules of art. Still, what a comfort it was, after the blurred outlines and smudged profiles many of us possess—seen to best advantage, I think, in church on Sundays, crowned with flower-decked bonnets, listening calmly serene to favorite ministers, unconscious of noses! When Christine had finished her laugh—and she never hurried anything—she stretched out her arm carelessly and patted Felipa's curly head. The child caught the descending hand and kissed the long white fingers.

It was a wild place where we were, yet not new or crude—the coast of Florida, that old-new land, with its deserted plantations, its skies of Paradise, and its broad wastes open to the changeless sunshine. The old house stood on the edge of the dry land, where the pine-barren ended and the salt-marsh began; in front curved the tide-water river that seemed ever trying to come up close to the barren and make its acquaintance, but could not quite succeed, since it must always turn and flee at a fixed hour, like Cinderella at the ball, leaving not a silver slipper behind, but purple drift-wood and bright seaweeds, brought in from the Gulf Stream outside. A planked platform ran out into the marsh from the edge of the barren, and at its end the boats were moored; for, although at high tide the river was at our feet, at low tide it was far away out in the green waste somewhere, and if we wanted it we must go and seek it. We did not want it, however; we let it glide up to us twice a day with its fresh salt odors and flotsam of the ocean, and the rest of the time we wandered over the barrens or lay under the trees looking up into the wonderful blue above, listening to the winds as they rushed across from sea to sea. I was an artist, poor and painstaking. Christine was my kind friend. She had brought me South because my cough was troublesome, and here because Edward Bowne recommended the place. He and three fellow sportsmen were down at the Madre Lagoon, farther south; I thought it probable we should see him, without his three fellow sportsmen, before very long.

"Who were the three women you have seen, Felipa?" said Christine.

"The grandmother, an Indian woman of the Seminoles who comes sometimes with baskets, and the wife of Miguel of the island. But they are all old, and their skins are curled: I like better the silver skin of the señora."

Poor little Felipa lived on the edge of the great salt-marsh alone with her grandparents, for her mother was dead. The yellow old couple were slow-witted Minorcans,[2] part pagan, part Catholic, and wholly ignorant; their minds rarely rose above the level of their orange-trees and their fish-nets. Felipa's father was a Spanish sailor, and, as he had died only the year before, the child's Spanish was fairly correct, and we could converse with her readily, although we were slow to comprehend the patois of the old people, which seemed to borrow as much from the Italian tongue and the Greek as from its mother Spanish. "I know a great deal," Felipa remarked confidently, "for my father taught me. He had sailed on the ocean out of sight of land, and he knew many things. These he taught to me. Do the gracious ladies think there is anything else to know?"

One of the gracious ladies thought not, decidedly. In answer to my remonstrance, expressed in English, she said, "Teach a child like that, and you ruin her."

"Ruin her?"

"Ruin her happiness—the same thing."

Felipa had a dog, a second self—a great gaunt yellow creature of unknown breed, with crooked legs, big feet, and the name Drollo. What Drollo meant, or whether it was an abbreviation, we never knew; but there was a certain satisfaction in it, for the dog was droll: the fact that the

Minorcan title, whatever it was, meant nothing of that sort, made it all the better. We never saw Felipa without Drollo. "They look a good deal alike," observed Christine—"the same coloring."

"For shame!" I said.

But it was true. The child's bronzed yellow skin and soft eyes were not unlike the dog's, but her head was crowned with a mass of short black curls, while Drollo had only his two great flapping ears and his low smooth head. Give him an inch or two of skull, and what a creature a dog would be! For love and faithfulness even now what man can match him? But, although ugly, Felipa was a picturesque little object always, whether attired in boy's clothes or in her own forlorn bodice and skirt. Olive-hued and meager-faced, lithe and thin, she flew over the pine-barrens like a creature of air, laughing to feel her short curls toss and her thin childish arms buoyed up on the breeze as she ran, with Drollo barking behind. For she loved the winds, and always knew when they were coming—whether down from the north, in from the ocean, or across from the Gulf of Mexico: she watched for them, sitting in the doorway, where she could feel their first breath, and she taught us the signs of the clouds. She was a queer little thing: we used to find her sometimes dancing alone out on the barren in a circle she had marked out with pine-cones, and once she confided to us that she talked to the trees. "They hear," she said in a whisper; "you should see how knowing they look, and how their leaves listen."

Once we came upon her most secret lair in a dense thicket of thorn-myrtle and wild smilax—a little bower she had made, where was hidden a horrible-looking image formed of the rough pieces of saw-palmetto grubbed up by old Bartolo from his garden. She must have dragged these fragments thither one by one, and with infinite pains bound them together with her rude withes of strong marsh-grass, until at last she had formed a rough trunk with crooked arms and a sort of a head, the red hairy surface of the palmetto looking not unlike the skin of some beast, and making the creature all the more grotesque. This fetich was kept crowned with flowers, and after this we often saw the child stealing away with Drollo to carry to it portions of her meals or a new-found treasure—a sea-shell, a broken saucer, or a fragment of ribbon. The food always mysteriously disappeared, and my suspicion is the Drollo used to go back secretly in the night and devour it, asking no questions and telling no lies: it fitted in nicely, however, Drollo merely performing the ancient part of the priests of Jupiter, men who have been much admired. "What a little pagan she is!" I said.

"Oh, no, it is only her doll," replied Christine.

I tried several times to paint Felipa during these first weeks, but those eyes of hers always evaded me. They were, as I have said before, yellow— that is, they were brown with yellow lights—and they stared at you with the most inflexible openness. The child had the full-curved, half-open mouth of the tropics, and a low Greek forehead. "Why isn't she pretty?" I said.

"She is hideous," replied Christine; "look at her elbows."

Now Felipa's arms *were* unpleasant: They were brown and lean, scratched and stained, and they terminated in a pair of determined little paws that could hold on like grim Death. I shall never forget coming upon a tableau one day out on the barren—a little Florida cow and Felipa, she holding on by the horns, and the beast with its small fore feet stubbornly set in the sand; girl pulling one way, cow the other; both silent and determined. It was a hard contest, but the girl won.

"And if you pass over her elbows, there are her feet," continued Christine languidly. For she was a sybaritic lover of the fine linens of life, that friend of mine—a pre-Raphaelite[3] lady with clinging draperies and a mediaeval clasp on her belt. Her whole being rebelled against ugliness, and the mere sight of a sharp-nosed, light-eyed woman on a cold day made her uncomfortable.

"Have we not feet too?" I replied sharply.

But I knew what she meant. Bare feet are not pleasant to the eye nowadays, whatever they may have been in the days of the ancient Greeks; and Felipa's little brown insteps were half the time torn or bruised by the thorns of the chaparral. Besides, there was always the disagreeable idea that she might step upon something cold and squirming when she prowled through the thickets knee-deep in the matted grasses. Snakes abounded, although we never saw them; but Felipa went up to their very doors, as it were, and rang the bell defiantly.

One day old Grandfather Bartolo took the child with him down to the coast: she was always wild to go to the beach, where she could gather shells and sea-beans, and chase the little ocean-birds that ran along close to the waves with that swift gliding motion of theirs, and where she could listen to the roar of the breakers. We were several miles up the salt-marsh, and to go down to the ocean was quite a voyage to Felipa. She bade us good-by joyously; then ran back to hug Christine a second time, then to the boat again; then back.

"I thought you wanted to go, child?" I said, a little impatiently; for I was reading aloud, and these small irruptions were disturbing.

"Yes," said Felipa, "I want to go; and still— Perhaps if the gracious señora would kiss me again—"

Christine only patted her cheek and told her to run away: she obeyed, but there was a wistful look in her eyes, and, even after the boat had started, her face, watching us from the stern, haunted me.

"Now that the little monkey has gone, I may be able at last to catch and fix a likeness of her," I said; "in this case a recollection is better than the changing quicksilver reality."

"You take it as a study of ugliness?"

"Do not be hard upon the child, Christine."

"Hard? Why, she adores me," said my friend, going off to her hammock under the tree.

Several days passed, and the boat returned not. I accomplished a fine amount of work, and Christine a fine amount of swinging in the hammock and dreaming. At length one afternoon I gave my final touch, and carried my sketch over to the pre-Raphaelite lady for criticism. "What do you see?" I said.

"I see a wild-looking child with yellow eyes, a mat of curly black hair, a lank little bodice, her two thin brown arms embracing a gaunt old dog with crooked legs, big feet, and turned-in toes."

"Is that all?"

"All."

"You do not see latent beauty, courage, and a possible great gulf of love in that poor wild little face?"

"Nothing of the kind," replied Christine decidedly. "I see an ugly little girl; that is all."

Felipa

The next day the boat returned, and brought back five persons, the old grandfather, Felipa, Drollo, Miguel of the island, and—Edward Bowne.

"Already?" I said.

"Tired of the Madre, Kitty; thought I would come up here and see you for a while. I knew you must be pining for me."

"Certainly," I replied; "do you not see how I have wasted away?"

He drew my arm through his and raced me down the plank-walk toward the shore, where I arrived laughing and out of breath.

"Where is Christine?" he asked.

I came back into the traces at once. "Over there in the hammock. You wish to go to the house first, I suppose?"

"Of course not."

"But she did not come to meet you, Edward, although she knew you had landed."

"Of course not, also."

"I do not understand you two."

"And of course not, a third time," said Edward, looking down at me with a smile. "What do peaceful little artists know about war?"

"Is it war?"

"Something very like it, Kitty. What is that you are carrying?"

"Oh! my new sketch. What do you think of it?"

"Good, very good. Some little girl about here, I suppose?"

"Why, it is Felipa!"

"And who is Felipa? Seems to me I have seen that old dog, though."

"Of course you have; he was in the boat with you, and so was Felipa; but she was dressed in boy's clothes, and that gives her a different look."

"Oh! that boy? I remember him. His name is Philip. He is a funny little fellow," said Edward calmly.

"Her name is Felipa, and she is not a boy or a funny little fellow at all," I replied.

"Isn't she? I thought she was both," replied Ned carelessly; and then he went off toward the hammock. I turned away, after noting Christine's cool greeting, and went back to the boat.

Felipa came bounding to meet me. "What is his name?" she demanded.

"Bowne."

"Buon—Buona; I can not say it."

"Bowne, child—Edward Bowne."

"Oh! Eduardo; I know that. Eduardo—Eduardo—a name of honey."

She flew off singing the name, followed by Drollo carrying his mistress's palmetto basket in his big patient mouth; but when I passed the house a few moments afterward she was singing, or rather talking volubly of, another name—"Miguel," and "the wife of Miguel," who were apparently important personages on the canvas of her life. As it happened, I never really saw that wife of Miguel, who seemingly had no name of her own; but I imagined her. She lived on a sand-bar in the ocean not far from the mouth of our salt-marsh; she drove pelicans like ducks with a long switch, and she had a tame eagle; she had an old horse also, who dragged the driftwood across the sand on a sledge, and this old horse seemed like a giant horse always, outlined as he was against the flat bar and the sky. She went out at dawn, and she went out at sunset, but during the middle of the burning day she sat at home and polished sea-beans, for which she obtained untold sums; she was very tall, she was very yellow, and she had but one eye. These items, one by one, had been dropped by Felipa at various times, and it was with curiosity that I gazed upon the original Miguel, the possessor of this remarkable spouse. He was a grave-eyed, yellow man, who said little and thought less, applying *cui bono?*[4] to mental much as the city man applies it to bodily exertion, and therefore achieving, I think, a finer degree of inanition. The tame eagle, the pelicans, were nothing to him; and, when I saw his lethargic, gentle countenance, my own curiosity about them seemed to die away in haze, as though I had breathed in an invisible opiate. He came, he went, and that was all; exit Miguel.

Felipa was constantly with us now. She and Drollo followed the three of us wherever we went—followed the two also whenever I staid behind to sketch, as I often staid, for in those days I was trying to catch the secret of the salt-marsh; a hopeless effort—I know it now. "Stay with me, Felipa," I said; for it was natural to suppose that the lovers might like to be alone. (I call them lovers for want of a better name, but they were more like haters; however, in such cases it is nearly the same thing.) And then Christine, hearing this, would immediately call "Felipa!" and the child would dart after them, happy as a bird. She wore her boy's suit now all the time, because the señora had said she "looked well in it." What the señora really said was, that in boy's clothes she looked less like a grasshopper. But this had been translated as above by Edward Bowne when Felipa suddenly descended upon him one day and demanded to be instantly told what the gracious lady was saying about her; for she seemed to know by intuition when we spoke of her, although we talked in English and mentioned no names. When told, her small face beamed, and she kissed Christine's hand joyfully and bounded away. Christine took out her handkerchief and wiped the spot.

"Christine," I said, "do you remember the fate of the proud girl who walked upon bread?"

"You think that I may starve for kisses some time?" said my friend, going on with the wiping.

"Not while I am alive," called out Edward from behind. His style of courtship *was* of the sledge-hammer sort sometimes. But he did not get much for it on that day; only lofty tolerance, which seemed to amuse him greatly.

Edward played with Felipa very much as if she was a rubber toy or a little trapeze performer. He held her out at arm's length in mid-air, he poised her on his shoulder, he tossed her up into the low myrtle-trees, and dangled her by her little belt over the claret-colored pools on the barren; but he could not frighten her; she only laughed and grew wilder and wilder, like a squirrel. "She has muscles and nerves of steel," he said admiringly.

"Do put her down; she is too excitable for such games." I said in French, for Felipa seemed to divine our English now. "See the color she has."

For there was a trail of dark red over the child's thin oval cheeks which made her look unlike herself. As she caught our eyes fixed upon her, she suddenly stopped her climbing and came and sat at Christine's feet. "Some day I shall wear robes like the señora's," she said, passing her hand over the soft fabric; "and I think," she added after some slow consideration, "that my face will be like the señora's too."

Edward burst out laughing. The little creature stopped abruptly and scanned his face.

"Do not tease her," I said.

Quick as a flash she veered around upon me. "He does not tease me," she said angrily in Spanish; "and, besides, what if he does? I like it." She looked at me with gleaming eyes and stamped her foot.

"What a little tempest!" said Christine.

Then Edward, man-like, began to explain. "You could not look much like this lady, Felipa," he said, "because you are so dark, you know."

"Am I dark?"

"Very dark; but many people are dark, of course; and for my part I always liked dark eyes," said this mendacious person.

"Do you like my eyes?" asked Felipa anxiously.

"Indeed I do: they are like the eyes of a dear little calf I once owned when I was a boy."

The child was satisfied, and went back to her place beside Christine. "Yes, I shall wear robes like this," she said dreamily, drawing the flowing drapery over her knees clad in the little linen trousers, and scanning the effect; "they would trail behind me—so." Her bare feet peeped out below the hem, and again we all laughed, the little brown toes looked so comical coming out from the silk and the snowy embroideries. She came down to reality again, looked at us, looked at herself, and for the first time seemed to comprehend the difference. Then suddenly she threw herself down on the ground like a little animal, and buried her head in her arms. She would not speak, she would not look up: she only relaxed one arm a little to take in Drollo, and then lay motionless. Drollo looked at us out of one eye solemnly from his uncomfortable position, as much as to say: "No use; leave her to me." So after a while we went away and left them there.

That evening I heard a low knock at my door. "Come in," I said, and Felipa entered. I hardly knew her. She was dressed in a flowered muslin gown which had probably belonged to her mother, and she wore her grandmother's stockings and large baggy slippers; on her mat of curly hair was perched a high-crowned, stiff white cap adorned with a ribbon streamer; and her lank little neck, coming out of the big gown, was decked with a chain of large sea-beans, like exaggerated lockets. She carried a

Cuban fan in her hand which was as large as a parasol, and Drollo, walking behind, fairly clanked with the chain of sea-shells which she had wound around him from head to tail. The droll tableau and the supreme pride on Felipa's countenance overcame me, and I laughed aloud. A sudden cloud of rage and disappointment came over the poor child's face: she threw her cap on the floor and stamped on it; she tore off her necklace and writhed herself out of her big flowered gown, and, running to Drollo, nearly strangled him in her fierce efforts to drag off his shell chains. Then, a half-dressed, wild little phantom, she seized me by the skirts and dragged me toward the looking-glass. "You are not pretty either," she cried. "Look at yourself! look at yourself!"

"I did not mean to laugh at you, Felipa," I said gently; "I would not laugh at any one; and it is true I am not pretty, as you say. I can never be pretty, child; but, if you will try to be more gentle, I could teach you how to dress yourself so that no one would laugh at you again. I could make you a little bright-barred skirt and a scarlet bodice: you could help, and that would teach you to sew. But a little girl who wants all this done for her must be quiet and good."

"I am good," said Felipa; "as good as everything."

The tears still stood in her eyes, but her anger was forgotten: she improvised a sort of dance around my room, followed by Drollo dragging his twisted chain, stepping on it with his big feet, and finally winding himself up into a knot around the chair-legs.

"Couldn't we make Drollo something too? dear old Drollo!" said Felipa, going to him and squeezing him in an enthusiastic embrace. I used to wonder how his poor ribs stood it: Felipa used him as a safety-valve for her impetuous feelings.

She kissed me good night, and then asked for "the other lady."

"Go to bed, child," I said; "I will give her your good night."

"But I want to kiss her too," said Felipa.

She lingered at the door and would not go; she played with the latch, and made me nervous with its clicking; at last I ordered her out. But on opening my door half an hour afterward there she was sitting on the floor outside in the darkness, she and Drollo, patiently waiting. Annoyed, but unable to reprove her, I wrapped the child in my shawl and carried her out into the moonlight, where Christine and Edward were strolling to and fro under the pines. "She will not go to bed, Christine, without kissing you," I explained.

"Funny little monkey!" said my friend, passively allowing the embrace.

"Me too," said Edward, bending down. Then I carried my bundle back satisfied.

The next day Felipa and I in secret began our labors; hers consisted in worrying me out of my life and spoiling material—mine in keeping my temper and trying to sew. The result, however, was satisfactory, never mind how we got there. I led Christine out one afternoon: Edward followed. "Do you like tableaux?" I said. "There is one I have arranged for you."

Felipa sat on the edge of the low, square-curbed Spanish well, and Drollo stood behind her, his great yellow body and solemn head serving as a background. She wore a brown petticoat barred with bright colors, and a little scarlet bodice fitting her slender waist closely; a chemisette of soft cream-color with loose sleeves covered her neck and arms, and set off the dark hues of her cheeks and eyes; and around her curly hair a red scarf was twisted, its fringed edges forming a drapery at the back of the head, which, more than anything else, seemed to bring out the latent character of her face. Brown moccasins, red stockings, and a quantity of bright beads completed her costume.

"By Jove!" cried Edward, "the little thing is almost pretty."

Felipa understood this, and a great light came into her face: forgetting her pose, she bounded forward to Christine's side. "I am pretty, then?" she said with exultation; "I *am* pretty, then, after all? For now you yourself have said it—have said it."

"No, Felipa," I interposed, "the gentleman said it." For the child had a curious habit of confounding the two identities which puzzled me then as now. But this afternoon, this happy afternoon, she was content, for she was allowed to sit at Christine's feet and look up into her fair face unmolested. I was forgotten, as usual.

"It is always so," I said to myself. But cynicism, as Mr. Aldrich [5] says, is a small brass field-piece that eventually bursts and kills the artilleryman. I knew this, having been blown up myself more than once; so I went back to my painting and forgot the world. Our world down there on the edge of the salt-marsh, however, was a small one: when two persons went out of it there was a vacuum.

One morning Felipa came sadly to my side. "They have gone away," she said.

"Yes, child."

"Down to the beach to spend all the day."

"Yes, I know it."

"And without me!"

This was the climax. I looked up. Her eyes were dry, but there was a hollow look of disappointment in her face that made her seem old; it was as though for an instant you caught what her old-woman face would be half a century on.

"Why did they not take me?" she said. "I am pretty now: she herself said it."

"They can not always take you, Felipa," I replied, giving up the point as to who had said it.

"Why not? I am pretty now: she herself said it," persisted the child. "In these clothes, you know: she herself said it. The clothes of the son of Pedro you will never see more: they are burned."

"Burned?"

"Yes, burned," replied Felipa composedly. "I carried them out on the barren and burned them. Drollo singed his paw. They burned quite nicely. But they are gone, and I am pretty now, and yet they did not take me! What shall I do?"

"Take these colors and make me a picture," I suggested. Generally, this was a prized privilege, but to-day it did not attract; she turned away, and a few moments after I saw her going down to the end of the plank-walk, where she stood gazing wistfully toward the ocean. There she staid all day, going into camp with Drollo, and refusing to come to dinner in spite of old Dominga's calls and beckonings. At last the patient old grand-mother went down herself to the end of the long walk where they were, with some bread and venison on a plate. Felipa ate but little, but Drollo, after waiting politely until she had finished, devoured everything that was left in his calmly hungry way, and then sat back on his haunches with one paw on the plate, as though for the sake of memory. Drollo's hunger was of the chronic kind; it seemed impossible either to assuage it or to fill him. There was a gaunt leanness about him which I am satisfied no amount of food could ever fatten. I think he knew it too, and that accounted for his resignation. At length, just before sunset, the boat returned, floating up the marsh with the tide, old Bartolo steering and managing the brown sails. Felipa sprang up joyfully; I thought she would spring into the boat in her eagerness. What did she receive for her long vigil? A short word or two; that was all. Christine and Edward had quarreled.

How do lovers quarrel ordinarily? But I should not ask that, for these were no ordinary lovers: they were extraordinary.

"You should not submit to her caprices so readily," I said the next day while strolling on the barren with Edward. (He was not so much cast down, however, as he might have been.)

"I adore the very ground her foot touches, Kitty."

"I know it. But how will it end?""

"I will tell you: some of these days I shall win her, and then—she will adore me."

Here Felipa came running after us, and Edward immediately challenged her to a race: a game of romps began. If Christine had been looking from her window she might have thought he was not especially disconsolate over her absence; but she was not looking. She was never looking out of anything or for anybody. She was always serenely content where she was. Edward and Felipa strayed off among the pine-trees, and gradually I lost sight of them. But as I sat sketching an hour afterward Edward came into view, carrying the child in his arms. I hurried to meet them.

"I shall never forgive myself," he said; "the little thing has fallen and injured her foot badly, I fear."

"I do not care at all," said Felipa; "I like to have it hurt. It is *my* foot, isn't it?"

These remarks she threw at me defiantly, as though I had laid claim to the member in question. I could not help laughing.

"The other lady will not laugh," said the child proudly. And in truth Christine, most unexpectedly, took up the *rôle* of nurse. She carried Felipa to her own room—for we each had a little cell opening out of the main apartment—and as white-robed Charity she shone with new radiance, "Shone" is the proper word; for through the open door of the dim cell, with the dark little face of Felipa on her shoulder, her white robe and skin seemed fairly to shine, as white lilies shine on a dark night. The old grandmother left the child in our care and watched our proceedings wistfully, very much as a dog watches the human hands that extract the thorn from the swollen foot of her puppy. She was grateful and asked no questions; in fact, thought was not one of her mental processes. She did not think much; she felt. As for Felipa, the child lived in rapture during those days in spite of her suffering. She scarcely slept at all—she was too happy: I heard her voice rippling on through the night, and Christine's low replies. She adored her beautiful nurse.

The fourth day came: Edward Bowne walked into the cell. "Go out and breathe the fresh air for an hour or two," he said in the tone more of a command than a request.

"The child will never consent," replied Christine sweetly.

"Oh, yes, she will; I will stay with her," said the young man, lifting the feverish little head on his arm and passing his hand softly over the bright eyes.

"Felipa, do you not want me?" said Christine, bending down.

"He stays; it is all the same," murmured the child.

"So it is.—Go, Christine," said Edward with a little smile of triumph.

Without a word Christine left the cell. But she did not go to walk; she came to my room, and, throwing herself on my bed, fell in a moment into a deep sleep, the reaction after her three nights of wakefulness. When she awoke it was long after dark, and I had relieved Edward in his watch.

"You will have to give it up," he said as our lily came forth at last with sleep-flushed cheeks and starry eyes shielded from the light. "The spell is broken; we have all been taking care of Felipa, and she likes one as well as the other."

Which was not true, in my case at least, since Felipa had openly derided my small strength when I lifted her, and beat off the sponge with which I attempted to bathe her hot face, "They" used no sponges, she said, only their nice cool hands; and she wished "they" would come and take care of her again. But Christine had resigned *in toto*. If Felipa did not prefer her to all others, then Felipa should not have her; she was not a common nurse. And indeed she was not. Her fair face, ideal grace, cooing voice, and the strength of her long arms and flexible hands, were like magic to the sick, and—distraction to the well; the well in this case being Edward Bowne looking in at the door.

"You love them very much, do you not, Felipa?" I said one day when the child was sitting up for the first time in a cushioned chair.

"Ah, yes; it is so strong when they carry me," she replied. But it was Edward who carried her.

"He is very strong," I said.

"Yes; and their long soft hair, with the smell of roses in it too," said Felipa dreamily. But the hair was Christine's.

"I shall love them for ever, and they will love me for ever," continued the child. "Drollo too." She patted the dog's head as she spoke, and then concluded to kiss him on his little inch of forehead; next she offered him all her medicines and lotions in turn, and he smelled at them grimly. "He likes to know what I am taking," she explained.

I went on: "You love them, Felipa, and they are fond of you. They will always remember you, no doubt."

"Remember!" cried Felipa, starting up from her cushions like a Jack-in-a-box. "They are not going away? Never! never!"

"But of course they must go some time, for—"

But Felipa was gone. Before I could divine her intent she had flung herself out of her chair down on the floor, and was crawling on her hands and knees toward the outer room. I ran after her, but she reached the door before me, and, dragging her bandaged foot behind her, drew herself toward Christine. "You are *not* going away! You are not! you are not!" she sobbed, clinging to her skirts.

Christine was reading tranquilly; Edward stood at the outer door mending his fishing-tackle. The coolness between them remained, unwarmed by so much as a breath. "Run away, child; you disturb me," said Christine, turning over a leaf. She did not even look at the pathetic little bundle at her feet. Pathetic little bundles must be taught some time what ingratitude deserves.

"How can she run, lame as she is?" said Edward from the doorway.

"You are not going away, are you? Tell me you are not," sobbed Felipa in a passion of tears, beating on the floor with one hand, and with the other clinging to Christine.

"I am not going," said Edward. "Do not sob so, you poor little thing!"

She crawled to him, and he took her up in his arms and soothed her into stillness again; then he carried her out on the barren for a breath of fresh air.

"It is a most extraordinary thing how that child confounds you two," I said. "It is a case of color-blindness, as it were—supposing you two were colors."

"Which we are not," replied Christine carelessly. "Do not stray off into mysticism, Catherine."

"It is not mysticism; it is a study of character—"

"Where there is no character," replied my friend.

I gave it up, but I said to myself: "Fate, in the next world make me one of those long, lithe, light-haired women, will you? I want to see how it feels."

Felipa's foot was well again, and spring had come. Soon we must leave our lodge on the edge of the pine-barren, our outlook over the salt-marsh, with the river sweeping up twice a day, bringing in the briny odors of the ocean; soon we should see no more the eagles far above us or hear the night-cry of the great owls, and we must go without the little fairy flowers of the barren, so small that a hundred of them scarcely made a tangible bouquet, yet what beauty! what sweetness! In my portfolio were sketches and studies of the salt-marsh, and in my heart were hopes. Somebody says somewhere: "Hope is more than a blessing; it is a duty and a virtue." But I fail to appreciate preserved hope—hope put up in cans and served out in seasons of depression. I like it fresh from the tree. And so when I hope it *is* hope, and not that well-dried, monotonous cheerfulness which makes one long to throw the persistent smilers out of the window. Felipa danced no more on the barrens; her illness had toned her down; she seemed content to sit at our feet while we talked, looking up dreamily into our faces, but no longer eagerly endeavoring to comprehend. We were there; that was enough.

"She is growing like a reed," I said; "her illness has left her weak."

"-Minded," suggested Christine.

At this moment Felipa stroked the lady's white hand tenderly and laid her brown cheek against it.

"Do you not feel reproached?" I said.

"Why? Must we give our love to whoever loves us? A fine parcel of paupers we should all be, wasting our inheritance in pitiful small change! Shall I give a thousand beggars a half hour's happiness, or shall I make one soul rich his whole life long?"

"The latter," remarked Edward, who had come up unobserved.

They gazed at each other unflinchingly. They had come to open battle during those last days, and I knew that the end was near. Their words had been cold as ice, cutting as steel, and I said to myself, "At any moment." There would be a deadly struggle, and then Christine would yield. Even I comprehended something of what that yielding would be.

"Why do they hate each other so?" Felipa said to me sadly.

"Do they hate each other?"

"Yes, for I feel it here," she answered, touching her breast with a dramatic little gesture.

"Nonsense! Go and play with your doll, child." For I had made her a respectable, orderly doll to take the place of the ungainly fetich out on the barren.

Felipa gave me a look and walked away. A moment afterward she brought the doll out of the house before my very eyes, and, going down to the end of the dock, deliberately threw it into the water; the tide was flowing out, and away went my toy-woman out of sight, out to sea.

"Well!" I said to myself. "What next?"

I had not told Felipa we were going; I thought it best to let it take her by surprise. I had various small articles of finery ready as farewell gifts, which should act as sponges to absorb her tears. But Fate took the whole matter out of my hands. This is how it happened: One evening in the jasmine arbor, in the fragrant darkness of the warm spring night, the end came; Christine was won. She glided in like a wraith, and I, divining at once what had happened, followed her into her little room, where I found her lying on her bed, her hands clasped on her breast, her eyes open and veiled in soft shadows, her white robe drenched with dew. I kissed her fondly—I never could help loving her then or now—and next I went out to find Edward. He had been kind to me all my poor gray life; should I not go to him now? He was still in the arbor, and I sat down by his side quietly; I knew that the words would come in time. They came; what a flood! English was not enough for him. He poured forth his love in the rich-voweled Spanish tongue also; it has sounded doubly sweet to me ever since.

> "Have you felt the wool of the beaver?
> Or swan's down ever?
> Or have smelt the bud o' the brier?
> Or the nard in the fire?
> Or ha' tasted the bag o' the bee?
> Oh so white, oh so soft, oh so sweet is she!"

said the young lover; and I, listening there in the dark fragrant night, with the dew heavy upon me, felt glad that the old simple-hearted love was not entirely gone from our tired metallic world.

It was late when we returned to the house. After reaching my room I found that I had left my cloak in the arbor. It was a strong fabric; the dew could not hurt it, but it could hurt my sketching materials and various trifles in the wide inside pockets—*objets de luxe*[6] to me, souvenirs of happy times, little artistic properties that I hang on the walls of my poor studio when in the city. I went softly out into the darkness again and sought the arbor; groping on the ground I found, not the cloak, but—Felipa! She was crouched under the foliage, face downward; she would not move or answer.

"What is the matter, child?" I said, but she would not speak. I tried to draw her from her lair, but she tangled herself stubbornly still farther among the thorny vines, and I could not move her. I touched her neck; it was cold. Frightened, I ran back to the house for a candle.

"Go away," she said in a low hoarse voice when I flashed the light over her. "I know all, and I am going to die. I have eaten the poison things in your box, and just now a snake came on my neck and I let him. He has bitten me, and I am glad. Go away; I am going to die."

I looked around; there was my color-case rifled and empty, and the other articles were scattered on the ground. "Good Heavens, child!" I creid, "what have you eaten?"

"Enough," replied Felipa gloomily, "I knew they were poisons; you told me so. And I let the snake stay."

By this time the household, aroused by my hurried exit with the candle, came toward the arbor. The moment Edward appeared Felipa rolled herself up like a hedgehog again and refused to speak. But the old grandmother knelt down and drew the little crouching figure into her arms with gentle tenderness, smoothing its hair and murmuring loving words in her soft dialect.

"What is it?" said Edward; but even then his eyes were devouring Christine, who stood in the dark vine-wreathed doorway like a picture in a frame. I explained.

Christine smiled. "Jealousy," she said in a low voice. "I am not surprised."

But at the first sound of her voice Felipa had started up, and, wrenching herself free from old Dominga's arms, threw herself at Christine's feet. "Look at *me* so," she cried—"me too; do not look at him. He has forgotten poor Felipa; he does not love her any more. But *you* do not forget, señora; *you* love me—*you* love me. Say you do, or I shall die!"

We were all shocked by the pallor and the wild, hungry look of her uplifted face. Edward bent down and tried to lift her in his arms; but when she saw him a sudden fierceness came into her eyes; they shot out yellow light and seemed to narrow to a point of flame. Before we knew it she had turned, seized something, and plunged it into his encircling arm. It was my little Venetian dagger.

We sprang forward; our dresses were spotted with the fast-flowing blood; but Edward did not relax his hold on the writhing, wild little body he held until it lay exhausted in his arms. "I am glad I did it," said the child, looking up into his face with her inflexible eyes. "Put me down—put me down, I say, by the gracious señora, that I may die with the trailing of her white robe over me." And the old grandmother with trembling hands received her and laid her down mutely at Christine's feet.

AH, WELL! Felipa did not die. The poisons racked but did not kill her, and the snake must have spared the little thin brown neck so despairingly offered to him. We went away; there was nothing for us to do but to go away as quickly as possible and leave her to her kind. To the silent old grandfather I said: "It will pass; she is but a child."

"She is nearly twelve, señora. Her mother was married at thirteen."

"But she loved them both alike, Bartolo. It is nothing; she does not know."

"You are right, lady; she does not know," replied the old man slowly; "but *I* know. It was two loves, and the stronger thrust the knife."

THE STREET OF THE HYACINTH

I

IT WAS A STREET in Rome—narrow, winding, not overclean. Two vehicles meeting there could pass only by grazing the doors and windows on
either side, after the usual excited whip-cracking and shouts which make
the new-comer imagine, for his first day or two, that he is proceeding at a
perilous speed through the sacred city of the soul.

But two vehicles did not often meet in the street of the Hyacinth.[1] It
was not a thoroughfare, not even a convenient connecting link; it skirted
the back of the Pantheon,[2] the old buildings on either side rising so high
against the blue that the sun never came down lower than the fifth line of
windows, and looking up from the pavement was like looking up from the
bottom of a well. There was no foot-walk, of course; even if there had been
one no one would have used it, owing to the easy custom of throwing from
the windows a few ashes and other light trifles for the city refuse-carts,
instead of carrying them down the long stairs to the door below. They
must be in the street at an appointed hour, must they not? Very well,
then—there they were; no one but an unreasonable foreigner would
dream of objecting.

But unreasonable foreigners seldom entered the street of the Hyacinth. There were, however, two who lived there one winter not long ago,
and upon a certain morning in the January of that winter a third came to
see these two. At least he asked for them, and gave two cards to the Italian

maid who answered his ring; but when, before he had time to even seat himself, the little curtain over the parlor door was raised again, and Miss Macks entered, she came alone. Her mother did not appear. The visitor was not disturbed by being obliged to begin conversation immediately; he was an old Roman sojourner, and had stopped fully three minutes at the end of the fourth flight of stairs to regain his breath before he mounted the fifth and last to ring Miss Macks's bell. Her card was tacked upon the door: "Miss Ettie F. Macks." He surveyed it with disfavor, while the little, loose-hung bell rang a small but exceedingly shrill and ill-tempered peal, like the barking of a small cur. "Why in the world doesn't she put her mother's card here instead of her own?" he said to himself. "Or, if her own, why not simply 'Miss Macks,' without that nickname?"

But Miss Macks's mother had never possessed a visiting-card in her life. Miss Macks was the visiting member of the family; and this was so well understood at home, that she had forgotten that it might not be the same abroad. As to the "Ettie," having been called so always, it had not occurred to her to make a change. Her name was Ethelinda Faith, Mrs. Macks having thus combined euphony and filial respect—the first title being her tribute to aesthetics, the second her tribute to the memory of her mother.

"I am so very glad to see you, Mr. Noel," said Miss Macks, greeting her visitor with much cordial directness of voice and eyes. "I have been expecting you. But you have waited so long—three days!"

Raymond Noel, who thought that under the circumstances he had been unusually courteous and prompt, was rather surprised to find himself thus put at once upon the defensive.

"We are not always able to carry out our wishes immediately, Miss Macks," he replied, smiling a little. "I was hampered by several previously made engagements."

"Yes; but this was a little different, wasn't it? This was something important—not like an invitation to lunch or dinner, or the usual idle society talk."

He looked at her; she was quite in earnest.

"I suppose it to be different," he answered. "You must remember how little you have told me."

"I though I told you a good deal! However, the atmosphere of a reception is no place for such subjects, and I can understand that you did not take it in. That is the reason I asked you to come and see me here. Shall I begin at once? It seems rather abrupt."

"I enjoy abruptness; I have not heard any for a long time."

"That I can understand, too; I suppose the society here is all finished off—there are no rough ends."

"There are ends. If not rough, they are often sharp."

But Miss Macks did not stop to analyze this; she was too much occupied with her own subject.

"I will begin immediately, then," she said. "It will be rather long; but if you are to understand me you ought, of course, to know the whole."

"My chair is very comfortable," replied Noel, placing his hat and gloves on the sofa near him, and taking an easy position with his head back.

Miss Macks thought that he ought to have said, "The longer it is, the more interesting," or something of that sort. She had already described him to her mother as "not over-polite. Not rude in the least, you know—as far as possible from that; wonderfully smooth-spoken; but yet, somehow—awfully indifferent." However, he was Raymond Noel; and that, not his politeness or impoliteness, was her point.

"To begin with, then, Mr. Noel, a year ago I had never read one word you have written; I had never even heard of you. I suppose you think it strange that I should tell you this so frankly; but, in the first place, it will give you a better idea of my point of view, and, in the second, I feel a friendly interest in your taking measures to introduce your writings into the community where I lived. It is a very intelligent community. Naturally, a writer wants his articles read. What else does he write them for?"

"Perhaps a little for his own entertainment," suggested her listener.

"Oh no! He would never take so much trouble just for that."

"On the contrary, many would take any amount just for that. Successfully to entertain one's self—that is one of the great successes of life."

Miss Macks gazed at him; she had a very direct gaze.

"This is just mere talk," she said, not impatiently, but in a business-like tone. "We shall never get anywhere if you take me up so. It is not that your remarks are not very cultivated and interesting, and all that, but simply that I have so much to tell you."

"Perhaps I can be cultivated and interesting dumbly. I will try."

"You are afraid I am going to be diffuse; I see that. So many women are diffuse! But I shall not be, because I have been thinking for six months just what I should say to you. It was very lucky that I went with Mrs. Lawrence to that reception where I met you. But if it had not happened as it did I should have found you out all the same. I should have looked for your address at all the bankers', and if it was not there I should have inquired at all the hotels. But it was delightful luck getting hold of you in this way almost the very minute I enter Rome!"

She spoke so simply and earnestly that Noel did not say that he was immensely honored, and so forth, but merely bowed his acknowledgments.

"To go back. I shall give you simply heads,"[3] pursued Miss Macks. "If you want details, ask, and I will fill them in. I come from the West. Tuscolee Falls is the name of our town. We had a farm there, but we did not do well with it after Mr. Spurr's death, so we rented it out. That is how I come to have so much leisure. I have always had a great deal of ambition; by that I mean that I did not see why things that had once been done could not be done again. It seemed to me that the point was—just determination. And then, of course, I always had the talent. I made pictures when I was a very little girl. Mother has them still, and I can show them to you. It is just like all the biographics, you know. They always begin in childhood, and astonish the family. Well, I had my first lessons from a drawing-teacher who spent a summer in Tuscolee. I can show you what I did while with him. Then I attended, for four years, the Young Ladies' Seminary in the county-town, and took lessons while there. I may as well be perfectly frank and tell the whole, which is that everybody was astonished at my progress, and that I was myself. All sorts of things are prophesied out there about my future. You see, the neighborhood is a very generous-spirited one, and they like to think they have discovered a genius at their own doors. My telling you all this sounds, I know, rather conceited, Mr. Noel. But if you could see my motive, and how entirely without conceit my idea of myself really is, you would hold me free from that charge. It is only that I want you to know absolutely the whole."

"I quite understand," answered her visitor.

"Well, I hope you do. I went on at home after that by myself, and I did a good deal. I work pretty rapidly, you see. Then came my last lessons, from a third teacher. He was a young man from New York. He had consumption, poor fellow! and cannot last long. He wasn't of much use to me in actual work. His ideas were completely different from those of my other teachers, and, indeed, from my own. He was unreliable, too, and his temper was uneven. However, I had a good deal of respect for his opinion, and *he* told me to get your art-articles and read them. It wasn't easy. Some of them are scattered about in the magazines and papers, you know. However, I am pretty determined, and I kept at it until I got them all. Well, they made a great impression upon me. You see, they were new." She paused. "But I doubt, Mr. Noel, whether we should ever entirely agree," she added, looking at him reflectively.

"That is very probable, Miss Macks."

Miss Macks thought this an odd reply. "He is so queer, with all his smoothness!" she said to her mother afterwards. "He never says what you think he will say. Now, any one would suppose that he would have answered that he would try to make me agree, or something like that. Instead, he just gave it right up without trying! But I expect he sees how independent I am, and that I don't intend to *reflect any* one.

"Well, they made a great impression," she resumed. "And as you seemed to think, Mr. Noel, that no one could do well in painting who had not seen and studied the old pictures over here, I made up my mind to come over at any cost, if it was a possible thing to bring it about. It wasn't easy, but—here we are. In the lives of all—almost all—artists, I have noticed—haven't you?—that there comes a time when they have to live on hope and their own pluck more than upon anything tangible that the present has to offer. They have to take that risk. Well, I have taken it; I took it when we left America. And now I will tell you what it is I want from *you*. I haven't any hesitation in asking, because I am sure you will feel interested in a case like mine, and because it was your writings really that brought me here, you know. And so, then, first: I would like your opinion of all that I have done so far. I have brought everything with me to show you. Second: I want your advice as to the best teacher; I suppose there is a great choice in Rome. Third: I should be glad if you would give a general oversight to all I do for the next year. And last, if you would be so kind, I should much enjoy making visits with you to all the galleries and hearing your opinions again by word of mouth, because that is always so much more vivid, you know, than the printed page."

"My dear Miss Macks! you altogether over-estimate my powers," said Noel, astounded by these far-reaching demands, so calmly and confidently made.

"Yes, I know. Of course it strikes you so—strikes you as a great compliment that I should wish to put myself so entirely in your hands," answered Miss Macks, smiling. "But you must give up thinking of me as the usual young lady; you must not think of me in that way any more than I shall think of you as the usual young gentleman. You will never meet me at a reception again; now that I have found *you,* I shall devote myself entirely to my work."

"An alarming girl!" said Noel to himself. But, even as he said it, he knew that, in the ordinary acceptation of the term at least, Miss Macks was not alarming.

She was twenty-two; in some respects she looked older, in others much younger, than most girls of that age. She was tall, slender, erect, but not especially graceful. Her hands were small and finely shaped, but thin. Her features were well cut; her face oval. Her gray eyes had a clear directness in their glance, which, combined with the other expressions of her face, told the experienced observer at once that she knew little of what is called "the world." For, although calm, it was a deeply confident glance; it showed that the girl was sure that she could take care of herself, and even several others also, through any contingencies that might arise. She had little color; but her smooth complexion was not pale—it was slightly brown. Her mouth was small, her teeth small and very white. Her light-brown hair was drawn back smoothly from her forehead, and drawn up smoothly behind, its thickness braided in a close knot on the top of her head. This compact coiffure, at a time when most feminine foreheads in Rome and elsewhere were shaded almost to the eyebrows by curling locks, and when the arched outline of the head was left unbroken, the hair being coiled in a low knot behind, made Miss Macks look somewhat peculiar. But she was not observant of fashion's changes. That had been the mode in Tuscolee; she had grown accustomed to it; and, as her mind was full of other things, she had not considered this one. One or two persons, who noticed her on the voyage over, said to themselves, "If that girl had more color, and if she was graceful, and if she was a little more womanly—that is, if she would not look at everything in such a direct, calm, impartial, impersonal sort of way—she would be almost pretty."

But Miss Macks continued without color and without grace, and went on looking at things as impersonally and impartially as ever.

"I shall be most happy, of course, to do anything that I can," Noel had answered. Then to make a diversion, "Shall I not have the pleasure of seeing Mrs. Macks?" he asked.

"Mrs. Macks? Oh, you mean mother. My mother's name is Spurr—Mrs. Spurr. My father died when I was a baby, and some years afterwards she married Mr. Spurr. She is now again a widow. Her health is not good, and she sees almost no one, thank you."

"I suppose you are much pleased with the picturesqueness of Roman life, and—ah—your apartment?" he went on.

"Pleased?" said Miss Macks, looking at him in wonder. "With our apartment? We get along with it because we must; there seems to be no other way to live in Rome. The idea of having only a story of a house, and not a whole house to ourselves, is dreadful to mother; she cannot get used to it. And with so many families below us—we have a clock-mender, a dress-maker, an engraver, a print-seller, and a cobbler—and only one pair of stairs, it does seem to me dreadfully public."

"You must look upon the stairway as a street," said Noel. "You have established yourselves in a very short time."

"Oh yes. I got an agent, and looked at thirty places the very first day. I speak Italian a little, so I can manage the house-keeping; I began to study it as soon as we thought of coming, and I studied hard. But all this is of secondary importance; the real thing is to get to work. Will you look at my paintings now?" she said, rising as if to go for them.

"Thanks; I fear I have hardly time to-day," said Noel. He was thinking whether it would be better to decline clearly and in so many words the office she had thrust upon him, or trust to time to effect the same without an open refusal. He decided upon the latter course; it seemed the easier, and also the kinder to her.

"Well, another day, then," said Miss Macks, cheerfully, taking her seat again. "But about a teacher?"

"I hardly know—"

"Oh, Mr. Noel! you *must* know."

And, in truth, he did know. It came into his mind to give her the name of a good teacher, and then put all further responsibilities upon him.

Miss Macks wrote down the name in a clear, ornamental handwriting.

"I am glad it isn't a foreigner," she said. "I don't believe I should get on with a foreigner."

"But it is a foreigner."

"Why, it's an English name, isn't it?—Jackson."

"Yes, he is an Englishman. But isn't an Englishman a foreigner in Rome?"

"Oh, you take that view? Now, to me, America and—well, yes, perhaps England, too, are the nations. Everything else is foreign."

"The English would be very much obliged to you," said Noel, laughing.

"Yes, I know I am more liberal than most Americans; I really like the English," said Miss Macks, calmly. "But we keep getting off the track. Let me see— Oh yes. As I shall go to see this Mr. Jackson this afternoon, and as it is not likely that he will be ready to begin to-morrow, will you come then and look at my pictures? Or would you rather commence with a visit to one of the galleries?"

Raymond Noel was beginning to be amused. If she had shown the faintest indication of knowing how much she was asking, if she had betrayed the smallest sign of a desire to secure his attention as Raymond Noel personally, and not simply the art authority upon whom she had pinned her faith, his disrelish for various other things about her would have been heightened into utter dislike, and it is probable that he would never have entered the street of the Hyacinth again. But she was so unaware of any intrusion, or any exorbitance in her demands, probably so ignorant of— certainly so indifferent to—the degree of perfection (perfection of the most quiet kind, however) visible in the general appearance and manner of the gentleman before her, that (he said to himself) he might as well have been one of her own Tuscolee farmers, for all she knew to the contrary. The whole affair was unusual; and Noel rather liked the unusual, if it was not loud—and Miss Macks was, at least, not loud; she was dressed plainly in black, and she had the gift of a sweet voice, which, although very clear, was low-toned. Noel was an observer of voices, and he had noticed hers the first time he heard her speak. While these thoughts were passing through his mind, he was answering that he feared his engagements for the next day would, unfortunately, keep him from putting himself at her service.

Her face fell; she looked much disappointed.

"Is it going to be like this all the time?" she asked, anxiously. "Are you always engaged?"

"In Rome, in the winter, one generally has small leisure. It will be the same with you, Miss Macks, when you have been here a while longer; you will see. As to the galleries, Mr. Jackson has a class, I think, and probably the pupils will visit them all under his charge; you will find that very satisfactory."

"But I don't want Mr. Jackson for the galleries; I want *you,*" said Miss Macks. "I have studied your art criticisms until I know them by heart, and I have a thousand questions to ask about every picture you have mentioned. Why, Mr. Noel, I came to Europe to see you!"

Raymond Noel was rather at a loss what to answer to this statement, made by a girl who looked at him so soberly and earnestly with clear gray eyes. It would be of no avail again to assure her that his opinions would be of small use to her; as she had said herself, she was very determined, and she had made up her mind that they would be of great use instead of small. Her idea must wear itself out by degrees. He would try to make the degrees easy. He decided that he would have a little private talk with Jackson, who was a very honest fellow; and, for the present, he would simply take leave.

"You are very kind," he said, rising. "I appreciate it, I assure you. It has made me stay an unconscionable time. I hope you will find Rome all you expected, and I am sure you will; all people of imagination like Rome. As to the galleries, yes, certainly; a——ah——little later. You must not forget the various small precautions necessary here as regards the fever, you know."

"Rome will not be at all what I expected if *you* desert me," answered Miss Macks, paying no attention to his other phrases. She had risen, also, and was now confronting him at a distance of less than two feet; as she was tall, her eyes were not much below the level of his own.

"How can a man desert when he has never enlisted?" thought Noel, humorously. But he kept his thought to himself, and merely replied, as he took his hat: "Probably you will desert me; you will find out how useless I am. You must not be too hard upon us, Miss Macks; we Americans lose much of our native energy if we stay long over here."

"Hard?" she answered—"hard? Why, Mr. Noel, I am absolutely at your feet!"

He looked at her, slightly startled, although his face showed nothing of it; was she, after all, going to—But no; her sentence had been as impersonal as those which had preceded it.

"All I said about having contrary opinions, and all that, amounts to nothing," she went on, thereby relieving him from the necessity of making reply. "I desire but one thing, and that is to have you guide me. And I don't believe you are really going to refuse. You haven't an unkind face, although you *have* got such a cold way! Why, think of it: here I have come all this long distance, bringing mother, too, just to study, and to see you. I shall study hard; I have a good deal of perseverance. It took a good deal to get here in the first place, for we are poor. But I don't mind that at all; the only thing I should mind, the only thing that would take my courage away, would be to have you desert me. In all the troubles that I thought might happen, I assure you, I never once thought of *that*, Mr. Noel. I thought, of course, you would be interested. Why, in your books you are all interest. Are you different from your books?"

"I fear, Miss Macks, that writers are seldom good illustrations of their own doctrines," replied Noel.

"That would make them hypocrites. I don't believe you are a hypocrite. I expect you have a habit of running yourself down. Many gentlemen do that, and then they think they will be cried up. I don't believe you are going to be unkind; you *will* look at the pictures I have brought with me, won't you?"

"Mr. Jackson's opinion is worth a hundred of mine, Miss Macks; my knowledge is not technical. But, of course, if you wish it, I shall take pleasure in obeying." He added several conventional remarks as filling-up, and then, leaving his compliments for "your mother"—he could not recall the name she had given—he went towards the little curtained door.

She had brightened over his promise.

"You will come Monday, then, to see them, won't you?—as you cannot come to-morrow," she said, smiling happily.

When she smiled (and she did not smile often), showing her little white, child-like teeth, she looked very young. He was fairly caught, and answered, "Yes." But he immediately qualified it with a "That is, if it is possible."

"Oh, *make* it possible," she answered, still smiling and going with him herself to the outer door instead of summoning the maid. The last he saw of her she was standing in the open doorway, her face bright and contented, watching him as he went down. He did not go to see her pictures on the following Monday; he sent a note of excuse.

Some days later he met her.

"Ah, you are taking one of the delightful walks?" he said. "I envy you your first impressions of Rome."

"I am not taking a walk—that is, for pleasure," she answered. "I am trying to find some vegetables that mother can eat; the vegetables here are so foreign! You don't know how disappointed I was, Mr. Noel, when I got your note. It was such a setback! Why couldn't you come right home with me now—that is, after I have got the vegetables—and see the pictures? It wouldn't take you fifteen minutes."

It was only nine o'clock, and a beautiful morning. He thought her such a novelty, with her urgent invitations, her earnest eyes, and her basket on her arm, that he felt the impulse to walk beside her a while through the old streets of Rome; he was very fond of the old streets, and was curious to see whether she would notice the colors and outlines that made their picturesqueness. She noticed nothing but the vegetable-stalls, and talked of nothing but her pictures.

He still went on with her, however, amused by the questions she put to the vegetable-dealers (questions compiled from the phrase-books), and the calm contempt with which she surveyed the Roman artichokes they offered. At last she secured some beans, but of sadly Italian aspect, and Noel took the basket. He was much entertained by the prospect of carrying it home. He remarked to himself that of all the various things he had done in Rome this was the freshest. They reached the street of the Hyacinth and walked down its dark centre.

"I see you have the sun," he said, looking up.

"Yes; that is the reason we took the top floor. We will go right up. Everything is ready."

He excused himself.

"Some other time."

They had entered the dusky hallway. She looked at him without replying; then held out her hand for the basket. He gave it to her.

"I suppose you have seen Mr. Jackson?" he said, before taking leave.

She nodded, but did not speak. Then he saw two tears rise in her eyes.

"My dear young lady, you have been doing too much! You are tired. Don't you know that that is very dangerous in Rome?"

"It is nothing. Mother has been sick, and I have been up with her two nights. Then, as she did not like our servant, I dismissed her, and as we have not got any one else yet, I have had a good deal to do. But I don't mind that at all, beyond being a little tired; it was only your refusing to come up, when it seemed so easy. But never mind; you will come another day." And, repressing the tears, she smiled faintly, and held out her hand for good-bye.

"I will come now," said Noel. He took the basket again, and went up the stairs. He was touched by the two tears, but, at the same time, vexed with himself for being there at all. There was not one chance in five hundred that her work was worth anything; and, in the four hundred and ninety-nine, pray what was he to say?

She brought him everything. They were all in the four hundred and ninety-nine. In his opinion they were all extremely and essentially bad.

It was one of Raymond Noel's beliefs that, where women were concerned, a certain amount of falsity was sometimes indispensable. There were occasions when a man could no more tell the bare truth to a woman than he could strike her; the effect would be the same as a blow. He was an excellent evader when he chose to exert himself, and he finally got away from the little high-up apartment without disheartening or offending its young mistress, and without any very black record of direct untruth—

what is more, without any positive promise as to the exact date of his next visit. But all this was a good deal of trouble to take for a girl he did not know or care for.

Soon afterwards he met, at a small party, Mrs. Lawrence.

"Tell me a little, please, about the young lady to whom you presented me at Mrs. Dudley's reception—Miss Macks," he said, after some conversation.

"A little is all I can tell," replied Mrs. Lawrence. "She brought a letter of introduction to me from a far-away cousin of mine, who lives out West somewhere, and whom I have not seen for twenty years; my home, you know, is in New Jersey. How they learned I was in Rome I cannot imagine; but, knowing it, I suppose they thought that Miss Macks and I would meet, as necessarily as we should if together in their own village. The letter assures me that the girl is a great genius; that all she needs is an opportunity. They even take the ground that it will be a privilege for me to know her! But I am mortally tired of young geniuses; we have so many here in Rome! So I told her at once that I knew nothing of modern art—in fact, detested it—but that in any other way I should be delighted to be of use. And I took her to Mrs. Dudley's *omnium gatherum*." [4]

"Then you have not been to see her?"

"No; she came to see me. I sent cards, of course; I seldom call. What did you think of her?"

"I thought her charming," replied Noel, remembering the night-vigils, the vegetables, the dismissed servant, and the two tears of the young stranger—remembering, also, her extremely bad pictures.

"I am glad she has found a friend in you," replied Mrs. Lawrence. "She was very anxious to meet you; she looks upon you as a great authority. If she really has talent—of course *you* would know—you must tell me. It is not talent I am so tired of, but the pretence of it. She struck me, although wofully unformed and awkward, of course, as rather intelligent."

"She is intelligence personified," replied Noel, qualifying it mentally with "intelligence without cultivation." He perceived that the young stranger would have no help from Mrs. Lawrence, and he added to himself: "And totally inexperienced purity alone in Rome." To be sure, there was the mother; but he had a presentiment that this lady, as guardian, would not be of much avail.

The next day he went down to Naples for a week with some friends. Upon his return he stopped at Horace Jackson's studio one afternoon as he happened to be passing. His time was really much occupied; he was a favorite in Rome. To his surprise, Jackson seemed to think that Miss Macks had talent. Her work was very crude, of course; she had been brutally taught; teachers of that sort should simply be put out of existence with the bowstring. He had turned her back to the alphabet; and, in time, they— would see what she could do.

Horace Jackson was English by birth, but he had lived in Italy almost all his life. He was a man of forty-five—short, muscular, his thick, rather shaggy, beard and hair mixed with gray; there was a permanent frown over his keen eyes, and his rugged face had marked lines. He was a man of strong individuality. He had the reputation of being the most incorruptibly honest teacher in Rome. Noel had known him a long time, and liked him, ill-tempered though he was. Jackson, however, had not shown any especial signs of a liking for Noel in return. Perhaps he thought that, in the nature of things, there could not be much in common between a middle-aged, morose teacher, who worked hard, who knew nothing of society, and did not want to know, and a man like Raymond Noel. True, Noel was also an artist—that is, a literary one. But he had been highly successful in his own field, and it was understood, also, that he had an income of his own by inheritance, which, if not opulence, was yet sufficiently large to lift him quite above the usual *res angusta*⁵ of his brethren in the craft. In addition, Jackson considered Noel a fashionable man; and that would have been a barrier, even if there had been no other.

As the Englishman seemed to have some belief in Miss Macks, Noel did not say all he had intended to say; he did, however, mention that the young lady had a mistaken idea regarding any use he could be to her; he should be glad if she could be undeceived.

"I think she will be," said Jackson, with a grim smile, giving his guest a glance of general survey that took him in from head to foot; "she isn't dull."

Noel understood the glance, and smiled at Jackson's idea of him.

"She is not dull, certainly," he answered. "But she is rather—inexperienced." He dismissed the subject, went home, dressed, and went out to dinner.

One morning, a week later, he was strolling through the Doria gallery.[6] He was in a bad humor. There were many people in the gallery that day, but he was not noticing them; he detested a crowd. After a while some one touched his coat-sleeve from behind. He turned, with his calmest expression upon his face; when he was in an ill-humor he was impassively calm. It was Miss Macks, her eyes eager, her face flushed with pleasure.

"Oh, what good luck!" she said. "And to think that I almost went to the Borghese, and might have missed you! I am so delighted that I don't know what to do. I am actually trembling." And she was. "I have so longed to see these pictures with you," she went on. "I have had a real aching disappointment about it, Mr. Noel."

Again Noel felt himself slightly touched by her earnestness. She looked prettier than usual, too, on account of the color.

"I always feel a self-reproach when with you, Miss Macks," he answered—"you so entirely over-estimate me."

"Well, if I do, live up to it," she said, brightly.

"Only an archangel could do that."

"An archangel who knows about Art! I have been looking at the Caraccis; what do you think of them?"

"Never mind the Caraccis; there are better things to look at here." And then he made the circuit of the gallery with her slowly, pointing out the best pictures. During this circuit he talked to her as he would have talked to an intelligent child who had been put in his charge in order to learn something of the paintings; he used the simplest terms, mentioned the marked characteristics, and those only of the different schools, and spoke a few words of unshaded condemnation here and there. All he said was in broad, plain outlines. His companion listened earnestly. She gave him a close attention, almost always a comprehension, but seldom agreement. Her disagreement she did not express in words, but he could read it in her eyes. When they had seen everything—and it took some time—

"Now," he said, "I want you to tell me frankly, and without reference to anything I have said, your real opinion of several pictures I shall name—that is, if you can remember?"

"I remember everything. I always remember."

"Very well. What do you think, then, of the Raphael double portrait?"

"I think it very ugly."

"And the portrait of Andrea Doria, by Sebastian del Piombo?"

"Uglier still."

"And the Velasquez?"

"Ugliest of all."

"And the two large Claude Lorraines?"

"Rather pretty; but insipid. There isn't any reality or meaning in them."

"The Memling?"

"Oh, *that* is absolutely hideous, Mr. Noel; it hasn't a redeeming point."[7]

Raymond Noel laughed with real amusement, and almost forgot his ill-humor.

"When you have found anything you really admire in the galleries here, Miss Macks, will you tell me?"

"Of course I will. I should wish to do so in any case, because, if you are to help me, you ought to thoroughly understand me. There is one thing more I should like to ask," she added, as they turned towards the door, "and that is that you would not call me Miss Macks. I am not used to it, and it sounds strangely; no one ever called me that in Tuscolee."

"What did they call you in Tuscolee?"

"They called me Miss Ettie; my name is Ethelinda Faith. But my friends and older people called me just 'Ettie'; I wish you would, too."

"I am certainly older," replied Noel, gravely (he was thirty-three); "but I do not like Ettie. With your permission, I will call you Faith."

"Do you like it? It's so old-fashioned! It was my grandmother's name."

"I like it immensely," he answered, leading the way down-stairs.

"You can't think how I've enjoyed it," she said, warmly, at the door.

"Yet you do not agree with my opinions?"

"Not yet. But all the same it was perfectly delightful. Good-bye."

He had signalled for a carriage, as he had, as usual, an engagement. She preferred to walk. He drove off, and did not see her for ten days.

Then he came upon her again and again in the Doria gallery. He was fond of the Doria, and often went there, but he had no expectation of meeting Miss Macks this time; he fancied that she followed a system, going through her list of galleries in regular order, one by one, and in that case she would hardly have reached the Doria on a second round. Her list was a liberal one; it included twenty. Noel had supposed that there were but nine in Rome.

This time she did not see him; she had some sheets of manuscript in her hand, and was alternately reading from them and looking at one of the pictures. She was much absorbed. After a while he went up.

"Good-morning, Miss Macks."

She started; her face changed, and the color rose. She was as delighted as before. She immediately showed him her manuscript. There he beheld, written out in her clear handwriting, all he had said of the Doria pictures, page after page of it; she had actually reproduced from memory his entire discourse of an hour.

There were two blank spaces left.

"There, I could not exactly remember," said Miss Macks, apologetically. "If you would tell me, I should be so glad; then it would be quite complete."

"I shall never speak again. I am frightened," said Noel. He had taken the manuscript, and was looking it over with inward wonder.

"Oh, please do."

"Why do you care for my opinions, Miss Macks, when you do not agree with them?" he asked, his eyes still on the pages.

"You said you would call me Faith. Why do I care? Because they are yours, of course."

"Then you think I know?"

"I am sure you do."

"But it follows, then, that you do not."

"Yes; and there is where my work comes in; I have got to study up to you. I am afraid it will take a long time, won't it?"

"That depends upon you. It would take very little if you would simply accept noncombatively."

"Without being convinced? That I could never do."

"You want to be convinced against your will?"

"No; my will itself must be convinced to its lowest depths."

"This manuscript won't help you."

"Indeed, it has helped me greatly already. I have been here twice with it. I wrote it out the evening after I saw you. I only wish I had one for each of the galleries! But I feel differently now about asking you to go."

"I told you you would desert me."

"No, it is not that. But Mr. Jackson says you are much taken up with the fashionable society here, and that I must not expect you to give me so much of your time as I had hoped for. He says, too, that your art articles will do me quite as much good as you yourself, and more; because you have a way, he says, like all society men, of talking as if you had no real convictions at all, and that would unsettle me."

"Jackson is an excellent fellow," replied Noel; "I like him extremely. And when would you like to go to the Borghese?"

"Oh, will you take me?" she said, joyfully. "Any time. To-morrow."

"Perhaps, Mrs.—your mother, will go, also," he suggested, still unable to recall the name; he could think of nothing but "stirrup," and of course it was not that.

"I don't believe she would care about it," answered the daughter.

"She might. You know we make more of mothers here than we do in America," he ventured to remark.

"That is impossible," said Miss Macks, calmly. Evidently she thought his remark frivolous.

He abandoned the subject, and did not take it up again. It was not his duty to instruct Miss Macks in foreign customs. In addition, she was not only not "in society," but she was an art student, and art students had, or took, privileges of their own in Rome.

"At what hour shall I come for you?" he said.

"It will be out of your way to come for me; I will meet you at the gallery," she answered, radiant at the prospect.

He hesitated, then accepted her arrangement of things. He would take her way, not his own. The next morning he went to the Borghese Palace ten minutes before the appointed time. But she was already there.

"Mother thought she would not come out—the galleries tire her so," she said; "but she was pleased to be remembered."

They spent an hour and a half among the pictures. She listened to all he said with the same earnest attention.

Within the next five weeks Raymond Noel met Miss Macks at other galleries. It was always very businesslike—they talked of nothing but the pictures; in truth, her systematic industry kept him strictly down to the subject in hand. He learned that she made the same manuscript copies of all he said, and, when he was not with her, she went alone, armed with these documents, and worked hard. Her memory was remarkable; she soon knew the names and the order of all the pictures in all the galleries, and had made herself acquainted with an outline, at least, of the lives of all the artists who had painted them. During this time she was, of course, going on with her lessons; but as he had not been again to see Jackson, or to the street of the Hyacinth, he knew nothing of her progress. He did not want to know; she was in Jackson's hands, and Jackson was quite competent to attend to her.

In these five weeks he gave to Miss Macks only the odd hours of his leisure. He made her no promises; but when he found that he should have a morning or half-morning unoccupied, he sent a note to the street of the Hyacinth, naming a gallery and an hour. She was always promptly there, and so pleased, that there was a sort of fresh aroma floating through the time he spent with her, after all—but a mild one.

To give the proper position to the place the young art student's light figure occupied on the canvas of Raymond Noel's winter, it should be mentioned that he was much interested in a French lady who was spending some months in Rome. He had known her and admired her for a long time; but this winter he was seeing more of her, some barriers which had heretofore stood in the way being down. Madame B——— was a charming product of the effects of finished cultivation and fashionable life upon a natural foundation of grace, wit, and beauty of the French kind. She was not artificial, because she was art itself. Real art is as real as real nature is natural. Raymond Noel had a highly artistic nature. He admired art. This did not prevent him from taking up occasionally, as a contrast to this lady, the society of the young girl he called "Faith." Most men of imagination, artistic or not, do the same thing once in a while; it seems a necessity. With Noel it was not the contrast alone. The French lady led him an uneasy life, and now and then he took an hour of Faith, as a gentle soothing draught of safe quality. She believed in him so perfectly! Now Madame appeared to believe in him not at all.

It must be added that, in his conversations with Miss Macks, he had dropped entirely even the very small amount of conventional gallantry that he had bestowed upon her in the beginning. He talked to her not as though she was a boy exactly, or an old woman, but as though he himself was a relative of mature age—say an uncle of benevolent disposition and a taste for art.

February gave way to March. And now, owing to a new position of his own affairs, Noel saw no more of Faith Macks. She had been a contrast, and he did not now wish for a contrast; or a soothing-draught, and a soothing-draught was not at present required. He simply forgot all about her.

In April he decided rather suddenly to leave Rome. This was because Madame B——— had gone to Paris, and had not forbidden her American suitor to follow her a few days later. He made his preparations for departure, and these, of course, included farewell calls. Then he remembered Faith Macks; he had not seen her for six weeks. He drove to the street of the Hyacinth, and went up the dark stairs. Miss Macks was at home, and came in without delay; apparently, in her trim neatness, she was always ready for visitors.

She was very glad to see him; but did not, as he expected, ask why he had not come before. This he thought a great advance; evidently she was learning. When she heard that he had come to say good-bye her face fell.

"I am so very sorry, please sit as long as you can, then," she said, simply. "I suppose it will be six months before I see you again; you will hardly return to Rome before October." That he would come at that time she did not question.

"My plans are uncertain," replied Noel. "But probably I shall come back. One always comes back to Rome. And you—where do you go? To Switzerland?"

"Why—we go nowhere, of course; we stay here. That is what we came for, and we are all settled."

He made some allusion to the heat and unhealthiness.

"I am not afraid," replied Miss Macks. "Plenty of people stay; Mr. Jackson says so. It is only the rich who go away, and we are not rich. We have been through hot summers in Tuscolee, I can tell you!" Then, without asking leave this time, as if she was determined to have an opinion from him before he departed, she took from a portfolio some of the work she had done under Mr. Jackson's instruction.

Noel saw at once that the Englishman had not kept his word. He had not put her back upon the alphabet, or, if he had done so, he had soon released her, and allowed her to pursue her own way again. The original faults were as marked as ever. In his opinion all was essentially bad.

He looked in silence. But she talked on hopefully, explaining, comparing, pointing out.

"What does Mr. Jackson think of this?" he said, selecting the one he thought the worst.

"He admires the idea greatly; he thinks it very original. He says that my strongest point is originality," she answered, with her confident frankness.

"He means—ah—originality of subject?"

"Oh yes; my execution is not much yet. But that will come in time. Of course, the subject, the idea, is the important thing; the execution is secondary." Here she paused; something seemed to come into her mind. "I know *you* do not think so," she added, thoughtfully, "because, you know, you said"—and here she quoted a page from one of his art articles with her clear accuracy. "I have never understood what you meant by that, Mr. Noel; or why you wrote it."

She looked at him questioningly. He did not reply; his eyes were upon one of the sketches.

"It would be dreadful for me if you were right!" she added, with slow conviction.

"I thought you believed that I was always right," he said, smiling, as he placed the sketches on the table.

But she remained very serious.

"You are—in everything but that."

He made some unimportant reply, and turned the conversation. But she came back to it.

"It would be dreadful," she repeated, earnestly, with the utmost gravity in her gray eyes.

"I hope the long summer will not tire you," he answered, irrelevantly. "Shall I not have the pleasure of saying good-bye—although that, of course, is not a pleasure—to Mrs.—to your mother?"

He should have made the speech in any case, as it was the proper one to make; but as he sat there he had thought that he really would like to have a look at the one guardian this young girl was to have during her long, lonely summer in Rome.

"I will tell her. Perhaps when she hears that you are going away she will feel like coming in," said Miss Macks.

She came back after some delay, and with her appeared a matron of noticeable aspect.

"My mother," she said, introducing her (evidently Noel was never to get the name); "this is Mr. Noel, mother."

"And very glad I am to see you, sir, I'm sure," said Mrs. Spurr, extending her hand with much cordiality. "I said to Ettie that I'd come in, seeing as 'twas you, though I don't often see strangers nowadays on account of poor health for a long time past; rheumatism and asthma. But I feel beholden to you, Mr. No-ul, because you've been so good to Ettie. You've been real kind."

Ettie's mother was a very portly matron of fifty-five, with a broad face, indistinct features, very high color, and a breathless, panting voice. Her high color—it really was her most noticeable feature—was surmounted by an imposing cap, adorned with large bows of scarlet ribbon; a worsted shawl, of the hue known as "solferino,"[8] decked her shoulders; under her low-necked collar reposed a bright blue necktie, its ends embroidered in red and yellow; and her gown was of a vivid dark green. But although her colors swore at each other, she seemed amiable. She was also voluble.

Noel, while shaking hands, was considering, mentally, with some retrospective amusement, his condition of mind if this lady had accepted his invitations to visit the galleries.

"You must sit down, mother," said Miss Macks, bringing forward an easy-chair. "She has not been so well as usual, lately," she said, explanatorily, to Noel, as she stood for a moment beside her mother's chair.

"It's this queer Eye-talian air," said Mrs. Spurr. "You see I ain't used to it. Not but what I ain't glad to be here on Ettie's account—real glad. It's just what she needs and oughter have."

The girl put her hand on her mother's shoulder with a little caressing touch. Then she left the room.

"Yes, I do feel beholden to you, Mr. No-ul. But, then, she'll be a credit to you, to whatever you've done for her," said Mrs. Spurr, when they were left alone. "Her taluntts are very remarkable. She was the head scholar of the Young Ladies' Seminary through four whole years, and all the teachers took a lot of pride in her. And then her paintings, too! I'm sorry you're going off so soon. You see, she sorter depends upon your opinion."

Noel felt a little stir at the edges of his conscience; he knew perfectly that his opinion was that Miss Macks, as an artist, would never do anything worth the materials she used.

"I leave her in good hands," he said.

After all, it was Jackson's responsibility, not his.

"Yes, Mr. Jackson thinks a deal of her. I can see that plain!" answered Mrs. Spurr, proudly.

Here the daughter returned, bringing a little notebook and pencil.

"Do you know what these are for?" she said. "I want you to write down a list of the best books for me to read this summer, while you are gone. I am going to work hard; but if I have books, too, the time won't seem so long."

Noel considered a moment. In one way her affairs were certainly none of his business; in another way they were, because she had thrust them upon him.

"I will not give you a list, Miss Macks; probably you would not be able to find the books here. But I will send you, from Paris or London, some things that are rather good, if you will permit me to do so."

She said he was very kind. Her face brightened.

"If she has appreciation enough to comprehend what I send her," he thought, "perhaps in the end she will have a different opinion about my 'kindness'!"

Soon afterwards he took leave. The next day he went to Paris.

II

THE EVENTS of Raymond Noel's life, after he left Rome that spring, were various. Some were pleasant, some unpleasant; several were quite unexpected. Their combinations and results kept him from returning to Italy the following winter, and the winter after that he spent in Egypt. When he again beheld the dome of St. Peter's he remembered that it lacked but a month of two full years since he had said good-bye to it; it was then April, and now it was March. He established himself in some pleasant rooms, looked about him, and then began to take up, one by one, the old threads of his Roman life—such, at least, as remained unbroken. He found a good many. Threads do not break in Rome. He had once said himself that the air was so soft and historic that nothing broke there—not even hearts. But this was only one of his little speeches. In reality he did not believe much in the breaking of hearts; he had seen them stretch so!

It may be said with truth that Noel had not thought of Miss Macks for months. This was because he had had other things to think of. He had sent her the books from Paris, with an accompanying note, a charming little note—which gave no address for reply. Since then his mind had been otherwise occupied. But as he never entirely forgot anything that had once interested him, even although but slightly (this was in reality a system of his; it gave him many holds on life, and kept stored up a large supply of resources ready for use when wanted), he came, after a while, on the canvas of his Roman impressions, to the figure of Miss Macks. When he came to it he went to see her; that is, he went to the street of the Hyacinth.

Of course, she might not be there; a hundred things might have happened to her. He could have hunted up Horace Jackson; but, on the whole, he rather preferred to see the girl herself first—that is, if she was there. Mrs. Lawrence, the only person among his acquaintances who had known her, was not in Rome. Reaching the street of the Hyacinth, he interrogated the old woman who acted as portress at the lower door, keeping up at the same time a small commerce in fritters; yes, the Americans were still on the fourth floor. He ascended the dark stairway. The confiding little "Ettie" card was no longer upon the door. In its place was a small framed sign: "Miss Macks' School."

This told a story!

However, he rang. It was the same shrill, ill-tempered little bell, and when the door opened it was Miss Macks herself who opened it. She was much changed.

The parlor had been turned into a school-room—at present empty of pupils. But even as a school-room it was more attractive than it had been before. He took a seat, and spoke the usual phrases of a renewal of acquaintance with his accustomed ease and courtesy; Miss Macks responded briefly. She said that her mother was not very well; she herself quite well. No, they had not left Italy, nor indeed the neighborhood of Rome; they had been a while at Albano.[9]

The expression of her face had greatly altered. The old direct, wide glance was gone; gone also what he had called her over-confidence; she looked much older. On the other hand, there was more grace in her bearing, more comprehension of life in her voice and eyes. She was dressed as plainly as before; but everything, including the arrangement of her hair, was in the prevalent style.

She did not speak of her school, and therefore he did not. But after a while he asked how the painting came on. Her face changed a little; but it was more in the direction of a greater calm than hesitation or emotion.

"I am not painting now," she answered.

"You have given it up temporarily?"

"Permanently."

"Ah—isn't that rather a pity?"

She looked at him, and a gleam of scorn filtered into the glance.

"You know it is not a pity," she said.

He was a little disgusted at the scorn. Of course, the only ground for him to take was the ground upon which she stood when he last saw her; at that time she proposed to pass her life in painting, and it was but good manners for him to accept her intentions as she had presented them.

"I never assumed to be a judge, you know," he answered. "When I last had the pleasure of seeing you, painting was, you remember, your cherished occupation!"

"When you last had the pleasure of seeing me, Mr. Noel," said Miss Macks, still with unmoved calm, "I was a fool."

Did she wish to go into the subject at length? Or was that merely an exclamation?

"When I last had the pleasure of seeing you, you were taking lessons of Mr. Jackson," he said, to give a practical turn to the conversation. "Is he still here? How is he?"

"He is very well, now. He is dead."

(She was going to be dramatic then, in any case.)

He expressed his regret, and it was a sincere one; he had always liked and respected the honest, morose Englishman. He asked a question or two. Miss Macks replied that he had died here in the street of the Hyacinth—in the next room. He had fallen ill during the autumn following Noel's departure, and when his illness grew serious, they—her mother and herself—had persuaded him to come to them. He had lived a month longer, and died peacefully on Christmas Eve.

"He was one of the most honest men I ever knew," said Noel. Then, as she did not reply, he ventured this: "That was the reason I recommended him when you asked me to select a teacher for you."

"Your plan was made useless by an unfortunate circumstance," she answered, with an evident effort.

"A circumstance?"

"Yes; he fell in love with me. If I did not consider his pure, deep, and devoted affection the greatest honor of my life I would not mention it. I tell you because it will explain to you his course."

"Yes, it explains," said Noel. As he spoke there came across him a realization of the whole of the strength of the love such a man as Horace Jackson would feel, and the way in which it would influence him. Of course, he saw to the full the imperfection of her work, the utter lack of the artist's conception, the artist's eye and touch; but probably he had loved her from the beginning, and had gone on hoping to win her love in return. She was not removed from him by any distance; she was young, but she was also poor, friendless, and alone. When she was his wife he would tell her the truth, and in the greatness of his love the revelation would be naught. "He was a good man," he said. "He was always lonely. I am glad that at last he was with your mother and you."

"His goodness was simply unbounded. If he had lived he would have remained always a faithful, kind, and respectful son to my dear mother. That, of course, would have been everything to me." She said this quietly, yet her tone seemed to hold intention.

For a moment he thought that perhaps she had married the Englishman, and was now his widow. The sign on the door bore her maiden name, but that might have been an earlier venture.

"Had you opened your school at that time?" he asked. "I may speak of it, since, of course, I saw the sign upon the door."

"Not until two months later; I had the sign made then. But it was of little use; day-schools do not prosper in Rome; they are not the custom. I have a small class twice a week, but I live by going out as day-governess. I have a number of pupils of that kind; I have been very successful. The old Roman families have a fancy for English-speaking governesses, you know. Last summer I was with the Princess C———, at Albano; her children are my pupils."

"Her villa is a delightful one," said Noel; "you must have enjoyed that."

"I don't know that I enjoyed, but I learned. I have learned a great deal in many ways since I saw you last, Mr. Noel. I have grown very old."

"As you were especially young when you saw me last it does not matter much," he answered, smiling.

"Yes, I was especially young." She looked at him soberly. "I do not feel bitterly towards you," she continued. "Strange! I thought I should. But now that I see you in person it comes over me that, probably, you did not intend to deceive me; that not only you tried to set me right by selecting Mr. Jackson as my teacher, but again you tried when you sent me those books. It was not much to do! But knowing the world as I now know it, I see that it was all that could have been expected. At first, however, I did not see this. After I went to Mr. Bellot, and, later, to Mr. Salviati, there were months when I felt very bitterly towards you. My hopes were false ones, and had been so from the beginning; you knew that they were, yet you did not set me right."

"I might have done more than I did," answered Noel. "I have a habit of not assuming responsibility, I suppose I have grown selfish. But if you went to Bellot, then it was not Jackson who told you?"

"He intimated something when he asked me to marry him; after that his illness came on, and we did not speak of it again. But I did not believe him. I was very obstinate. I went to Mr. Bellot the 1st of January; I wished him to take me as pupil. In answer he told me that I had not a particle of talent; that all my work was insufferably bad; that I better throw away my brushes and take in sewing."

"Bellot is always a brute!" said Noel.

"If he told the truth brutally, it was still the truth; and it was the truth I needed. But even then I was not convinced, and I went to Mr. Salviati. He was more gentle; he explained to me my lacks; but his judgment was the same. I came home; it was the 10th of January, a beautiful Roman winter day. I left my pictures, went over to St. Peter's, and walked there under its bright mosaics all the afternoon. The next day I had advertisements of a day-school placed at the bankers' and in the newspapers. I thought that I could teach better than I could sew." All this she said with perfect calm.

"I greatly admire your bravery, Miss Macks. Permit me to add that I admire, even more, the clear, strong, good sense which has carried you through."

"I had my mother to think of; my—good sense might not have been so faithful otherwise."

"You do not think of returning to America?"

"Probably not; I doubt if my mother could bear the voyage now. We have no one to call us back but my brother, and he has not been with us for years, and would not be if we should return; he lives in California. We sold the farm, too, before we came. No; for the present, at least, it is better for us to remain here."

"There is one more question I should like to ask," said Noel, later. "But I have no possible right to do so."

"I will give you the right. When I remember the things I asked you to do for me, the demands I made upon your time, I can well answer a few questions in return. I was a miracle of ignorance."

"I always did you justice in those respects, Miss Macks; all that I understood at once. My question refers to Horace Jackson: I see you appreciated his worth—which was rare—yet you would not marry him."

"I did not love him."

"Did any of his relatives come out from England?" he said, after a moment of silence.

"After his death a cousin came."

"As heir to what was left?"

"Yes."

"He should have left it to you."

"He wished to do so. Of course, I would not accept it."

"I thank you for answering. My curiosity was not an idle one." He paused. "If you will permit me to express it, your course has been very brave and true. I greatly admire it."

"You are kind," said Miss Macks.

There was not in her voice any indication of sarcasm. Yet the fact that he immediately thought of it made him suspect that it was there. He took leave soon afterwards. He was smarting a little under the sarcasm he had divined, and, as he was, it was like him to request permission to come again.

For Raymond Noel lived up with a good deal of determination to his own standard of what was manly; if his standard was not set on any very fine elevation of self-sacrifice or heroism, it was at least firmly established where it did stand, and he kept himself fairly near it. If Miss Macks was sarcastic, he had been at fault somewhere; he would try to atone.

He saw her four times during the five weeks of his stay in Rome; upon three other occasions when he went to the street of the Hyacinth she was not at home. The third week in April he decided to go to Venice. Before going he asked if there was not something he could do for her; but she said there was nothing, and he himself could think of nothing. She was well established in her new life and occupations, and needed nothing—at least, nothing that he could bestow.

The next winter he came back to Rome early in the season, before Christmas. By chance one of the first persons he encountered was Mrs. Lawrence. She began immediately to tell him a piece of American news, in which he, as an American, would of course be interested; the news was that "the brother of the Princess C——— —that is Count L———, you know—is determined to marry Ettie Macks. You remember her, don't you? I introduced you to her at the Dudley reception, three years ago."

Noel thought that probably he remembered her better than Mrs. Lawrence did, seeing that that lady had never troubled herself to enter the street of the Hyacinth. But he did her injustice. Mrs. Lawrence had troubled herself—lately.

"It seems that she has been out at Albano for two summers, as governess to his sister's children; it was there that he saw her. He has announced his determination to the family, and they are immensely disturbed and frightened; they had it all arranged for him to marry a second cousin down at Naples, who is rich——these Italians are so worldly, you know! But he is very determined, they say, and will do as he pleases in spite of them. He hasn't much money, but of course it's a great match for Ettie Macks. She will be a countess, and now, I suppose, more American girls will come over than ever before! Of course, as soon as I heard of it, I went to see her. I felt that she would need advice about a hundred things. In the beginning she brought a letter of introduction to me from a dear cousin of mine, and, naturally, she would rely upon me as her chief friend now. She is very much improved. She was rather silent; but, of course, I shall go again. The count is willing to take the mother, too, and that, under the circumstances, is not a small matter; she is a good deal to take. Until the other day I had not seen Mrs. Spurr! However, I suppose that her deficiencies are not apparent in a language she cannot speak. If her daughter would only insist upon her dressing in black! But the old lady told me herself, in the most cheerful way, that she liked 'a sprinkling of color.' And at the moment, I assure you, she had on five different shades of red!"

Noel had intended to present himself immediately at the street of the Hyacinth; but a little attack of illness kept him in for a while, and ten days had passed before he went up the dark stairway. The maid said that Miss Macks was at home; presently she came in. They had ten minutes of conversation upon ordinary topics, and then he took up the especial one.

"I am told that you are soon to be a countess," he said, "and I have come to give you my best good wishes. My congratulations I reserve for Count L———, with whom I have a slight acquaintance; he is, in my opinion, a very fortunate man."

"Yes, I think he is fortunate; fortunate in my refusal. I shall not marry Count L———."

"He is not a bad fellow."

"Isn't your praise somewhat faint?" This time the sarcasm was visible.

"Oh, I am by no means his advocate! All I meant was that, as these modern Romans go, he was not among the worst. Of course I should have expressed myself very differently if you had said you were to marry him."

"Yes; you would then have honored me with your finest compliments."

He did not deny this.

"Shall you continue to live in Rome?" he asked.

"Certainly. I shall have more pupils and patronage now than I know what to do with; the whole family connection is deeply obliged to me."

They talked awhile longer.

"We have always been unusually frank with each other, Miss Macks," he said, towards the end of his visit. "We have never stopped at conventionalities. I wonder if you will tell me why you refused him?"

"You are too curious. As to frankness, I have been frank with you; not you with me. And there was no conventionality, simply because I did not know what it was."

"I believe you are in love with some one in America," he said, laughing.

"Perhaps I am," answered Miss Macks. She had certainly gained greatly in self-possession during the past year.

He saw her quite frequently after this. Her life was no longer solitary. As she had said, she was over-whelmed with pupils and patronage from the friends of the Princess C———; in addition, the American girl who had refused a fairly-indorsed and well-appearing count was now something of a celebrity among the American visitors in Rome. That they knew of her refusal was not her fault; the relatives of Count L——— had announced their objections as loud and widely as the count had announced his determination. Apparently neither side had thought of a non-acceptance. Cards, not a few, were sent to the street of the Hyacinth; some persons even climbed the five flights of stairs. Mrs. Spurr saw a good deal of company— and enjoyed it.

Noel was very fond of riding; when in Rome he always rode on the Campagna. He had acted as escort to various ladies, and one day he invited Miss Macks to accompany him—that is, if she were fond of riding. She had ridden in America, and enjoyed it; she would like to go once, if he would not be troubled by an improvised habit. They went once. Then a second time, an interval of three weeks between. Then, after a while, a third time.

Upon this occasion an accident happened, the first of Noel's life; his horse became frightened, and, skilled rider though he was, he was thrown. He was dragged, too, for a short distance. His head came against some stones, and he lost consciousness. When it came back it did not come wholly. He seemed to himself to be far away, and the girl who was weeping and calling his name to be upon the other side of a wide space like an ocean, over which, without volition of his own, he was being slowly wafted. As he came nearer, still slowly, he perceived that in some mysterious way she was holding in her arms something that seemed to be himself, although he had not yet reached her. Then, gradually, spirit and body were reunited, he heard what she was saying, and felt her touch. Even then it was only after several minutes that he was able to move and unclose his heavy eyes.

When she saw that he was not dead, her wild grief was at once merged in the thought of saving him. She had jumped from her horse, she knew not how; but he had not strayed far; a shepherd had seen him, and was now coming towards them. He signalled to another, and the two carried Noel to a house which was not far distant. A messenger was sent to the city; aid came, and before night Noel was in his own rooms at the head of the Via Sistina, near the Spanish steps.

His injuries proved to be not serious; he had lost consciousness from the shock, and this, with his pallor and the blood from the cuts made by the stones, had given him the look of death. The cuts, however, were not deep; the effect of the shock passed away. He kept his bed for a week under his physician's advice; he had a good deal of time to think during that week. Later his friends were admitted. As has been said before, Noel was a favorite in Rome, and he had friends not a few. Those who could not come in person sent little notes and baskets of flowers. Among these Miss Macks was not numbered. But then she was not fashionable.

At the end of two weeks the patient was allowed to go out. He took a short walk to try his strength, and, finding that it held out well, he went to the street of the Hyacinth.

Miss Macks was at home. She was "so glad" to see him out again; and was he "really strong enough;" and he "should be very prudent for a while;" and so forth and so forth. She talked more than usual, and, for her, quite rapidly.

He let her go on for a time. Then he took the conversation into his own hands. With few preliminaries, and with much feeling in his voice and eyes, he asked her to be his wife.

She was overwhelmed with astonishment; she turned very white, and did not answer. He thought she was going to burst into tears. But she did not; she only sat gazing at him, while her lips trembled. He urged his point; he spoke strongly.

"You are worth a hundred of me," he said. "You are true and sincere; I am a dilettante in everything. But, dilettante as I am, in one way I have always appreciated you, and, lately, all other ways have become merged in that one. I am much in earnest; I know what I am doing; I have thought of it searchingly and seriously, and I beg you to say yes."

He paused. Still she did not speak.

"Of course I do not ask you to separate yourself from your mother," he went on, his eyes dropping for the moment to the brim of his hat, which he held in his hand; "I shall be glad if she will always make her home with us."

Then she did speak. And as her words came forth, the red rose in her face until it was deeply colored.

"With what an effort you said that! But you will not be tried. One gray hair in my mother's head is worth more to me, Mr. Noel, than anything you can offer."

"I knew before I began that this would be the point of trouble between us, Faith," he answered. "I can only assure you that she will find in me always a most respectful son."

"And when you were thinking so searchingly and seriously, it was *this* that you thought of—whether you could endure her! Do you suppose that I do not see the effort? Do you suppose I would ever place my mother in such a position? Do you suppose that you are of any consequence beside her, or that anything in this world weighs in my mind for one moment compared with her happiness?"

"We can make her happy; I suppose that. And I suppose another thing, and that is that we could be very happy ourselves if we were married."

"The Western girl, the girl from Tuscolee! The girl who thought she could paint, and could not! The girl who knew so little of social rules that she made a fool of herself every time she saw you!"

"All this is of no consequence, since it is the girl I love," answered Noel.

"You do not. It is a lie. Oh, of course, a very unselfish and noble one; but a lie, all the same. You have thought of it seriously and searchingly? Yes, but only for the last fourteen days! I understand it all now. At first I did not, I was confused; but now I see the whole. You were not unconscious out there on the Campagna; you heard what I said when I thought you were dying, or dead. And so you come—come very generously and self-sacrificingly, I acknowledge that—and ask me to be your wife." She rose; her eyes were brilliant as she faced him. "I might tell you that it was only the excitement, that I did not know or mean what I was saying; I might tell you that I did not know that I had said anything. But I am not afraid. I will not, like you, tell a lie, even for a good purpose. I did love you; there, you have it! I have loved you for a long time, to my sorrow and shame. For I do not respect you or admire you; you have been completely spoiled, and will always remain so. I shall make it the one purpose of my life from this moment to overcome the feeling I have had for you; and I shall succeed. Nothing could make me marry you, though you should ask me a thousand times."

"I shall ask but once," said Noel. He had risen also; and, as he did, he remembered the time when they had stood in the same place and position, facing each other, and she had told him that she was at his feet. "I did hear what you said. And it is of that I have been seriously thinking during the days of my confinement to the house. It is also true that it is what you said which has brought me here to-day. But the reason is that it has become precious to me—this knowledge that you love me. As I said before, in one way I have always done you justice, and it is that way which makes me realize to the full now what such a love as yours would be to me. If it is true that I am spoiled, as you say I am, a love like yours would make me better, if anything can." He paused. "I have not said much about my own feelings," he added; "I know you will not credit me with having any. But I think I have. I think that I love you."

"It is of little moment to me whether you do or not."

"You are making a mistake," he said, after a pause, during which their eyes had met in silence.

"The mistake would be to consent."

She had now recovered her self-possession. She even smiled a little.

"Imagine Mr. Raymond Noel in the street of the Hyacinth!" she said.

"Ah, I should hardly wish to live here; and my wife would naturally be with me."

"I hope so. And I hope she will be very charming and obedient and sweet." Then she dropped her sarcasms, and held out her hand in farewell. "There is no use in prolonging this, Mr. Noel. Do not think, however, that I do not appreciate your action; I do appreciate it. I said that I did not respect you, and I have not until now; but now I do. You will understand, of course, that I would rather not see you again, and refrain from seeking me. Go your way, and forget me; you can do so now with a clear conscience, for you have behaved well."

"It is not very likely that I shall forget you," answered Noel, "although I go my way. I see you are firmly resolved. For the present, therefore, all I can do is to go."

They shook hands, and he left her. As he passed through the small hall on his way to the outer door he met Mrs. Spurr; she was attired as opulently, in respect to colors, as ever, and she returned his greeting with much cordiality. He glanced back; Miss Macks had witnessed the meeting through the parlor door. Her color had faded; she looked sad and pale.

She kept her word; she did not see him again. If he went to the street of the Hyacinth, as he did two or three times, the little maid presented him with the Italian equivalent of "begs to be excused," which was evidently a standing order. If he wrote to her, as he did more than two or three times, she returned what he wrote, not unread, but without answer. He thought perhaps he should meet her, and was at some pains to find out her various engagements. But all was in vain; the days passed, and she remained invisible. Towards the last of May he left Rome. After leaving, he continued to write to her, but he gave no address for reply; she would now be obliged either to burn his letters or keep them, since she could no longer send them back. They could not have been called love-letters; they were friendly epistles, not long—pleasant, easy, sometimes amusing, like his own conversation. They came once a week. In addition he sent new books, and occasionally some other small remembrance.

In early September of that year there came to the street of the Hyacinth a letter from America. It was from one of Mrs. Spurr's old neighbors at Tuscolee, and she wrote to say that John Macks had come home—had come home broken in health and spirits, and, as he himself said, to die. He did not wish his mother to know; she could not come to him, and it would only distress her. He had money enough for the short time that was left him, and when she heard it would be only that he had passed away; he had passed from her life in reality years before. In this John Macks was sincere. He had been a ne'er-do-well, a rolling stone; he had not been a dutiful son. The only good that could be said of him, as far as his mother was concerned, was contained in the fact that he had not made demands upon her small purse since the sum he took from her when he first went away. He had written to her at intervals, briefly. His last letter had come eight months before.

But the Tuscolee neighbor was a mother herself, and, doing as she would be done by, she wrote to Rome. When her letter came Mrs. Spurr was overwhelmed with grief; but she was also stirred to an energy and determination which she had never shown before. For the first time in years she took the leadership, put her daughter decisively back into a subordinate place, and assumed the control. She would go to America. She must see her boy (the dearest child of the two, as the prodigal always is) again. But even while she was planning her journey illness seized her—her old rheumatic troubles, only more serious than before; it was plain that she could not go. She then required that her daughter should go in her place—go and bring her boy to Rome; this soft Italian air would give new life to his lungs. Oh, she should not die! Ettie need not be afraid of that. She would live for years just to get one look at him! And so it ended in the daughter's departure, an efficient nurse being left in charge; the physician said that although Mrs. Spurr would probably be crippled, she was in no danger otherwise.

Miss Macks left Rome on the 15th of September. On the 2d of December she again beheld the dome of St. Peter's rising in the blue sky. She saw it alone. John Macks had lived three weeks after her arrival at Tuscolee, and those three weeks were the calmest and the happiest of his unsuccessful—unworthy it may be—but also bitterly unhappy life. His sister did not judge him. She kissed him good-bye as he lost consciousness, and soon afterwards closed his eyes tenderly, with tears in her own. Although he was her brother, she had never known him; he went away when she was a child. She sat beside him a long time after he was dead, watching the strange, youthful peace come back to his worn face.

When she reached the street of the Hyacinth, a carriage was before the door; carriages of that sort were not often required by the dwellers on the floors below their own, and she was rather surprised. She had heard from her mother in London, the nurse acting as amanuensis; at that time Mrs. Spurr was comfortable, although still confined to her bed most of the day. As she was paying her driver she heard steps on the stairway within. Then she beheld this: The nurse, carrying a pillow and shawls; next, her mother, in an invalid-chair, borne by two men; and last, Raymond Noel.

When Mrs. Spurr saw her daughter she began to cry. She had not expected her until the next day. Her emotion was so great that the drive was given up, and she was carried back to her room. Noel did not follow her; he shook hands with the new-comer, said that he would not detain her, and then, lifting his hat, he stepped into the carriage which was waiting and was driven away.

For two days Mrs. Spurr wished for nothing but to hear, over and over again, every detail of her boy's last hours. Then the excitement and renewed grief made her dangerously ill. After ten days she began to improve; but two weeks passed before she came back to the present sufficiently to describe to her daughter all "Mr. No-ul's kind attentions." He had returned to Rome the first of October, and had come at once to the street of the Hyacinth. Learning what had happened, he had devoted himself to her "most as if he was my real son, Ettie, I do declare! Of course, he couldn't never be like my own darling boy," continued the poor mother, overlooking entirely, with a mother's sublime forgetfulness, the small amount of devotion her boy had ever bestowed; "but he's just done everything he could, and there's no denying that."

"He has not been mentioned in your letters, mother."

"Well, child, I just told Mrs. Bowler not to. For he said himself, frankly, that you might not like it; but that he'd make his peace with you when you come back. I let him have his way about it, and I *have* enjoyed seeing him. He's the only person I've seen but Mrs. Bowler and the doctor, and I'm mortal tired of both."

During Mrs. Spurr's second illness Noel had not come in person to the street of the Hyacinth; he had sent to inquire, and fruits and flowers came in his name. Miss Macks learned that these had come from the beginning.

When three weeks had passed Mrs. Spurr was back in her former place as regarded health. One of her first requests was to be taken out to drive; during her daughter's absence Mr. Noel had taken her five times, and she had greatly enjoyed the change. It was not so simple a matter for the daughter as it had been for Mr. Noel; her purse was almost empty; the long journeys and her mother's illness had exhausted her store. Still she did it. Mrs. Spurr wished to go to the Pincio.[10] Her daughter thought the crowd there would be an objection.

"It didn't tire me one bit when Mr. No-ul took me," said Mrs. Spurr, in an aggrieved tone; "and we went there every single time—just as soon as he found out that I liked it. What a lot of folks he does know, to be sure! They kept him a-bowing every minute."

The day after this drive Mr. Noel came to the street of the Hyacinth. He saw Miss Macks. Her manner was quiet, a little distant; but she thanked him, with careful acknowledgment of every item, for his kind attentions to her mother. He said little. After learning that Mrs. Spurr was much better he spoke of her own health.

"You have had two long, fatiguing journeys, and you have been acting as nurse; it would be well for you to give yourself entire rest for several weeks at least."

She replied, coldly, that she was perfectly well, and turned the conversation to subjects less personal. He did not stay long. As he rose to take leave, he said:

"You will let me come again, I hope? You will not repeat the 'not at home' of last spring?"

"I would really much rather not see you, Mr. Noel," she answered, after hesitating.

"I am sorry. But of course I must submit." Then he went away.

Miss Macks now resumed her burdens. She was obliged to take more pupils than she had ever accepted before, and to work harder. She had not only to support their little household, but there were now debts to pay. She was out almost the whole of every day.

After she had entered upon her winter's work Raymond Noel began to come again to the street of the Hyacinth. But he did not come to see her; his visits were to her mother. He came two or three times a week, and always during the hours when the daughter was absent. He sat and talked to Mrs. Spurr, or rather listened to her, in a way that greatly cheered that lady's monotonous days. She told him her whole history; she minutely described Tuscolee and its society; and, finally, he heard the whole story of "John." In addition, he sent her various little delicacies, taking pains to find something she had not had.

Miss Macks would have put an end to this if she had known how. But certainly Mr. Noel was not troubling *her,* and Mrs. Spurr resented any attempt at interference.

"I don't see why you should object, Ettie. He seems to like to come, and there's but few pleasures left to me, I'm sure! You oughtn't to grudge them!"

In this way two months passed, Noel continuing his visits, and Miss Macks continuing her lessons. She was working very hard. She now looked not only pale, but much worn. Count L———, who had been long absent, returned to Rome about this time. He saw her one day, although she did not see him. The result of this vision of her was that he went down to Naples, and, before long, the desirable second cousin with the fortune was the sister of the Princess C———.

One afternoon in March Miss Macks was coming home from the broad, new, tiresome piazza Indipendenza; the distance was long, and she walked with weariness. As she drew near the dome of the Pantheon she met Raymond Noel. He stopped, turned, and accompanied her homeward. She had three books.

"Give them to me," he said, briefly, taking them from her.

"Do you know what I have heard to-day?" he went on. "They are going to tear down your street of the Hyacinth. The Government has at last awakened to the shame of allowing all those modern accretions to disfigure longer the magnificent old Pagan temple. All the streets in the rear, up to a certain point, are to be destroyed. And the street of the Hyacinth goes first. You will be driven out."

"I presume we can find another like it."

He went on talking about the Pantheon until they entered the doomed street; it was as obstinately narrow and dark as ever. Then he dropped his Pagan temple.

"How much longer are you going to treat me in this way, Faith?" he said. "You make me very unhappy. You are wearing yourself out, and it troubles me greatly. If you should fall ill I think that would be the end. I should then take matters into my own hands, and I don't believe you would be able to keep me off. But why should we wait for illness? It is too great a risk."

They were approaching her door. She said nothing, only hastened her steps.

"I have been doing my best to convince you, without annoying you, that you were mistaken about me. And the reason I have been doing it is that I am convinced myself. If I was not entirely sure last spring that I loved you, I certainly am sure now. I spent the summer thinking of it. I know now, beyond the possibility of a doubt, that I love you above all and everything. There is no 'duty' or 'generosity' in this, but simply my own feelings. I could perfectly well have let the matter drop; you gave me every opportunity to do so. That I have not done it should show you—a good deal. For I am not of the stuff of which heroes are made. I should not be here unless I wanted to; my motive is the selfish one of my own happiness."

They had entered the dark hallway.

"Do you remember the morning when you stood here, with two tears in your eyes, saying 'Never mind; you will come another time'?" (Here the cobbler came down the stairs.) "Why not let the demolition of the street of the Hyacinth be the crisis of our fate?" he went on, returning the cobbler's bow. (Here the cobbler departed.) "If you refuse, I shall not give you up; I shall go on in the same way. But—haven't I been tried long enough?"

"You have not," she answered. "But, unless you will leave Rome, and—me, I cannot bear it longer."

It was a great downfall, of course; Noel always maintained that it was.

"But the heights upon which you had placed yourself, my dear, were too superhuman," he said, excusingly.

The street of the Hyacinth experienced a great downfall, also. During the summer it was demolished.

Before its demolition Mrs. Lawrence, after three long breaths of astonishment, had come to offer her congratulations—in a new direction this time.

"It is the most fortunate thing in the world," she said to everybody, "that Mrs. Spurr is now confined to her bed for life, and is obliged to wear mourning."

But Mrs. Spurr is not confined to her bed; she drives out with her daughter whenever the weather is favorable. She wears black, but is now beginning to vary it with purple and lavender.

AT THE CHÂTEAU OF CORINNE

ON THE SHORES of Lake Leman[1] there are many villas. For several centuries the vine-clad banks have been a favorite resting-place for visitors
from many nations. English, French, Germans, Austrians, Poles, and Russians are found in the circle of strangers whose gardens fringe the lake
northward from Geneva, eastward from Lausanne, and southward from
Vevey, Clarens, and Montreux. Not long ago an American joined this
circle. The American was a lady named Winthrop.

Mrs. Winthrop's villa was not one of the larger residences. It was an
old-fashioned square mansion, half Swiss, half French, ending in a high-
peaked roof, which came slanting sharply down over several narrowed
half-stories, indicated by little windows like dove-perches—four in the
broadest part, two above, then one winking all alone under the peak. On
the left side a round tower, inappropriate but picturesque, joined itself to
the square outline of the main building; the round tower had also a peaked
roof, which was surmounted by a contorted ornament of iron somewhat
resembling a letter S. Altogether the villa was the sort of a house which
Americans are accustomed to call "quaint." Its name was quaint also—
Miolans la Tour, or, more briefly, Miolans. Cousin Walpole pronounced
this "Miawlins."

Mrs. Winthrop had taken possession of the villa in May, and it was
now late in August; Lake Leman therefore had enjoyed her society for
three long months. Through all this time, in the old lake's estimation, and

notwithstanding the English, French, Germans, Austrians, Poles, and Russians, many of them titled, who were also upon its banks, the American lady remained an interesting presence. And not in the opinion of the old lake only, but in that also of other observers, less fluid and impersonal. Mrs. Winthrop was much admired. Miolans had entertained numerous guests during the summer; to-day, however, it held only the *bona fide* members of the family—namely, Mrs. Winthrop, her cousin Sylvia, and Mr. H. Walpole, Miss Sylvia's cousin. Mr. H. Walpole was always called "Cousin Walpole" by Sylvia, who took comfort in the name, her own (a grief to her) being neither more nor less than Pitcher. "Sylvia Pitcher" was not impressive, but "H. Walpole" could shine for two. If people supposed that H. stood for Horace, why, that was their own affair.[2]

Mrs. Winthrop, followed by her great white dog, had strolled down towards the lake. After a while she came within sight of the gate; some one was entering. The porter's lodge was unoccupied save by two old busts that looked out from niches above the windows, much surprised that no one knew them. The newcomer surveyed the lodge and the busts; then opened the gate and came in. He was a stranger; a gentleman; an American. These three items Mrs. Winthrop's eyes told her, one by one, as she drew nearer. He now caught sight of her—a lady coming down the water-path, followed by a shaggy dog. He went forward to meet her, raising his hat. "I think this is Mrs. Winthrop. May I introduce myself? I am John Ford."

"Sylvia will be delighted," said Mrs. Winthrop, giving her hand in courteous welcome. "We have been hoping that we should see you, Mr. Ford, before the summer was over."

They stood a few moments, and then went up the plane-tree avenue towards the house. Mrs. Winthrop spoke the usual phrases of the opening of an acquaintance with grace and ease; her companion made the usual replies. He was quite as much at his ease as she was, but he did not especially cultivate grace. Sylvia, enjoying her conversation with Cousin Walpole, sat just within the hall door; she was taken quite by surprise. "Oh, John, how you startled me! I thought you were in Norway. But how very glad I am to see you, my dear, dear boy!" She stood on tiptoe to kiss him, with a moisture in her soft, faded, but still pretty eyes.

Mrs. Winthrop remained outside; there were garden chairs in

the small porch, and she seated herself in one of them. She smiled a little
when she heard Sylvia greet this mature specimen of manhood as a "dear,
dear boy."

Cousin Walpole now came forward. "You are welcome, sir," he said,
in his slender little voice. Then bethinking him of his French, he added,
with dignity, "Welcome to Miaw-lins—Miaw-lins-lay-Tower."

Ford took a seat in the hall beside his aunt. She talked volubly: the
surprise had excited her. But every now and then she looked at him with
a far-off remembrance in her eyes: she was thinking of his mother, her sister, long dead. "How much you look like her!" she said at last. "The
same profile—exact. And how beautiful Mary's profile was! Every one
admired it."

Ford, who had been gazing at the rug, looked up; he caught Mrs.
Winthrop's glance, and the gleam of merriment in it. "Yes, my profile is
like my mother's, and therefore good," he answered, gravely. "It is a pity
that my full face contradicts it. However, I live in profile as much as
possible; I present myself edgewise."

"What do you mean, dear?" said Sylvia.

"I am like the new moon," he answered; "I show but a rim. All the
rest I keep dark."

Mrs. Winthrop laughed, and again Ford caught her glance. What he
had said of himself was true. He had a regular, clearly cut, delicately
finished profile, but his full face contradicted it somewhat, showing more
strength than beauty. His eyes were gray, without much expression, unless
calmness can be called an expression; his hair and beard, both closely cut,
were dark brown. As to his height, no one would have called him tall, yet
neither would any one have described him as short. And the same phrasing
might have been applied to his general appearance: no one would have
called him handsome, yet neither would any one have classed him as ordinary. As to what is more important than looks, namely, manner, although
his was quiet, and quite without pretension, a close observer could have
discovered in it, and without much effort, that the opinions of John Ford
(although never obtruded upon others) were in general sufficiently satisfactory to John Ford; and, furthermore, that the opinions of other people,
whether accordant or discordant with his own, troubled him little.

After a while all went down to the outlook to see the after-glow on Mont Blanc. Mrs. Winthrop led the way with Cousin Walpole, whose high, bell-crowned straw hat had a dignity which no modern head-covering could hope to rival.

Sylvia followed, with her nephew. "You must come and stay with us, John," she said. "Katharine has so much company that you will find it entertaining, and even at times instructive. I am sure I have found it so; and I am, you know, your senior. We are alone to-day; but it is for the first time. Generally the house is full."

"But I do not like a full house," said Ford, smiling down upon the upturned face of the little "senior" by his side.

"You will like this one. It is not a commonplace society—by no means commonplace. The hours, too, are easy; breakfast, for instance, from nine to eleven—as you please. As to the quality of the—of the bodily support, it is sufficient to say that Marches is housekeeper. You remember Marches?"

"Perfectly. Her tarts no one could forget."

"Katharine is indebted to me for Marches," continued Sylvia. "I relinquished her to Katharine upon the occasion of her marriage, ten years ago; for she was totally inexperienced, you know—only seventeen."

"Then she is now twenty-seven."

"I should not have mentioned that," said Miss Pitcher, instinctively. "It was an inadvertence. Could you oblige me by forgetting it?"

"With the greatest ease. She is, then, sensitive about her age?"

"Not in the least. Why should she be? Certainly no one would ever dream of calling twenty-seven *old!*" (Miss Pitcher paused with dignity.) "You think her beautiful, of course?" she added.

"She is a fine-looking woman."

"Oh, John, that is what they always say of women who weigh two hundred! And Katharine is very slender."

Ford laughed. "I supposed the fact that Mrs. Winthrop was handsome went without the saying."

"It goes," said Sylvia, impressively, "but not without the saying; I assure you, by no means without the saying. It has been said this summer many times."

"And she does not find it fatiguing?"

The little aunt looked at her nephew. "You do not like her," she said, with a fine air of penetration, touching his coat-sleeve lightly with one finger. "I see that you do not like her."

"My dear aunt! I do not know her in the least."

"Well, how does she impress you, then, *not* knowing her?" said Miss Pitcher, folding her arms under her little pink shawl with an impartial air.

He glanced at the figure in front. "How she impresses me?" he said. "She impresses me as a very attractive, but very complete, woman of the world."

A flood of remonstrance rose to Sylvia's lips; but she was obliged to repress it, because Mrs. Winthrop had paused, and was waiting for them.

"Here is one of our fairest little vistas, Mr. Ford," she said as they came up, showing him an oval opening in the shrubbery, through which a gleam of blue lake, a village on the opposite shore, and the arrowy, snow-clad Silver Needle, rising behind high in the upper blue, were visible, like a picture in a leaf frame. The opening was so narrow that only two persons could look through it. Sylvia and Cousin Walpole walked on.

"But you have seen it all before," said Mrs. Winthrop. "To you it is not something from fairy-land, hardly to be believed, as it is to me. Do you know, sometimes, when waking in the early dawn, before the prosaic little details of the day have risen in my mind, I ask myself, with a sort of doubt in the reality of it all, if this is Katharine Winthrop living on the shores of Lake Leman—herself really, and not her imagination only, her longing dream." It was very well uttered, with a touch of enthusiasm which carried it along, and which was in itself a confidence.

"Yes—ah—quite so. Yet you hardly look like a person who would think that sort of thing under those circumstances," said Ford, watching a bark, with the picturesque lateen-sails of Lake Leman, cross his green-framed picture from east to west.

Mrs. Winthrop let the hand with which she had made her little gesture drop. She stood looking at him. But he did not add anything to his remark, or turn his glance from the lateen-sails.

"What sort of a person, then, do I look like?" she said.

He turned. She was smiling; he smiled also. "I was alluding merely to the time you named. As it happened, my aunt had mentioned to me by chance your breakfast hours."

"That was not all, I think."

"You are very good to be interested."

"I am not good; only curious. Pray tell me."

"I have so little imagination, Mrs. Winthrop, that I cannot invent the proper charming interpretation as I ought. As to bald truth, of course you cannot expect me to present you with that during a first visit of ceremony."

"The first visit will, I hope, be a long one; you must come and stay with us. As to ceremony, if this is your idea of it——"

"——What must I be when unceremonious! I suppose you are thinking," said Ford, laughing. "On the whole, I had better make no attempts. The owl, in his own character, is esteemed an honest bird; but let him not try to be a nightingale."

"Come as owl, nightingale, or what you please, so long as you come. When you do, I shall ask you again what you meant."

"If you are going to hold it over me, perhaps I had better tell you now."

"Much better."

"I only meant, then, that Mrs. Winthrop did not strike me as at all the sort of person who would allow anything prosaic to interfere with her poetical, heart-felt enthusiasms."

She laughed gayly. "You are delightful. You have such a heavy apparatus for fibbing that it becomes fairly stately. You do not believe I have any enthusiasms at all," she added. Her eyes were dark blue, with long lashes; they were very fine eyes.

"I will believe whatever you please," said John Ford.

"Very well. Believe what I tell you."

"You include only what you tell in words?"

"Plainly, you are not troubled by timidity," said the lady, laughing a second time.

"On the contrary, it is excess of timidity. It makes me desperate and crude."

They had walked on, and now came up with the others. "Does he amuse you?" said Sylvia, in a low tone, as Cousin Walpole in his turn walked onward with the new-comer. "I heard you laughing."

"Yes; but he is not at all what you said. He is so shy and ill at ease that it is almost painful."

"Dear me!" said the aunt, with concern. "The best thing, then, will be for him to come and stay with us. You have so much company that it will be good for him; his shyness will wear off."

"I have invited him, but I doubt his coming," said the lady of the manor.

The outlook was a little terrace built out over the water. Mrs. Winthrop seated herself and took off her garden-hat (Mrs. Winthrop had a very graceful head, and thick, soft, brown hair). "Not so close, Gibbon," she said, as the shaggy dog laid himself down beside her.

"You call your dog Gibbon?" said Ford.

"Yes; he came from Lausanne, where Gibbon[3] lived; and I think he looks just like him. But pray put on your hat, Mr. Ford. A man in the open air, deprived of his hat, is always a wretched object, and always takes cold."

"I may be wretched, but I do not take cold," replied Ford, letting his hat lie.

"John *does* look very strong," said Sylvia, with pride.

"O fortunate youth—if he but knew his good-fortune!" said Cousin Walpole. "From the Latin, sir; I do not quote the original tongue in the presence of ladies, which would seem pedantic. You do look strong indeed, and I congratulate you. I myself have never been an athlete; but I admire, and with impartiality, the muscles of the gladiator."

"Sure, Cousin Walpole, there is nothing in common between John and a gladiator!"

"Your pardon, Cousin Sylvia. I was speaking generally. My conversation, sir," said the bachelor, turning to Ford, "is apt to be general."

"No one likes personalities, I suppose," replied Ford, watching the last hues of the sunset.

"On the contrary, I am devoted to them," said Mrs. Winthrop.

"Oh no, Katharine; you malign yourself," said Sylvia. "You must not believe all she says, John."

"Mr. Ford has just promised to do that very thing," remarked Mrs. Winthrop.

"Dear me!" said Sylvia. Her tone of dismay was so sincere that they all laughed. "You know, dear, you have so much imagination," she said, apologetically, to her cousin.

"Mr. Ford has not," replied the younger lady; "so the exercise will do him no harm."

The sky behind the splendid white mass of Mont Blanc was of a deep warm gold; the line of snowy peaks attending the monarch rose irregularly against this radiance from east to west, framed by the dark nearer masses of the Salève and Voirons.[4] The sun had disappeared, cresting with glory as he sank the soft purple summits of the Jura, and sending up a blaze of color in the narrow valley of the Rhone. Then, as all this waned slowly into grayness, softly, shyly, the lovely after-glow floated up the side of the monarch, tingeing all his fields of pure white ice and snow with rosy light as it moved onward, and resting on the far peak in the sky long after the lake and its shores had faded into night.

"This lake, sir," said Cousin Walpole, "is remarkable for the number of persons distinguished in literature who have at various times resided upon its banks. I may mention, cursorily, Voltaire, Sismondi, Gibbon, Rousseau, Sir Humphry Davy, D'Aubigné, Calvin, Grimm, Benjamin Constant, Schlegel, Châteaubriand, Byron, Shelley, the elder Dumas, and in addition that most eloquent authoress and noble woman Madame de Staël."[5]

"The banks must certainly be acquainted with a large amount of fine language," said Ford.

"And oh, how we have enjoyed Coppet, John! You remember Coppet?" said Miss Pitcher. "We have had, I assure you, days and conversations there which I, for one, can never forget. Do you remember, Katharine, that moment by the fish-pond, when, carried away by the influences of the spot, Mr. Percival exclaimed, and with such deep feeling, '*Etonnante femme!*'"[6]

"Meaning Mrs. Winthrop?" said Ford.

"No, John, no; meaning Madame de Staël," replied the little aunt.

Mr. Ford did not take up his abode at Miolans, in spite of his aunt's wish and Mrs. Winthrop's invitation. He preferred a little inn among the vineyards, half a mile distant. But he came often to the villa, generally rowing himself down the lake in a skiff. The skiff, indeed, spent most of its time moored at the water-steps of Miolans, for its owner accompanied the ladies in various excursions to Vevey, Clarens, Chillon,[7] and southward to Geneva.

"I thought you had so much company," he said one afternoon to Sylvia, when they happened to be alone. "I have been coming and going now for ten days, and have seen no one."

"These ten days were reserved for the Storms," replied Miss Pitcher. "But old Mrs. Storm fell ill at Baden-Baden, and what could they do?"

"Take care of her, I should say."

"Gilbert Storm was poignantly disappointed. He is, I think, on the whole, the best among Katharine's *outside* admirers."

"Then there are inside ones?"

"Several. You know Mr. Winthrop was thirty-five years older than Katharine. It was hardly to be expected, therefore, that she should love him—I mean in the *true* way."

"Whatever she might have done in the false."

"You are too cynical, my dear boy. There was nothing false about it; Katharine was simply a child. He was very fond of her, I assure you. And died most happily."

"For all concerned."

Sylvia shook her head. But Mrs. Winthrop's step was now heard in the hall; she came in with several letters in her hand. "Any news?" said Miss Pitcher.

"No," replied the younger lady. "Nothing ever happens any more."

"As Ronsard sang,

> "'Le temps s'en va, le temps s'en va, ma dame!
> Las! le temps non; mais nous nous en allons,'"[8]

said Ford, bringing forward her especial chair.

"That is true," she answered, soberly, almost sombrely.

That evening the moonlight on the lake was surpassingly lovely; there was not a ripple to break the sheen of the water, and the clear outline of Mont Blanc rose like silver against the dark black-blue of the sky. They all strolled down to the shore; Mrs. Winthrop went out with Ford in his skiff, "for ten minutes." Sylvia watched the little boat float up and down for twenty; then she returned to the house and read for forty more. When Sylvia was down-stairs she read the third canto of "Childe Harold";[9] in her own room she kept a private supply of the works of Miss Yonge. At ten Katharine entered. "Has John gone?" said the aunt, putting in her mark and closing the Byronic volume.

"Yes; he came to the door, but would not come in."

"I wish he would come and stay. He might as well; he is here every day."

"That is the very point; he also goes every day," replied Katharine.

She was leaning back in her chair, her eyes fixed upon the carpet. Sylvia was going to say something more, when suddenly a new idea came to her. It was a stirring idea; she did not often have such inspirations; she remained silent, investigating it. After a while, "When do you expect the Carrols?" she said.

"Not until October."

Miss Pitcher knew this perfectly, but she thought the question might lead to further information. It did. "Miss Jay has written," pursued Mrs. Winthrop, her eyes still fixed absently on the carpet. "But I answered, asking her to wait until October, when the Carrols would be here. It will be much pleasanter for them both."

"She has put them off!" thought the little aunt. "She does not want any one here just at present." And she was so fluttered by the new possibilities rising round her like a cloud that she said good-night, and went up-stairs to think them over; she did not even read Miss Yonge.

The next day Ford did not come to Miolans until just before the dinner hour. Sylvia was disappointed by this tardiness, but cheered when Katharine came in; for Mrs. Winthrop wore one of her most becoming dresses. "She wishes to look her best," thought the aunt. But at this moment, in the twilight, a carriage came rapidly up the driveway and stopped at the door. "Why, it is Mr. Percival!" said Sylvia, catching a glimpse of the occupant.

"Yes; he has come to spend a few days," said Mrs. Winthrop, going into the hall to greet her new guest.

Down fell the aunt's cloud-castle; but at the same moment a more personal feeling took its place in the modest little middle-aged breast; Miss Pitcher deeply admired Mr. Percival.

"You know who it is, of course?" she whispered to her nephew when she had recovered her composure.

"You said Percival, didn't you?"

"Yes; but this is Lorimer Percival—Lorimer Percival, the poet."

Katharine now came back. Sylvia sat waiting, and turning her bracelets round on her wrists. Sylvia's bracelets turned easily; when she took a book from the top shelf of the bookcase they went to her shoulders.

Before long Mr. Percival entered. Dinner was announced. The conversation at the table was animated. From it Ford gathered that the new guest had spent several weeks at Miolans early in the season, and that he had also made since then one or two shorter visits. His manner was that of an intimate friend. The intimate friend talked well. Cousin Walpole's little candle illuminated the outlying corners. Sylvia supplied an atmosphere of general admiration. Mrs. Winthrop supplied one of beauty. She looked remarkably well—brilliant; her guest—the one who was not a poet—noticed this. He had time to notice it, as well as several other things, for he said but little himself; the conversation was led by Mr. Percival.

It was decided that they would all go to Coppet the next day—"dear Coppet," as Sylvia called it. The expedition seemed to be partly sacred and partly sylvan; a pilgrimage-picnic. When Ford took leave, Mrs. Winthrop and Mr. Percival accompanied him as far as the water-steps. As his skiff glided out on the calm lake, he heard the gentleman's voice suggesting that they should stroll up and down awhile in the moonlight, and the lady's answer, "Yes; for ten minutes." He remembered that Mrs. Winthrop's ten minutes was sometimes an hour.

The next day they went to Coppet; Mrs. Winthrop and Mr. Percival in the carriage, Sylvia and Cousin Walpole in the phaeton,[10] and Ford on horseback.

"Oh! isn't this almost *too* delightful!" said Miss Pitcher, when they reached the gates of the old Necker château. Cousin Walpole was engaged in tying his horse, and Mr. Percival had politely stepped forward to assist her from the phaeton. It is but fair, however, to suppose that her exclamation referred as much to the intellectual influences of the home of Madame de Staël as to the attentions of the poet. "I could live here, and I could die here," she continued, with ardor. But as Mr. Percival had now gone back to Mrs. Winthrop, she was obliged to finish her sentence to her nephew, which was not quite the same thing. "Couldn't *you*, John?" she said.

"It would be easy enough to die, I should say," replied Ford, dismounting.

"We must all die," remarked Cousin Walpole from the post where he was at work upon the horse. He tied that peaceful animal in such intricate and unexpected convolutions that it took Mrs. Winthrop's coachman, later, fully twenty minutes to comprehend and unravel them.

The Necker homestead is a plain, old-fashioned château, built round three sides of a square, a court-yard within. From the end of the south side a long, irregular wing of lower outbuildings stretches towards the road, ending in a thickened, huddled knot along its margin, as though the country highway had refused to allow aristocratic encroachments, and had pushed them all back with determined hands. Across the three high, pale-yellow façades of the main building the faded shutters were tightly closed. There was not a sign of life, save in a little square house at the end of the knot, where, as far as possible from the historic mansion he guarded, lived the old custodian, who strongly resembled the portraits of Benjamin Franklin.

Benjamin Franklin knew Mrs. Winthrop (and Mrs. Winthrop's purse). He hastened through the knot in his shuffling woollen shoes, and unlocked the court-yard entrance.

"We must go all through the dear old house again, for John's sake," said Sylvia.

"Do not sacrifice yourselves; I have seen it," said her nephew.

"But not lately, dear John."

"I am quite willing to serve as a pretext," he answered, leading the way in.

They passed through the dark old hall below, where the white statue of Necker gleams in solitude, and went up the broad stairway, the old custodian preceding them, and throwing open the barred shutters of room after room. The warm sunshine flowed in and streamed across the floors, the dim tapestries, the spindle-legged, gilded furniture, and the Cupid-decked clocks. The old paintings on the walls seemed to waken slowly and survey them as they passed. Lorimer Percival seated himself in a yellow arm-chair, and looked about with the air of a man who was breathing a delicate aroma.

"This is the room where the 'incomparable Juliette' danced her celebrated gavotte," he remarked, "probably to the music of that old harpsichord—or is it a spinet?—in the corner."

"Pray tell us about it," entreated Sylvia, who had seated herself gingerly on the edge of a small ottoman embroidered with pink shepherd-esses on a blue meadow, and rose-colored lambs. Mrs. Winthrop mean-while had appropriated a spindle-legged sofa, and was leaning back against a tapestried Endymion.[11]

Percival smiled, but did not refuse Sylvia's request. He had not the objection which some men have to a monologue. It must be added, how-ever, that for that sort of thing he selected his audience. Upon this occa-sion the outside element of John Ford, strolling about near the windows, was discordant, but not enough so to affect the admiring appreciation of the little group nearer his chair.

"Madame de Staël," he began, with his eyes on the cornice, "was a woman of many and generous enthusiasms. She had long wished to behold the grace of her lovely friend Madame Récamier,[12] in her celebrated gavotte, well known in the salons of Paris, but as yet unseen by the exile of Coppet. By great good-fortune there happened to be in the village, upon the occasion of a visit from Madame Récamier, a French dancing-master. Madame de Staël sent for him, and the enchanted little man had the signal honor of going through the dance with the beautiful Juliette, in this room, in the presence of all the distinguished society of Coppet: no doubt it was the glory of his life. When the dance was ended, Corinne, carried away by admiration, embraced with transport—"

"The dancing-master?" said Cousin Walpole, much interested.

"No; her *ravissante amie*."[13]

Cousin Walpole, conscious that he had made a mistake, betook him-self to the portrait near by. "Superb woman!" he murmured, contemplat-ing it. "Superb!"

The portrait represented the authoress of *Corinne* standing, her talented head crowned by a majestic aureole of yellow satin turban, whose voluminous folds accounted probably for the scanty amount of material left for the shoulders and arms.

"If I could have had the choice," said Miss Pitcher, pensively gazing at this portrait, "I would rather have been that noble creature than any one else on history's page."

Later they went down to the old garden. It stretched back behind the house for some distance, shut in by a high stone wall. A long, straight alley, shaded by even rows of trees, went down one side like a mathematical line; on the other there was some of the stiff landscape-gardening of the last century. In the open space in the centre was a moss-grown fish-pond, and near the house a dignified little company of clipped trees. They strolled down the straight walk: this time Ford was with Mrs. Winthrop, while Sylvia, Mr. Percival, and Cousin Walpole were in front.

"I suppose she used to walk here," observed Mrs. Winthrop.

"In her turban," suggested Ford.

"Perhaps she has sat upon that very bench—who knows?—and mused," said Sylvia, imaginatively.

"Aloud, of course," commented her nephew. But these irreverent remarks were in undertone; only Mrs. Winthrop could hear them.

"No doubt they all walked here," observed the poet; "it was one of the customs of the time to take slow exercise daily in one of these dignified alleys. The whole society of Coppet was no doubt often here, Madame de Staël and her various guests, Schlegel, Constant, the Montmorency,[14] Sismondi, Madame Récamier, and many others."

"Would that I too could have been of that company!" said Cousin Walpole, with warmth.

"Which one of the two ladies would you have accompanied down this walk, if choice had been forced upon you?" said Mrs. Winthrop.

"Which one?—Madame de Staël, of course," replied the little bachelor, chivalrously.

"And you, Mr. Percival?"

"With the one who had the intellect," replied the poet.

"We must be even more lacking in beauty than we suppose, Sylvia, since they all chose the plain one," said Katharine, laughing. "But you have not spoken yet, Mr. Ford: What would your choice have been?"

"Between the two, there would hardly have been one."

"Isn't that a little enigmatical?"

"John means that he admires them equally," explained the aunt.

"That is it," said her nephew.

Lunch was spread upon the grass. Mrs. Winthrop's coachman had made an impromptu carpet of carriage rugs and shawls. Percival threw himself down beside the ladies; Cousin Walpole, after trying various attitudes, took the one denominated "cross-legged." Ford surveyed their group for a moment, then went off and came back with a garden bench; upon this he seated himself comfortably, with his back against a tree.

"You are not sufficiently humble, Mr. Ford," said Katharine.

"It is not a question of humility, but of grace. I have not the gifts of Mr. Percival."

Percival said nothing. He was graceful; why disclaim it?

"But you are very strong, John," said Sylvia, with an intention of consolation. "And if not exactly graceful, I am sure you are very well shaped."

Her hearers, including Ford himself, tried not to laugh, but failed. There was a burst of merriment.

"You think John does not need my encouragement?" said the little lady, looking at the laughers. "You think I forget how old he is? It is quite true, no doubt. But I remember him *so* well, you know, in his little white frock, with his dear little dimpled shoulders! He always would have bread and sugar, whether it was good for him or not, and he was so pretty and plump!"

These reminiscences provoked another peal.

"You may laugh," said Miss Pitcher, nodding her head sagely, "but he did eat a great deal of sugar. Nothing else would content him but that bowl on the high shelf."

"Do you still retain the same tastes, Mr. Ford?" said Katharine. "Do you still prefer what is out of reach—*on a high shelf?*"

"When one is grown," said Ford, "there is very little that is absolutely out of reach. It is, generally speaking, a question merely of determination, and—a long arm."

The sun sank; his rays came slanting under their tree, gilding the grass in bars. The conversation had taken a turn towards the society of the eighteenth century. Percival said the most. But a poet may well talk in a memorial garden, hushed and sunny, on a cushioned carpet under the trees, with a long-stemmed wineglass near his hand, and fair ladies listening in rapt attention. Ford, leaning back against his tree, was smoking a cigarette; it is to be supposed that he was listening also.

"Here is something I read the other day, at least as nearly as I can recall it," said the speaker. He was gazing at the tops of the trees on the other side of the pond. He had a habit of fixing his eyes upon something high above his hearers' heads when speaking. Men considered this an impertinence; but women had been known to allude to it as "dreamy."

"'Fair vanished ladies of the past,'" quoted the poet in his delightful voice, "'so charming even in your errors, do you merit the judgment which the more rigid customs of our modern age would pronounce upon you? Was that enthusiasm for virtue and for lofty sentiments with which your delicious old letters and memoirs, written in faded ink and flowing language, with so much wit and so much bad spelling, are adorned—was it all declamation merely, because, weighed in our severer balances, your lives were not always in accordance with it? Are there not other balances? And were you not, even in your errors, seeking at least an ideal that was fair? Striving to replace by a sensibility most devoted and tender a morality which, in the artificial society that surrounded you, had become well-nigh impossible? Let us not forget how many of you, when the dread hour came, faced with unfaltering courage the horrors of the Revolution, sustained by your example the hearts of strong men which had failed them, and atoned on the red guillotine for the errors and follies of your whole generation with your delicate lives.'"

He paused. Then, in a lighter tone, added: "Charming vanished dames, in your powder and brocade, I salute you! I, for one, enroll myself among your faithful and tender admirers."

Mr. Percival remained two weeks at Miolans. He was much with Mrs. Winthrop. They seemed to have subjects of their own for conversation, for on several occasions when Ford came over in the morning they were said to be "in the library," and Miss Pitcher was obliged to confess that she did not feel at liberty to disturb them. She remarked, with a sigh, that it must be "very intellectual," and once she asked her nephew if he had not noticed the poet's "brow."

"Oh yes; he is one of those tall, slim, long-faced, talking fellows whom you women are very apt to admire," said Ford.

Miss Pitcher felt as much wrath as her gentle nature allowed. But again her sentiments were divided, and she sacrificed her personal feelings. That evening she confided to Katharine, under a pledge of deepest secrecy, her belief that "John" was "jealous."

Mrs. Winthrop greeted this confidence with laughter. Not discouraged, the aunt the next day confided to her nephew her conviction that, as regarded the poet, Katharine had not yet "at all made up her mind."

"That is rather cruel to Percival, isn't it?" said Ford.

"Oh, he too has many, many *friends,*" said Sylvia, veering again.

"Fortunate fellow!"

At last Percival went. Ford was again the only visitor. And if he did not have long mornings in the library, he had portions not a few of afternoons in the garden. For if he came up the water-steps and found the mistress of the house sitting under the trees, with no other companion than a book, it was but natural that he should join her, and possibly make some effort to rival the printed page.

"You do not like driving?" she said, one day. They were in the parlor, and the carriage was coming round; she had invited him to accompany them, and he had declined.

"Not with a coachman, I confess."

"There is always the phaeton," she said, carelessly.

He glanced at her, but she was examining the border of her lace scarf. "On the whole, I prefer riding," he answered, as though it were a question of general preferences.

"And Katharine rides *so* well!" said Sylvia, looking up from her wax flowers. Sylvia made charming wax flowers, generally water-lilies, because they were "so regular."

"There are no good horses about here," observed Ford. "I have tried them all. I presume at home in America you keep a fine one?"

"Oh, in America! That is too far off. I do not remember what I did in America," answered Mrs. Winthrop.

A day or two later. "You were mistaken about there being no good saddle-horses here," she remarked. "My coachman has found two; they are in the stable now."

"If you are going to be kind enough to offer one of them to me," he said, rather formally, after a moment's silence, "I shall then have the pleasure of some rides with you, after all."

"Yes," answered Mrs. Winthrop. "As you say—after all!" She was smiling. He smiled too, but shook his head. Sylvia did not see this little by-play. Whatever it meant, however, it did not prevent Ford's riding with Mrs. Winthrop several times, her groom following. Miss Pitcher watched these little excursions with much interest.

Meanwhile letters from Lorimer Percival came to Miolans almost daily. "That is the Percival crest," said Sylvia to her nephew, one of these epistles, which had just arrived, being on the hall table, seal upward, as they passed. "*So* appropriate for a poet, I think—a flame."

"Ah! I took it for steam," said Ford.

Now the elder Percival had been a successful builder of locomotives. "John," said Miss Pitcher, solemnly, "do you mean that for derision?"

"Derision, my dear aunt! There is nothing in the world so powerful as steam. If I only had more, I too might be a poet. Or if my father had had more, I too might have enjoyed a fortune."

"Mr. Percival enjoys no fortune," said Sylvia, still solemnly.

"What has he done with it, then? Enjoyed it all out?"

"He tells me that it dissolved, like a mist, in his grasp."

"Yes; they call it by various names," said Ford.

Mrs. Winthrop, dressed in her habit, now came down the stairway; she took the letter and put it in her pocket. That day the groom could not accompany them: the horse he rode was lame. "We are sufficiently brave to do without him for one afternoon, are we not?" said the lady.

"I confess I am timid; but I will do my best," answered Ford, assisting her to mount. Sylvia, standing in the doorway, thought this a most unfortunate reply.

They rode southward. "Shall we stop for a few moments?" said Katharine, as they came towards Coppet.

"Yes; for ten," he answered.

The old custodian let them in, and threw open the windows as before. The visitors went out on the little shelf-like balcony which opened from the drawing-room.

"You notice there is no view, or next to none," said Ford, "although we are on the share of Lake Leman, and under the shadow of Mont Blanc. They did not care for views in the eighteenth century—that is, views of the earth; they were all for views of the 'soul.' Madame de Staël detested the country; to the last, Coppet remained to her a dreary exile. She was the woman who frankly said that she would not cross the room to look at the Bay of Naples, but would walk twenty miles to talk with an agreeable man."

"They were as rare then, it seems, as they are now," said Mrs. Winthrop. "But to-day we go more than twenty miles; we go to Europe."

"She did the same—that is, what was the same in her day; she went to Germany. There she found two rather agreeable men—Goethe and Schiller.[15] Having found them, she proceeded to talk to them. They confessed to each other, long afterwards, the deep relief they felt when that gifted woman departed."

"Ah, well, all she wanted, all she was seeking, was sympathy."

"She should have waited until it came to her."

"But if it never came?"

"It would—if she had not been so eager and voracious. The truth is, Corinne was an inordinate egotist. She expected all minds to defer to her superiority, while at the very moment she was engaged in extracting from them any poor little knowledge or ideas they might possess which could serve her own purposes. All her books were talked into existence; she talked them before she wrote them. It was her custom, at the dinner-table here at Coppet, to introduce the subject upon which she was engaged, and all her guests were expected, indeed forced, to discuss it with her in all its bearings, to listen to all she herself had to say, and never to depart from the given line by the slightest digression until she gave the signal. The next morning, closeted in her own room, she wrote out the results of all this, and it became a chapter."

"She was a woman of genius, all the same," said Mrs. Winthrop, in a disagreeing tone.

"A woman of genius! And what is the very term but a stigma? No woman is so proclaimed by the great brazen tongue of the Public unless she has thrown away her birthright of womanly seclusion for the miserable mess of pottage called 'fame.'"

"The seclusion of a convent? or a prison?"

"Neither. Of a home."

"You perhaps commend obedience, also?"

"In one way—yes."

"I'm glad to know there are other ways."

"I shall be very obedient to the woman I love in several of those other ways," replied Ford, gathering some of the ripening grapes near the balcony rail.

Mrs. Winthrop went back into the faded drawing-room. "It is a pity there is no portrait here of Madame Récamier," she remarked. "That you might have admired."

"The 'incomparable Juliette' was at least not literary. But in another way she was as much before the public as though she had been what you call a woman of genius. It may be said, indeed, that she had genius—a genius for attracting admiration."

"You are hard to please."

"Not at all; I ask only the simple and retiring womanly graces. But anything retiring was hard to find in the eighteenth century."

"You dislike literary women very much," said Mrs. Winthrop. She had crossed the room to examine an old mirror made of squares of glass, welded together by little leaden frames, which had once been gilded.

"Hardly. I pity them."

"You did not know, then, that I was one?"

He had crossed the room also, and was now standing behind her; as she asked the question she looked at his image in the glass.

"I did not know it," he answered, looking at hers.

"I am, anonymously."

"Better anonymously than avowedly."

"Will you read something I have written?"

"Thanks. I am not in the least a critic."

"I know that; you are too prejudiced, too narrow, to be one. All the same, will you read?"

"If you insist."

"I do insist. What is more, I have it with me. I have had it for several days, waiting for a good opportunity." She drew from her pocket a small flat package, and gave it to him.

"Must it be now?"

"Here and now. Where could we find a more appropriate atmosphere?"

He seated himself and opened the parcel; within was a small square book in flexible covers, in decoration paper and type, a daintily rich little volume.

"Ah! I know this," he said. "I read it when it first came out."

"So much the better. You can give me your opinion without the trouble of reading."

"It received a good deal of praise, I remember," he said, turning over the leaves.

She was silent.

"There was a charming little description somewhere—about going out on the Campagna[16] to gather the wild narcissus," he went on, after a pause.

And then there was another silence.

"But—" said Mrs. Winthrop.

"But, as you kindly suggest, I am no judge of poetry. I can say nothing of value."

"Say it, valuable or not. Do you know, Mr. Ford, that you have scarcely spoken one really truthful word to me since we first met. Yet I feel sure that it does not come natural to you, and that it has cost you some trouble to—to—"

"To decorate, as I have, my plain speech. But if that is true, is it not a compliment?"

"And do I care for your compliments? I have compliments in abundance, and much finer ones than yours. What I want from you is the truth, your real opinion of that little volume in your hand. You are the only man I have met in years who seems to feel no desire to flatter me, to make me think well of myself. I see no reason why I should not think well of myself; but, all the same, I am curious. I can see that you judge me impartially, even severely."

She paused. He did not look up or disclaim; he went on turning the pages of the little volume.

She had not seated herself; she was standing beside a table opposite him. "I can see that you do not in the least like me," she added, in a lower tone.

"My dear lady, you have so many to like you!" said Ford.

And then he did look up; their eyes met.

A flush came to her cheeks. He shut the little book and rose.

"Really, I am too insignificant a victim," he said, bowing as he returned it.

"You mean that I—that I have tried——"

"Oh no; you do it naturally."

For the moment her self-possession had failed her. But now she had it in hand again. "If I *have* tried, naturally or artificially, I have made a failure—have I not?"

"It must be a novel experience for Mrs. Winthrop."

She turned away and looked at a portrait of Voltaire. After some moments, "Let us come back to the real point between us," she said, as he did not speak—"that is, your opinion of my little book."

"Is that the real point between us?"

"Of course it is. We will walk up and down Corrine's old rooms, and you shall tell me as we walk."

"Why do you force me to say unpleasant things?"

"They are unpleasant, then? I knew it! Unpleasant for me."

"For us both."

"For you, I doubt it. For me, they cannot be more unpleasant than the things you have already said. Yet you see I forgive them."

"Yes; but I have not forgiven you, Mrs. Winthrop."

"For what, pray?"

"For proposing to make me a victim."

"Apparently you had small difficulty in escaping."

"As you say—apparently. But perhaps I conceal my wounds."

"You are trying to turn the subject, so that I will not insist about the little book."

"I wish, indeed, that you would not insist."

"But if I am the sort of woman you have indicated, I should think you would enjoy punishing me a little."

"A little, perhaps. But the punishment would be too severe."

They were walking slowly through the rooms; she turned her head and looked at him. "I have listened to you, Mr. Ford; I have let you say pretty much what you pleased to me, because it was amusing. But you cannot seriously believe that I really care for what you say, severe or otherwise?"

"Only as any right-minded woman must care."

"Say on. Now I insist."

"Good-bye to Miolans, then. You will never admit me within its gates again; that is, unless you have the unusual justice—unusual in a woman—to see that what I say is but the severity of a true friend."

"A friend is not severe."

"Yes, he is; in such a case as this, must be."

"Go on. I will decide afterwards."

They entered the third room. Ford reflected a moment; then began. "The poem, which you now tell me is yours, had, as its distinguishing feature, a certain daring. Regarding its other points: its rhythm was crude and unmelodious; its coloring was exaggerated—reading it, one was cloyed with color; its logic—for there was an attempt at logic—was utterly weak." He paused. Mrs. Winthrop was looking straight before her at the wall across the end of the last room in the vista. Her critic did not lift his eyes, but transferred his gaze from one section of the dark old floor to the next as they walked onward.

"All this, however," he resumed, "could be forgiven. We do not expect great poems from women any more than we expect great pictures; we do not expect strong logic any more than we expect brawny muscle. A woman's poetry is subjective. But what cannot be forgiven—at least in my opinion—is that which I have called the distinguishing feature of the volume, a certain sort of daring. This is its essential, unpardonable sin. Not because it is in itself dangerous; it has not force enough for that; but because it comes, and can be recognized at once as coming, from the lips of a woman. For a woman should not dare in that way. Thinking to soar, she invariably descends. Her mental realm is not the same as that of man; lower, on the same level, or far above, it is at least different. And to see her leave it, and come in all her white purity, which must inevitably be soiled, to the garish arena where men are contending, where the dust is rising, and the air is tainted and heavy—this is indeed a painful sight. Every honest

233

man feels like going to her, poor mistaken sibyl that she is, closing her lips with gentle hand, and leading her away to some far spot among the quiet fields, where she can learn her error, and begin her life anew. To the pity of it is added the certain truth that if the words she sang could be carried out to their logical end, if they were to be clothed in the hard realities of life and set up before her, they would strike first the poor creature who was chanting them, and crush her to the dust. Fortunately there is no danger of this; it is among the impossibilities. And sometimes the poor sibyls learn, and through the teachings of their own hearts, their great mistake." As he ended, for the first time he lifted his eyes from the floor and looked at her.

Katharine Winthrop's face was flushed; the dark color extended over her forehead and dyed even her throat, and there was an expression as though only by a strong effort was a tremor of the lips controlled. This gave to her mouth a fixed look. She was so unlike herself, veiled in that deep, steady, painful blush, that, involuntarily and earnestly, Ford said, "I beg you not to mind it so much."

"I mind only that you should dare to say such things to me," she answered, slowly, as though utterance was an effort.

"Remember that you forced me to speak."

"I did not expect—this."

"How could I know what you expected? But in one way I am glad you made me go on; it is well that you should have for once a man's true opinion."

"All men do not think as you think."

"Yes, they do; the honest ones."

"Mr. Percival does not."

"Oh, Percival! He's effeminate."

"So you judge him," said Mrs. Winthrop, to whose utterance anger had now restored the distinctness.

"We will not quarrel about Lorimer Percival," said Ford; "he is not worth it—at least, he is not worth it to me." Then, as they entered the last room, "Take it as I meant it, Katharine," he said, the tone of his voice changing—"take it as a true woman should. Show me the sweet side of your nature, the gentle, womanly side, and I will then be your suitor indeed, and a far more real and earnest one than though I had become the victim you intended me to be. You may not care for me; you may never care. But only let me see you accept for your own sake what I have said, in the right spirit, and I will at least ask you to care, as humbly and devotedly as man ever asked woman. For when she is her true self she is so far above us that we can only be humble."

The flush still covered her forehead; her eyes looked at him, strangely and darkly blue in all this red.

"Curious, isn't it, how things come about?" she said. "You have made me a declaration, after all."

"A conditional one."

"No, not conditional in reality, although you might have pleased yourself with the fancy. For I need not have been in earnest. I had only to pretend a little, to pretend to be the acquiescent creature you admire, and I could have turned you round my little finger. It is rather a pity I did not do it. It might have been entertaining."

He had watched her as she spoke. "I do not in the least believe you," he said, gravely.

"It is not of much consequence whether you believe me or not. I think, on the whole, however, that I may as well take this occasion to tell you what you seem not to have suspected: I am engaged to Mr. Percival."

"Of course, then, you were angry when I spoke of him as I did. But I beg you will do me the justice to believe that I never for a moment dreamed that he was anything to Mrs. Winthrop."

"Your dreams must be unobservant."

"I knew that he was with you, of course, and that you received his letters—there is one in your pocket now. But it made no impression upon me—that is, as far as you were concerned."

"And why not? Even in the guise of an apology, Mr. Ford, you succeed in insinuating your rudeness. What you have said, when translated, simply means that you never dreamed that Mrs. Winthrop could be interested in Mr. Percival. And why should she not be interested? But the truth is, there is such an infinite space between you that you cannot in the least comprehend him." She turned towards the door which led to the stairway.

"That is very possible," said Ford. "But I have not now the honor to be a rival of Mr. Percival's, even as an unfavored suitor; you did not comply with my condition."

They went down the stairs, past the shining statue of Necker, and out into the sunshine. Benjamin Franklin brought forward the horses, and Ford assisted her to mount. "You prefer that I should not go with you," he said; "but of course I must. We cannot always have things just as we wish them in this vexatious world, you know."

The flush on her face was still deep; but she had recovered herself sufficiently to smile. "We will select subjects that will act as safe conductors down to commonplace," she said. They did. Only at the gate of Miolans was any allusion made to the preceding conversation.

He had said good-bye; the two riding-gloves had formally touched each other. "It may be for a long time," he remarked. "I start towards Italy this evening; I shall go to Chambéry and Turin." [17]

She passed him; her horse turned into the plane-tree avenue. "Do not suppose that I could not have been, that I could not be—if I chose—all you described," she said, looking back.

"I know you could. It was the possibilities in you which attracted me, and made me say what I did."

"*That* for your possibilities!" she answered, making the gesture of throwing something lightly away.

He lifted his hat; she smiled, bowed slightly, and rode onward out of sight. He took his horse to the stables, went down to the water-steps, and unmoored his skiff. The next day Sylvia received a note from him; it contained his good-bye, but he himself was already on the way to Italy.

The following summer found Miss Pitcher again at Miolans. But although her little figure was still seen going down to the outlook at sunset, although she still made wax flowers and read (with a mark) "Childe Harold," it was evident that she was not as she had been. She was languid, mournful, and by August these adjectives were no longer sufficient to describe her condition, for she was now seriously ill. Her nephew, who was spending the summer in Scotland, was notified by a letter from Cousin Walpole. In answer he travelled southward to Lake Leman without an hour's delay; for Sylvia and himself were the only ones of their blood on the old side of the Atlantic, and if the gentle little aunt was to pass from earth in a strange land, he wished to be beside her.

But Sylvia did not pass. Her nephew read her case so skillfully, and with the others tended her so carefully, that in three weeks' time she was lying on a couch by the window, with "Childe Harold" again by her side. But if she was now well enough for a little literature, she was also well enough for a little conversation.

"I suppose you were much surprised, John, to find Katharine still Mrs. Winthrop?"

"No, not much."

"But she told me that she had mentioned to you her engagement."

"Yes, she mentioned it."

"You speak as though she was one of the women who make and break engagements lightly. But she is not, I assure you; far from it."

"She broke this one, it seems."

"One breaking does not make a—breaker," said Sylvia, thinking vaguely of "swallows," and nearly saying "summer." She paused, then shook her head sadly. "I have never understood it," she said, with a deep sigh. "It lasted, I know, until the very end of June. I think I may say, without exaggeration, that I spent the entire month of July, day and night, picturing to myself his sufferings."

"You took more time than he did. He was married before July was ended."

"Simply despair."

"Despair took on a cheerful guise. Some of the rest of us might not object to it in such a shape."

But Miss Pitcher continued her dirge. "So terrible for such a man! A mere child—only seventeen!"

"And he is—"

"Thirty-seven years, eight months, and nine days." answered the lady, in the tone of an obituary. "Twenty years younger than he is! Of course, she cannot in the least appreciate the true depth of his poetry."

"He may not care for that, you know, if she appreciates him," said Ford—Miss Pitcher thought, heartlessly.

During these three weeks of attendance upon his aunt he had, of course, seen Mrs. Winthrop daily. Generally he met her in the sick-room, where she gave to the patient a tender and devoted care. If she was in the drawing-room when he came down, Cousin Walpole was there also; he had not once seen her alone. He was not staying at Miolans, although he spent most of his time there; his abode nominally was a farm-house near by. Sylvia improved daily, and early in September her nephew prepared for departure. He was going to Heidelberg. One beautiful morning he felt in the mood for a long farewell ride. He sent word to Sylvia that he should not be at Miolans before evening, mounted, and rode off at a brisk pace. He was out all day under the blue sky, and enjoyed it. He had some wonderful new views of Mont Blanc, some exhilarating speed over tempting stretches of road, a lunch at a rustic inn among the vineyards, and the uninterrupted companionship of his own thoughts. Towards five o'clock, on his way home, he came by Coppet. Here the idle ease of the long day was broken by the small incident of his horse losing a shoe. He took him to the little blacksmith's shop in the village; then, while the work was in slow Swiss progress, he strolled back up the ascent towards the old château.

A shaggy white dog came to meet him; it was his friend Gibbon, and a moment later he recognized Mrs. Winthrop's groom, holding his own and his mistress's horse. Mrs. Winthrop was in the garden, so Benjamin Franklin said. He opened the high gate set in the stone wall and went down the long walk.

She was at the far end; her back was towards him, and she did not hear his step; she started when he spoke her name. But she recovered herself immediately, smiled, and began talking with much the same easy, graceful manner she had shown upon his first arrival at Miolans, when they met at the gate the year before. This meant that she had put him back as an acquaintance where he was then.

He did not seem unwilling to go. They strolled onward for ten minutes; then Mrs. Winthrop said that she must start homeward; they turned towards the gate. They had been speaking of Sylvia's illness and recovery. "I often think, when I look at my little aunt," said Ford, "how pretty she must have been in her youth. And, by-the-way, just before leaving Scotland I met a lady who reminded me of her, or rather of my idea of what she must have been. It was Mrs. Lorimer Percival."

"She is charming, I am told," said the lady beside him.

"I don't know about the charming; I dislike the word. But she is very lovely and very lovable."

"Did you see much of her?"

"I saw her several times; but only saw her. We did not speak."

"You judge, then, by appearance merely."

"In this case—yes. Her nature is written on her face."

"All are at liberty to study it, then. Pray describe her."

He was silent. Then, "If I comply," he said, "will you bear in mind that I am quite well aware that that which makes this little lady's happiness is something that Mrs. Winthrop, of her own accord, has cast aside as nothing worth?" As he rounded off this phrase he turned and looked at her.

But she did not meet his eyes. "I will remember," she answered.

He waited. But she said nothing more.

"Mrs. Percival," he resumed, "is a beautiful young girl, with a face like a wild flower in the woods. She has an expression which is to me enchanting—an expression of sweet and simple goodness, and gentle, confiding trust. One is thankful to have even seen such a face."

"You speak warmly. I am afraid you are jealous of poor Mr. Percival."

"He did not strike me as poor. If I was jealous, it was not the first time. He was always fortunate."

"Perhaps there are other wild flowers in the woods; you must search more diligently." She opened the gate, passed through, and signalled to her groom.

"That is what I am trying to do; but I do not succeed. It is terribly lonely work sometimes."

"What a confession of weakness!"

He placed her in the saddle. "It may be. At any rate, it is the truth. But women do not believe in truth for its own sake; it strikes them as crude."

"You mean cruel," said Katharine Winthrop. She rode off, the groom and Gibbon following. He went back to the blacksmith's shop. The next day he went to Heidelberg.

But he had not seen the last of Corinne's old château. On the 25th of October he was again riding up the plane-tree avenue of Miolans, this time under bare boughs.

"Oh, John! dear John!" said Miss Pitcher, hurrying into the drawing-room when she was told he was there. "How glad I am to see you! But how did you know—I mean, how did you get here at this time of year?"

"By railway and on horseback," he answered. "I like autumn in the country. And I am very glad to see you looking so well, Aunt Sylvia."

But if Sylvia was well in body, she was ill at ease in mind. She began sentences and did not finish them; she often held her little handkerchief to her lips as if repressing herself. Cousin Walpole had gone to Geneva, "on business for Katharine." No, Katharine was not with him; she was out riding somewhere. She was not well, and needed the exercise. Katharine, too, was fond of autumn in the country. But Sylvia found it rainy. After a while Ford took leave, promising to return in the evening. When he reached the country road he paused, looking up and down it for a moment; then he turned his horse southward. It was a dreary day for a ride; a long autumn rain had soaked the ground, clouds covered the sky, and a raw wind was blowing. He rode at a rapid pace, and when he came towards Coppet he again examined the wet track, then turned towards the château. He was not mistaken; Mrs. Winthrop's horse was there. There was no groom this time; the horse was tied in the court-yard. Benjamin Franklin said that the lady was in the garden, and he said it muffled in a worsted cap and a long wadded coat that came to his heels. No doubt he permitted himself some wonder over the lady's taste.

The lady was at the end of the long walk as before. But to-day the long walk was a picture of desolation; all the bright leaves, faded and brown, were lying on the ground in heaps so sodden that the wind could not lift them, strongly as it blew. Across one end of this vista stretched the blank stone wall, its grayness streaked with wet spots; across the other rose the old château among the bare trees, cold, naked, and yellow, seeming to have already begun its long winter shiver. But men do not mind such things as women mind them. A dull sky and stretch of blank stone wall do not seem to them the end of the world—as they seemed at that moment to Katharine Winthrop. This time she heard his step; perhaps he intended that she should hear it. She turned.

Her face was pale; her eyes, with the dark shadows under them, looked larger than usual. She returned his greeting quietly; her trouble, whatever it was, did not apparently connect itself with him.

"You should not be walking here, Mrs. Winthrop," he said as he came up; "it is too wet."

"It is wet; but I am going now. You have been at Miolans?"

"Yes. I saw my aunt. She told me you were out riding somewhere. I thought perhaps you might be here."

"Is that all she told you?"

"I think so. No; she did say that you were fond of autumn in the country. So am I. Wouldn't it be wise to stop at the old man's cottage, before remounting, and dry your shoes a little?"

"I never take cold."

"Perhaps we could find a pair in the village that you could wear."

"It is not necessary. I will ride rapidly; the exercise will be the best safeguard."

"Do you know why I have come back?" he said, abandoning the subject of the shoes.

"I do not," answered the lady. She looked very sad and weary.

"I have come back, Katharine, to tell you plainly and humbly that I love you. This time I make no conditions; I have none to make. Do with me as you please; I must bear it. But believe that I love you with all my heart. It has been against my will; I have not been willing to admit it to myself; but of late the certainty has forced itself upon me so overwhelmingly that I had no resource left save to come to you. I am full of faults; but—I love you. I have said many things that displeased you deeply; but—I love you. Do not deliberate. Send me away—if go I must—now. Keep me—if you will keep me—now. You can punish me afterwards."

They had been walking onward, but now he stopped. She stopped also; but she said nothing; her eyes were downcast.

"It is a real love I offer you," he said, in a low tone. Then, as still she did not speak, "I will make you very happy, Katharine," he added.

Her face had remained pale, but at this assertion of his a slight color rose, and a smile showed itself faintly. "You are always so sure!" she murmured. And then she laughed, a little low, sweet, sudden laugh.

"Let him laugh who wins," said Ford, triumphantly. The old streaked stone wall, if dreary, was at least high; no one saw him but one very wet and bedraggled little bird, who was in the tree above. This bird was so much cheered (it must have been that) that he immediately chirruped one note quite briskly, and coming out on a drier twig, began to arrange his soaked feathers.

"Now," said Ford, "we will have those shoes dried, whether you like it or not. No more imprudence allowed. How angry you were when I said we might find a pair in the village that you could wear! Of course I meant children's size." He had drawn her hand through his arm, and was going towards the gate.

But she freed herself and stopped. "It is all a mistake," she said, hurriedly. "It means nothing. I am not myself to-day. Do not think of it."

"Certainly I shall not trouble myself to think of it much when— what is so much better—I have it."

"No; it is nothing. Forget it. I shall not see you again. I am going back to America immediately—next week."

He looked at her as she uttered these short sentences. Then he took her hands in his. "I know about the loss of your fortune, Katharine; you need not tell me. No, Sylvia did not betray you. I heard it quite by chance from another source while I was still in Heidelberg. That is the reason I came."

"The reason you came!" she repeated, moving from him, with the old proud light coming back into her eyes. "You thought I would be overwhelmed—you thought that I would be so broken that I would be glad—you pitied me—you came to help me? And you were *sure*—" She stopped; her voice was shaking.

"Yes, Katharine, I did pity you. Yes, I came to help you if you would let me. But I was not sure. I was sure of nothing but my own obstinate love, which burst out uncontrollably when I thought of you in trouble. I have never thought of you in that way before; you have always had everything. The thought has brought me straight to your side."

But she was not softened. "I withdraw all I have said," she answered. "You have taken advantage."

"As it happens, you have said nothing. As to taking advantage, of course I took advantage: I was glad enough to see your pale face and sad eyes. But that is because you have always carried things with such a high hand. First and last, I have had a great deal of bad treatment."

"That is not true."

"Very well; then it is not. It shall be as you please. Do you want me to go down on my knees to you on this wet gravel?"

But she still turned from him.

"Katharine," he said, in a graver tone, "I am sorry on your account that your fortune is gone, or nearly gone; but on my own, how can I help being glad? It was a barrier between us, which, as I am, and as you are—but principally as you are—would have been, I fear, a hopeless one. I doubt if I should ever have surmounted it. Your loss brings you nearer to me—the woman I deeply love, love in spite of myself. Now if you are my wife—and a tenderly loved wife you will be—you will in a measure be dependent upon your husband, and that is very sweet to a self-willed man like myself. Perhaps in time I can even make it sweet to you."

A red spot burned in each of her cheeks. "It is very hard," she said, almost in a whisper.

"Well, on the whole, life *is* hard," answered John Ford. But the expression in his eyes was more tender than his words. At any rate, it seemed to satisfy her.

"Do you know what I am going to do?" he said, some minutes later. "I am going to make Benjamin Franklin light a fire on one of those old literary hearths at the château. Your shoes shall be dried in the presence of Corinne herself (who must, however, have worn a much larger pair). And while they are drying I will offer a formal apology for any past want of respect, not only to Corinne, but to all the other portraits, especially to that blue-eyed Madame Necker in her very tight white satin gown. We will drink their healths in some of the native wine. If you insist, I will even make an effort to admire the yellow turban."

He carried out his plan. Benjamin Franklin, tempted by the fee offered, and relying no doubt upon the gloomy weather as a barrier against discovery, made a bright fire upon one of the astonished hearths, and brought over a flask of native wine, a little loaf, and some fine grapes. Ford arranged these on a spindle-legged table, and brought forward an old tapestried arm-chair for Katharine. Then while she sat sipping her wine and drying her shoes before the crackling flame, he went gravely round the room, glass in hand, pausing before each portrait to bow ceremoniously and drink to its health and long life—probably in a pictorial sense. When he had finished the circuit, "Here's to you all, charming vanished ladies of the past," he said; "may you each have every honor in the picturesque, powdered, unorthographic age to which you belong, and never by any possibility step over into ours!"

"That last touch has spoiled the whole," said the lady in the tapestried chair.

But Ford declared that an expression in Madame Necker's blue eye approved his words.

He now came back to the hearth. "This will never do," he said. "The shoes are not drying; you must take them off." And with that he knelt down and began to unbutton them. But Katharine, agreeing to obey orders, finished the task herself. The old custodian, who had been standing in the doorway laughing at Ford's portrait pantomime, now saw an opportunity to make himself useful; he came forward, took one of the shoes, put it upon his hand, and, kneeling down, held it close to the flame. The shoes were little boots of dark cloth like the habit, slender, dainty, and made with thin soles; they were for riding, not walking. Ford brought forward a second arm-chair and sat down. "The old room looks really cheerful," he said. "The portraits are beginning to thaw; presently we shall see them smile."

Katharine too was smiling. She was also blushing a little. The blush and slight embarrassment made her look like a school-girl.

"Where shall we go for the winter?" said Ford. "I can give you one more winter over here, and then I must go home and get to work again. And as we have so little foreign time left, I suggest that we lose none of it, and begin our married life at once. Don't be alarmed; he does not understand a word of English. Shall we say, then, next week?"

"No."

"Are you waiting to know me better? Take me, and make me better."

"What are your principal faults—I mean besides those I already know?" she said, shielding her face from the heat of the fire with her riding gauntlets.

"I have very few. I like my own way; but it is always a good way. My opinions are rather decided ones; but would you like an undecided man? I do not enjoy general society, but I am extremely fond of the particular. I think that is all."

"And your obstinacy?"

"Only firmness."

"You are narrow, prejudiced; you do not believe in progress of any kind. You would keep women down with an iron hand."

"A velvet one."

The custodian now took the other shoe.

"He will certainly stretch them with that broad palm of his," said Ford. "But perhaps it is as well; you have a habit of wearing shoes that are too small. What ridiculous little affairs those are! Will twelve pairs a year content you?"

A flush rose in her cheeks; she made no reply.

"It will be very hard for you to give up your independence, your control of things," he said.

But she turned towards him with a very sweet expression in her eyes. "You will do it all for me," she answered.

He rose, walked about the room, coming back to lean over the gilded top of her chair and say, with emphasis, "What in the world does that old wretch mean by staying here so persistently all this time?"

She laughed. Benjamin Franklin, looking up from his task, laughed too—probably on general principles of sociability and appreciation of his fee.

"To go back to your faults," she said; "please come and sit down, and acknowledge them. You have a very jealous nature."

"You are mistaken. However, if you like jealousy, I can easily take it up."

"It will not be necessary. It is already there."

"You are thinking of some particular instance; of whom did you suppose I was jealous?"

But she would not say.

After a while he came back to it. "You thought I was jealous of Lorimer Percival," he said.

The custodian now announced that both shoes were dry; she put them on, buttoning them with an improvised button-hook made of a hair-pin. The old man stood straightening himself after his bent posture; he still smiled—probably on the same general principles. The afternoon was drawing towards its close; Ford asked him to bring round the horses. He went out; they could hear his slow, careful tread on each of the slippery stairs. Katharine had risen, she went to the mirror to adjust her riding-hat. Ford came up and stood behind her. "Do you remember when I looked at you in the glass, in this same way, a year ago?" he said.

"How you talked to me that day about my poor little book! You made me feel terribly."

"I am sorry. Forgive it."

"But you do not forgive the book?"

"I will forget it, instead. You will write no more."

"Always so sure! However, I will promise, if you acknowledge that you have a jealous disposition."

She spoke gayly. He watched her in the glass a moment, then drew her away. "Whether I have a jealous disposition or not I do not know," he answered. "But I was never jealous of Lorimer Percival; I held him in too light estimation. And I did not believe—no, not at any time—that you loved him; he was not a man whom you would love. Why you allowed yourself to become engaged to him I do not know; but I suspect it was because he flattered what you thought your literary talent. I do not believe you would ever have married him; you would have drawn back at the last moment. To be engaged to him was one thing, to marry him another. You kept your engagement along for months, when there was no reason at all for the delay. If you had married him I should have thought the less of you, but I should not have been jealous." He paused. "I might never have let you know it, Katharine," he went on, "but I prefer that there should be nothing but the truth between us. I know that it was Percival who broke the engagement at the last, and not you. I knew it when I was here in the summer. He himself told me when I met him in Scotland just after his marriage."

She broke from him. "How base are all men!" she said, in a voice unlike her own.

"In him it was simply egotism. He knew that I had known of his engagement to you, and he wished me to appreciate that in order to marry that sweet young girl, who was quite without fortune, he had been obliged to make, and had made, a great sacrifice."

"Great indeed!" she commented, bitterly. "You do well to commend him."

"I do not commend him. I simply say that he was following out his nature. Being a poet, he is what is called sympathetic, you know; and he wanted my appreciation and sympathy—I will not say applause."

She was standing with her back towards him. She now walked towards the door. But her courage failed, she sank into a chair and covered her face with her hands. "It is too much," she said. "You wait until I have lost my fortune and am overwhelmed; you wait until I am rejected, cast aside; and then you come and win from me an avowal of my love, telling me afterwards—*afterwards*"— Her voice broke, she burst into tears.

"Telling you afterwards nothing but that I love you. Telling you afterwards that I have not had one really happy moment since our conversation in this old house a year ago. Telling you afterwards that my life has resolved itself into but one unceasing, tormenting wish—the wish, Katharine, that you would love me, I suppose I ought to say a little, but I mean a great deal. Look at me; is this humble enough for you?"

Her drew her hands away; she saw that he was kneeling at her feet; and, not only that, but she saw also something very like a mist in the gray eyes she had always thought too cold.

In the library of Mr. John Ford, near New York, there hangs in the place of honor a water-color sketch of an old yellow château. Beneath it, ranged by themselves, are all the works of that eloquent authoress and noble woman, Madame de Staël.

"You admire her?" said a visitor recently, in some surprise. "To me she always seemed a—a little antique, you know."

"She is antiquity itself! But she once lent me her house, and I am grateful. By-the-way, Katharine, I never told you, although I found it out afterwards: Benjamin Franklin understood English, after all."

"MISS GRIEF"

꘎꘎꘎꘎꘎

"*A CONCEITED FOOL*" is a not uncommon expression. Now, I know that I am not a fool, but I also know that I am conceited. But, candidly, can it be helped if one happens to be young, well and strong, passably good looking, with some money that one has inherited and more that one has earned—in all, enough to make life comfortable—and if upon this foundation rests also the pleasant superstructure of a literary success? The success is deserved, I think: certainly it was not lightly gained. Yet even with this I fully appreciate its rarity. Thus, I find myself very well entertained in life: I have all I wish in the way of society, and a deep, though of course carefully concealed, satisfaction in my own little fame; which fame I foster by a gentle system of non-interference. I know that I am spoken of as "that quiet young fellow who writes those delightful little studies of society, you know"; and I live up to that definition.

A year ago I was in Rome, and enjoying life particularly. I had a large number of my acquaintances there, both American and English, and no day passed without its invitation. Of course I understood it: it is seldom that you find a literary man who is good tempered, well dressed, sufficiently provided with money, and amiably obedient to all the rules and requirements of "society." "When found, make a note of it";[1] and the note was generally an invitation.

One evening, upon returning to my lodgings, my man Simpson informed me that a person had called in the afternoon, and upon learning that I was absent had left not a card, but her name—"Miss Grief." The title lingered—Miss Grief! "Grief has not so far visited me here," I said to myself, dismissing Simpson and seeking my little balcony for a final smoke, "and she shall not now. I shall take care to be 'not at home' to her if she continues to call." And then I fell to thinking of Isabel Abercrombie, in whose society I had spent that and many evenings: they were golden thoughts.

The next day there was an excursion; it was late when I reached my rooms, and again Simpson informed me that Miss Grief had called.

"Is she coming continuously?" I said, half to myself.

"Yes, sir: she mentioned that she should call again."

"How does she look?"

"Well, sir, a lady, but not so prosperous as she was, I should say," answered Simpson, discreetly.

"Young?"

"No, sir."

"Alone?"

"A maid with her, sir."

But once outside in my little high-up balcony with my cigar, I again forgot Miss Grief and whatever she might represent. Who would not forget in that moonlight, with Isabel Abercrombie's face to remember?

The stranger came a third time, and I was absent; then she let two days pass, and began again. It grew to be a regular dialogue between Simpson and myself when I came in at night: "Grief today?"

"Yes, sir."

"What time?"

"Four, sir."

"Happy the man," I thought, "who can keep her confined to a particular hour!"

But I should not have treated my visitor so cavalierly if I had not felt sure that she was eccentric and unconventional—qualities extremely tiresome in a woman no longer young or attractive. If she were not eccentric, she would not have persisted in coming to my door day after day in this silent way, without stating her errand, leaving a note, or presenting her credentials in any shape. I made up my mind that she had something to sell—a bit of carving or some intaglio supposed to be antique. It was known that I had a fancy for oddities. I said to myself, "She has read or heard of my 'Old Gold' story, or else 'The Buried God,' and she thinks me an idealizing ignoramus upon whom she can impose. Her sepulchral name is at least not Italian; probably she is a sharp countrywoman of mine, turning, by means of the present aesthetic craze, an honest penny when she can."

She had called seven times during a period of two weeks without seeing me, when one day I happened to be at home in the afternoon, owing to a pouring rain and a fit of doubt concerning Miss Abercrombie. For I had constructed a careful theory of that young lady's characteristics in my own mind, and she had lived up to it delightfully until the previous evening, when with one word she had blown it to atoms and taken flight, leaving me standing, as it were, on a desolate shore, with nothing but a handful of mistaken inductions wherewith to console myself. I do not know a more exasperating frame of mind, at least for a constructor of theories. I could not write, and so I took up a French novel (I model myself a little on Balzac).[2] I had been turning over its pages but a few moments when Simpson knocked, and, entering softly, said, with just a shadow of a smile on his well-trained face, "Miss Grief." I briefly consigned Miss Grief to all the Furies,[3] and then, as he still lingered—perhaps not knowing where they resided—I asked where the visitor was.

"Outside, sir—in the hall. I told her I would see if you were at home."

"She must be unpleasantly wet if she had no carriage."

"No carriage, sir: they always come on foot. I think she *is* a little damp, sir."

"Well, let her in; but I don't want the maid. I may as well see her now, I suppose, and end the affair."

"Yes, sir."

I did not put down my book. My visitor should have a hearing, but not much more: she had sacrificed her womanly claims by her persistent attacks upon my door. Presently Simpson ushered her in. "Miss Grief," he said, and then went out, closing the curtain behind him.

A woman—yes, a lady—but shabby, unattractive, and more than middle-aged.

I rose, bowed slightly, and then dropped into my chair again, still keeping the book in my hand. "Miss Grief?" I said interrogatively as I indicated a seat with my eyebrows.

"Not Grief," she answered—"Crief: my name is Crief."

She sat down, and I saw that she held a small flat box.

"Not carving, then," I thought—"probably old lace, something that belonged to Tullia or Lucrezia Borgia."[4] But, as she did not speak, I found myself obliged to begin: "You have been here, I think, once or twice before?"

"Seven times; this is the eighth."

A silence.

"I am often out; indeed, I may say that I am never in," I remarked carelessly.

"Yes; you have many friends."

"—Who will perhaps buy old lace," I mentally added. But this time I too remained silent; why should I trouble myself to draw her out? She had sought me; let her advance her idea, whatever it was, now that entrance was gained.

But Miss Grief (I preferred to call her so) did not look as though she could advance anything: her black gown, damp with rain, seemed to retreat fearfully to her thin self, while her thin self retreated as far as possible from me, from the chair, from everything. Her eyes were cast down; an old-fashioned lace veil with a heavy border shaded her face. She looked at the floor, and I looked at her.

I grew a little impatient, but I made up my mind that I would continue silent and see how long a time she would consider necessary to give due effect to her little pantomime. Comedy? Or was it tragedy? I suppose full five minutes passed thus in our double silence; and that is a long time when two persons are sitting opposite each other alone in a small still room.

At last my visitor, without raising her eyes, said slowly, "You are very happy, are you not, with youth, health, friends, riches, fame?"

It was a singular beginning. Her voice was clear, low, and very sweet as she thus enumerated my advantages one by one in a list. I was attracted by it, but repelled by her words, which seemed to me flattery both dull and bold.

"Thanks," I said, "for your kindness, but I fear it is undeserved. I seldom discuss myself even when with my friends."

"I am your friend," replied Miss Grief. Then, after a moment, she added slowly, "I have read every word you have written."

I curled the edges of my book indifferently; I am not a fop, I hope, but—others have said the same.

"What is more, I know much of it by heart," continued my visitor. "Wait: I will show you"; and then, without pause, she began to repeat something of mine word for word, just as I had written it. On she went, and I—listened. I intended interrupting her after a moment, but I did not, because she was reciting so well, and also because I felt a desire gaining upon me to see what she would make of a certain conversation which I knew was coming—a conversation between two of my characters which was, to say the least, sphinx-like, and somewhat incandescent as well. What won me a little, too, was the fact that the scene she was reciting (it was hardly more than that, though called a story) was secretly my favorite among all the sketches from my pen which a gracious public has received with favor. I never said so, but it was; and I had always felt a wondering annoyance that the aforesaid public, while kindly praising beyond their worth other attempts of mine, had never noticed the higher purpose of this little shaft, aimed not at the balconies and lighted windows of society, but straight up toward the distant stars. So she went on, and presently reached the conversation: my two people began to talk. She had raised her eyes now, and was looking at me soberly as she gave the words of the woman, quiet, gentle, cold, and the replies of the man, bitter, hot, and scathing. Her very voice changed, and took, though always sweetly, the different tones required, while no point of meaning, however small, no breath of delicate emphasis which I had meant, but which the dull types could not give, escaped an appreciative and full, almost overfull, recognition which startled me. For she had understood me—understood me almost better than I had understood myself. It seemed to me that while I had labored to interpret, partially, a psychological riddle, she, coming after, had comprehended its bearings better than I had, though confining herself strictly to my own words and emphasis. The scene ended (and it ended rather suddenly), she dropped her eyes, and moved her hand nervously to and fro over the box she held; her gloves were old and shabby, her hands small.

I was secretly much surprised by what I had heard, but my ill humor was deep-seated that day, and I still felt sure, besides, that the box contained something which I was expected to buy.

"You recite remarkably well," I said carelessly, "and I am much flattered also by your appreciation of my attempt. But it is not, I presume, to that alone that I owe the pleasure of this visit?"

"Yes," she answered, still looking down, "it is, for if you had not written that scene I should not have sought you. Your other sketches are interiors—exquisitely painted and delicately finished, but of small scope. *This* is a sketch in a few bold, masterly lines—work of entirely different spirit and purpose."

I was nettled by her insight. "You have bestowed so much of your kind attention upon me that I feel your debtor," I said, conventionally. "It may be that there is something I can do for you—connected, possibly, with that little box?"

It was impertinent, but it was true; for she answered, "Yes."

I smiled, but her eyes were cast down and she did not see the smile.

"What I have to show you is a manuscript," she said after a pause which I did not break; "it is a drama. I thought that perhaps you would read it."

"An authoress! This is worse than old lace," I said to myself in dismay.—Then, aloud, "My opinion would be worth nothing, Miss Crief."

"Not in a business way, I know. But it might be—an assistance personally." Her voice had sunk to a whisper; outside, the rain was pouring steadily down. She was a very depressing object to me as she sat there with her box.

"I hardly think I have the time at present—" I began.

She had raised her eyes and was looking at me; then, when I paused, she rose and came suddenly toward my chair. "Yes, you will read it," she said with her hand on my arm—"you will read it. Look at this room; look

253

at yourself; look at all you have. Then look at me, and have pity."

I had risen, for she held my arm, and her damp skirt was brushing my knees.

Her large dark eyes looked intently into mine as she went on: "I have no shame in asking. Why should I have? It is my last endeavor; but a calm and well-considered one. If you refuse I shall go away, knowing that Fate has willed it so. And I shall be content."

"She is mad," I thought. But she did not look so, and she had spoken quietly, even gently. "Sit down," I said, moving away from her. I felt as if I had been magnetized; but it was only the nearness of her eyes to mine, and their intensity. I drew forward a chair, but she remained standing.

"I cannot," she said in the same sweet, gentle tone, "unless you promise."

"Very well, I promise; only sit down."

As I took her arm to lead her to the chair, I perceived that she was trembling, but her face continued unmoved.

"You do not, of course, wish me to look at your manuscript now?" I said, temporizing; "it would be much better to leave it. Give me your address, and I will return it to you with my written opinion; though, I repeat, the latter will be of no use to you. It is the opinion of an editor or publisher that you want."

"It shall be as you please. And I will go in a moment," said Miss Grief, pressing her palms together, as if trying to control the tremor that had seized her slight frame.

She looked so pallid that I thought of offering her a glass of wine; then I remembered that if I did it might be a bait to bring her here again, and this I was desirous to prevent. She rose while the thought was passing through my mind. Her pasteboard box lay on the chair she had first oc-cupied; she took it, wrote an address on the cover, laid it down, and then, bowing with a little air of formality, drew her black shawl round her shoulders and turned toward the door.

I followed, after touching the bell. "You will hear from me by letter," I said.

Simpson opened the door, and I caught a glimpse of the maid, who was waiting in the anteroom. She was an old woman, shorter than her mistress, equally thin, and dressed like her in rusty black. As the door opened she turned toward it a pair of small, dim, blue eyes with a look of furtive suspense. Simpson dropped the curtain, shutting me into the inner room; he had no intention of allowing me to accompany my visitor further. But I had the curiosity to go to a bay window in an angle from whence I could command the street door, and presently I saw them issue forth in the rain and walk away side by side, the mistress, being the taller, holding the umbrella: probably there was not much difference in rank between persons so poor and forlorn as these.

It grew dark. I was invited out for the evening, and I knew that if I should go I should meet Miss Abercrombie. I said to myself that I would not go. I got out my paper for writing, I made my preparations for a quiet evening at home with myself; but it was of no use. It all ended slavishly in my going. At the last allowable moment I presented myself, and—as a punishment for my vacillation, I suppose—I never passed a more disagreeable evening. I drove homeward in a murky temper; it was foggy without, and very foggy within. What Isabel really was, now that she had broken through my elaborately built theories, I was not able to decide. There was, to tell the truth, a certain young Englishman—But that is apart from this story.

I reached home, went up to my rooms, and had a supper. It was to console myself; I am obliged to console myself scientifically once in a while. I was walking up and down afterward, smoking and feeling somewhat better, when my eye fell upon the pasteboard box. I took it up; on the cover was written an address which showed that my visitor must have walked a long distance in order to see me: "A. Crief."—"A Grief," I thought; "and so she is. I positively believe she has brought all this trouble upon me: she has the evil eye." I took out the manuscript and looked at it. It was in the form of a little volume, and clearly written; on the cover was the word "Armor" in German text, and, underneath, a pen-and-ink sketch of a helmet, breastplate, and shield.

"Grief certainly needs armor," I said to myself, sitting down by the table and turning over the pages. "I may as well look over the thing now; I could not be in a worse mood." And then I began to read.

Early the next morning Simpson took a note from me to the given address, returning with the following reply: "No; I prefer to come to you; at four; A. Grief." These words, with their three semicolons, were written in pencil upon a piece of coarse printing paper, but the handwriting was as clear and delicate as that of the manuscript in ink.

"What sort of a place was it, Simpson?"

"Very poor, sir, but I did not go all the way up. The elder person came down, sir, took the note, and requested me to wait where I was."

"You had no chance, then, to make inquiries?" I said, knowing full well that he had emptied the entire neighborhood of any information it might possess concerning these two lodgers.

"Well, sir, you know how these foreigners will talk, whether one wants to hear or not. But it seems that these two persons have been there but a few weeks; they live alone, and are uncommonly silent and reserved. The people round there call them something that signifies 'the Madames American, thin and dumb.'"

At four the "Madames American" arrived; it was raining again, and they came on foot under their old umbrella. The maid waited in the anteroom, and Miss Grief was ushered into my bachelor's parlor. I had thought that I should meet her with great deference; but she looked so forlorn that my deference changed to pity. It was the woman that impressed me then, more than the writer—the fragile, nerveless body more than the inspired mind. For it was inspired; I had sat up half the night over her drama, and had felt thrilled through and through more than once by its earnestness, passion, and power.

No one could have been more surprised than I was to find myself thus enthusiastic. I thought I had outgrown that sort of thing. And one would have supposed, too (I myself should have supposed so the day before), that the faults of the drama, which were many and prominent, would have chilled any liking I might have felt, I being a writer myself, and therefore critical; for writers are as apt to make much of the "how," rather than the "what," as painters, who, it is well known, prefer an exquisitely rendered representation of a commonplace theme to an imperfectly executed picture of even the most striking subject. But in this case, on the contrary, the scattered rays of splendor in Miss Grief's drama had made me forget the dark spots, which were numerous and disfiguring; or, rather, the splendor had made me anxious to have the spots removed. And this also was a philanthropic state very unusual with me. Regarding unsuccessful writers, my motto had been "Væ victis!" [5]

My visitor took a seat and folded her hands; I could see, in spite of her quiet manner, that she was in breathless suspense. It seemed so pitiful that she should be trembling there before me—a woman so much older than I was, a woman who possessed the divine spark of genius, which I was by no means sure (in spite of my success) had been granted to me—that I felt as if I ought to go down on my knees before her, and entreat her to take her proper place of supremacy at once. But there! one does not go down on one's knees, combustively, as it were, before a woman over fifty, plain in feature, thin, dejected, and ill dressed. I contented myself with taking her hands (in their miserable old gloves) in mine, while I said cordially, "Miss Crief, your drama seems to me full of original power. It has roused my enthusiasm: I sat up half the night reading it."

The hands I held shook, but something (perhaps a shame for having evaded the knees business) made me tighten my hold and bestow upon her also a reassuring smile. She looked at me for a moment, and then, suddenly and noiselessly, tears rose and rolled down her cheeks. I dropped her hands and retreated. I had not thought her tearful: on the contrary, her voice and face had seemed rigidly controlled. But now here she was bending herself over the side of the chair with her head resting on her arms, not sobbing aloud, but her whole frame shaken by the strength of her emotion. I rushed for a glass of wine; I pressed her to take it. I did not quite know what to do, but, putting myself in her place, I decided to praise the drama; and praise it I did. I do not know when I have used so many adjectives. She raised her head and began to wipe her eyes.

"Do take the wine," I said, interrupting myself in my cataract of language.

"I dare not," she answered; then added humbly, "that is, unless you have a biscuit here or a bit of bread."

I found some biscuit; she ate two, and then slowly drank the wine, while I resumed my verbal Niagara. Under its influence—and that of the wine too, perhaps—she began to show new life. It was not that she looked radiant—she could not—but simply that she looked warm. I now perceived what had been the principal discomfort of her appearance heretofore: it was that she had looked all the time as if suffering from cold.

At last I could think of nothing more to say, and stopped. I really admired the drama, but I thought I had exerted myself sufficiently as an anti-hysteric, and that adjectives enough, for the present at least, had been administered. She had put down her empty wineglass, and was resting her hands on the broad cushioned arms of her chair with, for a thin person, a sort of expanded content.

"You must pardon my tears," she said, smiling; "it was the revulsion of feeling. My life was at a low ebb: if your sentence had been against me, it would have been my end."

"Your end?"

"Yes, the end of my life; I should have destroyed myself."

"Then you would have been a weak as well as wicked woman," I said in a tone of disgust. I do hate sensationalism.

"Oh no, you know nothing about it. I should have destroyed only this poor worn tenement of clay. But I can well understand how *you* would look upon it. Regarding the desirableness of life, the prince and the beggar may have different opinions. We will say no more of it, but talk of the drama instead." As she spoke the word "drama" a triumphant brightness came into her eyes.

I took the manuscript from a drawer and sat down beside her. "I suppose you know that there are faults," I said, expecting ready acquiescence.

"I was not aware that there were any," was her gentle reply.

Here was a beginning! After all my interest in her—and, I may say under the circumstances, my kindness—she received me in this way! However, my belief in her genius was too sincere to be altered by her whimsies; so I persevered. "Let us go over it together," I said. "Shall I read it to you, or will you read it to me?"

"I will not read it, but recite it."

"That will never do; you will recite it so well that we shall see only the good points, and what we have to concern ourselves with now is the bad ones."

"I will recite it," she repeated.

"Now, Miss Crief," I said bluntly, "for what purpose did you come to me? Certainly not merely to recite: I am no stage manager. In plain English, was it not your idea that I might help you in obtaining a publisher?"

"Yes, yes," she answered, looking at me apprehensively, all her old manner returning.

I followed up my advantage, opened the little paper volume and began. I first took the drama line by line, and spoke of the faults of expression and structure; then I turned back and touched upon two or three glaring impossibilities in the plot. "Your absorbed interest in the motive of the whole no doubt made you forget these blemishes," I said apologetically.

But, to my surprise, I found that she did not see the blemishes—that she appreciated nothing I had said, comprehended nothing. Such unaccountable obtuseness puzzled me. I began again, going over the whole with even greater minuteness and care. I worked hard: the perspiration stood in beads upon my forehead as I struggled with her—what shall I call it—obstinacy? But it was not exactly obstinacy. She simply could not see the faults of her own work, any more than a blind man can see the smoke that dims a patch of blue sky. When I had finished my task the second time, she still remained as gently impassive as before. I leaned back in my chair exhausted, and looked at her.

Even then she did not seem to comprehend (whether she agreed with it or not) what I must be thinking. "It is such a heaven to me that you like it!" she murmured dreamily, breaking the silence. Then, with more animation, "And *now* you will let me recite it?"

I was too weary to oppose her; she threw aside her shawl and bonnet, and standing in the center of the room, began.

And she carried me along with her: all the strong passages were doubly strong when spoken, and the faults, which seemed nothing to her, were made by her earnestness to seem nothing to me, at least for that moment. When it was ended, she stood looking at me with a triumphant smile.

"Yes," I said, "I like it, and you see that I do. But I like it because my taste is peculiar. To me originality and force are everything—perhaps because I have them not to any marked degree myself—but the world at large will not overlook as I do your absolutely barbarous shortcomings on account of them. Will you trust me to go over the drama and correct it at my pleasure?" This was a vast deal for me to offer; I was surprised at myself.

"No," she answered softly, still smiling. "There shall not be so much as a comma altered." Then she sat down and fell into a reverie as though she were alone.

"Have you written anything else?" I said after a while, when I had become tired of the silence.

"Yes."

"Can I see it? Or is it *them?*"

"It is *them*. Yes, you can see all."

"I will call upon you for the purpose."

"No, you must not," she said, coming back to the present nervously. "I prefer to come to you."

At this moment Simpson entered to light the room, and busied himself rather longer than was necessary over the task. When he finally went out, I saw that my visitor's manner had sunk into its former depression: the presence of the servant seemed to have chilled her.

"When did you say I might come?" I repeated, ignoring her refusal.

"I did not say it. It would be impossible."

"Well, then, when will you come here?" There was, I fear, a trace of fatigue in my tone.

"At your good pleasure, sir," she answered humbly.

My chivalry was touched by this: after all, she was a woman. "Come tomorrow," I said. "By the way, come and dine with me then; why not?" I was curious to see what she would reply.

"Why not, indeed? Yes, I will come. I am forty-three: I might have been your mother."

This was not quite true, as I am over thirty: but I look young, while she—Well, I had thought her over fifty. "I can hardly call you 'mother,' but we might compromise upon 'aunt,'" I said, laughing. "Aunt what?"

"My name is Aaronna," she gravely answered. "My father was much disappointed that I was not a boy, and gave me as nearly as possible the name he had prepared—Aaron."

"Then come and dine with me tomorrow, and bring with you the other manuscripts, Aaronna," I said, amused at the quaint sound of the name. On the whole, I did not like "aunt."

"I will come," she answered.

It was twilight and still raining, but she refused all offers of escort or carriage, departing with her maid, as she had come, under the brown umbrella. The next day we had the dinner. Simpson was astonished—and more than astonished, grieved—when I told him that he was to dine with the maid; but he could not complain in words, since my own guest, the mistress, was hardly more attractive. When our preparations were complete, I could not help laughing: the two prim little tables, one in the parlor and one in the anteroom, and Simpson disapprovingly going back and forth between them, were irresistible.

I greeted my guest hilariously when she arrived, and, fortunately, her manner was not quite so depressed as usual: I could never have accorded myself with a tearful mood. I had thought that perhaps she would make, for the occasion, some change in her attire; I have never known a woman who had not some scrap of finery, however small, in reserve for that unexpected occasion of which she is ever dreaming. But no: Miss Grief wore the same black gown, unadorned and unaltered. I was glad that there was no rain that day, so that the skirt did not at least look so damp and rheumatic.

She ate quietly, almost furtively, yet with a good appetite, and she did not refuse the wine. Then, when the meal was over and Simpson had removed the dishes, I asked for the new manuscripts. She gave me an old green copybook filled with short poems, and a prose sketch by itself; I lit a cigar and sat down at my desk to look them over.

"Perhaps you will try a cigarette?" I suggested, more for amusement than anything else, for there was not a shade of Bohemianism about her; her whole appearance was puritanical.

"I have not yet succeeded in learning to smoke."

"You have tried?" I said, turning round.

"Yes: Serena and I tried, but we did not succeed."

"Serena is your maid?"

"She lives with me."

I was seized with inward laughter, and began hastily to look over her manuscripts with my back toward her, so that she might not see it. A vision had risen before me of those two forlorn women, alone in their room with locked doors, patiently trying to acquire the smoker's art.

But my attention was soon absorbed by the papers before me. Such a fantastic collection of words, lines, and epithets I had never before seen, or even in dreams imagined. In truth, they were like the work of dreams: they were *Kubla Khan,*[6] only more so. Here and there was radiance like the flash of a diamond, but each poem, almost each verse and line, was marred by some fault or lack which seemed wilful perversity, like the work of an evil sprite. It was like a case of jeweller's wares set before you, with each ring unfinished, each bracelet too large or too small for its purpose, each breast-pin without its fastening, each necklace purposely broken. I turned the pages, marvelling. When about half an hour had passed, and I was leaning back for a moment to light another cigar, I glanced toward my visitor. She was behind me, in an easy chair before my small fire, and she was—fast asleep! In the relaxation of her unconsciousness I was struck anew by the poverty her appearance expressed; her feet were visible, and I saw the miserable worn old shoes which hitherto she had kept concealed.

After looking at her for a moment, I returned to my task and took up the prose story; in prose she must be more reasonable. She was less fantastic perhaps, but hardly more reasonable. The story was that of a profligate and commonplace man forced by two of his friends, in order not to break the heart of a dying girl who loves him, to live up to a high imaginary ideal of himself which her pure but mistaken mind has formed. He has a handsome face and sweet voice, and repeats what they tell them. Her long, slow decline and happy death, and his own inward ennui and profound weariness of the rôle he has to play, made the vivid points of the story. So far, well enough, but here was the trouble: through the whole narrative moved another character, a physician of tender heart and exquisite mercy, who practiced murder as a fine art, and was regarded (by the author) as a second Messiah! This was monstrous. I read it through twice, and threw it down; then, fatigued, I turned round and leaned back, waiting for her to wake. I could see her profile against the dark hue of the easy chair.

Presently she seemed to feel my gaze, for she stirred, then opened her eyes. "I have been asleep," she said, rising hurriedly.

"No harm in that, Aaronna."

But she was deeply embarrassed and troubled, much more so than the occasion required; so much so, indeed, that I turned the conversation back upon the manuscripts as a diversion. "I cannot stand that doctor of yours," I said, indicating the prose story; "no one would. You must cut him out."

Her self-possession returned as if by magic. "Certainly not," she answered haughtily.

"Oh, if you do not care—I had labored under the impression that you were anxious these things should find a purchaser."

"I am, I am," she said, her manner changing to deep humility with wonderful rapidity. With such alternations of feeling as this sweeping over her like great waves, no wonder she was old before her time.

"Then you must take out that doctor."

"I am willing, but do not know how," she answered, pressing her hands together helplessly. "In my mind he belongs to the story so closely that he cannot be separated from it."

Here Simpson entered, bringing a note for me: it was a line from Mrs. Abercrombie inviting me for that evening—an unexpected gathering, and therefore likely to be all the more agreeable. My heart bounded in spite of me; I forgot Miss Grief and her manuscripts for the moment as completely as though they had never existed. But, bodily, being still in the same room with her, her speech brought me back to the present.

"You have had good news?" she said.

"Oh no, nothing especial—merely an invitation."

"But good news also," she repeated. "And now, as for me, I must go."

Not supposing that she would stay much later in any case, I had that morning ordered a carriage to come for her at about that hour. I told her this. She made no reply beyond putting on her bonnet and shawl.

"You will hear from me soon," I said; "I shall do all I can for you."

She had reached the door, but before opening it she stopped, turned and extended her hand. "You are good," she said: "I give you thanks. Do not think me ungrateful or envious. It is only that you are young, and I am so—so old." Then she opened the door and passed through the anteroom without pause, her maid accompanying her and Simpson with gladness lighting the way. They were gone. I dressed hastily and went out—to continue my studies in psychology.

Time passed; I was busy, amused and perhaps a little excited (sometimes psychology is exciting). But, though much occupied with my own affairs, I did not altogether neglect my self-imposed task regarding Miss Grief. I began by sending her prose story to a friend, the editor of a monthly magazine, with a letter making a strong plea for its admittance. It should have a chance first on its own merits. Then I forwarded the drama to a publisher, also an acquaintance, a man with a taste for phantasms and a soul above mere common popularity, as his own coffers knew to their cost. This done, I waited with conscience clear.

Four weeks passed. During this waiting period I heard nothing from Miss Grief. At last one morning came a letter from my editor. "The story has force, but I cannot stand that doctor," he wrote. "Let her cut him out, and I might print it." Just what I myself had said. The package lay there on my table, travel worn and grimed; a returned manuscript is, I think, the most melancholy object on earth. I decided to wait, before writing to Aaronna, until the second letter was received. A week later it came. "Armor" was declined. The publisher had been "impressed" by the power displayed in certain passages, but the "impossibilities of the plot" rendered it "unavailable for publication"—in fact, would "bury it in ridicule" if brought before the public, a public "lamentably" fond of amusement, "seeking it, undaunted, even in the cannon's mouth." I doubt if he knew himself what he meant. But one thing, at any rate, was clear: "Armor" was declined.

Now, I am, as I have remarked before, a little obstinate. I was determined that Miss Grief's work should be received. I would alter and improve it myself, without letting her know: the end justified the means. Surely the sieve of my own good taste, whose mesh had been pronounced so fine and delicate, would serve for two. I began; and utterly failed.

I set to work first upon "Armor." I amended, altered, left out, put in, pieced, condensed, lengthened; I did my best, and all to no avail. I could not succeed in completing anything that satisfied me, or that approached, in truth, Miss Grief's own work just as it stood. I suppose I went over that manuscript twenty times: I covered sheets of paper with my copies. But the obstinate drama refused to be corrected; as it was it must stand or fall.

Wearied and annoyed, I threw it aside and took up the prose story: that would be easier. But, to my surprise, I found that that apparently gentle "doctor" would not out: he was so closely interwoven with every part of the tale that to take him out was like taking out one especial figure in a carpet: that is, impossible, unless you unravel the whole. At last I did unravel the whole, and then the story was no longer good, or Aaronna's: it was weak, and mine. All this took time, for of course I had much to do in connection with my own life and tasks. But, though slowly and at my leisure, I really did try my best as regarded Miss Grief, and without success. I was forced at last to make up my mind that either my own powers were not equal to the task, or else that her perversities were as essential a part of her work as her inspirations, and not to be separated from it. Once during this period I showed two of the short poems to Isabel, withholding of course the writer's name. "They were written by a woman," I explained.

"Her mind must have been disordered, poor thing!" Isabel said in her gentle way when she returned them—"at least, judging by these. They are hopelessly mixed and vague."

Now, they were not vague so much as vast. But I knew that I could not make Isabel comprehend it, and (so complex a creature is man) I do not know that I wanted her to comprehend it. These were the only ones in the whole collection that I would have shown her, and I was rather glad that she did not like even these. Not that poor Aaronna's poems were evil: they were simply unrestrained, large, vast, like the skies or the wind. Isabel was bounded on all sides, like a violet in a garden bed. And I liked her so.

One afternoon, about the time when I was beginning to see that I could not "improve" Miss Grief, I came upon the maid. I was driving, and she had stopped on the crossing to let the carriage pass. I recognized her at a glance (by her general forlornness), and called to the driver to stop. "How is Miss Grief?" I said. "I have been intending to write to her for some time."

"And your note, when it comes," answered the old woman on the crosswalk fiercely, "she shall not see."

"What?"

"I say she shall not see it. Your patronizing face shows that you have no good news, and you shall not rack and stab her any more on *this* earth, please God, while I have authority."

"Who has racked or stabbed her, Serena?"

"Serena, indeed! Rubbish! I'm no Serena: I'm her aunt. And as to who has racked and stabbed her, I say you, *you*—YOU literary men!" She had put her old head inside my carriage, and flung out these words at me in a shrill, menacing tone. "But she shall die in peace in spite of you," she continued. "Vampires! you take her ideas and fatten on them, and leave her to starve. You know you do—*you* who have had her poor manuscripts these months and months!"

"Is she ill?" I asked in real concern, gathering that much at least from the incoherent tirade.

"She is dying," answered the desolate old creature, her voice softening and her dim eyes filling with tears.

"Oh, I trust not. Perhaps something can be done. Can I help you in any way?"

"In all ways if you would," she said, breaking down and beginning to sob weakly, with her head resting on the sill of the carriage window. "Oh, what have we not been through together, we two! Piece by piece I have sold all."

I am goodhearted enough, but I do not like to have old women weeping across my carriage door. I suggested, therefore, that she should come inside and let me take her home. Her shabby old skirt was soon beside me, and, following her directions, the driver turned toward one of the most wretched quarters of the city, the abode of poverty, crowded and unclean. Here, in a large bare chamber up many flights of stairs, I found Miss Grief.

As I entered I was startled: I thought she was dead. There seemed no life present until she opened her eyes, and even then they rested upon us vaguely, as though she did not know who we were. But as I approached a light came into them: she recognized me, and this sudden revivification, this return of the soul to the almost deserted body, was the most wonderful thing I ever saw. "You have good news of the drama?" she whispered as I bent over her: "tell me. I *know* you have good news."

What was I to answer? Pray, what would you have answered, puritan?

"Yes, I have good news, Aaronna," I said. "The drama will appear." (And who knows? Perhaps it will in some other world.)

She smiled, and her now brilliant eyes did not leave my face.

"He knows I'm your aunt: I told him," said the old woman, coming to the bedside.

"Did you?" whispered Miss Grief, still gazing at me with a smile. "Then please, dear Aunt Martha, give me something to eat."

Aunt Martha hurried across the room, and I followed her. "It's the first time she's asked for food in weeks," she said in a husky tone.

She opened a cupboard door vaguely, but I could see nothing within. "What have you for her?" I asked with some impatience, though in a low voice.

"Please God, nothing!" answered the poor old woman, hiding her reply and her tears behind the broad cupboard door. "I was going out to get a little something when I met you."

"Good Heavens! is it money you need? Here, take this and send; or go yourself in the carriage waiting below."

She hurried out breathless, and I went back to the bedside, much disturbed by what I had seen and heard. But Miss Grief's eyes were full of life, and as I sat down beside her she whispered earnestly, "Tell me."

And I did tell her—a romance invented for the occasion. I venture to say that none of my published sketches could compare with it. As for the lie involved, it will stand among my few good deeds, I know, at the judgment bar.

And she was satisfied. "I have never known what it was," she whispered, "to be fully happy until now." She closed her eyes, and when the lids fell I again thought that she had passed away. But no, there was still pulsation in her small, thin wrist. As she perceived my touch she smiled. "Yes, I am happy," she said again, though without audible sound.

The old aunt returned; food was prepared, and she took some. I myself went out after wine that should be rich and pure. She rallied a little, but I did not leave her: her eyes dwelt upon me and compelled me to stay, or rather my conscience compelled me. It was a damp night, and I had a little fire made. The wine, fruit, flowers, and candles I had ordered made the bare place for the time being bright and fragrant. Aunt Martha dozed in her chair from sheer fatigue—she had watched many nights—but Miss Grief was awake, and I sat beside her.

"I make you my executor," she murmured, "as to the drama. But my other manuscripts place, when I am gone, under my head, and let them be buried with me. They are not many—those you have and these. See!"

I followed her gesture, and saw under her pillows the edges of two more copybooks like the one I had. "Do not look at them—my poor dead children!" she said tenderly. "Let them depart with me—unread, as I have been."

Later she whispered, "Did you wonder why I came to you? It was the contrast. You were young—strong—rich—praised—loved— successful: all that I was not. I wanted to look at you—and imagine how it would feel. You had success—but I had the greater power. Tell me, did I not have it?"

"Yes, Aaronna."

"It is all in the past now. But I am satisfied."

After another pause she said with a faint smile, "Do you remember when I fell asleep in your parlor? It was the good and rich food. It was so long since I had had food like that!"

I took her hand and held it, conscience stricken, but now she hardly seemed to perceive my touch. "And the smoking?" she whispered. "Do you remember how you laughed? I saw it. But I had heard that smoking soothed—that one was no longer tired and hungry—with a cigar."

In little whispers of this sort, separated by long rests and pauses, the night passed. Once she asked if her aunt was asleep, and when I answered in the affirmative she said, "Help her to return home—to America: the drama will pay for it. I ought never to have brought her away."

I promised, and she resumed her bright-eyed silence.

I think she did not speak again. Toward morning the change came, and soon after sunrise, with her old aunt kneeling by her side, she passed away.

All was arranged as she had wished. Her manuscripts, covered with violets, formed her pillow. No one followed her to the grave save her aunt and myself; I thought she would prefer it so. Her name was not "Crief," after all, but "Moncrief"; I saw it written out by Aunt Martha for the coffin plate, as follows: "Aaronna Moncrief, aged forty-three years, two months, and eight days."

I never knew more of her history than is written here. If there was more that I might have learned, it remained unlearned, for I did not ask.

And the drama? I keep it here in this locked case. I could have had it published at my own expense; but I think that now she knows its faults herself, perhaps, and would not like it.

I keep it; and, once in a while, I read it over—not as a *memento mori* [7] exactly, but rather as a memento of my own good fortune, for which I should continually give thanks. The want of one grain made all her work void, and that one grain was given to me. She, with the greater power, failed—I, with the less, succeeded. But no praise is due to me for that. When I die "Armor" is to be destroyed unread: not even Isabel is to see it. For women will misunderstand each other; and, dear and precious to me as my sweet wife is, I could not bear that she or anyone should cast so much as a thought of scorn upon the memory of the writer, upon my poor dead, "unavailable," unaccepted "Miss Grief."

"MISS WOOLSON"

꘎꘎꘎꘎꘎

by Henry James

FLOODED as we have been in these latter days with copious discussion as to
the admission of women to various offices, colleges, functions, and privileges, singularly little attention has been paid, by themselves at least, to the
fact that in one highly important department of human affairs their cause is
already gained—gained in such a way as to deprive them largely of their
ground, formerly so substantial, for complaining of the intolerance of man.
In America, in England, to-day, it is no longer a question of their admission
into the world of literature: they are there in force; they have been admitted, with all the honours, on a perfectly equal footing. In America, at
least, one feels tempted at moments to exclaim that they are in themselves
the world of literature. In Germany and in France, in this line of production, their presence is less to be perceived. To speak only of the latter
country, France has brought forth in the persons of Madame de Sévigné,
Madame de Staël, and Madame Sand,[1] three female writers of the first
rank, without counting a hundred ladies to whom we owe charming memoirs and volumes of reminiscence; but in the table of contents of the Revue
des Deux Mondes,[2] that epitome of the literary movement (as regards everything, at least, but the famous doctrine, in fiction, of "naturalism"), it is
rare to encounter the name of a female contributor. The covers of American and English periodicals tell a different story; in these monthly joints of
the ladder of fame the ladies stand as thick as on the staircase at a crowded
evening party.

"Miss Woolson" by Henry James

There are, of course, two points of view from which this free possession of the public ear may be considered—as regards its effect upon the life of women, and as regards its effect upon literature. I hasten to add that I do not propose to consider either, and I touch on the general fact simply because the writer whose name I have placed at the head of these remarks happens to be a striking illustration of it. The work of Miss Constance Fenimore Woolson is an excellent example of the way the door stands open between the personal life of American women and the immeasurable world of print, and what makes it so is the particular quality that this work happens to possess. It breathes a spirit singularly and essentially conservative—the sort of spirit which, but for a special indication pointing the other way, would in advance seem most to oppose itself to the introduction into the feminine lot of new and complicating elements. Miss Woolson evidently thinks that lot sufficiently complicated, with the sensibilities which even in primitive ages women were acknowledged to possess; fenced in by the old disabilities and prejudices, they seem to her to have been by their very nature only too much exposed, and it would never occur to her to lend her voice to the plea for further exposure—for a revolution which should place her sex in the thick of the struggle for power. She sees it in preference surrounded certainly by plenty of doors and windows (she has not, I take it, a love of bolts and Oriental shutters), but distinctly on the private side of that somewhat evasive and exceedingly shifting line which divides human affairs into the profane and the sacred. Such is the turn of mind of the author of *Rodman the Keeper* and *East Angels,* and if it has not prevented her from writing books, from competing for the literary laurel, this is a proof of the strength of the current which to-day carries both sexes alike to that mode of expression.[3]

Miss Woolson's first productions were two collections of short tales, published in 1875 and 1880, and entitled respectively *Castle Nowhere* and *Rodman the Keeper.* I may not profess an acquaintance with the former of these volumes, but the latter is full of interesting artistic work. Miss Woolson has done nothing better than the best pages in this succession of careful, strenuous studies of certain aspects of life, after the war, in Florida, Georgia and the Carolinas. As the fruit of a remarkable minuteness of observation and tenderness of feeling on the part of one who evidently did not glance and pass, but lingered and analysed, they have a high value, especially when regarded in the light of the *voicelessness* of the conquered and reconstructed South. Miss Woolson strikes the reader as having a compassionate sense of this pathetic dumbness—having perceived that no social revolution of equal magnitude had ever reflected itself so little in literature, remained so unrecorded, so unpainted and unsung. She has attempted to give an impression of this circumstance, among others, and a sympathy altogether feminine has guided her pen. She loves the whole region, and no daughter of the land could have handled its peculiarities more indulgently, or communicated to us more of the sense of close observation and intimate knowledge. Nevertheless it must be confessed that the picture, on the whole, is a picture of dreariness—of impressions that may have been gathered in the course of lonely afternoon walks at the end of hot days, when the sunset was wan, on the edge of rice-fields, dismal swamps, and other brackish inlets. The author is to be congratulated in so far as such expeditions may have been the source of her singularly exact familiarity with the "natural objects" of the region, including the negro of reality. She knows every plant and flower, every vague odour and sound, the song and flight of every bird, every tint of the sky and murmur of the forest, and she has noted scientifically the dialect of the freedmen. It is not too much to say that the negroes in *Rodman the Keeper* and in *East Angels* are a careful philological study, and that if Miss Woolson preceded Uncle Remus[4] by a considerable interval, she may have the credit of the initiative—of having been the first to take their words straight from their lips.

No doubt that if in *East Angels,* as well as in the volume of tales, the sadness of Miss Woolson's South is more striking than its high spirits, this is owing somewhat to the author's taste in the way of subject and situation, and especially to her predilection for cases of heroic sacrifice—sacrifice sometimes unsuspected and always unappreciated. She is fond of irretrievable personal failures, of people who have had to give up even the memory of happiness, who love and suffer in silence, and minister in secret to the happiness of those who look over their heads. She is interested in general in secret histories, in the "inner life" of the weak, the superfluous, the disappointed, the bereaved, the unmarried. She believes in personal renunciation, in its frequency as well as its beauty. It plays a prominent part in each of her novels, especially in the last two, and the interest of *East Angels* at least is largely owing to her success in having made an extreme case of the virtue in question credible to the reader. Is it because this element is weaker in *Anne,* which was published in 1882, that *Anne* strikes me as the least happily composed of the author's works? The early chapters are charming and full of promise, but the story wanders away from them, and the pledge is not taken up. The reader has built great hopes upon Tita, but Tita vanishes into the vague, after putting him out of countenance by an infant marriage—an accident in regard to which, on the whole, throughout her stories, Miss Woolson shows perhaps an excessive indulgence. She likes the unmarried, as I have mentioned, but she likes marriages even better, and also sometimes hurries them forward in advance of the reader's exaction. The only complaint it would occur to me to make of *East Angels* is that Garda Thorne, whom we cannot think of as anything but a little girl, discounts the projects we have formed for her by marrying twice; and somehow the case is not bettered by the fact that nothing is more natural than that she should marry twice, unless it be that she should marry three times. We have perceived her, after all, from the first, to be peculiarly adapted to a succession of pretty widowhoods.

For the Major has an idea, a little fantastic perhaps, but eminently definite. This idea is the secret effort of an elderly woman to appear really as young to her husband as (owing to peculiar circumstances) he believed her to be when he married her. Nature helps her (she happens to preserve, late in life, the look of comparative youth), and art helps nature, and her husband's illusions, fostered by failing health and a weakened brain, help them both, so that she is able to keep on the mask till his death, when she pulls it off with a passionate cry of relief—ventures at last, gives herself the luxury, to be old. The sacrifice in this case has been the sacrifice of the maternal instinct, she having had a son, now a man grown, by a former marriage, who reappears after unsuccessful wanderings in far lands, and whom she may not permit herself openly to recognise. The sacrificial attitude is indeed repeated on the part of her step-daughter, who, being at last taken into Madam Carroll's confidence, suffers the young man—a shabby, compromising, inglorious acquaintance—to pass for her lover, thereby discrediting herself almost fatally (till the situation is straightened out), with the Rev. Frederick Owen, who has really been marked out by Providence for the character, and who cannot explain on any comfortable hypothesis her relations with the mysterious Bohemian. Miss Woolson's women in general are capable of these refinements of devotion and exaltations of conscience, and she has a singular talent for making our sympathies go with them. The conception of Madam Carroll is highly ingenious and original, and the small stippled portrait has a real fascination. It is the first time that a woman has been represented as painting her face, dyeing her hair, and "dressing young," out of tenderness for another: the effort usually has its source in tenderness for herself. But Miss Woolson has done nothing of a neater execution than this fanciful figure of the little ringleted, white-frocked, falsely juvenile lady, who has the toilet-table of an actress and the conscience of a Puritan.

The author likes a glamour, and by minute touches and gentle, conciliatory arts, she usually succeeds in producing a valid one. If I had more space I should like to count over these cumulative strokes, in which a delicate manipulation of the real is mingled with an occasionally frank appeal to the romantic muse. But I can only mention two of the most obvious: one the frequency of her reference to the episcopal church as an institution giving a tone to American life (the sort of tone which it is usually assumed that we must seek in civilisations more permeated with ecclesiasticism); the other her fondness for family histories—for the idea of perpetuation of race, especially in the backward direction. I hasten to add that there is nothing of the crudity of sectarianism in the former of these manifestations, or of the dreariness of the purely genealogical passion in the latter; but none the less is it clear that Miss Woolson likes little country churches that are dedicated to saints not vulgarised by too much notoriety, that are dressed in greenery (and would be with holly if there were any), at Christmas and Easter; that have "rectors," well connected, who are properly garmented, and organists, slightly deformed if possible, and addicted to playing Gregorian chants in the twilight, who are adequately artistic; likes also generations that have a pleasant consciousness of a few warm generations behind them, screening them in from too bleak a past, from vulgar draughts in the rear. I know not whether for the most part we are either so Anglican or so long-descended as in Miss Woolson's pages we strike ourselves as being, but it is certain that as we read we protest but little against the soft impeachment. She represents us at least as we should like to be, and she does so with such discretion and taste that we have no fear of incurring ridicule by assent. She has a high sense of the picturesque; she cannot get on without a social atmosphere. Once, I think, she has looked for these things in the wrong place—at the country boardinghouse denominated Caryl's, in *Anne,* where there must have been flies and grease in the dining-room, and the ladies must have been over-dressed; but as a general thing her quest is remarkably happy. She stays at home, and yet gives us a sense of being "abroad"; she has a remarkable faculty of making the new world seem ancient. She succeeds in represent-ing Far Edgerly, the mountain village in *For the Major,* as bathed in the precious medium I speak of. Where is it meant to be, and where was the place that gave her the pattern of it? We gather vaguely, though there are no negroes, that it is in the south; but this, after all, is a tolerably indefinite part of the United States. It is somewhere in the midst of forests, and yet it has as many idiosyncrasies as Mrs. Gaskell's *Cranford,*[5] with added possibili-ties of the pathetic and the tragic. What new town is so composite? What composite town is so new? Miss Woolson anticipates these questions; that is she prevents us from asking them: we swallow Far Edgerly whole, or say at most, with a sigh, that if it couldn't have been like that it certainly ought to have been.

It is, however, in *East Angels* that she has been most successful in this feat of evoking a local tone, and this is a part of the general superiority of that very interesting work, which to my mind represents a long stride of her talent, and has more than the value of all else she has done. In *East Angels* the attempt to create an atmosphere has had, to a considerable degree, the benefit of the actual quality of things in the warm, rank penin-sula which she has studied so exhaustively and loves so well. Miss Woolson found a tone in the air of Florida, but it is not too much to say that she has left it still more agreeably rich—converted it into a fine golden haze. Wonderful is the tact with which she has pressed it into the service of her story, draped the bare spots of the scene with it, and hung it there half as a curtain and half as a background. *East Angels* is a performance which does Miss Woolson the highest honour, and if her talent is capable, in another novel, of making an advance equal to that represented by this work in relation to its predecessors, she will have made a substantial contribution to our new literature of fiction. Long, comprehensive, copious, still more elaborate than her other elaborations, *East Angels* presents the interest of a large and well-founded scheme. The result is not flawless at every point, but the undertaking is of a fine, high kind, and, for the most part, the effect produced is thoroughly worthy of it. The author has, in other words, proposed to give us the complete natural history, as it were, of a group of persons collected, in a complicated relationship, in a little winter-city on a southern shore, and she has expended on her subject stores of just observation and an infinite deal of the true historical spirit. How much of this spirit and of artistic feeling there is in the book, only an attentive perusal will reveal. The central situation is a very interesting one, and is triumphantly treated, but I confess that what is most substantial to me in the book is the writer's general conception of her task, her general attitude of watching life, waiting upon it and trying to catch it in the fact. I know not what theories she may hold in relation to all this business, to what camp or league she may belong; my impression indeed would be that she is perfectly free—that she considers that though camps and leagues may be useful organisations for looking for the truth, it is not in their own bosom that it is usually to be found. However this may be, it is striking that, artistically, she has had a fruitful instinct in seeing the novel as a picture of the actual, of the characteristic—a study of human types and passions, of the evolution of personal relations. In *East Angels* she has gone much farther in this direction than in either of her other novels.

The book has, to my sense, two defects, which I may as well mention at once—two which are perhaps, however, but different faces of the same. One is that the group on which she has bent her lens strikes us as too detached, too isolated, too much on a desert island. Its different members go to and fro a good deal, to New York and to Europe, but they have a certain shipwrecked air, as of extreme dependence on each other, though surrounded with every convenience. The other fault is that the famous "tender sentiment" usurps among them a place even greater perhaps than that which it holds in life, great as the latter very admittedly is. I spoke just now of their complicated relationships, but the complications are almost exclusively the complications of love. Our impression is of sky and sand— the sky of azure, the sand of silver—and between them, conspicuous, immense, against the low horizon, the question of engagement and marriage. I must add that I do not mean to imply that this question is not, in the very nature of things, at any time and in any place, immense, or that in a novel it should be expected to lose its magnitude. I take it indeed that on such a simple shore as Miss Woolson has described, love (with the passions that flow from it), is almost inevitably the subject, and that the perspective is not really false. It is not that the people are represented as hanging together by that cord to an abnormal degree, but that, there being few accessories and circumstances, there is no tangle and overgrowth to disguise the effect. It is a question of effect, but it is characteristic of the feminine, as distinguished from the masculine hand, that in any portrait of a corner of human affairs the particular effect produced in *East Angels,* that of what we used to call the love-story, will be the dominant one. The love-story is a composition in which the elements are distributed in a particular proportion, and every tale which contains a great deal of love has not necessarily a title to the name. That title depends not upon how much love there may be, but upon how little of other things. In novels by men other things are there to a greater or less degree, and I therefore doubt whether a man may be said ever to have produced a work exactly belonging to the class in question. In men's novels, even of the simplest strain, there are still other references and other explanations; in women's, when they are of the category to which I allude, there are none but that one. And there is certainly much to be said for it.

In *East Angels* the sacrifice, as all Miss Woolson's readers know, is the great sacrifice of Margaret Harold, who immolates herself—there is no other word—deliberately, completely, and repeatedly, to a husband whose behaviour may as distinctly be held to have absolved her. The problem was a very interesting one, and worthy to challenge a superior talent—that of making real and natural a transcendent, exceptional act, representing a case in which the sense of duty is raised to exaltation. What makes Margaret Harold's behaviour exceptional and transcendent is that, in order to render the barrier between herself and the man who loves her, and whom she loves, absolutely insurmountable, she does her best to bring about his marriage, endeavours to put another woman into the frame of mind to respond to him in the event (possible, as she is a woman whom he has once appeared to love) of his attempting to console himself for a bitter failure. The care, the ingenuity, the precautions the author has exhibited, to make us accept Mrs. Harold in her integrity, are perceptible on every page, and they leave us finally no alternative but to accept her; she remains exalted, but she remains at the same time thoroughly sound. For it is not a simple question of cleverness of detail, but a question of the larger sort of imagination, and Margaret Harold would have halted considerably if her creator had not taken the supreme precaution of all, and conceived her from the germ as capable of a certain heroism—of clinging at the cost of a grave personal loss to an idea which she believes to be a high one, and taking such a fancy to it that she endeavours to paint it, by a refinement of magnanimity, with still richer hues. She is a picture, not of a woman indulging in a great spasmodic flight or moral *tour de force,* but of a nature bent upon looking at life from a high point of view, an attitude in which there is nothing abnormal, and which the author illustrates, as it were, by a test case. She has drawn Margaret with so close and firm and living a line that she seems to put us in the quandary, if we repudiate her, of denying that a woman *may* look at life from a high point of view. She seems to say to us: "Are there distinguished natures, or are there not? Very well, if there are, that's what they can do—they can try and provide for the happiness of others (when they adore them) even to their own injury." And we feel that we wish to be the first to agree that there *are* distinguished natures.

Garda Thorne is the next best thing in the book to Margaret, and she is indeed equally good in this, that she is conceived with an equal clearness. But Margaret produces her impression upon us by moving before us and doing certain things, whereas Garda is more explained, or rather she explains herself more, tells us more about herself. She says somewhere, or some one says of her, that she doesn't narrate, but in fact she does narrate a good deal, for the purpose of making the reader understand her. This the reader does, very constantly, and Garda is a brilliant success. I must not, however, touch upon the different parts of *East Angels,* because in a work of so much patience and conscience a single example carries us too far. I will only add that in three places in especial the author has been so well inspired as to give a definite pledge of high accomplishment in the future. One of these salient passages is the description of the closing days of Mrs. Thorne, the little starved yet ardent daughter of the Puritans, who has been condemned to spend her life in the land of the relaxed, and who, before she dies, pours out her accumulations of bitterness—relieves herself in a passionate confession of everything she has suffered and missed, of how she has hated the very skies and fragrances of Florida, even when, as a consistent Christian, thankful for every mercy, she has pretended most to appreciate them. Mrs. Thorne is the pathetic, tragic form of the type of which Mrs. Stowe's Miss Ophelia[6] was the comic. In almost all of Miss Woolson's stories the New England woman is represented as regretting the wholesome austerities of the region of her birth. She reverts to them, in solemn hours, even when, like Mrs. Thorne, she may appear for a time to have been converted to mild winters. Remarkably fine is the account of the expedition undertaken by Margaret Harold and Evert Winthrop to look for Lanse in the forest, when they believe him, or his wife thinks there may be reason to believe him, to have been lost and overtaken by a storm. The picture of their paddling the boat by torchlight into the reaches of the river, more or less smothered in the pestilent jungle, with the personal drama, in the unnatural place, reaching an acute stage between them— this whole episode is in a high degree vivid, strange, and powerful. Lastly, Miss Woolson has risen altogether to the occasion in the scene in which Margaret "has it out," as it were, with Evert Winthrop, parts from him and, leaving him baffled and unsurpassably sore, gives him the measure of her determination to accept the necessity of her fate. These three episodes are not alike, yet they have, in the high finish of Miss Woolson's treatment of them, a family resemblance. Moreover, they all have the stamp which I spoke of at first—the stamp of the author's conservative feeling, the implication that for her the life of a woman is essentially an affair of private relations.

THE LADY OF LITTLE FISHING

1. Sir Francis Bacon (1561–1626) was an English writer and politician.

2. In Genesis 29–46, Reuben is Jacob's eldest son by Leah and tries to save Joseph from the treachery of his brothers. He loses his right of double inheritance for sleeping with his father's concubine.

3. The Northwest and Hudson Bay Companies were English corporations that owned vast territories and monopolized fur trading in Canada and northwestern America.

4. bateaux: small boats used to collect furs from hunters' and trappers' camps.

5. Sault Ste. Marie is at the eastern end of Lake Superior.

6. St. Paul writes to the Romans that "the wages of sin are death, but the gift of God is eternal life through Jesus Christ our Lord" (Rom. 6:23).

7. In Wagner's opera, *The Flying Dutchman* (1843), a sea captain is doomed to sail forever without entering port until he can find a woman who will be eternally faithful to him.

8. paste: pastry.

9. sidling (or sideling): oblique, sloping.

10. Martin Luther (1483–1548), German religious reformer and translator of the Bible.

11. *voyageurs:* men who traveled in small boats collecting furs from trappers' camps.

12. wanting: lacking in intelligence.

13. In Matthew 8 : 12, Jesus is impressed by the faith of a Roman centurion, and says many like him will enter the Kingdom of Heaven while Israelites without faith will "be cast out into outer darkness; there shall be weeping and gnashing of teeth."

CASTLE NOWHERE

1. British America refers to Canada.

2. Sonnet XXX.

3. In Psalm 55, attributed to David, the psalmist, grieved by his friend's betrayal, wishes for the wings of a dove to fly away to the wilderness.

4. Old Nick is the devil.

5. The Old Testament prophet Amos was a shepherd in a savage wilderness, where he learned how to survive amid constant dangers. Although he accepted God's call to become a prophet, he retained his detached nomadic life.

6. "Rejoice, O young man, in thy youth," says Ecclesiastes 11 : 9, "but know thou, that for all these things God will bring thee into judgment. . . . Childhood and youth are vanity."

7. In "The Rime of the Ancient Mariner," by English Romantic poet and critic Samuel Taylor Coleridge (1772 – 1834), a sailor does lifelong penance for his sin in killing an albatross, a bird of good fortune associated with Christ. The mariner's compulsive need to confess the story of his crimes against life and human community to the person who most needs to hear it is reflected in Fog's eventual narration of his crimes to Waring.

8. In Greek myth, Sisyphus was condemned for eternity to push a boulder up a hill, and see it roll back to the bottom, so that he must begin again.

9. In Genesis 25 – 27, Jacob withholds food from his starving twin brother Esau to force him to sell his right to inherit a double share of their father's property. Esau, with whom Waring identifies himself, was "a skillful hunter, a man of the field," but is twice tricked out of his privileges as first-born son. Jacob himself suffered from trickery; after working seven years for his uncle Laban for the right to marry his daughter Rachel, he is given her older sister Leah on his wedding night, and forced to work another seven years for Rachel.

10. While searching for a bride, Jacob dreamed of a ladder reaching from earth to heaven, on which angels ascended and descended. At the top stood God, who promised to protect him and see that his descendents would fill the land.

11. The flesh-pots of Egypt where meat was cooked were lamented by the Hebrews starving in the wilderness with Moses (Exod. 16:3).

12. Orange is another name for the servant Lorez. Apparently Woolson forgot she had used the other name, an unusual slip for so careful a writer.

13. Noah released a dove from his ark to see if it could find dry land, signaling an end to the flood. Then the ark settled on Mount Ararat, understood to be the highest part of the world (Gen. 8:4). Japheth was Noah's third son.

14. After Cain murdered his brother Abel, and God punished him with a fugitive's life, God protected him from human punishment by putting a mark on him (Gen. 4:15).

15. In Job 1:7 and 2:2, Satan reports to God that he has been "going to and fro in the earth, and walking up and down in it."

16. In Psalms 139:9–10, the psalmist marvels at God's universal presence and knowledge of him, even if "I take the wings of the morning, and dwell in the uttermost parts of the sea; Even there shall thy hand lead me, and thy right hand shall hold me."

17. Mormon doctrine permits men more than one wife. "The Mormon problem" involved polygamy and the remarkable prosperity of the Mormons, as well as the crimes Woolson refers to. The founder of the church, Joseph Smith, was lynched by a mob in Illinois in 1844 and twenty thousand of his followers driven from their destroyed city.

ST. CLAIR FLATS

1. The St. Clair River forms a lake between Lake Erie and Lake Huron.

2. In Greek myth, Ariadne gives her lover Theseus a clew, or a ball of thread, to guide him out of the maze or labyrinth after he has killed the Minotaur—a man with the head of a bull—imprisoned there.

3. A misquotation of Edgar Allan Poe's poem "Annabel Lee"; *sotto voce* means spoken under one's breath.

4. Apollyon is an angel of destruction in Revelations 9:11 who guards a bottomless pit.

5. St. Paul wrote from prison to the community of Christians at Philippi to beware of wicked men who are like dogs in trusting to the flesh (by urging circumcision as necessary to salvation). Christians should worship God in spirit "and have no confidence in the flesh" (Phil. 3:2–3).

6. In Exodus 14, after the Israelites pass through the sea on dry land "in the morning watch," God drowns the pursuing Egyptians.

7. After losing the Battle of Waterloo, Napoleon was exiled to the island of St. Helena, where he died in 1821.

8. In Matthew 6:28–29, Jesus urges his followers not to be anxious about their bodily needs for food or clothing, but to "consider the lilies of the field" and trust to God to meet their needs.

9. Faust, a scholar who sold his soul to the devil for knowledge and power, was the subject of operas by Hector Berlioz, Ludwig Spohr, Charles Gounod, and Arrigo Boito, as well as plays by Christopher Marlowe and Johann Wolfgang von Goethe.

10. *Te Deum:* a hymn of praise to God.

11. Mount Tabor is traditionally identified as the mountain on which Jesus appeared before his disciples transfigured, talking to Moses and Elijah (Matt. 17:1–8, Mark 9:2–8, Luke 9:28–36).

12. Jacob Boehmen (1575–1624) was a German mystic who believed that God's wisdom was revealed to individuals independently of churches. Chiliasm is the doctrine that Christ will come to earth in visible form, establish a theocratic kingdom over all the earth, and usher in the millennium.

13. Prime was one of two brothers who edited the *New York Observer* and wrote popular works of travel in the mid-nineteenth century.

14. Brunswick was a German state belonging to the house of Welfen (Woolson uses Wolfen) with its capital once at Wolfenbüttel.

15. In medieval legend, a Jew who offended Jesus was sentenced by him to wander the earth until the Second Coming.

16. "Melons," an essay by Bret Harte (1836–1902), is a heavily ironic piece about a small boy named Melons who whistled a popular song about the famous abolitionist John Brown, executed after his attack on the Harper's Ferry Arsenal in 1859. The song says that "John Brown's body lies a'mouldering in the grave, / His soul goes marching on."

17. chirk: cheerful.

18. In editing "St. Clair Flats" for inclusion in her collection of short stories entitled *Castle Nowhere,* Woolson removed the following passage which had been part of the story as originally published in *Appleton's Journal* on October 4, 1873. The men's debate on the relative merits of men and women, on spirituality versus materialism, is central to the story's theme. Woolson may have thought the passage was too explicit, or that it might have involved her in the debate on women's rights, from which she kept her distance.

"'What a complete unlikeness!' I said, as we struggled with the difficulties of undressing by match-light.

'Simply the result of such a marriage,' replied Raymond. 'An ignorant, commonplace woman falls in love with a poetical, imaginative man; we see such cases all around us, both in high life and low. What is the result? Inevitable misery. In this case the man has taken refuge in religious fanaticism. The higher nature always suffers most.'

'I disagree with you—I utterly disagree with you,' I said, hotly. 'Why, this poor woman is heroic, absolutely heroic! Has she not given up her parents, her home, her little household gods, to follow her husband out into this wild, lonely waste? Does she not work while he is idle?'

'Yes, she works; but this is the least she could do after dragging this man down.'

'She loved him, you cynic! Where would he be without her?'

'Better off.'

'You mean in a lunatic asylum, perhaps; for there is where he would have been, long since, without her tender care. Her love for him is something sublime; her poor, plain face, her dull eyes, and her rough hands, are transformed by it into something higher than beauty. Do you hear what I say, Raymond,' I called out; for by this time we were in our respective mounds. No answer. 'Very well,' I went on, angrily, for Raymond's cynical creed always annoyed me, 'all I can say is, Raymond Lowell, that no woman will ever love *you* as this poor Roxana loves her visionary husband. *You*, at least, will not be troubled by any excessive affection.'

Years afterward I found that Raymond had thrown away his love upon a fickle heart. If he could have forgotten her! But he could not; and never did."

19. "Folded their tents like the Arabs, and silently stolen away" is adapted from "The Day Is Done" by Henry Wadsworth Longfellow (1807–82).

MISS ELISABETHA

1. Edgar Fawcett (1847–1904) was an American poet, novelist, dramatist, and essayist.

2. St. Cecilia was an early Christian martyr regarded as the patron saint of music.

3. Minorcans were people from the island of Minorca off the east coast of

Spain. They were originally brought to Florida in 1766, along with Greeks and Italians, by an English corporation as indentured laborers to cultivate indigo, sugar cane, and fruit trees. At the end of their indenture, they received lands.

4. *coquina:* limestone made of broken shells and coral cemented together.

5. *gondelieds:* an adaptation of a German word for gondolier's songs.

6. In 2 Kings 5:18, Naaman, commander of the Syrian army, is cured of his leprosy by the Hebrew prophet Elisha, and acknowledges that Jehovah is the only god. But Naaman asks to be pardoned when he accompanies his king to the temple of Rimmon and must bow down to that god.

7. Paul and Virginia are brought up together in innocence and poverty, removed from society and its corruptions, in a sentimental romance called *Paul et Virginie* (1787) written by Bernardin de Saint-Pierre (1737–1814). The idealized pastoral life they live reflects the influence of Rousseau.

IN THE COTTON COUNTRY

1. Paul Hamilton Hayne (1830–86) was a Southern American poet with whom Woolson had a long correspondence following his appreciative response to her work early in her career.

2. Henry Timrod (1828–67) was a Southern American poet, and a close friend of Hayne's.

3. William Wordsworth (1770–1850) writes these words in "Stepping Westward." The speaker of the poem says that the country woman's greeting "seemed to give me spiritual right / To travel through that region bright" where the sky's color contrasted with the "dewy ground" which "was dark and cold; / Behind all gloomy to behold."

4. Giant Despair appears in *The Pilgrim's Progress* by John Bunyan (1628–88). He captures Christian and Hopeful on their way to the Celestial City, and casts them in the dungeon of his Doubting Castle. After beating them severely, he advises them to commit suicide, but Christian finally remembers he has a key "called Promise" which opens all the locks and lets them escape.

5. General William Tecumseh Sherman (1820–91) said "War is hell."

6. In Matthew 24:20, Jesus tells his disciples of the tribulations that will precede the end of the world and the Second Coming, when all will need to flee from the destruction. He adds, "And pray ye that your flight be not in the winter."

7. Deuteronomy 34:6 describes the death of Moses after seeing Judea but

not being allowed to enter it. The mystery of his burial place—"no man knoweth his sepulchre unto this day"—suits his role as the greatest of Israel's prophets.

8. "Le roi est mort, vive le roi!" (the king is dead, long live the king) was traditionally spoken to confirm the continuity of the French monarchy when a king died and was succeeded by his heir.

9. "Is there any sorrow like unto my sorrow?" is spoken in Lamentations 1:2 by a woman who personifies Jerusalem devastated by the Babylonians.

10. The great march to the sea was General Sherman's (above, n. 5) 1864 march from Atlanta to the sea, which destroyed everything in his path and cut the Confederacy in half.

11. In Exodus 13:21, God leads the Israelites out of Egypt with a pillar of cloud by day and of fire by night.

12. In Acts 7:18, Stephen says "A new king arose that knew not Joseph" as an example of how the prophets had always been persecuted.

FELIPA

1. Sidney Lanier (1842–81) was a Southern American poet, musician, and critic.

2. See note 3 to "Miss Elisabetha."

3. Pre-Raphaelites were members of a nineteenth-century art movement that rejected the conventions of academic painting in favor of exact detail; the movement later deteriorated into a fashionable aesthetic featuring long-necked ladies in medieval costumes.

4. *cui bono* (Lat.): Who will be the better for it? What good will it do?

5. Thomas Bailey Aldrich (1836–1907) was an American poet, editor, and writer of short stories.

6. *objets de luxe:* objects of wealth and value.

THE STREET OF THE HYACINTH

1. In Greek myth, Hyacinth was beloved by Apollo, who accidentally killed him while teaching him to throw the discus.

2. The Pantheon is a massive building in Rome, still intact, built in the first century to honor all the Roman gods.

3. heads: headings, as in an outline.

4. *omnium gatherum* (Lat.): a miscellaneous collection of people or things.

5. *res angusta* (Lat.): scanty necessities of life, or poverty.

6. The Doria and the Borghese galleries (mentioned in the next paragraph) are among the major collections of paintings in Rome.

7. In rejecting the painters Noel mentions, Ettie is rejecting masters of the fifteenth through seventeenth centuries, representing major movements in art history: Raphael (1483–1520), Italian painter and great stylistic innovator; Sebastian del Piombo (1485–1547), Italian painter closely associated with Michelangelo, his subject, Andrea Doria (1468–1560), Italian admiral and statesman; Velasquez (1599–1660), Spanish painter known for his portraits and landscapes; Claude Lorraine (1600–82), French landscape painter; Memling (c. 1430–94), Flemish painter of religious subjects.

8. solferino: a shade of red.

9. Albano is a summer resort with Roman ruins south of Rome.

10. The Pincio is a parapet in the Borghese Gardens overlooking Rome. A popular place for walking and driving, it is the locale of an important scene in Henry James's first successful story, *Daisy Miller.*

AT THE CHÂTEAU OF CORINNE

Corinne is a novel by Madame de Staël (Anne-Louise Germaine Necker, 1766–1817) about a young woman of immense poetic genius who dies of a broken heart when her fiancé abandons her for a more conventional woman. The author's brilliance and her tumultuous life led her to be identified with her heroine Corinne. The château at Coppet, a village on Lake Leman north of Geneva, is the estate of Staël's father, the distinguished statesman and financier, Jacques Necker. After the family was exiled from Paris by Napoleon, Staël's mother Suzanne held salons at Coppet attended by the most brilliant literary, political, and financial figures of the age. Their daughter grew up in the company of these people. When she was not traveling throughout Europe, Madame de Staël lived much of her life at Coppet, and is buried there.

1. Lake Leman, also called the Lake of Geneva, runs east from the city of Geneva along the boundary of France and Switzerland. Lausanne, Vevey, Clarens, and Montreux are resorts along its northern shore.

2. Horace Walpole (1717–97) was an English author best known for his Gothic romance, *The Castle of Otranto.*

3. English historian Edward Gibbon (1737–94) was best known for *The History of the Decline and Fall of the Roman Empire*.

4. Mont Blanc is the highest peak in western Europe; it is in the Alps on the French-Italian border. Salève and Voirons are mountain ranges that overlook Geneva. The Jura Mountains run along the French and Swiss borders from the Rhone River to the Rhine.

5. The writers mentioned are identified as follows: Voltaire, the pen name of François Marie Arouet (1694–1778), French author of tragedies, poems, history, philosophy, and criticism; Jean Charles Léonard di Sismondi (1773–1842), Swiss historian and economist; Jean-Jacques Rousseau (1712–78), French writer and philosopher whose social and educational theories were very influential; Sir Humphrey Davy (1778–1824), English scientist; Théodore Agrippa d'Aubigné (1552–1630), French writer and ardent follower of Calvin; John Calvin (1509–64), French Protestant reformer and theologian; Friedrich Melchior Grimm (1723–1807), German literary critic and editor; Benjamin Constant (1767–1830), French novelist, orator, and politician, and one of Madame de Staël's lovers, as well as her protégé; August Wilhelm von Schlegel (1767–1845), German poet and critic who traveled extensively with Madame de Staël; René de Chateaubriand (1768–1848), French Romantic author and statesman; George Gordon, Lord Byron (1788–1824) and Percy Bysshe Shelley (1792–1822), English Romantic poets who lived at Lake Leman when they were ostracized in England for leaving their wives and living with other women (in Shelley's case, with Mary Godwin, who wrote *Frankenstein* during their stay on Lake Leman); Alexandre Dumas (1802–70), French novelist and dramatist, best known for *The Count of Monte Cristo* and *The Three Musketeers*.

6. *Etonnante femme:* astonishing woman.

7. Chillon is a castle at the eastern end of Lake Leman where François Bonnivard was imprisoned in the sixteenth century for his defense of Swiss liberties. He is the hero of Byron's poem, "The Prisoner of Chillon."

8. Pierre de Ronsard (1524–85) was the leading French poet of the Renaissance. The verses mean "Time passes, time passes, my lady! / Alas! time does not, but we pass away."

9. "Childe Harolde's Pilgrimage" is a popular poem by Byron, which takes its romantic hero through western Europe. Charlotte Yonge (1823–1901) was an English author of popular and didactic historical romances.

10. phaeton: a light horse-drawn carriage.

11. In Greek myth, Endymion is a beautiful youth loved by Silene, the moon goddess.

12. Madame Récamier (Jeanne Françoise Julie Bernard, 1777–1849) was a

French writer who had a stormy friendship with Madame de Staël. She was famous for her beauty, her wit, her salon, and her Dance of the Shawl which Staël describes in *Corinne* and in *Delphine*.

13. *ravissante amie:* extraordinarily charming friend.

14. The Montmorency was Mathieu de Montmorency-Laval (1767–1826), a French aristocrat who served in the American Revolution, supported the French Revolution, led nobles to sacrifice some of their privileges, and finally became an ultraroyalist. He was a lover of Madame de Staël, who rescued him as well as others from the revolutionary Reign of Terror.

15. Johann Wolfgang von Goethe (1749–1832), German poet, dramatist, novelist, philosopher, and statesman, was best known for his romantic novel, *The Sorrows of Young Werther,* and for his tragedy *Faust*. His close friend Johann Christoph Schiller (1759–1805) was a German poet, dramatist and historian.

16. The Campagna is a large plain around Rome.

17. Chambéry lies between Geneva and Grenoble, France. Turin is in northwestern Italy.

"MISS GRIEF"

1. "When found, make a note of it" is from *Dombey and Son* by Charles Dickens (1812–70).

2. Honoré de Balzac (1799–1850) was a founder of realism in the French novel. He is best known for his comprehensive study of French society, *La comédie humaine*.

3. In Greek and Roman mythology, the Furies were winged women who avenged crime, especially crimes against ties of kinship. They hounded Orestes to madness for the murder of his mother, Clytemnestra.

4. In Roman legendary history, Tullia stirred her husband, Tarquinius Superbus, to oust her father from his throne, then drove her chariot over her father's murdered body. Lucrezia Borgia (1480–1519), patron of learning and the arts, was from an Italian family noted for its cruelties and murders.

5. Vae victis (Lat.): Woe to the vanquished.

6. *Kubla Khan* is a poem about poetric inspiration by Coleridge (see "Castle Nowhere," n. 7). He called it "a vision in a dream," and claimed to have written it in a reverie brought on by opium.

7. *memento mori* (Lat.): reminder of death.

"MISS WOOLSON"

1. Madame de Sévigné (1626–96) is famous for her correspondence with her daughter. George Sand was the pseudonym of Amadine Aurore Lucile Dupin, Baroness Dudevant (1804–76), prolific and unconventional novelist and play-wright. Madame de Staël is identified in the headnote to "At the Château of Corinne."

2. *Revue des Deux Mondes* is an immensely influential French periodical founded in 1829, which publishes literary criticism as well as literary and political writings.

3. When he edited this essay for publication in *Partial Portraits* (1888), James omitted the following passage which came at this point in the essay he first published in *Harper's Weekly* the previous year:

"It would not be hidden from a reader of *Anne* and *East Angels* that the author is a native of New England, who may have been transplanted to a part of the country open in some degree to the imputation of being 'out West,' who may then have lived for a considerable time in the South, and who may meanwhile constantly have retained as a part of her essence certain myste-rious and not unvalued affinities with the State of New York. Such, in fact, so far as my knowledge goes, has been the succession of events in Miss Wool-son's history. She was born, like her father, Dr. Charles Jarvis Woolson, before her, at Claremont, New Hampshire, and taken as a child to live at Cleveland. She was educated partly in that city and partly at a French school in New York—an establishment which she has sketchily commemorated (if, indeed, the term 'sketchy' may ever be applied to her earnest, lingering manner) in certain chapters of *Anne.* Such at least is my inference; the charming figure of Madame Moreau, in that novel, may be assumed to be a reminiscence of the late celebrated Madame Chegaray. On the death of her father, in 1869, she entered with her mother upon an unbroken residence of several years in the Southern States, principally in Florida, where, as is manifest in every page of *East Angels,* she conceived a high appreciation of orange gardens and white beaches, pine-barrens and rivers smothered in jungles, and a peculiar affection for that city of the past, so rapidly becoming a city of the future, St. Augustine. Her early summers she was accustomed to spend, in the Cleveland phrase, 'up the lakes,' and particularly amid the beautiful scenery of Mackinaw, in the straits between Michigan and Huron. Mackinaw is obviously the rather tormentingly nameless island represented in the early chapters of *Anne,* represented with a vividness which causes the reader of that story to rage not a little at the perversity which leads the author to desert the brilliant frozen straits and the little snow-bound United States military post for scenes less remunerative—the only case that I can remember, by the way, in which she abandoned an opportunity without having conscientiously pressed it out. Miss Woolson must have known Mackinaw by winter as well as by summer, and none of her novels contains an episode better executed than those interrupted pages of *Anne* which give the sense of the snow-glare beating into small, hot, bare interiors, the dog trains jogging over the white expanse, and the black forests staring for long months at the channel of ice. When it is added that Miss Woolson is by her mother a grandniece of Fenimore Cooper, and that she cherishes a devotion for the charming little town on Lake Otsego which bears, for good reasons, the name of the great romancer, her stories will have been accounted for so far as the distribution of her years, superficially speaking, may account for them.

That is, there is one one element unaccounted for—the inevitable European element, which, oddly enough, is nowadays almost the sign and hallmark of American experience. Miss Woolson has, I believe, of late years lived much in Europe, and yet there is nothing about Europe in her writings. She has not pressed it into service; she appears to have an unassuming suspicion that she can get on without it. Her characters sometimes sail for foreign countries (in general they move about a great deal, and take many journeys), but she does not even accompany them to the plank of the steamer, to the office where they take their berths; it is the most if she will renew acquaintance with them when they come back. Has she a story about Europe in reserve (I remember two or three very short ones, which, apparently, she has been shy of republishing), or does she propose to maintain her distinguished independence? It will be interesting to see, and meanwhile we may note this independence as an unusual phenomenon, taken in connection with her personal familiarity with Rome, Florence, Venice, and other irrepressible cities. The habit of introducing these cities usually exhibits itself in connection with a want of familiarity with them."

4. Uncle Remus is the narrator in several collections of Southern black folk tales published between 1876 and 1900 by Joel Chandler Harris (1848–1908).

5. Elizabeth Gaskell (1810–65), English novelist and biographer of Charlotte Brontë, published *Cranford* in 1853. It describes English village life in the mid-nineteenth century.

6. In Harriet Beecher Stowe's influential antislavery novel, *Uncle Tom's Cabin* (1851–52), Miss Ophelia is a strong-minded New England spinster.